# The Power to Choose

Bangladeshi Women and Labour Market
Decisions in London and Dhaka

## NAILA KABEER

**VERSO**
London • New York

First published by Verso 2000
© Naila Kabeer 2000
All rights reserved

**Verso**
UK: 6 Meard Street, London, W1V 3HR
US: 180 Varick Street, New York, NY 10014–4606

Verso is the imprint of New Left Books

ISBN 1–85984–804–4

**British Library Cataloguing in Publication Data**
A catalogue record for this book is available from the British Library

**Library of Congress Cataloging-in-Publication Data**
A catalog record for this book is available from the Library of Congress

Typeset in 9/11pt ITC New Baskerville by
SetSystems Ltd, Saffron Walden, Essex
Printed by Biddles Ltd, Guildford and King's Lynn

This book is dedicated to my mother, Rokeya Rahman Kabeer,
and to my friend, Shireen Huq

# Contents

PREFACE AND ACKNOWLEDGEMENTS     vii

1   Labour standards, double standards? Selective
    solidarity in international trade     1

2   'Rational fools' or 'cultural dopes'? Stories of structure
    and agency in the social sciences     16

3   The changing face of *shonar Bangla*: background to
    the Dhaka study     54

4   Renegotiating purdah: women workers and labour
    market decision making in Dhaka     82

5   Individualised entitlements: factory wages and intra-
    household power relations     142

6   Across seven seas and thirteen rivers: background to
    the London study     193

7   Reconstituting structure: homeworkers and labour
    market decision making in London     230

8   Mediated entitlements: home-based piecework and
    intra-household power relations     284

9   Exclusion and economics in the labour market:
    explaining the paradox     312

10   The power to choose and 'the evidence of things not
    seen': revisiting structure and agency     326

11  Weak winners, powerful losers: the politics of
    protectionism in international trade                    364

APPENDIX 1   METHODOLOGICAL NOTE                           405

APPENDIX 2   STATISTICAL BACKGROUND TO THE
             DHAKA STUDY                                   412

APPENDIX 3   STATISTICAL BACKGROUND TO THE LONDON
             STUDY                                         421

BIBLIOGRAPHY                                               433

INDEX                                                     451

# Preface and acknowledgements

The idea for this book came about in response to an apparent paradox relating to the work patterns of two groups of Bangladeshi women workers living several thousand miles apart. The first group came to my attention when I visited Bangladesh in 1984 after an absence of three years. I was struck then by the sight of thousands of young women moving briskly around on the streets of Dhaka. In a city, and a country, where women had been conspicuous by their absence in the public domain, this was not merely a new phenomenon, but a remarkable one. I was told that they worked in the new garment factories which had sprung into existence almost overnight in response to incentives put in place by the government in 1982 to promote export-oriented manufacturing.

Very soon after this, as a result of my involvement in a campaign which I describe in Chapter 1 of the book, I heard about another group of Bangladeshi women also working in the clothing industry, but this time in the East End of London. However, they had been incorporated into a very different form of employment in the industry. While much of the clothing industry in the UK is dominated by female labour, Bangladeshi women were largely absent from its factories and small, outdoor units. They worked instead as home-based machinists, paid on a piecework basis. At a time when research based on official statistics in the UK had declared that manufacturing homework was a 'relative rarity', an anachronism from the last century, these women represented a rising trend in the British garment industry of subcontracting out the machining stages of production to home-based outworkers.

It was not the fact that Bangladeshi women took up different forms of paid work in the garment industries in these two contexts that was puzzling – they were, after all, located in different labour markets in different parts of the world – but rather the counter-intuitive forms that their work had taken in the two contexts. In Bangladesh, a country where strong norms of purdah, or female seclusion, had always confined women to the precincts of the home and where female participation in public forms of employment had historically been low, the apparent ease with which women appeared to have abandoned old norms in response to new oppor-tunities went against the grain of what has been presented in the development literature as one of the least negotiable patriarchies in the world. By contrast, in Britain, a secular country accustomed to the presence of women in the public arena, and with a tradition of female factory employment going back over a hundred years, particularly in the clothing industry, Bangladeshi women were largely found working from home, in apparent conformity with purdah norms.

A reading of the literature on the international division of labour in the garment industry suggested that this paradoxical set of labour market outcomes could be explained at a number of different levels. There was an explanation at the global level which stressed the extensive geographical restructuring of textile and garment manufacturing since the late 1960s and the very different patterns of employment it gave rise to in different parts of the world. There was an explanation at the national level, which explored the local organisation of the garment industry in different countries and the demand for different categories of labour which this generated. And finally, there was a third, micro-level set of explanations which relates to the lives and circumstances of individ-ual workers and their motivations for taking up particular forms of employment in different contexts.

It is this third level of analysis which forms the main substance of this book. The book can be seen as drawing on two different kinds of explanatory narratives which have a bearing directly, or indirectly, on the labour market outcomes outlined above. The first set of narratives are those related in the third person: in other words, they are narratives *about* the women workers in question. Some of these are populist in origin, the accounts of journalists, trade unionists, feminist activists and employers, a range of people who had, or claimed to have, some form of first- or second-hand knowledge of the workers. Others are more academic and take the form of theories about the behaviour of social actors in general, of whom the women workers described above represent particular examples. The various rationales put forward for women's labour market behaviour within these diverse narratives constitute one kind of explanation for our paradox. In addition to these third-person narratives, however, there are also first-person narratives, those told *by* women workers everywhere about themselves. Such narratives contain the workers' own accounts of their behaviour, of the motivations which led them to seek paid work and to opt for one form of employment rather than another. Such narratives offer an alternative set of explanations for our paradox which may or may not converge with the first set.

## Objectives

I have attempted to bring together both sets of narratives in order to achieve a number of objectives. The first objective is a straightforward empirical one. It is to find out the reasons for the paradoxical labour market choices made by Bangladeshi women in the contexts of Britain and Bangladesh. The second objective is more theoretical in nature and seeks to compare the 'fit' between the accounts of their labour market behaviour, and its implications, provided by Bangladeshi women workers in the two contexts and the theoretical accounts of women's labour market behaviour put forward in the social science literature.

Finally, I had a third and more political objective for undertaking this research and for adopting the particular methodology which has guided it. The two sets of narratives I have outlined above embody, implicitly or explicitly, models of the human actor, either in a general abstract sense, or more concretely, in the shape of Third World women workers. They also contain explicit or implicit claims about what these workers' interests might be and how they might best be served in the context of the rapid expansion and growing interdependence of international trade. However, these views do not always converge, and indeed may be in conflict. The gap between these views is partly theoretical, reflecting differing conceptualisations of human agency and social structure. It is partly informational, reflecting the extent and accuracy of the knowledge base on which they are built. And it is partly political, a reflection of the strategic positioning of different stakeholders in public debates about appropriate policies in international trade. That there is a power imbalance involved can be deduced from the fact that it was the third-person narratives about Third World women workers which commanded attention in the public debates at the time when I decided to do this study, while the views of Third World women workers themselves were largely unsought and unheard.

The politics of this gap has been dissected in passionate and polemical terms by Linda Lim (1990). She pointed to the convergence of expediency, ideology and politics which had led to an unlikely coalition of actors to make claims on behalf of the Third World women workers who were being drawn into the manufacturing labour force by the changing international division of labour. This coalition included feminists from both north and south who saw the super-exploitation of these women workers as the product of a merger between patriarchy and capital; anti-imperialists committed to challenging the predatory operations of multinational corporations; and a protectionist constituency of domestic capital, labour movements and local communities in the advanced industrialised countries whose interests were threatened by the import of Third World manufactured goods which competed with domestically produced alternatives.

What allowed these different groups to make claims on behalf of women workers in the Third World was the remarkably homogeneous image of the 'average' Third World worker which underpinned their claims. She was young, single, cheap, docile and dispensable. She was ruthlessly exploited by multinational employers who paid her a pittance, subjected her to a harsh factory discipline, played on her cultural deference to authority and laid her off when the going got tough. She had little choice in the matter because the imperatives of poverty forced her to take up work wherever she could find it, but she benefited very little from her new identity as a worker because she remained subject to the seamless patriarchal discipline of family, community and capitalist work relations.

The construction of this stereotype partly reflected the ideological and political predilections of its adherents. It was reinforced by the considerable social distances of location, language, class and culture that separated many of those who spoke about women workers in global manufacturing and the women workers they spoke about. Much of the talking, writing and theorising in this early discourse tended to be couched as broad generalisations, derived from a meagre empirical base or 'read off' from a structural analysis of the interests of global capital. It was rarely based on any detailed concrete analysis of the circumstances which had led Third World women to accept these apparently exploitative jobs.

The third objective in undertaking the research for this book derived from these observations. I wanted to move beyond abstract, structuralist debates about the exploitation of women workers in global manufacturing in general to a more concrete analysis of the lives of particular groups of workers who had been drawn into these jobs in order to understand their motivations and what these jobs might have meant to them. I hoped that this more situated analysis of the 'supply side' of the story would help to clarify how women workers viewed their own interests and the extent to which these converged with the claims being made on their behalf by those with the power to be heard in international forums.

## Structure

The structure and content of the book reflects the fact that it is comparing the lives and situations of two groups of Bangladeshi women, who presumably shared similar cultural beliefs and values but lived in two very different parts of the world. While both were working in the clothing industries in their respective locations, they had been incorporated into very different forms of employment. Part of the reason for this was that the industry itself was organised somewhat differently in the two contexts. The industry in Bangladesh was largely export-oriented and relatively new. Unlike some other Third World countries, export manufacturing in Bangladesh was not primarily located in special export-processing zones. Instead garment factories were dispersed across the main cities of Dhaka and Chittagong. Representatives of the major retailers and mail-order firms in Europe and the US either set up direct contact with factory owners or worked through middlemen located in Hong Kong or Singapore. The Dhaka factories we visited, which were probably typical of the industry as a whole at that time, generally hired between 200 to 500 production workers, predominantly female. While some men were also employed as machinists, cutting, packing and ironing was done entirely by men. There was only one shift, lasting from around 8 in the morning to 5 or 6 in the evening, but overtime in the busy season was frequent and compulsory.

The London industry, on the other hand, was producing largely for the domestic market, for high-street chain stores as well as small boutiques. It was a much older industry but it had shrunk considerably since the 1970s, partly as a result of competition from other European as well as Third World countries. There were very few large factories left by the time the fieldwork was done. Instead, it was made up of a complex network of small factories and outdoor units. Women from ethnic minorities dominated the industry but there were also large numbers of Bangladeshi men working as machinists and sub-contractors. In addition, there was also a large but unknown number of home-based machinists, predominantly women, who were subcontracted in to do simple 'flat' machining. Bangladeshi women were mainly to be found in this group. Employers or middlemen supplied the homeworkers with orders and made the arrangements to have the completed work picked up. The women owned their own sewing machines and paid for their own electricity; the employers supplied the materials and thread.

Differences in the organisation of garment manufacturing, and corresponding differences in labour force requirements, therefore partly accounted for the differences in the way in which Bangladeshi women had been incorporated into the Dhaka and London industries. However, the underlying premise of the research was that employment patterns are not merely artefacts of the demand for labour, they also represent the responses of workers and their households to perceived opportunities and constraints. The main substance of the book is taken up with an investigation of the factors which led two groups of women workers, with presumably similar views about gender roles and cultural constraints, to respond to labour market opportunities in such counter-intuitive ways.

The first chapter deals with the international level of explanation for the incorporation of Bangladeshi women into the garment industry in the two contexts under study. It documents the global restructuring of the garment industry, the changing geography of production it generated and the employment opportunities it gave rise to in Dhaka and London. The discussion in this chapter also touches on some of the ways in which Third World women workers have been brought into popular as well as academic narratives about the causes and implications of these changes. Chapter 2 focuses more explicitly on the social science literature dealing with women's labour market behaviour, the 'supply side' of the story, distinguishing between economic accounts which focus on individual choice, sociological accounts which emphasise structural constraint and a third set of explanations which attempt to integrate the analysis of choice and constraint.

The next six chapters of the book deal with empirical material, the first three with the Bangladesh component of the research and the next three with the London component. Chapters 3 and 6 provide a brief account of the clothing industry and labour markets in Dhaka and London, the backdrop against which the women workers' stories unfold. Chapters 4, 5, 7 and 8 deal with the key research questions that the book sets out to explore. Chapters 4 and 7 deal with the factors underlying women's decisions to take up particular forms of paid work, while Chapters 5 and 8 explore the personal and social ramifications of these decisions. Together these chapters illuminate how similarities in cultural norms and values helped to shape what women and their families in the two contexts considered to be acceptable forms of behaviour, including acceptable forms of employment. As we will see, the two groups of women had a great deal in common in these matters and there is considerable overlap in many aspects of their testimonies. However, the chapters also provide an explanation for why these definitions of 'acceptable' behaviour led to such different labour market choices in the two contexts.

Chapters 9, 10 and 11 return us to the three objectives of the research outlined earlier. Chapter 9 pulls together the findings from the Dhaka and London components of the research in order to provide an integrated explanation for the paradoxical labour market outcomes which constituted the starting point for the research. Chapter 10 evaluates the explanatory power of various theoretical accounts of women's labour market behaviour through the lens provided by their own accounts. Finally, Chapter 11 explores the politics of protectionism when the interests of powerful 'losers' in international trade appear to go against those of 'weak' winners.

This book has taken a long time to write because, in the course of writing it, it became a very different book from the one I set out to write. Given my own disciplinary training, it had originally been intended as a critique of neo-classical theories of choice. However, it became quickly apparent from a reading of the literature on Bangladeshi women's labour market behaviour that 'choice' was not a concept which featured a great deal in the explanations. Rather, the literature was framed primarily by structuralist concepts of purdah, poverty and patriarchy. While these are important concepts for the analysis of gender relations and outcomes in Bangladesh, and have featured in my own earlier work, it was clear that they would have to be considerably rethought in order to accommodate the questions I wanted to raise in the book. Consequently, the book evolved into a critique not only of the way in which neo-classical economists have explained choice but also of how sociologists have conceptualised structure.

## Acknowledgements

There are many different people who have contributed in many different ways to the writing of this book. However, my first debt is to my friend Shireen Huq. We had hoped to do this research as a collaborative venture which would bring together our shared experiences in Bangladesh and in Britain. We worked together in conceptualising the project, inspired by the same concerns about the portrayal of Bangladeshi women workers in the academic literature as well as in the popular press, and moved by same curiosity about why Bangladeshi women in Dhaka and London had made the labour market choices they had. We also managed to carry out the first phase of the fieldwork, the interviews with women workers in the Bangladesh context, before Shireen had to leave the project. Her ideas and her spirit have remained a strong presence throughout the writing of the book however and, for that reason, I have dedicated the book to her.

My family in Bangladesh are always an indispensable part of the work I do there and I want to acknowledge my debt to them. Some made a direct contribution to the work; others were helpful in more indirect ways, sending me features and articles they thought might be useful, letting me endlessly discuss my ideas about the work. They include my mother, Rokeya Rahman Kabeer, to whom this book is also dedicated; my aunt, Ruby Ghuznavi; and my cousins, Khushi Kabir, Farah Ghuznavi and Zein Ghuznavi. There are also a number of uncles who all played generally supportive roles: Rezaur Rahman, Mizanur Rahman and Farhad Ghuznavi.

Then there is the wider group of people who all helped and contributed in different ways and at different times: Iram Rahman, Kazi Rokeya, Haseria Akhter, Nuzhat Shahzadir, Sharmin Sonia Murshad, Julie Begum, Afia Begum, Shaheena Joaddar, Adrian Wood, Ramya Subrahmanian, Maithrayee Mukhopadhyay, Ann Whitehead, Shahra Razavi, Mathew Lockwood, Alison Evans, Susanna Moorehead, Martin Greeley, Swasti Mitter, Ruth Pearson, Diane Elson and Susan Joekes. I am grateful to a number of people working on similar issues to those covered in this book who shared their work with me in unpublished form, particularly Margaret Newby, Nazli Kibria and Petra Dannecker. Thanks also to Ameerah Haq who gave me the refuge of her house and garden at extremely short notice when I needed it. I would like to thank John Toye for his encouragement when I was starting the book and Keith Bezanson for his patience when I was finishing it. At Verso, I would like to thank Robin Blackburn, Jane Hindle, Sara Barnes and, of course, Colin Robinson for their support. I want to acknowledge my gratitude to Altaf Gauhar for helping me to get the project off the ground. And finally, as always, I owe Chris Leaf special thanks for his patience with the drawn-out process of writing the book.

A number of publications based on some of the chapters in the book have appeared in various forms at earlier stages. A very preliminary version of Chapter 4 came out as an article entitled 'Cultural Dopes or Rational Fools? Women and labour supply in the Bangladesh garment industry' in the *European Journal of Development Research*, volume 3, no. 1, 1991, and was subsequently reprinted in a collection of essays entitled *Muslim Women's Choices: Religious Belief and Social Reality* edited by Camillia Fawzi El-Soh and Judy Mabro. An early version of Chapter 7 came out in *Development and Change*, vol. 25, no. 2, 1994, entitled 'The structure of "revealed" preference: race, community and female labour supply in the London clothing industry' and was subsequently reprinted in *Academic Readings: Reading and Writing Across Disciplines*, compiled by Janet Giltrow, Broadview Press, 1995, Ontario. An early version of Chapter 5 came out initially as IDS Working Paper 25 in 1995 and entitled 'Necessary, sufficient or irrelevant? Women, wages and intra-household power relations in urban Bangladesh'. It was subsequently published in *Development and Change* vol. 28, no. 2, 1997. These earlier versions have all been substantially revised for inclusion in this book.

In terms of financial support I am very grateful to the Third World Foundation, to the Economic and Social Research Council and to DFID, UK. The project also benefited from small grants from the Nuffield Foundation and CIDA. I also owe the Rockefeller Foundation enormous thanks for a wonderful month's residency at the Bellagio Conference Centre in Italy and for the opportunity to meet, and make friends, with some wonderful people.

# Labour standards, double standards?
## Selective solidarity in international trade

The international restructuring of the garment industry, which began in the early 1960s, was itself part of a larger phenomenon which was initially termed 'the new international division of labour', but which has subsequently been subsumed under the more general term of globalisation. The 'old' international division of labour was one in which the advanced industrialised countries specialised in the production and export of manufactured goods while poorer, developing countries produced and exported primary commodities. Although many in the latter category had sought to develop their own manufacturing capacity behind a wall of protective barriers, the aim had been import substitution rather than export promotion.

What was 'new' about the new international division of labour was the growth of an export-oriented manufacturing sector in a number of countries in Asia and Latin America, exemplified in the popular imagination by the four East Asian 'tigers': Hong Kong, Singapore, South Korea and Taiwan. All four had opted for a more open economic policy, with active government support for export-oriented manufacturing. The hospitable environment provided in these contexts, together with the availability of large supplies of low-cost labour, led a number of industries to relocate all, or part, of their production processes from the high wage economies of the advanced industrialised countries to these new locations in the south. The industries most affected by the process of relocation tended to be those which were particularly labour-intensive and hence had a high ratio of labour to overall costs; older industries like textiles and clothing and new ones like electronics. Given the focus of the book on the clothing industries of Britain and Bangladesh, I will briefly summarise some of the factors behind the changing international division of labour in this industry, with specific reference to the experience of these two countries.

## The international restructuring of the garment industry

A major factor in the changing international division of labour in industries like clothing was the rising cost of labour in advanced industrialised countries. Full employment, the increasing incorporation of women into the labour market in the post-war period and the successful claims of a highly organised trade union movement had led to extremely high overall wages in these countries, with particular implications for the level of profits in labour-intensive industries like clothing. Because competition in the mass clothing market revolved primarily around price, major clothing retailers were constantly driven by the need to respond to fashion-led fluctuations in the demand for clothing at increasingly more competitive prices. The search for ever-cheaper sources of clothing led to the opening up of production sites in some of the low-wage, export-oriented economies of the south.

However, anxieties about the levels of import penetration of developed country markets threatened by this restructuring process led to the adoption in 1973 of the Multifibre Arrangement (MFA) in 1974, which brought together various disparate attempts to regulate the rapid growth in Third World exports of clothing and textiles in the interests of 'orderly trade'. The agreement set the acceptable rate of increase in exports from developing to developed countries at 6 per cent and an 'anti-surge' clause was put in place to guard against sudden increases in exports from any particular country to any other, beyond bilaterally agreed levels. With world recession in the early 1970s exacerbating the effects of the steady expansion in clothing imports from the East Asian economies, the MFA was invoked by several signatories to impose quotas on further imports from these countries.

However, the imposition of quotas did not succeed in dissipating the flow of cheap imports. Instead, it gave rise to the enterprising practice of 'quota hopping' as producers and buyers from Hong Kong, Singapore and other newly industrialising countries went in search of fresh, low-wage sites which were still 'quota-free'. It was at this stage that Bangladesh came into the picture, since it met all these requirements. By the late 1970s a small number of sub-contracting factories had been set up in the country, largely by domestic entrepreneurs, but with the assistance of east Asian technology, connections and knowledge of international markets. It was only after 1982, however, when the Bangladesh government put in place its New Industrial Policy offering various incentives for export-oriented manufacturing, that the industry really took off, growing from a handful in 1976 to around 700 in 1985, located largely in the cities of Chittagong and Dhaka (*Economist*, 23 September 1989). Estimates as to the number of jobs created varied between 80,000 and 250, 000, but it was generally agreed that 85 per cent of them were held by women (World Bank, 1990).

The international restructuring of the clothing industry, which gave rise to these new jobs for women in Bangladesh, had a very different effect in the British context, since the industry there was much older, dating back to the mid-nineteenth century, and women workers had been involved in it from its inception. They accounted for around 80 per cent of the total labour force at the end of the 1970s (Coyle, 1982). Here, the impact of import penetration since the 1960s, exacerbated by the effects of the recession in the 1970s, led to a process of internal restructuring, based on the three basic options open to garment manufacturers: 'automate, relocate or evaporate' (Phizacklea, 1990, p. 9). The high fashion end of the manufacturing industry retained a competitive advantage with the major retailers because their products could not be so easily replicated by an unskilled labour force. It was the firms that produced cheap standardised clothing for the mass market that were most vulnerable to 'evaporation'. Clothing production in the UK fell by 29 per cent between 1979 and 1983, while one third of the registered work force lost their jobs. In 1978, there were 307,000 registered workers in the industry; in 1983, there were 207,400 (Phizacklea, 1990). Of the firms that survived, some chose to 'automate', adopting computer-aided techniques for the design, cutting and finishing, the more skilled stages of the production process. However, the sewing of garments, which required few skills beyond the ability to handle a sewing machine competently, did not lend itself readily to mechanisation because of the 'limp' quality of cloth. This remained the most labour-intensive stage of production, accounting for four-fifths of the labour time in producing garments. The 'relocation' option was relevant primarily at this stage.

In some cases, relocation took an international form whereby all or part of the production process was subcontracted to a low-wage location elsewhere in the world. In London, however, relocation was largely internal, with firms increasingly subcontracting the labour-intensive machining stages to much cheaper, unorganised labour working in the 'outdoor units' and as domestic outworkers in the 'hidden' economy of the depressed inner city areas of Britain. Given that the Bangladeshi community in the UK was largely concentrated in the East End of London, which was also where the London industry was largely located, it was not surprising that Bangladeshi women benefited from the increasing supply of homework in this area. What is less clear is why they had not taken up factory jobs in the first place or why they did not take advantage of the increased supply of work to the 'outdoor' units.

## Patriarchy reconstituted: theories of gender and capital in the international division of labour

One of the features of the rise of the export-oriented manufacturing industry in the developing countries which had begun to draw a great deal of attention in the 1980s was the female-intensiveness of its work force. The phenomenon appeared to suggest that women in low-income countries who had hitherto worked as family labour in 'traditional' agriculture were now being drawn into 'modern' industry as waged workers. There were both optimistic and pessimistic readings of this. This was a period when Boserup's path-breaking book (1980) documenting the marginalisation of women from the benefits of development had helped to put women's issues explicitly on the international development agenda for the first time. Many agencies interpreted the call to 'integrate women into the development process' which came out of the UN Conference for International Women's Year 1975 as a demand to integrate women more effectively into the labour market (Elson and Pearson, 1981).

There thus appeared to be a happy coincidence between the discovery of women as the preferred labour force in the new world market factories springing up in different parts of the Third World and the new 'women and development' policy agenda identifying employment as the most effective route to the goal of integration. Indeed, the idea that paid employment held the key to ending women's subordinate status was subscribed to by a wide spectrum of opinion, from the World Bank to Marxist scholars, who all shared a view of market forces as gender-neutral, even if they disagreed fundamentally in their views of the relationship between capital and labour within the market place (Elson and Pearson, 1981).

A great deal of critical feminist scholarship at the time was aimed at countering this optimistic orthodoxy. It pointed out that it was the 'comparative advantage of women's disadvantage' (Arizpe and Aranda, 1981) which explained their status as the preferred labour force for these industries. A number of factors were thought to lie behind this preference. These industries relied on largely unskilled labour, but their intensive use of such labour meant that wage costs formed the major portion of their overall costs. Furthermore, the seasonality of demand in industries like clothing, as well as its exposure to international competition, introduced an inherent instability into their production cycle. They needed a cheap labour force to cut down on their costs and they needed a 'flexible' labour force which could be drawn into, and expelled from, employment, in response to changing levels of demand.

As feminist scholars pointed out, young, unmarried women in the Third World constituted an ideal work force on grounds which reflected an intersection of the 'economics' of demand and the 'culture' of supply. This genre of studies produced some fascinating insights into the ways in which apparently modern factory organisation drew on, and indeed actively promoted, cultural norms of femininity which helped to legitimate employers' 'super-exploitation' of their predominantly female work force. Elson and Pearson (1981), for instance, cited the following invest- ment brochure issued by the Malaysian government as an example of the 'cultural construction' of the 'oriental female worker', stressing the advantages of both 'nature' and 'inheritance' in making her ideal for assembly line production:

> The manual dexterity of the oriental female is famous the world over. Her hands are small and she works with extreme care. Who, therefore, could be better qualified by nature and inheritance to contribute to the efficiency of a bench-assembly production line than the oriental girl? No need for a Zero Defects program here! By nature, they will 'quality control' them- selves. (*Far Eastern Economic Review*, 18 May 1979, p. 76)

Studies pointed to the deliberate promotion of various cultural practices in the work place by employers in their attempts to extract maximum profit from their female work force: Western-style beauty contests and sporting activities to promote competitiveness among workers; Japanese-style authoritarian paternalism to ensure docility and discipline; conformity with local cultural values to build loyalty among the work force and the community for respecting its norms (Lim, 1978; Arrifin, 1983; Mather, 1985). Still other studies explained the recruitment of young, single women in terms of patriarchal traditions which allowed the smooth transfer of their submission to patriarchal authority from the family patriarch to the capitalist patriarch (Safa, 1990; Salaff, 1981). Mather's study from Indonesia drew attention to the alliance between factory manage- ment and the local Islamic elite to use traditional authority within the community to create a compliant labour force and to neutralise any threat that the community might feel at the prospect of young girls entering factory work: 'indeed there (was) a convergence of opinion between the incoming capitalists and the village patriarchs, who both see women and young people as submissive, dominated objects' (p. 171).

However, intriguing as these various insights were into the way in which apparently traditional norms and practices were drawn upon in the labour practices of modern, profit-maximizing fac- tories, oriented to producing for the world market, they were predominantly focused on the needs and strategies of employers. They did little to illuminate the 'supply side' of the picture. They told us that most of the women who worked in these factories were young, often unmarried, that many had migrated from traditional rural cultures to take up factory jobs and that it was these features, and what they signified to employers, which explained their predominance in the industrial work force. The few studies that explored the *effects* of women's entry into the paid labour force on other aspects of their lives generally concluded that it had done little to challenge the structures of patriarchy within the family and community (Joekes, 1982; Salaff, 1981; Greenhalgh, 1985).

Thus, in comparison to the detailed attention paid to employers' motivations in hiring a young and female work force, there was a deafening silence in these early studies on who these women were, why they had sought factory employment and what their jobs meant to them. They were treated as 'undifferentiated, homogenous, faceless and voiceless' (Wolf, 1992), members of a puppet-like reserve army of labour whose behavioural strings were pulled by capital, not social actors who thought about, struggled against and acted upon their own conditions (Beneria and Roldan, 1987). As Ong (1988, p. 84) pointed out, such approaches attributed far more animation and personality to capital than to the female labour it exploited.

A great deal of the pessimism which characterised this first wave of feminist scholarship on the feminisation of export-oriented factory labour, followed logically from its analytical objective of countering the prevailing orthodoxy that market forces were gender-neutral. Re-evaluating her own widely cited (co-authored) contribution to some of this early literature 'through the lens of time', Pearson (1998) comments: 'Our eagerness to examine the processes which connect the "modern" experiences of industrial employment with "traditional" modes of gender control allowed us to posit for heuristic purposes an uncontested and undifferentiated notion of traditional gender identities and controls, and an experience of interaction which was structurally determined by capital and patriarchy rather than open to negotiation and reconstitution by women workers themselves' (p. 180). Given this stance, the preoccupation of much of the early literature with 'the expression of patriarchy and the ways in which it easily mates with the relations of domination inherent in capitalism, as both are enacted through the oppression of women within the factory workplace' (Wolf, 1992, p. 8) was not surprising.

However, as long as the analytical focus was confined to the undeniable problems of hazardous working conditions, harsh discipline and insecurity of employment, the possibility that access to such employment might have any positive implications tended to be ruled out a priori. Employers clearly exercise a great deal of power in the labour market and in the work place, particularly so in situations of labour surplus. Yet women workers do not only exist as artefacts of employers' strategies nor is the quality of their lives fully determined by their experiences in the work place. Quoting Pearson again:

> To understand fully the implications of industrialization for women we would also need to examine the impact of women's earnings on intra-household income distribution and decision making. In other words, we would need to analyse whether earning a wage empowers women within the households, and increases their autonomy and ability to resist coercion or oppression. We would also need to examine whether employment in factories is 'women's choice', or whether such employment carries costs such as reduced access to education, restrictions in timing and choice of marriage partner, or alternatively, whether employment actually increases women's choices in these spheres. (1992, p. 246)

These were not, however, questions to which a great deal of attention was paid in most of the early studies. It was only as a number of later studies began to focus on women workers in the contexts of their families, households and communities, that a much more complex and contradictory picture of the relationships between women, employment and family has begun to emerge (Wolf, 1992; Ong, 1988; Beneria and Roldan, 1987).

## The selective visibility of exploitation in the global division of labour

My own dissatisfaction with the prevailing mode of feminist analysis of the situation of Third World women workers, and with the politics it gave rise to, crystallised in 1985 when it became Bangladesh's turn to pay the price of its success in international export markets. That year, Britain, France and the United States all imposed quotas on clothing imports from Bangladesh on the grounds that the rapidity with which they had grown was threatening to disrupt the domestic markets of these countries and hence constituted grounds for invoking the 'anti-surge' clause of the Multi Fibre Arrangements (MFA). The quotas were extremely punishing for the Bangladesh industry, particularly when it was considered that the 'surges' in question started from a very low base. In the UK, for instance, while the rate of growth in imports from Bangladesh did indeed exceed the 6 per cent permitted under the MFA, in actual terms, it took Bangladesh's share of total clothing imports into Britain from a mere 0.01 in 1980 to 0.11 in 1985, a share that was totally dwarfed at all times by the more established suppliers like Hong Kong (Jackson, 1992). The effects on the Bangladesh industry were brutal: 'Shipments of garments were stopped on their way to the docks, investors panicked and the bottom fell out of the booming market. With no experience of quotas and no system in place to manage them, there was chaos' (Jackson, 1992, p. 29). As quota-induced uncertainty spread, around two-thirds of the factories had closed down within three months and over 100,000 women workers were thrown out of work, many into destitution and hunger (Ahmed and Rahman, 1991, cited in Jackson, 1992).

Restrictions on imports under the MFA were generally supported in the UK by trade associations, trade unions and domestic employers as well as by the Labour Party whose consultative document on 'Labour and Textiles & Clothing' called for a 'tough' MFA to insulate the domestic industry while it underwent a process of planned restructuring. As Labour Party representatives in the House of Commons debate on the MFA on 9 May 1985 put it, what they wanted was 'fair trade', not 'free trade' and quotas had to be supported in the interests of 'order and stability'. Trade unionists also argued in favour of quotas on the grounds that the extremely exploitative conditions which prevailed in Third World factories gave employers from these countries an unfair advantage in the international market.

However, there was also opposition to the quotas from a range of differing political perspectives. The Silberston Report, commissioned by the Thatcher government, expressed a perspective which echoed the then-government's free-market philosophy. It pointed out that the restrictive practices permitted by the MFA militated against the efficient allocation of resources along lines of comparative advantage and represented a net cost to the consumer, who had to pay for more expensive locally-produced goods. The World Bank pointed to the contradictions that MFA quotas on Bangladesh exports represented to the overall commitment to free trade expressed by the very countries imposing them. Indeed, it led to the anomalous situation that the US government, on the one hand, sought to restrict clothing imports from Bangladesh at the behest of a protectionist domestic lobby, but on the other, put forward through its aid agency, USAID, a proposal for a consultant to advise the Bangladesh government how to get around the American quota (Chisholm et al. 1986)! Canada, Sweden and West Germany had refused to impose quotas on Bangladesh expressly on the grounds that it would be inconsistent with their aid policy which sought to promote both free trade and industrialisation in that country.[1]

In addition, opposition to the quota on clothing imports from Bangladesh also came from those of us who believed the quota system symbolised the way in which powerful countries not only wrote 'the rules of the game' in international trade, but were able to interpret them in their own interests. Bangladesh, for instance, would have been an obvious candidate for exemption from anti-surge quotas under Article 13 of the MFA, which required participating countries to be conscious of the problems posed by their restrictions on exports from new entrants and small suppliers. It was, after Ethiopia, the world's poorest country at that time with

1. Although Canada did subsequently yield to protectionist pressure.

an income per head of $150, less than one-hundredth of that of the United States. Shortly after the quotas were announced, the World Development Movement (WDM) in Britain launched a campaign to rule out the imposition of any quotas on imports from the fifty poorest countries of the world. Its rationale was that for such countries, production of clothing and textiles for a wider export market offered a promising, and indeed at the time, the only route, out of the 'trade trap' which bound so many poor countries into dependence on a limited range of primary commodities, the prices of which had been systematically declining in the past decades.

The campaign also pointed out that, although 'cheap imports from the Third World' were frequently cited as the major cause of job losses in Britain, thereby fuelling public and political support for an ever-more restrictive MFA stance towards the Third World, the major threat to jobs in the UK did not in fact come from the Third World at all, let alone from the poorer countries of the Third World. In 1984, 34 per cent of domestic demand for clothing in Britain was met by imports (Chisolm et al., 1986). Hong Kong, one of the wealthiest fastest-growing economies of the Third World, was also its largest individual supplier, accounting for 23 per cent of imports. However, the remaining imports were fairly evenly shared between industrialised and developing countries. Almost a third of imports were from within the EEC, with Italy as the dominant supplier, followed by Portugal, France and the Irish Republic. In addition, the WDM argued that the major factor in job losses was not in fact the increase in imports, but an economic climate in which crippling interest rates, a soaring exchange rate and the slump in domestic demand had all adversely affected domestic production, employment and capacity.

However, despite these facts, trade union support for the imposition of quotas on imports made by 'cheap' Third World women workers persisted. Elson (1983) provided a perceptive deconstruction of the meanings embedded in this persistent, and stigmatising, equation of 'Third World women' with 'cheap labour'. She noted, first of all, how the equation served to legitimise demands by workers in the First World for greater protection from unfair competition:

Women workers in the Third World are often stigmatised as 'cheap labour', willing to work in appalling conditions which undermines the position of women workers in the First World countries of North America, Western Europe and Australasia. There is often a feeling that Third World women are at fault; that they won't stand up for their rights, and thus jeopardise any attempt by women in the First World to stand up for theirs.

Tighter restrictions on imports of garments and textiles are often seen as the only strategy for women in the First World to protect themselves against the supposed menace of 'cheap labour' founded on 'oriental submissiveness. (p. 6)

She went on to point to the pejorative subtext of the discourse of 'cheap labour':

The term 'cheap labour' carries with it condemnation of the workers themselves. There is something of an implication that workers who are cheap labour must be lacking in self-respect. . . . Frequently, it also has racist implications when applied to non-white people – the implication that people of colour are 'cheap labour' because they are culturally backward. When used to describe women in the Third World (or of Third World origin) sexism and racism are often combined – as in the myth of the submissive Oriental girl. (p. 10)

Many of us who were involved in the campaign against the MFA quotas experienced at first hand this combination of self-interest and prejudice which characterised the attitudes of many trade unionists in the north towards workers in the south. It was brought home to me personally after a conference organised by the WDM campaign which brought in trade unionists from the Philippines and Bangladesh to present the case against quotas from the perspective of Third World workers. At the end of the conference, a woman from the Scottish TUC told me, in private, that their arguments had made little headway with her. As she put it: 'There is no way we can be expected to compete with these people. All you have to do is throw them a handful of rice and they are prepared to work all hours of the day'.

Kumudhini Rosa, a Sri Lankan feminist activist with several years of experience organising women workers in the free trade zones around Colombo, also encountered similar attitudes in the course of her interactions with northern trade unionists:

I think there is very little awareness of the international nature of the textile industry; western workers, even trade union officials, have little knowledge of the movement of capital, and the effects of this in the West or in the Third World. A German trade unionist I met was very hostile towards the movement of capital, and really blamed the whole thing on the workers of the South. I met a group of Belgian workers, about 70–100 of whom had been displaced when a factory moved to Sri Lanka. One man kept asking "Why is your labour so cheap? Why can't you make it expensive?" For me trying to explain to them why our workers are so cheap was like talking to a wall. (cited in Chisolm et al., 1986, p. 75)

Bangladeshi trade unionists also expressed their frustration at finding their efforts to improve the conditions of women workers in the garment factories in Bangladesh sabotaged by the lurid sensationalism which characterised the efforts of the northern labour movement to promote 'protectionism with a human face'. As the General Secretary of the National Garment Workers in Bangladesh pointed out, Bangladeshi women workers needed *better* rather than *fewer* jobs:

We want to see the garment industry flourish in Bangladesh and at the same time workers' conditions improve. We need international support in our struggle to improve the conditions of garment workers. But not buying Bangladeshi shirts isn't going to help us, it will just take away people's jobs. The shock tactics – such as the pictures I have seen from America of Bangladeshi shirts dripping with blood – should stop ... Instead they should concentrate on putting pressure on buyers in their own country to make sure they buy from factories with decent conditions ... As workers, we give an emphatic "yes" to the campaign *against* the quotas. (cited in Jackson, 1992, p. 28)

In addition to giving me first-hand experience of the resistance of the British labour movement to the idea that jobs in the Third World might be worth defending, my involvement with the WDM campaign also brought me indirectly into contact with another group of Bangladeshi women garment workers, this time within Britain itself. As a part of the campaign, a colleague, Nick Chisolm, and I, were asked to carry out a small research project in London in order to explore the views of clothing producers and trade unionists in the industry, some of the staunchest supporters of protection against 'unfair' competition from the Third World. We did not actually interview any homeworkers, but visited a number of factories scattered across the east and north of London, where the clothing industry was largely located. In the course of this research, it became clear that none of the employers we spoke to actually employed any Bangladeshi women either in larger factories we visited or in the smaller sweatshop units, although we came across many who employed Bangladeshi men. A colleague, Swasti Mitter, who wrote up the final report with us and had done some previous work on the clothing industry in the East End of London, told us that this absence was deceptive and there were in fact large numbers of Bangladeshi women employed as machinists at home.

I became increasingly struck by the contrast between the high visibility of the Bangladeshi women workers whom I had observed on their way to and from work on the streets of Dhaka, and the near-invisibility of the Bangladeshi women who worked as domestic outworkers for the industry in London. There was also next to no research at all in existence at the time on this latter group of women who occupied a shadowy presence in discussions about the decline of the British clothing industry. To some extent, this was part of a more general ignorance of the situation of homeworkers. As Allen and Wolkowitz (1987) pointed out, with few exceptions, it had been largely neglected by researchers: 'the frameworks within which work is usually analysed tend to marginalise homeworking and perpetuate its invisibility' (p. 28). It had received some attention in studies by organisations like the Low Pay Unit, but attempts to regulate homeworking conditions through parliamentary bills in 1979 and 1981 received little support in parliament and the issue subsequently languished.

At the time of the WDM campaign, manufacturing outwork was being dismissed by some as a minor problem, affecting a few unfortunate women during their child bearing years and by others as a logical outcome of ethnic cultural practices. However, apart from Mitter's brief study of the exploitative conditions under which Bangladeshi women worked in the clothing industry in London, and some occasional headlines about the unsafe conditions in the sweatshops of East London, the community as a whole was largely absent from public consciousness. This silence on the situation of

Bangladeshi clothing workers in East London by the British labour movement was in marked contrast to the vehemence of their condemnation of the exploitation of Third World women workers abroad and the unfair competition it gave rise to.

Clearly, the logic of justice requires that the decision to make claims on behalf of one group of workers, and to remain silent on behalf of another, should be grounded in concrete information about the lives of the workers in question, the conditions under which they work, the reasons for their choice of work and the implications of these choices for other aspects of their lives. Such information was, however, conspicuously missing as were the voices of the workers themselves, both those in Bangladesh whose working conditions were the focus of so much attention, and those in London, who were largely invisible in these discussions. It was partly to fill this gap that the research for this book was initiated and why the methodology of seeking out women workers' own testimonies on their labour market behaviour was adopted. However, as I point out in the Preface, in the course of exploring these issues from the perspectives of the women workers, I also became interested in evaluating the extent to which the insights offered by their narratives related to social science accounts of such behaviour. Consequently, in the next chapter, I review some of this social science literature and draw out the competing hypotheses it generates about women's labour market behaviour. These then form the organising framework around which the empirical analysis in this book is arranged.

# 2

# 'Rational fools' or 'cultural dopes'? Stories of structure and agency in the social sciences

Economics is all about how people make choices. Sociology is all about why they don't have any choices to make. (Duesenberry, 1960, pp. 231–234)

The *purely* economic man is indeed close to being a social moron. Economic theory has been much preoccupied with this rational fool decked in the glory of his *one* all-purpose preference ordering. (Sen, 1982, p. 99)

Voluntarism here . . . becomes largely reduced to making space in social theory for an account of motivation, connected via norms to the characteristics of social systems . . . Parson's actors are cultural dopes . . . (Giddens, 1979, p. 52)

In this book I am concerned primarily with explaining the differing, and counter-intuitive, patterns of labour market behaviour which characterised two groups of women with similar cultural beliefs and values, but located in different parts of the world. In order to formulate some hypotheses as to the factors which lay behind these labour market outcomes, I want to review the main accounts put forward in the social sciences to explain why people act in the way they do, focusing in particular on those which have a bearing on women's labour market behaviour. I will be organising my discussion around two extreme versions of these thereotical approaches, which are summarised in Duesenberry's famous aphorism quoted at the start of this chapter.

The 'economics' referred to by Duesenberry is mainstream neoclassical economics which focuses on the individual as its unit of analysis and portrays all human behaviour as the product of individual choice and action. The 'sociology' in question refers to forms of analysis which focus on the properties of larger social structures for their explanations of human behaviour. Over the years, dissatisfaction with each of these extremes has led to the emergence of a theoretical 'middle ground' where the useful insights from each tradition are drawn on to modify the extremes of the other. This chapter provides a brief overview of both the extreme versions outlined above as well as the key features of this convergent middle ground.

## Choice as decision making: constructing 'the rational fool'

The idea that human behaviour can be explained in terms of the choices that people make, given limited resources, has an immediate intuitive appeal. However, choice in economic theory has the much more restrictive meaning of 'rational choice'. While this refers to the attempts of individuals to achieve the maximum possible satisfaction of their desires, given unlimited desires, but limited means, economists are generally not interested in what determines individual desire, what makes people choose what they do. Instead, tastes and preferences are either taken to be subjectively determined, varying randomly and idiosyncratically across the population or else they are assumed to be stable over time and roughly the same for all people: 'one does not argue over tastes for the same reason that one does not argue over the Rocky mountains – both are there, will be there next year, too, and are the same to all men' (Stigler and Becker, 1977).

Either way, tastes and preferences are treated as exogenous to the rational choice calculus. All that is necessary for economic analysis to take place is that individuals have consistent preference orderings over the full range of possible choices, so that every good or service can be ranked as preferred to, or as equivalent of, every

other other, in terms of the satisfaction yielded. Individual preference orderings can then be aggregated into individual utility functions which weight different goods and services, or bundles of goods
and services, according to the satisfaction yielded. The exercise of
'rational choice' requires each individual to choose the particular
bundle of goods and services which gives them the greatest level of
satisfaction, given the resources at their disposal. Consequently,
while individual preferences cannot be directly observed, embedded as they are in the human psyche, they are 'revealed' by
individual choice: if x is chosen over y, then x is 'revealed' to be
preferred to y.

Early versions of rational choice theory portrayed the labour
supply decision as the process by which individual workers weighed
the utility to be derived from income earned in the market place
versus the utility derived from leisure, before deciding how much
time to allocate to each. However, as economists began to focus on
women's labour supply patterns, it became clear that the decision
about use of individual labour time could not be treated as the act
of an isolated individual, nor could it be reduced to a simple choice
between work and leisure.[1] The New Household Economics, associated in particular with the work of Becker, was the principal
response to this discovery by mainstream economists. It represented
an attempt to shift the focus of analysis from individual to household decision making and to incorporate unpaid household work,
including child care, into the choice calculus as an additional
possible use of individual time.

The Beckerian household, which emerged out of this analysis,
was seen as the site of both production as well as consumption.
Decision making was depicted as a two-stage process: first of all, the
allocation of household resources to the productive effort so as to
maximise returns to each input, followed by the allocation of the
resulting output to different members so as to achieve maximum
levels of joint satisfaction. Utility was seen to inhere in certain final
commodities which could either be purchased directly from the

---

1. As Dex (1985) has pointed out, an economic model which assumed the labour
supply decision to entail a simple individual choice between work and leisure could only
have been the product of a male imagination.

market place, using income earned by household members, or else produced at home, using purchased inputs, household technology and the labour of household members. Household labour availability was thus a critical factor in the achievement of utility and the narrow monetary income constraint of earlier models was replaced with a 'full income constraint' which measured the total income flows available to the household together with unpaid labour, valued at its imputed market wage. Welfare maximisation required that each member's time was allocated between paid market-oriented activities, unpaid domestic activities and leisure, according to their marginal returns in these activities and, hence, according to their expected marginal contributions to household welfare.

The widely observed gender division of labour within the household, with women specialising in unpaid domestic chores while men played a greater role in market-related activities, was explained by adherents to the New Household Economics in terms of a 'trade' metaphor (McCrate, 1988): women were seen to have a comparative advantage over men in child bearing and breastfeeding, based on their 'genetic endowments'. A rational choice calculus dictated that they specialised in those activities, including unpaid domestic labour, which allowed them to make the most of this advantage, leaving male family members to specialise in market-related activities and earn the primary income of the household. An increase in the market value of women's time of a sufficient magnitude would bring about a re-allocation in this division of labour, with women increasing their time into market-oriented activities while men reallocated some of their time into domestic or other non-paid uses of their time.

A major problem for the rational choice approach of this shift from the individual to the household as the locus of decision making was the problem of aggregating individual preferences into a single welfare function for maximising purposes. While it could plausibly be maintained that individuals knew, and hence were able to act on, their own preferences, and while members of a collectivity might be individually capable of knowing, and acting on, their own preferences, the assumption that they would also be able to know, and to agree, on what would maximise their joint welfare levels could not be similarly taken for granted. It was possible that individual preference orderings might dictate very differing, and perhaps conflicting, calculations of what constituted joint household welfare.

The problem of aggregation was dealt with by neo-classical economists by essentially side-stepping it. Some cited the special nature of the family – 'blood is thicker than water' – to imply full interdependence of utility functions so that each member of the same household obtained as much satisfaction from the satisfaction of the others as they did from their own (Samuelson, 1956; Schultz, 1973). Others conceded the possibility of self-interested behaviour among household members, but confined it to 'rotten kids'. The assumption of welfare-maximisation was retained intact by positing that all resources were pooled under the authority of a 'benevolent dictator' who then allocated them along welfare-maximising lines.

The New Household Economics attracted a number of adherents among those who were persuaded by its extension of the choice-theoretic framework to domains of decision making not normally associated with economics: birth, death, love, marriage, child care, divorce and so on. Others, however, both within and outside the discipline, greeted with some incredulity its claims that *all* decision making, whether it involved: 'money prices or imputed shadow prices, repeated or infrequent decisions, large or minor decisions, emotional or mechanical ends, rich or poor persons, men or women, adults or children, brilliant or stupid persons, businessmen or politicians, teachers or students' (Becker, 1976, p. 8) could be explained in terms of a rational choice calculus. Attempts to critique such sweeping claims have led to an alternative economics of the middle ground which eschews the idea of 'rational economic man' in favour of the more realistic and recognisable 'imperfectly rational, somewhat economic person' (Folbre, 1994, p. 20). In the sections which follow, I will be focusing in greater detail on specific aspects of this critique which are of particular relevance to the themes of this book: the economic conceptualisation of choice and its treatment of conflict, particularly in the context of the household, where decisions about women's labour supply are largely made.

## Qualifying choice: individual preferences and social context

A major appeal of rational choice analysis for its adherents is the 'parsimony' of its approach, its ability to explain all aspects of human behaviour through a limited number of variables relating to prices and incomes. However, as Hodgson (1988) has pointed out, it is one of the paradoxes of neo-classical economics that while economists pride themselves on the parsimony of their own deliberations, a rational choice calculus requires economic agents to engage in the statistical analysis of information on a scale and complexity that is likely to defy the cognitive capacity and material resources of any human individual. For instance, if we take the time allocation decision of an average individual as an example, it would require that individual to conduct an information search on all the job opportunities available to someone with their particular qualifications, a comparison of the immediate and longer-term returns to each of these jobs with returns to alternative uses of their time in unpaid activities, and then a calculation of the 'winning' combination of activities which would maximise the expected returns to his or her time use. If that individual lived in a household, rather than alone, these calculations would immediately have to be multiplied to take account of the relative returns to each and every other household member.

A realistic evaluation of the scale of effort, information and cognitive capacity entailed in 'global rationality' has led to the development of a more 'bounded' notion of rationality which accommodates 'inertness' or non-decision making as an aspect of human behaviour. 'Inertness' reflects the fact that many aspects of behaviour are governed by rules and norms which have evolved over time on the basis of recurring events and which help to create routines and customs in different domains of decision making. Such rules and norms serve to remove certain forms of action from the purposive deliberation of individual actors, leaving them free to utilise a rational choice calculus on other less predictable and less routine decisions.

Economic critics of global rationality tended to focus on information costs and cognitive limitations as the explanation for rule-governed behaviour. However, a more sociologically-informed interpretation of rules and norms would focus attention on their role in defining and maintaining the social order. Here it would be necessary to distinguish, as economists generally do not, between rules which are relatively value-free (for example, the Highway Code), and those which are more value-laden (rules of inheritance, for example). A rule that cars must stop when traffic lights turn to red has the practical purpose of facilitating an orderly flow of traffic, and applies to specific actors in specific contexts. A rule which says that only sons will inherit parental property is of a very different order. It expresses more widely held values about who matters in a society, why they matter and how they matter, values which are deeply entrenched within the traditions of that society and which cut across its various domains. Value-laden rules, and the behaviour which they give rise to, are likely to be more enduring, and difficult to change than practical rules, such as those of the Highway Code. They do not merely exist 'out there' as a legally-defined set of guidelines for human behaviour, but are assimilated by individuals in the process of acquiring their sense of selfhood and identity. The more closely bound up these norms and conventions are with the 'core identity' of individuals in particular societies, their sense of who they are and what their place is in the greater scheme of things, the more value-laden they are likely to be and the more 'inert' or resistant to change are the forms of behaviour which they govern.

One of the arguments that will be made in this book is that the norms, beliefs, customs and values through which societies differentiate between women and men, their approved models of gender difference, are an important dimension of the core identity of individuals, shaping their preferences, defining their interests and regulating their behaviour in ways that cannot easily be shaken off simply because there has been a change in prices or income. Such identities are acquired very early in life and influence the individuals' experiences of affection and intimacy, their understanding of their own sexuality and emotional needs, and their expectations and obligations in relation to others. At the same time, however, individual identities and the preferences they generate, are not simply frozen in childhood: they evolve over the course of a person's lifetime, reflecting their social positioning, their individual experiences and their changing circumstances. Furthermore, the human capacity for purposeful deliberation can be brought to bear on questions of identity and preferences as much as it can on questions of buying and selling (Folbre, 1994; Hirschman, 1985; McCrate, 1988). As McCrate points out: 'While we may not quibble about tastes over many of the choices we make, we do struggle regularly with ourselves over who we are and who we want to be: we have second-order preferences about our preferences concerning such fundamental issues as manhood and womanhood' (1988, p. 237).

Such modifications to our understanding of the interaction between the subjective and the social in how people perceive their choices gives the idea of 'preferences' a far more central role in the analysis of human behaviour than is customary in mainstream economics, but it suggests varying orders of preferences in place of the '*one* all-purpose preference ordering' which characterises rational economic man (Sen, 1982, p. 99). In particular, it distinguishes between preferences which are highly personal to the individual, what have been described as 'wanton' preferences, formed out of whim or passion, 'impulsive, uncomplicated, haphazard, publicity-induced' and higher order or 'meta' preferences which are a result of conscious reflection (Hirshmann, 1985, p. 9). As Hirshmann points out, individual tastes are almost by definition a form of preference about which there can be no argument: 'de gustibus non est disputandum'. By contrast, a taste or preference about which there can be an argument – with others or with *one's self* – 'ceases ipso facto being a taste – it turns into a value'. While wanton preferences can change equally wantonly, higher order preferences tend to be more enduring, embodying as they do the norms of a society or the ethical values of the individual.

## Qualifying choice:
### preferences and power within the household

A second paradox of neoclassical economics relates to its depiction of individual agency. Economists claim to provide a theory of choice: as Buchanan, a Nobel Prize winning economist put it, 'Economists, almost alone, understand the notion of choice itself . . . and economists who believe in homo economicus must not be duped or lulled into the neglect of elementary principles' (1988). In actual fact, however, 'homo economicus' is denied very much choice at all. *Real* choice means that the individual actor could have always chosen otherwise. For the economic actor, on the other hand, 'there is almost always but one preferred or rational course of action', to their situations, 'and this is always followed' (Lawson, 1997, p. 9). As long as empirical outcomes are compatible with the predictions of a rational choice calculus, they are assumed to embody such a calculus. Where they are not, it is assumed that the model has not been properly specified. However, the underlying assumption of rational choice is never questioned and actual decision making processes rarely investigated.

In reality, the assumption of rational choice as the guiding principle of behaviour is problematic, even at the individual level. As already noted, it assumes that people know their own prefer-ences, that their preferences are consistent and that they have the information and cognitive capacity necessary to carry out a rational choice calculus. However, decision making is rarely of an individual nature. Most decisions are taken in the context of collectivities – firms, trade unions, non-government organisations and, of course, households. In such situations, the assumption of maximising behaviour is not only problematic but frequently misleading. Let me illustrate this with reference to the household, the arena of decision making which is the main focus of this book.

Although the New Household Economics represented an attempt by economists to take account of the collective nature of the household, the shift from individual to collective decision making was, in fact, more apparent than real. By assuming a unified household preference function, based on interdependent utility functions or benevolent dictatorship, economists were able to sidestep the real challenge to rational choice theory posed by collective decision making: conflicts over what might constitute the joint welfare of the household and the ability of some members to promote their own interests at the expense of others in non-welfare-maximising ways. These assumptions have now come under increasing challenge in the face of accumulating empirical evidence of widespread age and gender inequalities within the household in many regions of the world. In some regions (including Bangladesh), these inequalities have taken such extreme forms that they result in markedly higher levels of mortality, malnutrition and ill-health among women and girls (see, for instance, contributions to Townsend and Momsen, 1987).

Such inequalities are difficult to explain away simply in terms of differences in tastes and preferences. They have given rise to alternative ways of conceptualising the household which dispense with the assumption of unified preferences. These take a more institutional approach to household analysis, seeking to replace the orthodox portrayal of the household as a collection of individuals, differentiated only by their human capital characteristics and genetic endowments, with a more considered analysis of what is specific to the household as an institutional form, differentiating it as a decision making entity, both from the individual as well as from other collectivities in society.

The distinctive characteristics of the household are seen to lie in the particular activities which are usually carried out within it and in the social relationships through which these activities are carried out. Households represent a specific institutional response to the desire of individuals for long-term stable environments in which to bear and bring up children, to care for each other through sickness and health, disability and old age and to plan their lives in a world, characterised by risk and uncertainty. The institutional advantage of the household lies in the close intertwining of interests and emotions which characterises its relationships. Its members are related to each other by blood or marriage, have known each other for much of their lives and are likely to be more trustworthy and reliable than a group of strangers. Nevertheless, behaviour within the household is not simply a spontaneous outcome of the affection and loyalty its members might feel towards each other. It is also underwritten by a series of 'implicit contracts' which spells out the claims and obligations of different members to each other and which are backed by the norms and rules of the wider society.

An institutional analysis of the household thus accommodates areas of 'inertia' in household decision making. Its members are unlikely to be as responsive to economic incentives as neo-classical economists assume them to be because many aspects of their behaviour are governed by the prior commitments embodied in the implicit contracts of the family. An illuminating illustration of the difference relates to the widely documented empirical observation that women's domestic workloads tend to be higher than men's in much of the world, regardless of their hours of work in market-related activity. A Beckerian explanation might point to women's stronger predilection for housework and to lags in response to an increase in their market involvement (Rosensweig, 1986). An institutional explanation, on the other hand, would stress the contractual underpinnings of the intra-household division of labour which assigns domestic tasks primarily to women. These contractual obligations are likely to take precedence over individual preferences and any desire to change them would entail a process of often protracted renegotiation of the domestic contract between family members.

However, the ability of household members to act on their individual preferences is not only constrained by their contractual obligations. Once the household is treated as a genuine collection of individuals, rather than as an individual disguised as a collectivity, the possibility of conflicting preferences between its members becomes a real possibility. There is no a priori reason why, in such situations, the preferences of each individual member will be given equal weight in household decision making processes; indeed, it is possible that some preferences may be given no weight at all. In other words, once conflicting preferences are recognised as a possibility within the household – or any other collectivity – the possibility of inequalities of power in the resolution of such conflict also has to be recognised.

One way in which power has been accommodated within these alternative approaches has been through a game-theoretic bargaining framework. As we saw earlier, an institutional approach explains household co-operation as a response to the need for stability in critical areas of people's lives. Its members agree to be bound by certain contractual obligations to each other, perhaps making rational choice decisions within this framework of co-operation, as long as the gains from co-operation outweigh the gains from what menbers could achieve on their own. The problem arises in situations where there are a range of co-operative solutions which are all preferable to any solution which could be achieved in the absence of co-operation, but where individual members disagree as to which one of this range of possible co-operative solutions they prefer. There would still be an incentive to find a co-operative solution, but conflicts are likely to arise over which particular one. In such situations, bargaining and negotiation between individual members is likely to come into play to determine which solution will be adopted, with the final decision reflecting the preferences of the household member, or members, with the greatest bargaining power.

While this conceptualisation of co-operation and conflict is common to a range of institutional approaches to household decision making, there is some variation in how differences in bargaining power are conceptualised, depending on how seriously the institutional character of the household is taken. Most versions of the bargaining approach posit differences in the bargaining power of different members in terms of the levels of utility they would enjoy should co-operation break down, variously called their 'fall-back', 'breakdown' or 'threat' positions. In more economistic versions, differences in fall-back position are conceptualised in terms of differences in the economic characteristics of individuals, such as their relative earnings and wealth. Other versions have expanded the notion to include a range of 'extra environmental parameters', which can be seen as an attempt to incorporate aspects of the wider social context in which decision making takes place. McElroy (1990), for instance, in her analysis of bargaining between married couples suggests that such parameters may include sex ratios in the relevant marriage markets, laws concerning alimony/child support settlements, women's ability to return to their natal homes after marital breakdown, as well as the cultural acceptability of outside work.

Sen (1990) moves away from a formalised approach to household bargaining in order to incorporate questions of ideology and perceptions into his model. He draws attention to the ways in which these might serve to differentiate, not only the ability of different household members to exercise bargaining power, but also how they define their preferences. One set of perceptions relates to the valuation given to the contribution of different members such that those who are perceived to contribute to the welfare of the household are seen to 'deserve' a greater say in household decision making. Such perceptions often have very little to do with the actual amount of time and effort invested by household members in different activities. Rather, they are influenced by the form taken by these contributions. Orientation to the market rather than to subsistence production, the location of the work in the public domain rather than in the privacy of the home, the type of remuneration (cash rather than kind) and its magnitude, are some of the factors which help to influence the perceived economic value of a contribution.

Perceptions are also brought into the analysis of bargaining via their influence on the individual's sense of their own self-worth, what Sen calls the 'perceived interest response'. If certain individuals, or categories of individuals, perceive their longer-term interests to be best served by sacrificing their personal well-being for that of others, then they are less likely to press their own individual claims in the bargaining process. There are a number of alternative interpretations as to how the 'perceived interest response' works, depending on whether the emphasis is on conscious or unconscious processes.

Sen, for instance, makes the point that there might be an unconscious adjustment by women in their behaviour and expectations to take account of their opportunities and circumstances. As he points out: 'There is much evidence in history that acute inequalities often survive precisely by making allies out of the deprived. The underdog comes to accept the legitimacy of the unequal order and becomes an implicit accomplice' (1990, p. 126). Sen explains this complicity on the part of subordinate groups as a case of 'adapted perceptions', of people learning to make the best of their lot. The fact that in many cultures, women appear to attach less value to their own well-being than to the well-being of other family members, suggests that the 'perceived interest response' partly operates through differences in internalised views of self-worth, in other words, through differences in the extent to which interests are perceived in individuated terms or subsumed within the interests of the larger collectivity. This version of the 'perceived interest response' links up to the earlier discussion about the significance of gender identity as a source of differences in the preferences that women and men bring to their choices.[2]

However, the perceived interest response may also work at a conscious strategic level. Agarwal (1997), for instance, suggests that women's awareness of their weaker fallback positions may curtail their ability to press openly for their own advantage within household decision making processes – although it need not preclude them from doing so covertly: compliance, in other words, need not imply collusion. She notes various clandestine ways in which women in the South Asian context seek to secure their own self-interest while appearing to comply with the cultural norms of self-subordination. For Agarwal, therefore, the emphasis should be more on the external constraints to women acting overtly in their self-interest and less on a lack of awareness on their part as to where their interests lie. However, regardless of which particular version of perceived interest response is assumed to be dominant in decision making processes, the effect in terms of bargaining power is the same. Women are less likely than men within the family to press for outcomes which reflect their personal well-being or their individual interests.

These different determinants of bargaining power are by no means mutually exclusive. In fact, patriarchal power in most cultures reflects the fact that, for any given class, these determinants tend to coalesce in favour of men as a category, forming the bedrock of rules and resources from which they are able to shape, and indeed impose, 'co-operative' solutions which favour their own well-being and self-interest should they wish to. The institutionalist approach to the household thus allows us to dispense with the simplifying fiction of the benevolent dictator and to grapple with issues of power and decision making in a more realistically portrayed collectivity. It recognises the possibility that a range of utility functions may co-exist within the household for different kinds of

---

2. It also echoes the point made by a number of feminists that women and men are brought up with very different degrees of 'connectedness' and 'separation' in how they perceive the relationship between their interests and those of other family members.

decisions, from the purely selfish (in which satisfaction is gained primarily from devoting resources to own wants, needs and preferences) at one end of the spectrum, to the purely selfless (where satisfaction is entirely gained from devoting resources to the wants, needs and preferences of others).

Furthermore, it recognises that decision making outcomes within the household need not invariably represent the equitably-weighted aggregation of individual preferences, as implied by the logic of the unified preference approach. They may also reflect the distribution of bargaining power within the household, and hence the preferences of dominant members. The formulation thus reverses the positive association posited for the Beckerian household between power and altruism (exemplified in the concept of the 'benevolent dictator') and offers the intuitively more plausible hypothesis that selfishness within the household is much more likely to 'reveal' power just as apparent 'selflessness' is more intuitively indicative of powerlessness. This gels with a point that Folbre makes (1986, p. 251):

> The suggestion that women and female children 'voluntarily' relinquish leisure, education, and food would be somewhat more persuasive if they were in a position to demand their fair share. It is the juxtaposition of women's lack of economic power with the unequal allocation of household resources that lends the bargaining power approach much of its persuasive appeal.

## Qualifying choice:
## preferences and power in the wider context

Households and household behaviour obviously represent one form of challenge to the 'atomised' model of decision making at the core of neo-classical theories of choice. However, collective forms of behaviour are not confined to the family-kinship nexus, but are a routine feature of the wider social context in which this nexus is located. Nor is gender the only basis on which inequality exists in a society. While gender inequality is central to the analysis carried out in this book because of the nature of the research questions it addresses, we will also be encountering evidence of other forms of social inequalities which have to be taken into account in how we answer these questions.

Folbre (1994) attempts to capture the multiple and intersecting inequalities which characterise social relationships in different societies through the idea of structures of collective constraint viz. the asset distributions, political rules, cultural norms and individual preferences which combine to assign individuals to different social groupings within a society, groupings which stand in hierarchical relationships to each other. The structure of rules and resources help to spell out the material interests of these different groups while social norms and individual preferences give their members a sense of identity and affiliation with the different groups to which they belong. These structures of collective constraint reflect inequalities of gender, of class, of race and so on which characterise different societies, particular 'matrices of domination' in which the same individual may occupy a subordinate position as a member of certain social groups, but a dominant position in others. However, such social inequalities do not simply exist as a result of 'given' configurations of assets distributions, political rules, cultural norms and individual preferences. They are actively sustained by the collective action of dominant groups to defend their privileges through a variety of means, which include the overt exercise of discrimination as well as the covert mobilisation of institutional bias. Equally, of course, they are likely to be challenged, overtly or covertly, by subordinate groups who will mobilise whatever material or symbolic resources are available to them to undermine the structures of inequality. There is thus a constant, dynamic interplay between the creation of privilege and disprivilege as part of the process of social change in a society.

Folbre makes a distinction between different social groupings in society on the basis of whether they are given or chosen. Membership of chosen groups, as the name suggests, are voluntary: people join them in order to pursue shared interests, based on some shared aspect of their positions, and are free to leave them when they wish. Trade unions, feminist organisations, political parties or housing associations are examples of such collectivities. 'Given' groups, on the other hand, are not easily joined or abandoned, although there may be some scope for negotiation. Race, gender, ethnicity, class and so on are examples of such 'given' groups where membership is not chosen but may nevertheless create ties of solidarity between members based on affinities of identity and interests. While such group solidarity is often based on trust between people who have had similar life experiences and share the same aspirations, solidarity also has its darker side: 'it governs exclusion as well as inclusion, unifying privileged as well as disadvantaged groups' (p. 42). There can in other words, be no 'us' without a 'them'.

Some of the examples of this darker side of solidarity noted by Folbre have a particular resonance for the subject of this book. For instance, she points out that, while it is usually in the employers' interests to create divisions among their workers, based on attributes such as race or gender, in order to weaken their bargaining power, it is also in the interests of groups of workers, once they have gained privileged access to market opportunities, to collude with employers to protect themselves from competition from the weaker sections of the labour force through various forms of boundary demarcation: white workers will collude against black workers and male workers against female. Thus, along with Folbre's 'given' and 'chosen' groups, we could add the cross-cutting categories of 'open' and 'closed' groups, where the differential use of access and closure are used as ways of perpetuating exclusion and defending privilege (Parkin, 1979).

Group solidarity can take nationalist lines as well. Harsh restrictions on labour immigration have long served to defend the 'labour aristocracy' of advanced industrialised countries from low-wage competition from the rest of the world, perpetuating the international wage differentials which help to support their higher living standards. And when the restructuring of manufacturing industry of the kind discussed in the previous chapter threatens to erode this advantage, protectionist measures, this time restricting the import of low-wage goods, can be brought to bear once again to restrict 'unfair' competition and defend privilege.

Gender is thus not the sole, or always the most salient, aspect of inequality and disadvantage in people's lives. However, it is one that was, until very recently, an unquestioned, taken-for-granted, aspect of social reality and rarely the subject of social science analysis. For that reason it continues to merit special attention. The dominant focus of the book will be on gender relations, and on gender inequalities, as they play out in the domain of the household, where power and preference, constraint and consent, are most difficult to disentangle. However, as we will be arguing, the nature of gender inequalities within the household, their persistence or transformation, have to be located and understood in relation to other forms of inequality and interests operating in the wider society and economy. In the course of this book, we will be seeing how intra-household relationships of co-operation and conflict are influenced by the collective identities and interests of race, class and community, and how actions taken within the household in turn act upon these wider collective structures.

## Structure as non-decision making: the sociological actor as 'cultural dope'

At the other end of the spectrum to explanations of individual choice as the wellspring of human behaviour are explanations of behaviour which give priority to structure over agency, to the extent of leaving very little scope at all for the exercise of individual choice. Explanations of women's labour supply patterns in terms of modes of productions or 'the needs of capital', examples of which were briefly referred to in Chapter 1, represent one genre of structuralist explanation, where the structures in question are largely economic. However, my main interest for the purposes of this book is in another genre of structuralist analysis, one which emphasises culture. Within this culturalist paradigm, individual actors have so completely internalised the norms and values of their society that individual behaviour is merely a re-enactment of social norm: culture becomes a word for describing 'that which constrains us ... in the most effective way possible, by shaping our 'will' that seeks to assert its 'freedom' (Wallerstein, 1990, p. 64).

The idea of individuals as 'cultural dopes' is of particular relevance to the concerns of this book, because it is so frequently fore-grounded in studies which deal with Third World women and even more strikingly so when the analytical focus is on Muslim women. As Kandiyoti remarks: 'A cursory glance at writings on the question of women and Islam reveals a widespread tendency to treat Islam as a unitory ideology from which practices relating to women can be automatically read off in any Islamic society' (1987, p. 1). There are understandable reasons why social norms and values should play a prominent role in attempts to understand gendered phenomena, given well-documented evidence of a 'geography of gender deprivation' created by strong empirical correlations between the norms and practices of particular regions in the world and marked gender inequalities in basic well-being, including life expectancy, nutritional status, and health status which prevail in these regions. The concept of purdah occupies a central role in much of this analysis, partly because of its empirical association with regions of inequality and partly because of the very real limits it is seen to place on women's life choices. Purdah has been explained in terms of the logic of patrilineal descent rules whereby family name and property is transmitted largely through male offspring. The paternity of children becomes a crucial social issue in such contexts, engendering rigid controls over female sexuality and reproductive capacity. Purdah is central to the institutional arrangements through which such control is exercised.

At the core of purdah is the notion that family *izzat* (honour) resides in the virtue and modesty of its women; constant surveil-lance is necessary to ensure that women do nothing to bring *sharam* (shame) on their kin. Purdah literally means 'veil' or 'curtain' and expresses the symbolic, physical and economic demarcation of the universe along gender lines. It operates most obviously at a physical and spatial level, dividing off the hidden and domestic sphere of women from the public and visible sphere of men. It is also a behavioural principle, regulating female behaviour by defining the norms of modesty and virtue: 'The female voice should not reach male ears outside the household. She must therefore speak in a low voice. Girls are admonished by their mother, "you are female and should speak in a soft voice", the virtue of softness and submissiveness is thus inculcated in girls . . .' (Islam, 1979, p. 227).

Purdah is often used to refer to the concealing clothing that women put on to protect themseves when they venture outside the home.

Purdah also has an economic dimension, since it restricts women's income-earning opportunities to those which can be carried out within the home. While feminist critiques of official labour force statistics have pointed to various forms of gender bias which have led to the underestimation of women's actual labour force participation, it remains the fact that in regions where the ideological link between the maintenance of female purity and family honour requires the seclusion of women, women's participation in paid activity outside the home has in reality been very low and their reliance on a male breadwinner correspondingly high.

A final dimension of purdah relates to the Islamic view of female sexuality as active and dangerous, threatening moral chaos and disorder (*fitna*) if not properly regulated (Mernissi, 1975). The Muslim universe is consequently constructed along sexually segregated lines, in which men belong to the Umma, the public domain of religion, belief and the moral order while women are contained within the domestic sphere, the realm of family, legitimised sexuality and reproduction. By minimising interaction between the sexes, the principle of segregation seeks to protect men from sexual temptation; a woman who transgresses these boundaries and enters traditionally male space is guilty of provoking men to thoughts of *zina* (illicit intercourse), endangering his peace of mind, social prestige and allegiance to the moral order (Mernissi, 1975, p. 85). Hence, the stress on seclusion and veiling of women and the admonishments to women to conceal anything of their person which might provoke thoughts of *zina* in a man who is not their husband. Hence, also, the emphasis on the power of the gaze in such societies: the eye has the power to provoke and women must lower their gaze in the presence of male strangers. Men can dishonour women with their gaze as much as they can through more physical forms of contact. Men's response to unveiled women in public space can be interpreted as a logical response to the provocation that this is seen to represent: 'pursuing the woman for hours, pinching her if the occasion is propitious, eventually assaulting her verbally, all in the hope of convincing her to carry out her

exhibitionist propositioning to its implied end' (Mernissi, op. cit.,
p. 86).

Purdah is therefore much more than the simple veiling of
women. According to Mernissi, it is central to the entrenchment of
patriarchal power, linking the territorial regulation of female sexuality and the institutionalisation of male power in the societies
where it is practised: 'Institutionalised boundaries dividing parts of
the society express the recognition of power in one part at the
expense of the other. Any transgression of the boundaries is a
danger to the social order because it is an attack on the unacknowledged allocation of power. The link between boundaries and
power is particularly salient in a society's sexual patterns' (Mernissi,
op. cit., p. 81).

## Gender and agency in the Bangladesh literature: local constructions of 'the cultural dope'

Purdah norms prevail in much of the Indian subcontinent among
Hindus as well as Muslims, but is adhered to more strongly in its
northern plains, among higher caste Hindus, among Muslims in
general and among their wealthier families in particular. The
seclusion of female family members from public forms of economic
activity, or their withdrawal from such work once it is affordable, is
an important means of signalling social status within these communities. However, while the low rates of female labour force
participation which characterises much of this region can be partly
attributed to the value attached to female seclusion, there has often
been an unthinking tendency in some of the analysis of women's
behaviour to attribute a degree of passivity, of mechanical conformity to cultural norms, to them which is not warranted by the
evidence provided. I would like to provide some examples of these
representations of women as 'cultural dopes' from the Bangladesh
context before going on to consider alternative frameworks which
take the power of cultural norms and practices seriously without
totally obliterating all possibility of individual agency.

Research on gender relations in Bangladesh really began after its
independence in 1971, a period which coincided with a time when

women were being 'discovered' in the international development
agenda and research funding being made available for this topic
for the first time. However, the dearth of knowledge about women's
lives meant that such research had to begin from first principles.[3]
Early research inevitably, and perhaps necessarily, took the form of
compiling 'cultural inventories' (Connell, 1987), the documenta-
tion of the various norms and practices which helped to explain
women's subordinate position in the context of Bangladesh society.
However, the preoccupation with the overarching culture of constraint gave rise to a body of literature in which every aspect of
women's lives, including their personalities and behaviour, were
explained as manifestations of such constraint. Purdah norms were
viewed as antithetical to any exercise of rational choice, a point
made explicitly by Boserup (1982) in her preface to an influential
study of the lives of rural women in Bangladesh:

> In countries with purdah systems women lose status if they perform work
> which requires them to leave the confines of their own household.
> Therefore they cannot make a rational choice between different types of
> money earning activities nor can they decide how to allocate their time
> between income earning and domestic work. (Boserup, 1982)

The portrayal of Bangladeshi women, particularly rural women, as
submerged in tradition, mechanically acting out its dictates, surfaced repeatedly in these early studies:

> (Village) women feel no urge to view themselves with detachment in
> relation to their culture; they do not seem to display any conscious
> inclination towards analysis or objectivity in regard to their pursuits. They
> do not explain the reasons for doing what they do, for behaving as they
> behave. They simply perform their 'duty' and behave according to custom.
> (S. Begum, 1982, cited in Alam and Matin, 1984, p. 8)

> In a situation of poverty and scarcity women suffer most in the traditional
> society of Bangladesh. The sanctification of motherhood, self-sacrifice, and

---

3. As one of the first studies in the post-independence era noted 'The lives of Bangali
women rarely appears as the subject matter of any literary or research work. The
available writing is mostly based on Hindu women, discussing the problems of unbreak-
able marriage bonds, persecution of widows and 'suttee' or presenting biographies of
illustrious ladies' (Abdullah, 1974, p. 2).

obedience to the husband as head of the family leads to women putting their own interest last – always . . . Less educated in general than men their greater ignorance keeps them fearful of the outside world. They lack time and freedom from family duties to seek any remunerative employment outside the household. (Gerard, 1979, p. 13)

Brought up from childhood to believe that she exists only as daughter, wife and mother to some men, her whole existence is oriented to serve and please men. She is ignorant of the world outside the home and develops no outlook on life. She has no ambition in life and no desire or urge to improve her lot. (Islam, 1979, p. 228)

As Giddens has pointed out, such representations of people as structurally determined automatons is frequently generated by analytical approaches which do not allow any space for the exploration of individual agents' own understanding of themselves and the circumstances of their actions. The significance of structures tends to be inflated in such analysis to such an extent that individual behaviour takes on the appearance of the 'blind' unfolding of structures in action. The exaggeration of structural constraint also characterises research in which there is considerable social distance between 'researcher' and 'researched', a distance which permits those who are positioned as 'experts' to attribute social incompetence and passivity to those of different class, locational and cultural backgrounds to themselves (Giddens, 1979, p. 72). This social distance is certainly a characteristic of some of the studies cited above, taking separate but overlapping forms: the social distance of the privileged, middle-class, urban-based and, frequently, expatriate researcher attempting to analyse the lives of poor, illiterate, rural women. The distance was evident in the standpoint of 'modernity' from which many of the early writers commented on the lives of 'traditional' village women:

Village life seems to have another time, an existence of its own almost untouched by time as we know it in the urban world, the modern world. (Sattar, 1974, p. 17)

The sad fact is that their intelligence has been blunted and their thinking capacity lulled by the pressure of tradition. (Begum, 1982, p. 109)

It was also evident in the very different motivations and impacts attributed to the employment of poorer, rural women and those from urban, middle-class backgrounds to which many of the Bangladeshi researchers belonged. Urban, middle-class women were seen to be working 'for personal fulfilment and a sense of independence' or to improve their family's standard of living (Enayet, 1979). They either ran their own businesses or worked in professional or salaried occupations in teaching, social work or government service where they enjoyed some degree of job security, regular hours and leave privileges. The implications of their employed status was portrayed in positive terms: 'That they have become more and more involved in gainful employment has improved their economic status as members of society and at the household level they have improved the condition of their families and the welfare of their children' (Enayet, 1979, p. 184).

By contrast, economic desperation was seen as the major factor behind the search for employment by poorer, rural women:

> Women under extreme economic pressures are forced to work as casual labourers or swarm the city pavements in search of employment or begging. Destitute women have shed their social inhibitions and seek employment in rice mills, factories or construction work outdoors even with men. They are desperate to seek sources of employment whenever and wherever possible to avoid starvation for themselves and their families. (Huq, 1979, p. 144)

Access to paid work had little impact on the lives of these women. According to Huq (1979), 'even when a woman was a wage earner, the female wage was usurped by the male master of the household who is also the decision maker' (Huq, p. 142). Islam suggested that poorer rural women who migrated into the towns in search of work kept their links with their families in the village, making them 'psychologically' no different from those still in the countryside. Forced by their poverty to work outside the home, they suffered from a guilty conscience. Through their devotion and deference to their husbands, they tried to maintain their adherence to the normative ideals.

These representations of Bangladeshi women are local examples of a strand in the wider development literature which often portrays Third World women, particularly those from the poorer sections of the population, as the passive dupes of patriarchal culture.[4] They were scathingly dismissed by Alam and Matin (1984, p. 8) as 'an amorphous collection of socio-anthropological explanations' which offered a depiction of Bangladeshi women as 'hardworking but weak and pitiable'; 'functioning as robots and ants do – without volition, understanding or vision – and inherently incapable of solving their own problems', cardboard figures waiting to be 'helped' rather than as 'vibrant, alive, protesting, outraged, even when they are denied direct expression': 'nowhere is there an attempt to acknowledge the wisdom, the tongue-in-cheek sarcasm of village women'.

## Accommodating agency:
## conjugal contracts and patriarchal bargains

I have dealt so far with forms of analysis in which culture is brought in as pure 'constraint', and as constraint of such magnitude, that individual actors appear totally overshadowed by its workings. I want to turn now to alternative conceptualisations of culture which depict individuals as competent and purposeful social actors, but which are also mindful of the very real boundaries within which their agency must operate. The idea of implicit contracts reappears in many of these attempts as a conceptual bridge between the understanding of culture as a broad and vaguely specified set of social rules and norms, and the more explicit consideration of how these rules and norms operate to shape individual motivations and strategies in specific institutional contexts.

Whitehead's study of the workings of the 'conjugal contract' in different socio-economic contexts was an early example of this form of analysis. Examining the 'politics of domestic budgeting', she pointed out that the relative power of husbands and wives did not simply mirror their relative wages in the labour market, pre-

---

4. See discussion in Kabeer, 1994, Chapter 3 and Mohanty, 1991 for some different perspectives on this strand of the literature.

cisely because familial ideologies about roles and responsibilities intervened to differentiate how male and female earnings were translated into control over, and hence disposal of, these earnings (Whitehead, 1981). In particular, what she called 'ideologies of maternal altruism' often led women to deny themselves the resources to satisfy their own needs and preferences in favour of other members of the family. However, she also noted that such altruism often contained a self-interested dimension. Inasmuch as women's fortunes were bound up with the fortunes of the household collectivity to a larger degree than those of male members in the context that she was studying, their longer-term interests were likely to be better served through forms of altruistic behaviour which helped to preserve household solidarity and co-operation.

The analysis of the implicit contracts of the family, and of 'the conjugal contract' in particular, has a resonance beyond the domestic domain. As Whitehead pointed out, the cluster of claims, obligations, resources and responsibilities embodied in such contracts illuminates not only the terms on which women and men make claims and meet obligations within the family, but also tell us something about how their society views their nature, aptitudes and dispositions and hence constructs gender difference in the broader context. The idea of 'contract' is important here because it draws attention to structures as 'resources' as well as 'rules'. The following quote from Cain et al. (1979) which can be seen as a description of the centrality of purdah in the patriarchal contract in the context of Bangladesh, illustrates this mutuality of claims and obligations, power and responsibility:

> Purdah is a complex institution that entails much more than restrictions on women's physical mobility and dress. It denies women access to many opportunities and aspects of everyday life and at the same time confers upon them social status as a protected group. Thus, in theory, purdah both controls women and provides them with shelter and security. While men have power and authority over women, they are also normatively obligated to provide them with food, clothing and shelter. (p. 408)

While the concept of 'contracts' is a useful way of capturing shared understanding about rights and obligations within the family,

sociological interpretations of the idea of bargaining draws attention to the possibility for negotiations over the terms of the
contract, the scope for which is partly defined by the contract itself.
Kandiyoti (1988), for instance, suggested that such contracts created very differing sets of gender interests in different social
contexts and very different possibilities for pursuing these interests.
She used the idea of 'the patriarchal bargain' as a way of capturing
the generalised state of play between the genders within particular
social contexts, and the specific combination of strategies that they
embodied. In contexts where women had some degree of independence in their access to resources and economic opportunities, as
in parts of sub-Saharan Africa, the relationship between the spouses
was likely to be characterised by an overt bargaining element. Any
attempt to infringe women's economic autonomy could result in
open conflict, often ending with women leaving their husbands to
set up their own households.

By contrast, the strategies adopted by women in areas of 'strong
patriarchy', such as South Asia, appeared to be one of adhering as
closely and as long as possible to cultural 'rules' even where these
rules served to express their own devalued status within society.
Such strategies reflected the fundamental asymmetry in the contractual basis of gender relations, captured in the quote from Cain
et al. cited earlier, whereby male authority over women within the
family had a material base, but male responsibility was normatively
controlled. Normative control, while powerful, is nevertheless relatively malleable in the face of economic imperative.

This marked dependence on men for economic needs and social
protection leaves women particularly vulnerable to what Cain et al.
term 'patriarchal risk', the likelihood of abrupt declines in their
economic welfare and social status should they find themselves
bereft of male guardianship. The risks and uncertainties attendant
on women's dependent status within such systems paradoxically
engender in them greater incentives to comply with, rather than
challenge, male dominance, and to manipulate the norms of male
obligation and protection to shore up their own position within
their families. 'Maternal altruism' takes a gender-discriminatory
form in such contexts as it is in women's interests to have as many
sons as possible, to assure their position within the marriage, and

to win their sons' loyalty and affection as a way of ensuring their own longer-term security: in other words, to buy into, rather than counter, norms of son preference prevalent in such societies. The obverse of this is the devaluation and neglect of daughters.

## Accommodating agency: 'invention within limits'

The work of Bourdieu (1977) offers a valuable framework for integrating sociological concerns with norms and custom with the concerns of conventional economics in order to produce a more culturally nuanced approach to the analysis of choice, interests, strategies and power. It also helps to integrate the analysis of gender and intra-household relations with the broader processes by which social inequalities of various kinds are sustained in daily life and over time – without the open exercise of power or the emergence of overt conflict. For Bourdieu, the collective life of a community is organised around hierarchies of age, gender and relationship to means of production, hierarchies which embody a conceptual schema which represent the community's official account of its own social relations, its ideologies about itself. Membership of these hierarchical relationships offers access to resources and opportunities to exercise agency, but within the terms and meanings laid out by these official accounts. Consequently, many aspects of individual behaviour will be 'relatively unmotivated', governed by community codes of conduct, although they will vary according to upbringing, experience and position within the community.

Bourdieu uses the concept of 'habitus' to capture this socially-structured aspect of subjectivity in social practice. Because habitus generates aspirations and practices which reflect, and are compatible with, the objective range of possibilities available in given social contexts, it serves to delineate the improbable and the unthinkable within particular situations from what is possible, desirable or indeed inevitable. This 'sense of limits' which a social order produces in its members, which is also their 'sense of reality', underpins their adherence to the social order by 'naturalising' some aspects of reality, placing the behaviour associated with them in the realm of unquestioned routine, habit and tradition, the realm of 'doxa'.

However, within the limits of habitus, individual behaviour takes the form of purposive agency, based on the calculation of interests. Bourdieu uses the concept of 'strategies' to describe the diverse ways in which interests are addressed and meanings negotiated by social actors. The aim of these strategies is to draw on the resources and conventions available to them in order to accumulate both 'material capital', the tangible means through which they meet their material needs and wants, as well as what Bourdieu calls 'symbolic capital', the creation and maintenance of various social relationships among kin and in the wider community. As he points out, the accumulation of symbolic capital is not easily intelligible in terms of neo-classical notions of rationality because it appears to involve the diversion of scarce time, effort and resources from the acquisition of concrete material goods into the pursuit of such nebulous and intangible achievements as the prestige and honour of the family, a good reputation or social standing within the community. However, if it is recognised that the fund of duties, debts, claims and obligations built up through investments in social relationships can be converted into material resources in times of need, such investments will be seen to have had a material dimension to them rather than being purely symbolic. At the same time, it is a paradoxical feature of such investments that they are most effective precisely when they can be presented in purely symbolic terms, valued only in, and for themselves, with no consideration for their additional material advantage.

Social hierarchies are sustained over time, not only because they embody differences in the capacity of social actors to mobilise material capital, but also because the actors are positioned un-equally in relation to the accumulation of symbolic capital. It is also in the nature of such hierarchies that those who have a position of dominance within them are also best placed to pursue *officialising* strategies, i.e. strategies by which the considerations of the private advantage likely to accrue to them from particular forms of sym-bolic capital can be disguised as the 'disinterested, collective, publicly avowable, legitimate interests' of the wider collectivity (p. 40). We will come across a number of examples in the course of this book of the ways in which the ideologies and practices which characterise different hierarchies also produce an equation between the self-interests of privileged groups and that of the 'larger' social good. In particular, we will see how men's pursuit of private advantage is often presented as being in the legitimate interests of their households and the wider community and, hence, given official status. Women, by contrast, tend to resort to unofficial, private and often clandestine, strategies to achieve their individual goals.

Bourdieu's emphasis on individual practice as enacting the structuring principles of social location has, as Moore points out, left him open to the charge of 'a theory that appears to have little space for agency and/or social change' (1994, p. 77). However, the enactment of social norms in Bourdieu's analysis is very different from that described in the structuralist tradition described earlier. The notion of agency in Bourdieu's work is associated with the creative *interpretation* of rules rather than with their mechanical *execution*. Interests are always to the forefront in these interpretations; conformity occupies a secondary place. Consequently, individual actors may strategise within the framework spelt out by the community's codes of conduct, but their interpretation of these codes brings into play a far more diverse range of practical outcomes than would be suggested by a formal inventory of cultural rules. An understanding of how such rules are invoked in practice and what this implies for the reconstitution or modification of the structures which generate these rules helps to illuminate 'the structuring of structures' over time.

The possibility of social change is brought into Bourdieu's analysis through a distinction beween different levels of adherence to the established order. As long as the subjective assessments of individual actors are largely congruent with the objectively organised possibilities available to them, the world of doxa, the taken-for-granted character of routines, customs and conventions, remains intact: tradition 'goes without saying because it comes without saying'. Adherence to the social order does not require dominant groups to defend their interests actively because it rests on the consent created by an unquestioned and impenetrable 'sense of limits' which is shared by all members of the community. The passage from doxa to 'discourse' occurs when the taken-for-granted way of organising social life legitimised by the social order begins to lose its 'naturalised' character and reveal its arbitrariness and when the congruence between its objective possibilities and its subjective evaluation is undermined, radically or gradually and unevenly.

The emergence of discourse, of opinions and arguments about what was previously unquestioned, implies the co-existence of competing 'possibles'. However, it need not necessarily imply the emergence of an explicit critique if the silence of doxa is broken only by the discourse of dominant groups who seek to defend their interests through 'orthodoxy', the explicitly defensive rationalisations of social convention which come into play when tradition is no longer taken for granted. 'Heterodoxy', the critical discourses through which the arbitrariness of the social order is revealed to the subordinated groups, are only possible when they have the material as well as the symbolic means to reject dominant systems for classifying and defining the social order. The silence of doxa is thus the two-fold silence of what goes without saying as well as of what cannot be said because the vocabulary to say it is not available. By providing such a vocabulary to question what had been previously 'naturalised', discourse destabilises power: 'Words wreak havoc when they find a name for what had up to then been lived namelessly' (Sartre, cited in Bourdieu, p. 170).

## Summarising the middle ground: the duality of structure and agency

We can see why the extremes of methodological individualism in economics and methodological structuralism in sociology have not proven particularly useful in grappling with the problems of structure and agency in the real world. One portrayed economic actors as abstract ciphers, undifferentiated by context or biography, the bearer of 'one all-purpose preference ordering' which applies to all decisions in their lives, regardless of how trivial or how momentous. The other presented the individual as a 'cultural dope' whose choices, practices and perceptions were blurred and out-of-focus because of the relentless pre-occupation with overarching structures.

However, as we have documented, critics of both traditions have helped to carve out a convergent middle ground in which the agency of individuals can be recognised without losing sight of the constraining structures within which they exercise their agency. Rationality is given a more 'situated' or 'substantive' interpretation which draws attention to the fact that individual actors care about more than the hedonistic pursuit of self-interest, and that what they care about is partly unique to them, but is also shaped in socially situated ways (McCrate, 1992; Lawson, 1997). Such a formulation still allows us to appreciate the 'conscious, deliberative aspects of human agency', to ask what actions of individuals reveal about their purpose and 'explore the ways in which calculations of economic consequences may influence their decisions' (Folbre, 1994, p. 27). There has also been a move away from a preoccupation with structure as 'the intractability of the social world' (Connell, 1987, p. 92) to a greater concern with strategic conduct on the part of individuals and their capacity for 'invention within limits'. Interests are recognised as the well-spring of human behaviour, with conformity as secondary concern, but these interests are constituted and pursued within social frameworks of meaning and discourse.

One of the valuable features of this theoretical middle ground is a view of the relationship between structure and agency as one of duality, of mutual interdependence, rather than of dichotomy: 'Human practice always presupposes social structure, in the sense that practice necessarily calls into play social rules and resources. Structure is always emergent from practice and is constituted by it' (Connell, 1987, p. 94). Individual agency is modified in these accounts through the recognition of the power of the social: society exists prior to those who are born into it and places demands upon them: 'there are values and norms to be appropriated and internalised, institutions and things to be understood, language and customs with which to come to terms' (Wright, 1985, p. 7). However, if individual agency is socially constrained, society also needs to be lived and put into action. It must be reconstituted by individual practice so that determination can be seen to cut both ways.

The idea of the duality of structure and agency opens up a far richer set of possibilities for the analysis of social change than permitted by approaches which give analytical primacy to either agency or structure. Recognition of their interdependence can still accommodate the idea of behavioural change as the product of changes in prices and incomes, as specified by economists or as the result of significant 'exogenous' events, such as war, ecological disasters, technological innnovation or exposure to the value systems of other societies. In all these cases, however, change will be mediated by the pre-existing configurations of rules and resources within which people's responses are formulated. In addition, however, a duality paradigm allows for change to occur 'endogenously' as the intended or unintended consequence of individual actions on the rules and resources which make up structural constraint. Even highly stable structures can generate a sufficient diversification of strategies to lead to a modification of these structures over time. Any influence, Giddens (1979) points out, that leads to the questioning of 'traditional practices' has the potential for bringing about social change. It may simply entail the replacement of one set of restrictive norms and beliefs with another equally restrictive set or it may take the form of divergent interpretations of existing beliefs and values.

However, even if all that happens is the replacement of 'tradition' with 'traditions', the existence of competing possibilities pushes back the boundaries of 'doxa' and opens up the space for manoeuvre available to subordinate groups. Finally, and most importantly, given that human beings have the power of introspection and reflexivity, change can come about as the result of purposive action. Women and men have the ability 'to step back from their "revealed" wants, volitions and preferences, to ask themselves whether they really want these wants and prefer these preferences (Hirschman, 1985). Human agency can be turned against what constrains it through the explicit disavowal of the oppressive aspects of past practice. Structure, in other words, can be made the object of practice (Connell, 1987).

## Agency, structure and women's labour market decisions: the key hypotheses of the research

It will be clear from the discussion in this chapter that there are many different and competing accounts for why Bangladeshi women take up employment, why they take up particular forms of employment and what their employment implies for their status as subordinate actors. For economists, in general, labour supply decisions, regardless of context and culture, reflect comparative advantage considerations, the weighing up of marginal returns from different uses of time, by individuals or by households. Structuralist approaches emphasise tradition and custom as the basis for 'conformist' forms of employment and economic desperation for any observed deviation. Between these extremes we would expect to find less deterministic approaches which would accept that changes in market signals are likely to induce changes in individual behaviour, but suggest that the relationship between the two will be mediated by a complex set of deliberations which weigh up the material and non-material costs and benefits of responses by different individuals within the household. Purely instrumentalist rationality of the choice-theoretic kind is more relevant to some forms of decision making than others: where decisions impinge on behaviour governed by value-laden rules and norms, they are likely to entail greater emotional costs and to be more resistant to change.

As far as the *impact* of women's access to paid work is concerned, neither individualist nor structuralist perspectives attach a great deal of transformatory potential to women's earnings, but for very different reasons. For Beckerian economists, power is not in any case a factor in intra-household relations and the identity of who earns and who does not is consequently irrelevant to decision making. In more structuralist approaches to the analysis of gender, women's earning capacity would also be irrelevant, but this time because their earnings are likely to be appropriated by the malevolent patriarch pursuing his own self-interests.

However, other approaches *do* attach some degree of transformatory potential to women's earning capacity, although they vary as to how unqualified they see this potential to be. For some, access to paid work is considered a sufficient condition to bring about a shift in intra-household power relations. This view is most likely to characterise those who subscribe to a straightforward bargaining model of the household, or its sociological counterpart which focuses on the 'comparative resourcefulness' of different members (Blood and Wolfe, 1960). It is put forward, for instance, by Joekes (1987), for whom the crucial distinction in terms of its transforma-tory potential is between work that receives a monetary reward, and work that does not, 'regardless of whether the level of remunera-tion in the former case is in some sense appropriate or fair'. With the increased monetisation of economies, she suggests that the value given to labour effort is likely to be measured in direct monetary terms so that women who earn will acquire some leverage in intra-household bargaining.

Finally, there are those who have suggested that paid employ-ment may be a *necessary* condition for challenging intra-household hierarchies, but it is not *sufficient*. They draw attention to the role of the gender norms and practices governing the distribution of resources and responsibilities within the household which will mediate women's access to earnings and its translation into impact within the household (Whitehead, 1981; Standing, 1991; Wolf, 1992). In addition, they highlight the significance of the labour processes through which women acquire income (Whitehead, 1985; Sen, 1990; Beneria and Roldan, 1987). They suggest that, in general, women are more likely to exercise control over the pro-ceeds of their labour when it is carried out in forms of production which are independent of male household members and in social relationships outside the familial sphere of command. The magni-tude and form of their remuneration is also likely to be significant.

These various social science 'stories' are useful in transforming broad, abstract propositions relating to human behaviour into empirically researchable hypotheses about what *might* have hap-pened in particular situations, but they do not constitute a genuine explanation which is one that tells us what *actually* happened (Elster, 1989). For a genuine explanation, we need a 'more finely grained knowledge' about the situation of the women workers, the reasons for their labour market decisions and the implications of their decisions. The most obvious and logical source of such information appeared to be the women workers themselves and their accounts of their actions and its implications are indeed the main data used to explore the competing hypotheses outlined above. A more detailed description of the approach to data collection adopted for the research is given in Appendix 1. Here, however, I would like to comment on some of the methodological problems raised by this approach of 'testimony-based hypothesis testing'.

The idea of asking people for their own accounts of why they did what they did – and what it meant to them – may appear an obvious way of proceeding in research, but it is by no means uncontroversial. Mainstream neo-classical economists are notoriously reluctant to rely on people's own accounts of their preferences and motivations because they suspect that people are not willing to own up to the kinds of narrow self-interest which neo-classical economics attributes to them (Arrow, 1991). Many sociologists similarly begin their accounts by discounting people's own explanations of their actions in order to discover the 'real' reasons for their behaviour. The assumption is that institutions and structures work 'behind the backs' of social actors who have no worthwhile understanding of their environment or the circumstances of their actions (Giddens, 1979, p. 71). Other social scientists have also questioned the idea that the stated perceptions of subordinated groups are necessarily complete truths if they have internalised dominant values and hence appear to 'consent' to their subordinate status. This is precisely the implication of Sen's point about 'adapted perceptions' which we cited earlier.

There are clearly valid reasons for exercising caution in making the leap from people's accounts of their own actions and the actual realities of their situation. But, equally, I have pointed to the distortions which characterise attempts to analyse the actions of subordinated groups without giving any space to their own understandings of why they do what they do. Personal testimonies can enrich social science analysis by providing us with access to the reflections and reactions of social actors who are directly involved in, and affected by, the structures of oppression. At the same time, it is important to point out that my purpose in seeking out the voices of those whose actions are the subject of this research was not simply to 'give voice' to the excluded. While this is clearly an important goal, and there are several excellent books that testify to the richness of the result (see, for instance, Viramma et al., 1997; Stree Shakti Sanghatana, 1987), this is a different kind of book. My aim was to find out what light women's testimonies could throw on the key questions that this research set out to answer and to explore the 'fit' between their accounts and those provided by the social sciences.

Consequently, I have not relied purely on women's testimonies in my analysis, but located them in what I could find out about the wider context of their lives. If we take the idea of individuals as purposive actors with a wide-ranging and intimate knowledge of the societies of which they are members seriously, then we have to accept that they do things for a reason. These reasons can be seen as a first-order set of explanations for their behaviour. However, as Giddens points out, what an actor knows as a competent – but historically and spatially located – member of society 'shades off' in contexts that stretch beyond those of his or her everyday activity (1979, p. 73). To rely solely on their explanations would consequently provide a very partial insight on the phenomena being studied. Consequently, I have sought a second and deeper level of analysis, the 'explanation for their explanations'. This entailed going beyond the immediate causal relationships identified by the women workers to an exploration of the underlying structures which are likely to have been thrown up by these relationships. In other words, I have sought to analyse their testimonies in relation to the broader context in which they live their lives, some aspects of which may be discernible in these testimonies, but other aspects of which form the unacknowledged conditions in which they make their choices. By grounding the analysis of women's voices in the empirical context of their lives, I have tried to explore their own understanding of the limits embodied by this larger context, and their willingness as well as their ability to transform it. Let me conclude this chapter with a quote from Wolf which succinctly summarises the challenge that such an approach poses:

> A subject-mediated approach must constantly move back and forth between the 'raw data' – the subjects – and theory, continuously modifying and

confronting the latter in an attempt to understand and contextualise the former. Clearly, as social scientists we are interpreters, not ventriloquists; we have access to our subjects' mediated representations of themselves and can only portray our own mediated understanding and representation of them as best we can. Despite such problems with mediation, representation and subjectivity, it is important and useful to engage with such narratives and weave them into our attempts to understand structural transformation. (Wolf, 1992, p. 25)

# 3

# The changing face of *shonar Bangla*: background to the Dhaka study

This chapter provides a background to the Dhaka component of our study. Given the concern of the book with issues of protectionism in the textile and clothing industries, this chapter reminds us that these are not new issues for Bangladesh. It tracks the historical decline of textile manufacturing in Bengal and the role played by protectionism in bringing this about. It also documents the emergence of Bangladesh as a separate nation and some of the economic and social trends which have marked its post-independence history and which help to explain the emergence of a female industrial work force some time in the early 1980s. Finally, it explores some of the factors which help to explain employer preference for female labour in a country where men have long been perceived as the primary breadwinners of the family and hence enjoyed privileged entitlement to mainstream forms of employment.

## Textiles and protectionism in Bangladesh: the historical record

Bangladesh's involvement in international trade is by no means a twentieth-century phenomenon. It goes back several centuries. As part of greater Bengal, it was one of the most prosperous regions in the Indian subcontinent, drawing traders, pirates, travellers and immigrants from distant cultures from a very early period. It was the Arab merchants who came to trade in the port of Chittagong as early as the eighth century who brought Islam to Bengal. Since the sixteenth century, Europeans also began to trade with Bengal, lured in particular by its legendary cotton textile industry. Dhaka muslin was in demand in the court of the Mughal emperor and among the aristocracy of Europe as the finest textile in the world and descriptions of its delicacy and beauty abound in the historical literature.

With the decline of Mughal rule in Bengal, the British East India Company was one of several contending powers seeking control of the province, which it achieved after a military victory over the local ruler in 1757. The next hundred years saw the destruction of local manufacturing industry as trade deteriorated into outright plunder. By 1787, William Fullerton, a British MP, observed of Bengal that 'such has been the restless energy of our misgovernment that within the short space of 20 years many parts of this country have been reduced to a desert' (cited in Dutt, 1940).

It was the profits from the lucrative trade in Bengal textiles, combined with a policy of protection for the nascent British textile industry, which helped to finance Britain's industrial revolution. The following comments of the House of Commons Select Committee 1783, in response to a proposal of the East India Company to introduce restrictions on Bengal's textile industry, provides a neat encapsulation of official British attitudes at the time:

> This letter contains a perfect plan of policy, both of compulsion and encouragement which must in a very considerable degree operate destructively to the manufactures of Bengal. Its effects must be (so far as it could operate without being eluded) to change the whole face of the industrial country, in order to render it a field for the produce of crude materials subservient to the manufactures of Great Britain. (quoted in Government of Bengal, 1940)

As the British textile industry mechanised, Britain sought to eliminate competition from Bengal's textiles through an elaborate network of restrictions and prohibitive duties. Duties of up to 70 and 80 per cent had to be placed on Indian goods in order to protect the nascent British textile industry and, even within India, the sale of Bengal cloth was restricted, so as to favour British products: 'Had this not been the case, had not such positive prohibitory duties and decrees existed, the mills of Paisley and Manchester would have stopped in their outset, and could scarcely have been set in motion, even by the power of steam' (H.H. Wilson, quoted in Government of Bengal, 1940).

However, British industry developed at the expense of Bengal's. By 1835, the Governor-General of the East India Company was reporting to London: 'The misery hardly finds a parallel in the history of commerce. The bones of the cotton weavers are bleaching the plains of India' (cited in Mukherjee, 1974, p. 304), while Sir Charles Trevelyan of the East India Company wrote in 1840 that:

> the peculiar kind of silky cotton formerly grown in Bengal, from which the fine Dacca muslins used to be made is hardly ever seen; the population of the town of Dacca has fallen from 150,000 to 30,000 or 40,000 and the jungle and malaria are encroaching fast upon the town ... Dacca which used to be the Manchester of India has fallen off from a flourishing town to a very poor and small one. (cited in Hartmann and Boyce, ibid., pp. 537–538)

Bengal was indeed, as predicted, transformed into a 'field for the produce of crude materials subservient to the manufactures of Great Britain'. Its cultivators were reduced to near-slavery conditions producing indigo for British plantation owners until a peasant revolt led the plantation owners to move on to Bihar. In the mid-1870s, as international trade expanded and the demand for a cheap packaging material grew, jute became the main cash crop of East Bengal. By the end of British rule, the region had become a primarily agrarian economy with jute as its main export.

## Economic trends in the post-independence era

India's independence from British rule in 1947 was accompanied by the partition of the subcontinent and a so-called 'homeland' for Muslims, Pakistan, was created out of an unlikely union between four Muslim-majority provinces in the north-west corner of India and Muslim-dominated East Bengal in its eastern corner. However, a country whose people were divided, not only physically by over

1000 miles of hostile Indian territory but also symbolically by culture, language, history, apparel, diet, calendar and even by standard time was unlikely to cohere as a nation merely because it shared the same religion. In 1971, Bangladesh emerged as a sovereign and secular state under the nationalist government of the Awami League, under the leadership of Sheikh Mujib.

Committed to a mix of 'nationalism, socialism, secularism and democracy', the Awami League nationalised banks and key industries and instituted protective controls to promote domestic industry. However, the euphoria of independence soon gave way to despair and political instability as corruption and inefficiency within the ruling party led to its inability to overcome the deep-rooted problems of poverty and unemployment. The growing political instability in the country culminated in the assassination of Mujib in 1976 in an army-led coup. The leaders who came after him sought to reverse many of the Awami League policies and, in an effort to woo the international aid community, put in place a programme of economic liberalisation with the support of the World Bank and the IMF. This included the 1982 New Industrial Policy for the promotion of export-oriented manufacturing, of which the garment industry which is the focus of this book, was one result.

The 1970s were, in many ways, a watershed decade in Bangladesh, entailing not only an intensification of economic trends, which were already in motion, but a qualitative transformation in people's lives. Crises are not by any means unknown in Bangladesh, but the 1970s were exceptional in the swift succession with which one crisis followed another. It began with a devastating cyclone in 1970; it was followed by a brief and bloody war of liberation in 1971, entailing large-scale genocide and rape by the Pakistan army and the massive dislocation of the economy; the first years of independence were marred by the economic and social aftermath of the war; an extended period of rising prices, exacerbated by the international oil crisis, culminated in massive crop failure leading to famine in 1974–75; growing political instability was coupled with the growing authoritarianism of the government. Mujib was assassinated in 1976 and his successor was assassinated in 1981. This was a period when many of the economic trends which were already evident in earlier decades were intensified. Landlessness, a relatively unknown phenomenon at the start of the century, had begun to increase gradually over its course, but accelerated during the 1970s from 33 per cent in 1960 to 41 per cent in 1977 before declining again to 37 per cent in 1982. Poverty levels also rose dramatically from about 40 per cent in the mid-1960s to around 80 per cent in the mid-1980s before declining again in the late 1980s. The growth in the rural population, the decline in the size of landholdings and the increase in the number of landless labourers, combined with limited growth in the agricultural sector, led to intensified competition within the rural economy. One response was the increasing diversification of rural livelihoods out of agriculture into a range of other occupations, including trade and service, transport, small-and-cottage industry and construction.[1]

The diversification of livelihoods also took a geographical form through migration. Initially, the flow of migration was from the more densely populated districts of Faridpur, Comilla, Noakhali and Mymmensingh to the less densely populated districts of Rangpur, Sylhet, Rajshahi and Jessore, but over the years, there was also an increasing flow into urban areas, mainly Dhaka and Chittagong. There has consequently been a steady increase in the percentage of the total population living in urban areas from around 2 per cent according to the 1881 census to around 12 per cent in 1981. Seventy-four per cent of the total increase in the population of Dhaka city between 1961 and 1974 was due to rural–urban migration (Khan, 1982) while Islam (1996) found in a more recent study that 81 per cent of household heads in the metropolitan area were of migrant status and only 19 per cent had lived in the city since birth. Dhaka is thus, quintessentially, a city of migrants (Islam, 1998; Shankland Cox et al., 1981). Most migrants were absorbed into the urban informal sector where they composed around 70 per cent of the labour force (Amin, 1986).

Qualitative studies offer other insights into the changing nature

---

1. The declining significance of agriculture as a source of employment which began around this period is documented by Osmani (1990) who points out that while more than half of the incremental labour force between 1961 and 1974 had been absorbed by the agricultural sector, not only did the sector fail to absorb any additional labour in the subsequent decade, it actually registered a decline in the numbers employed within it.

of society and the economy during this period. Arthur and Mc-Nicoll note how the combined effects of population growth, declining farm size, growth in landlessness, an increasingly strained labour market and the commercialisation of agriculture set in motion a shift, from an older economy based on small-scale peasant ownership, ties of kinship and patronage and localised labour markets, into a more monetised economy based on impersonal wage labour relationships (Arthur and McNicoll, 1978). Reviewing evidence provided by village studies between 1942 and 1988, Adnan (1990) also testified to the gradual change in the nature of the rural labour markets, from ones characterised by reliance on primordial links, personalised labour relationships and payments in kind to markets based on wage labour and the formalisation of labour contracts and underpinned by a long-term decline in real rural wages under conditions of increasing uncertainty.[2]

Not surprisingly in a class-riven society like Bangladesh, all sections of the population were not uniformly affected by these changes. Wealthy farmers were able to divert their surpluses out of local patronage networks, a traditional source of power and prestige in rural society, and reinvest them in accordance with the new values and opportunities which came with technological change and increased urban contact: new agricultural technology, non-agricultural forms of economic activity, such as business, trade or commerce, financing of children's higher education or of the employment of sons abroad (Ahmed et al., 1990). In addition, educated sections of the urban middle classes and the rural elite who were able to access salaried employment, particularly in the government sector which took on a greater significance after Bangladesh's independence, benefited from a regular, secure and well-paid source of income.

The majority of the population, however, had neither the requisite land, capital, education or social networks necessary to make this transition. Faced with declining returns to their labour in the agricultural sector, they sought work in small-scale manufacturing, construction and various makeshift, irregular and seasonal forms of

---

2. Real agricultural wages in 1981 were 88% of those in 1974, 77% of those in 1970 and 64% of those in 1964 (World Bank, 1983).

self-employment. Diversification among the poor involved 'complex arrangements of agriculture and non-agriculture activity, includes all family members, and range from programme participation in NGO or government programmes . . . to piecework in rural industries or migration to areas where greater employment opportunities are thought to exist' (Ahmed et al., 1990, p. 26).

## Socio-economic change and gender relations in Bangladesh

Along with the class-specific implications of these changes in economy and society, there were also inevitable gender implications. The decline in the significance of family-based farming as the basis for accumulation in the countryside had eroded the traditional productive role of women as well as men, but the norms of female seclusion remained powerful enough to make it difficult for women to follow men into the wider cash economy in search of alternative employment opportunities. The economic devaluation of women which accompanied the transition of the economy from its predominantly subsistence-oriented agricultural base to a more diversified monetised one probably accounts for one of the key changes in gender relations in the course of this century: the shift in the direction of marriage payments from earlier practices which favoured the bride and her family (*pon*) to the new practice of *daabi* or 'demand' dowry[3] which favours the groom and his family (Lindenbaum, 1981).

Estimates vary as to the actual timing of this shift in the direction of marriage payments. Blei has used case studies of marriage practices dating back to 1925 to argue persuasively that the trend began to be discernible in the 1950s, became more widespread in the 1960s and emerged as actual 'demand' dowry – where demands are made by the groom's side as a condition for the marriage to take place rather than gifts being indicated by the bride's side – in the 1970s when the emergence of Bangladesh as an independent

3. The English word 'demand' in reference to this new version of dowry was in widespread use by villagers both in Faridpur where I did my fieldwork in 1979/80 and in the village in Dhaka district studied by Ahmad and Naher (op. cit).

state opened up a range of new avenues of employment for men in the bureaucracy, armed forces as well as in commerce and the professions. It is generally agreed that dowry first emerged among wealthy families in urban areas, whose sons were more likely to enter these highly coveted forms of salaried employment. However, the practice spread to all sectors of the population until even the most impoverished households were able to demand dowry for their sons.

While the emergence of dowry reflected these gender asymmetries in the changing structure of economic opportunities in the country, it also served to intensify them. It further reinforced women's economic devaluation and as far as parents were concerned, turned daughters into a major economic liability, since the need to pay dowry to marry their daughters off put intolerable burdens on parents who were often already impoverished. As Van Schendel commented in his study of processes of impoverishment in Bangladesh, 'A household with many daughters was sure to experience economic deterioration as a result of their marriages. As it was out of the question to leave a girl unmarried, girls were viewed as liabilities to their parents, while boys were viewed as assets' (1981, p. 109).

It has also been suggested that the rise of dowry contributed to the fragility of marital relations and increased incidence of divorce, separation and abandonment. This was particularly the case among poorer sections, where social sanctions against such practices are weakest. While families from all strata have used the substantial assets acquired through the marriage of sons to secure or initiate greater diversification in their economic activities, frequent remarriage was a particularly profitable avenue of accumulation for men from poorer households who were denied access to other sources of capital (Alam, 1985; Ahmad and Naher, 1987; Islam, 1979; Adnan, 1988; Chaudhury and Ahmad, 1980; Abdullah and Zeidenstein, 1980; Kabeer, 1985).

Other evidence of the fragility of traditional family ties under economic pressure lies in the emergence of female-headed households, and its greater incidence among poorer sections of the population. While estimates vary, the 1981 Population Census, the Bangladesh Bureau of Statistics as well as the 1988 Agricultural

Sector Review (Safilios-Rothschild and Mahmud, 1988) found around 15–17 per cent of rural households were female-headed, while the latter found that figures increased to 25 per cent among the landless. A recent participatory assessment exercise carried out by the UNDP (1996) with poor groups across the country identified dowry as one of their major problems and confirmed that the failure to pay dowry was perceived to be a key factor in marital instability and violence.

What these various changes in women's lives added up to was a major deterioration in the terms of the patriarchal contract in Bangladesh. As the following insightful comment by Cain et al. (1979) writing during this period put it:

> While men have both power and authority over women, they are also normatively obligated to provide them with food, clothing, and shelter . . . (T)he normative obligations of men towards women – the principal protection women have against loss of status – have probably never been universally honoured, but there are indications that, under the pressure of increasing poverty, male normative commitment has eroded. . . . As the bonds of obligation between kin erode under the pressure of poverty, the risk of precipitous decline in status increases. (pp. 408 and 432)

The significance of this observation lay in its suggestion that the erosion of family ties in the context of growing poverty was beginning to expose women's vulnerability *as women*, their social and economic dependence on men, and the likelihood of a precipitious decline in status should they find themselves deprived of male support. While the loss of male support was far more likely to occur among poorer women, 'patriarchal risk' applied in principle to women of all classes. One obvious way for women to have secured themselves against their growing exposure to such risk with the increasing instability of patriarchal contract would have been for them to seek out paid employment to make up for the erosion in their traditional economic roles.

However, this does not seem to have occurred. Official labour force statistics showed low, and largely unchanging, rates of female labour force participation: women's share of total employment rose from 5 per cent in 1967 to just 7 per cent in 1987 (World Bank, 1990). In addition, women appeared to be confined to a very limited range of paid activities, primarily those which could be carried out from within the precincts of the home. Not surprisingly, a great deal of the research on the nature of gender relations in Bangladesh has been concerned with explaining these phenomena. Also not surprisingly, in view of the undeniable reality of purdah and patriarchy in the Bangladesh context, structuralist forms of explanation tended to dominate in these explanations.

As we saw in the previous chapter, the earliest studies tended towards narrowly culturalist explanations, explaining women's absence from, or very low levels of participation in, the market place, in terms of their desire to conform to the strictures of purdah. Female waged employment was consequently seen as a symptom of extreme poverty, and women labourers were described in such terms as 'destitute' (implying lack of male support), 'marginal', 'drifting', 'vagrant', all of which served to convey their deviance from the statistical and social norm. Later analysis continued to give an important place to the 'internal' nature of the constraints on women's labour supply. Cain et al., for instance, pointed to the internalisation of purdah norms by women as a result of their 'sex role socialisation' and suggested that the associated 'psychic' costs experienced by women outside the accepted boundaries of the home explained the functional and spatial segregation of women's economic activity. In functional terms, it confined women to a few, primarily home-based jobs: e.g. cottage industry, post-harvest crop processing and domestic labour. Spatially, it influenced the distance women were prepared to travel, or were permitted to travel, in search of work. Based on their village study, Cain et al. estimated that 'the physical limits of the market for a particular woman's labour [were] described by a radius of 200–400 meters, with her homestead as the center of the circle' (p. 428).

However, there was also growing evidence that even where women were prepared to go the extra distance in search of work, they faced powerful external constraints on the kind of work that they were able to do. These external constraints were not just 'given' by social norms but reconstituted through the active mobilisation of powerful interest groups in defence of their privileged position in the social order. Subsequent studies helped to spell out in greater detail the role played by such institutions as *shamaj* and *shalish* in operationalising purdah as a constraint in the lives of women (Adnan, 1988; Chen, 1986). *Shamaj* was the 'moral economy' at the village level, a community based on the face-to-face interaction of its members, who recognised reciprocal rights and obligations to each other and co-operated at critical life cycle rituals, such as births, deaths and marriages. It also acted as the guardian of the social and moral order, representing the interests of the rich and powerful, through its dominance of the *shalish*, informal village courts which met to settle disputes and pronounced on approved behaviour for all sections of its membership.

It was able to back its authority within village society in both material and social terms, since employment opportunities, support in times of crisis, protection from the police and a variety of other resources were distributed through the networks of *shamaj*. Any form of 'deviant' behaviour could thus be censured economically and socially. Religious functionaries also played an important role in the regulation of women's behaviour, bringing to bear the authority of the sacred texts to dominant models of gender propriety within the community. Thus, 'restrictions regarding the participation of women in the social arena are imposed by dominant males amongst the community *as a whole* rather than the particular male guardians from the family or kinsmen of the women concerned' (Adnan, 1988, p. 8).

However, it was not only within the family and local community that barriers to women's labour force participation were to be found. They were constructed by the representatives of the state as well. The role played by government officials in excluding women from economic opportunities first came to public attention in the aftermath of the 1974 famine when the government set up food-for-work programmes to provide employment in periods of food shortage. Over a million casual wage labourers came forward to seek work on these schemes, of whom a small percentage were women. Although Bangladesh had a considerable history of public works programmes for relief purposes, the phenomenon of women putting themselves forward for such work was perceived to be a departure from the norm. Local programme officials, conditioned by the long-established tradition that women did not seek outside work, turned them away.[4] Official attitudes only started to change after a study documented the economic desperation of these women who, while not all strictly 'destitute' in the official sense of the word (i.e. destitute of a male breadwinner), came from households where male earnings were insufficient to support the whole family. Many had come in the face of considerable resistance from family and community (Chen and Ghuznavi, 1979; WFP, 1979).[5]

Despite their adoption of the rhetoric of Women in Development (WID), which became a part of the dominant development discourse in the 1970s, both the state and the international agencies operating in the country remained tied, in practice, to an extremely limited, urban, middle class and frequently Westernised set of ideas about what constituted 'proper' work for women. At a conference held in 1977 to discuss WID issues in Bangladesh, McCarthy et al. (1979) made the following exasperated intervention:

> Agencies conceive of helping women by shunting them into handicrafts or programs for cookery, nutrition, child care and a model of housewifery that is basically Western in design. . . . The foreign agency idea of a good program for rural women is some specialized project like charka spinning, sericulture or bee-keeping. These are done in the home, and may bring some income into the family, but only small amounts and only at the costs of extending the actual labor of women. These programs do not encourage rural women into new ventures, to develop new social roles and skills, or to increase their independence. Rather most programs implicitly assume that the best place for a woman is in the home and hence indirectly support the present status quo in the villages. (pp. 368 and 369)

They were equally scathing on government efforts:

4. One local official was prepared to acccept women from villages other than his own, protesting that there were no 'needy' women in this village. The needy women from his village were forced to request work through another official (WFP, 1979, p. 27).

5. One of the memorable figures that came out of the study was Saleha, a woman who had been forced by the loss of her husband's land, to seek waged employment wherever she could find it. Her testimony provides a reminder of how unusual it still was in the early 1970s for women to work outside the home. Aware of public disapproval at the idea of a woman doing public manual labour, she avoided working in the open: 'I worked in the fields at night, by moonlight, or at times when there was the least likelihood of being seen' (p. 35).

The ideas of many top civil servants and government officials about women are extremely Western in orientation and not applicable to the lives of village women. Other civil servants hold strong stereotypes that village women do not do any work, only housework, or that they only cook and look after children. Other common assumptions are that rural women are ignorant, inexperienced or shy and that not much can be done with them. (p. 368)

A minority of women, those from better-off families, who had some education, benefited from jobs reserved for women in the public sector and from the employment generated by the major expansion in government family planning programmes undertaken in the mid-1970s. However, although a plethora of women's income-generating projects sprang into existence at around this time, there was no serious attempt to address the livelihood needs of women from poorer rural families who were the main casualties of the changing economics of gender in Bangladesh.

As McCarthy and Feldman (1984) pointed out, most social service agencies were organised by elite women to provide literacy training and income-generating opportunities for destitute women along welfarist lines which defined poorer women as 'clients' dependent on the project for direction, funds, training and market-ing support. Indeed, the distinction made in the official discourse between 'employment' for men and 'income-generation' for women was strikingly symbolic of the mainstream/residual gender distinction which characterised much of the government's devel-opment efforts. Nor did NGO activity manage to shift these atti-tudes. Despite the expansion of NGO efforts explicitly targeting women for various income-generating activities, the direct impact of NGOs on women's labour force participation remained mar-ginal, hampered partly by the limited numbers of women they could reach but also by their very mixed track record in designing sustainable forms of livelihood for women.

It is not surprising that this evidence of powerful cultural con-straints on women's mobility, backed by the patriarchal authority of family, kinship and community led most observers at the time to stress the non-negotiability of patriarchal constraint in the foresee-able future. Returning to the analysis provided by Cain et al., this was their gloomy prognosis:

The picture that emerges from our analysis of patriarchy and women's work in rural Bangladesh is bleak. Male dominance is grounded in control of material resources and supported by interlocking and reinforcing elements of the kinship, political, and religious systems. Powerful norms of female seclusion extend to labor markets, severely limiting women's opportunities for independent income generation. . . . Potential agents of change and sources of resistance to the current system of patriarchy are undermined by the interaction of age, sex and class hierarchies . . . The systemic nature of patriarchy suggests that solutions to the problem of women's vulnerability and lack of income-earning opportunities will not be easily reached. (p. 434)

In other words, the possibility of paid employment as a way for women to mitigate their economic dependence was not considered an option by the authors because of the perceived inflexibility and pervasiveness of patriarchal constraint. Instead, they saw women's only option to lie in their continued reliance on bearing as many children as possible in order to secure a 'safe' number of sons to act as their primary form of insurance against 'patriarchal risk' and an uncertain future.

In reality, however, change was already under way. While fertility rates had been declining very gradually since the 1950s (Dyson, 1996), a radical decline in fertility began some time in late 1970s, bringing average fertility rates down from around 7 to 3 or 4 by the end of the 1980s (Cleland et al., 1994). There is evidence to suggest that this decline started earlier among poorer groups and and went furthest among them (Kabeer, 1998). Furthermore, while government statistics continued to record low and unchanging rates of female economic activity, small-scale quantitative surveys and qualitative studies carried out in the late 1970s and early 1980s showed a very different picture. They documented a gradual, uneven but perceptible increase in women's labour force participation rates. These studies generally affirmed the link between poverty and female employment, suggesting that in some villages, one-fourth of all rural households had female members in wage employment, with proportions rising to two-thirds among landless and functionally landless households (Rahman, 1986; Begum and Greely, 1983; Westergaard, 1983). However, the vast majority of these women remained confined to casualised forms of employment on the margins of the labour market, where they generally eluded the efforts of official data collection exercises.[6]

The other response by women from poorer households in search of work was migration to the cities, partly a response to the greater perceived likelihood of employment in the interstices of the urban economy and partly to escape the restrictive confines of village *shamaj*. In a country where independent migration has always been a largely male phenomenon, with women migrating in association with their families, the increase in independent female migration was not easily recognised by official circles. The systematic increase in the presence of women in the urban population over the last fifty years, with ratios of women to men increasing from 100: 163 in 1951, to 100: 118 males in 1991, was initially attributed by census officials to 'improved coverage'. Once again, a different interpretation was made possible by some of the micro-level urban studies conducted during the 1970s which found a significant proportion of women who reported themselves as recent migrants were divorced or deserted women from poor rural families seeking employment in the cities (Farouk, 1976; Jahan, 1979). A study of two urban slums in Dhaka carried out in 1988/89 found a disproportionate number of households with no adult males in them (Islam and Zeitlin, 1989). The Matlab Demographic Surveillance Report (ICDDRB, 1985) corroborated these findings from the rural perspective, through its estimates that independent female migration in pursuit of better livelihoods or subsequent to marital

6. The failure of the official statistics to capture forms of economic activity in the casualised sectors of the labour market where women and children from poorer, landless households were likely to be concentrated has been demonstrated in a number of studies. Ahmad and Quasen (1991), for instance, found that 34 per cent of children aged between 6 and 14 in their four-village study were economically active compared to the figure of 13 per cent recorded by the 1983–84 Labour Force Survey. They also noted that the discrepancy was greater for girls than boys: only 4 per cent of girls were economically active according to the Labour Force Survey compared to 29%, according to their estimates. The corresponding estimates for boys were 23 per cent compared to 39 per cent. Rahman's study of four villages in Faridpur district (1986) also highlighted the divergence between official estimates of around 3 per cent in 1981 and her finding that between 8–20 per cent of households sent their women in search of wage employment. Among landless households, the figure rose to 50–77 per cent. A larger data set on 46 villages in the same district found that 11–24 per cent of households, and 60 per cent of landless households, had a female member in wage employment.

dissolution constituted a third of total female out-migration from the area.

In the end, however, it took market forces, and the advent of an export-oriented garment manufacturing industry, to achieve what a decade of government and non-government efforts had failed to do: to create a female labour force of sufficient visibility, and on such a scale, that it could no longer be overlooked by official data gathering exercises. As we saw in Chapter 1, the garment factories first opened in Bangladesh in the late 1970s as a result of the quota-hopping strategies of East Asian capital. However, domestic entrepreneurs also began to take an interest in response to the incentives provided by the New Industrial Policy in 1982. These allowed producers to import fabrics duty-free, provided they were made into garments for export. In addition, the 'back-to-back' letter-of-credit scheme allowed factory owners to obtain cloth from foreign suppliers without having to pay up front until the factory itself has been paid. From the point of view of local entrepreneurs, entry into the industry was relatively easy. The initial outlay was limited – it cost about £200,000 to equip a medium-sized factory of about 500 workers with what it needed: modern sewing machines, pressing irons and button machines (Jackson, 1992).

As a result of these incentives, the industry mushroomed from 8 units in 1977 to around 700 in 1985. Aside from twenty-five factories in the Chittagong export-processing zones, the remainder were scattered in different parts of Dhaka, Chittagong and Narayanganj. Garment exports went from $4 million in 1981 to $117 million in 1985 (WBN, 1989), ousting the jute industry as the primary source of foreign exchange earnings in the country.

In addition, of course, several thousand women were drawn into jobs in the new factories,[7] a largely first-generation female industrial proletariat, dramatically changing the profile of female labour force participation in the country. Whereas in 1951, nearly 90 per cent of employed men and women in Bangladesh were to be found working in agriculture, by 1985/86, only 11 per cent of working women remained in agriculture compared to 63 per cent of

7. As we saw in Chapter 1, estimates of jobs generated ranged between 80,000 and 250,000 by 1985, with around 85 per cent of them female.

working men (Ahmad, 1991, p. 252). The urban manufacturing
sector was a major factor behind the changing pattern of female
labour force participation. Between 1974 and 1985/86, the percentage of working women in manufacturing rose from 4 to 55 while
urban female labour force participation rose from around 12 per
cent in 1983/84 to 20.5 per cent in 1995/96.

## Explaining employer preference for female labour: the 'demand' side of the story

As I pointed out in the preface, the initial motivation for undertaking the research for this book was the sheer unexpectedness of
large numbers of women, married, unmarried, widowed and
divorced, emerging from their homes to take up factory work with
such rapidity and on such a scale. This unexpectedness reflected a
number of factors. First and foremost, it appeared to go against
cherished ideas about women's place at home and about the power
of purdah norms in ensuring it. Until the change actually happened, most observers would have agreed with the prognosis
offered by Cain et al. only a few years previously that '(t)he systemic
nature of patriarchy suggests that solutions to the problem of
women's vulnerability and lack of income-earning opportunities
will not be easily reached' (1979, p. 434).

Secondly, the preference for female labour in reasonably well-
paid work in a country where men have traditionally assumed the
breadwinning role, and where there was a large pool of male
unemployment, appeared to be a cultural anomaly. And finally,
tailoring in Bangladesh had traditionally been a craft-based male
activity, carried out in small workshops for the domestic market.
Indeed, the tendency of official development programmes for
women to offer training in sewing had come under criticism from
Women-in-Development specialists. In the article cited earlier,
McCarthy et al. (1979, p. 367) had pointed out that it reflected
Western ideas about suitable feminine tasks, whereas in Bangladesh, 'men are the tailors and serve a long apprenticeship in
learning the trade. Women will therefore have great difficulty
competing with men in this kind of work in the immediate future.'

In the next chapter, we will be exploring in greater detail some of the explanations that women gave for their willingness to go against the cultural grain in terms of their labour market behaviour. Here, however, I would like to touch briefly on the 'demand' side of the story, the perspectives of the employers who were responsible for the recruitment of female labour into their factories in order to find out why they too were prepared to go against the social norm. This part of the analysis is based on interviews with twelve of the employers associated with the factories in which we carried out our research. Their responses suggested that higher female productivity in certain tasks – the 'nimble fingers' argument – was not a major factor in their preference for female labour. In fact, most employers maintained that men were more productive on the machines: 'girls learn quicker but men are faster'; 'women are neater, but men are faster'; 'women are slower; men work the machines faster and learn faster'; 'men can make ten shirts a day to women's five'. Indeed, the majority had started out with a much higher percentage of men in their workforce than they currently reported and at least one of those quoted below started out with an entirely male workforce. However, one factor overrode all others in explaining their preference for female labour: men made trouble (*chele-ra ganjam kore*):

We started with only men in our workforce, they all came from Faridpur, the partner here comes from Faridpur. But it was like a football match here ... no discipline. I came here in May 1986 when there were two-hundred and seventy-five men. They were sacked with three months' benefits and we brought women in. First of all, as helpers, then they learnt the work and replaced the men.

Why women? Because men smoke, drink tea, talk a lot, disturb everybody ... they are very vociferous, demand holidays, they have tough friends, football fans ... We want as little talk as possible on the machines. There is no problem if they confine their talk to the lunch hour. That is something women are prepared to do.

Men in groups will immediately start agitating for more pay. Women go straight home after work because of domestic responsibilities or because it gets dark. Women listen better and they don't talk back. Men won't take instructions or accept authority easily. And women are cheaper because they have fewer choices – in terms of physical location of work and in terms of their physical ability to do different kinds of work.

Female docility thus compensated for male productivity. The need to meet the deadlines imposed by their buyers, compulsory overtime, the locking of the factory gates to ensure that workers did not smuggle out duty-free fabrics intended for export production, all of these required a compliant labour force. Such docility on the part of women workers is hardly surprising in a country where women are brought up from childhood to defer to male authority, to speak in a soft and pleasing voice and to remain within the shelter of the home. In addition, it was reinforced by women's exclusion (in common with, but to a greater extent than women workers in many other parts of the world) from other more mainstream employment opportunities and their confinement to a narrow range of jobs on the margins of the labour market. One of the employers cited made this point bluntly: 'Women are cheaper because they have fewer choices'.[8]

However, employers also expressed a preference for *certain types* of female labour over others. They preferred young 'unencumbered' women: 'mothers tend to be inattentive to machines because they worry if their child is hungry'. They also wanted some basic literacy and numeracy: 'they need to be able to read bundle sizes and batch numbers and so on, and to match the pieces'; 'they need to be able to sign their names when they take their pay'. From this more selective perspective, the supply of female labour was not infinitely elastic and the employers had to make certain compromises. Many had started out making eight years of education as a minimum qualification, but had settled for women who could at

8. This point was not lost on the women workers. Explaining employer preference, one of the women workers we interviewed gave the following eloquent version of 'the competitive advantage of women's disadvantage' in the Bangladesh context: 'You see, as women, one of our wings is broken. We don't have the nerve that a man has, because we know we have a broken wing. A man can sleep anywhere, he can just lie down on the street and go to sleep. A woman cannot do that. She has to think about her body, about her security. So the garment factory owner prefers to hire women because men are smarter about their opportunities, you train them and they move on. Even when he compares a small boy and an older girl, he will think, "She's only a girl, she can't wander too far away"'.

least sign their own names.[9] Married women were also accepted as long as they worked regularly and did not object to compulsory overtime. The greatest bottleneck that employers faced was in the supply of experienced machinists. Very few women arrived in the factory with prior machining skills; they learnt on the job, either officially as trainee operators or unofficially as helpers, practising on the machine in their lunch hour. Once a woman had acquired 'machine control', she would seek to be assigned to the next grade up. Sometimes she would leave and seek a job in another factory where she could present herself as more experienced than she was and hence negotiate for a higher level of pay.

Competition between employers for skilled machinists gave them a stake in ensuring work conditions that would attract and retain such workers. Despite persistent rumours to the effect that the factories were hotbeds of sexual scandal, and the evidence of misbehaviour on the part of some employers and managers, it was generally in the interests of employers, as much as those of their workers, to keep the factories free of such behaviour. A factory's reputation for discipline, order and propriety was an important asset, integral to its ability to draw, and retain, a smooth supply of suitable female labour. As one employer put it, the factory had to be seen as a place 'where you could send your wife or your daughter to work'. One employer explained why he had sacked a male worker who had been making advances to one of the women: 'After all, there are 250 women here. What would happen if they had decided to take a stand because of the behaviour of one man? We cannot take the risk.'

One important way in which factories maintained both discipline and propriety was through the reproduction of the gender segregation – and hierarchy – which characterised the wider society. All the factories had a largely male management and a largely female production force. Among the production workers, there was a further gender segregation and hierarchy. Machinists were largely female, as were the helpers who cut threads, ran errands and were generally 'helpful'. The children employed by the industry, usually

9. We later found out from the women workers we interviewed that some of them had learnt how to sign their names just before they came to the interviews.

young girls, tended to be employed as helpers. Men predominated in the cutting section. There was a more even distribution in the finishing section, where tasks included pressing, folding, ironing, bagging, packing and binding, but women tended to be concentrated in certain tasks. Using survey data, Zohir and Paul-Majumder (1996) estimated that women made up 80 per cent of machinists, 11 per cent of workers in the cutting section and 43 per cent in the finishing section, where they were assigned to a limited range of tasks. Men tended to predominate in supervisory positions: overwhelmingly in the finishing section and about 75 per cent in the sewing section. Male-dominated tasks on the whole tended to be better paid. Male machinists were also paid higher on average than female machinists,[10] although employers explained this as a reflection of productivity rather than gender differentials.

These various tasks tended to be described by managers and workers alike in terms which were also explanations of why they were 'male'or 'female'. There may have been some objective basis for this gender differentiation of tasks. Cutting, for instance, was considered to require a great deal of skill and many of the male workers employed in the cutting rooms had previous experience as tailors or as tailors' apprentices. Similarly, there was probably an objective basis to the perception that carrying bales of material around the factory and 'laying' the material was too heavy for women. Explanations which associated the supervisory role with the norm of male authority also had some basis in social practice: 'if the job were done by a woman, the other women would not be as scared of her'. However, the descriptions also relied on some creative interpretation of prevailing ideologies of gender difference. Machining, for instance, was described as particularly suited to women because they had the necessary temperament to sit in the same place all day whereas men got 'dizzy' or 'fidgety'. Men's predominance in the ironing section was described in terms of women's unsuitability to dealing with electricity.[11]

10. In Zohir and Paul-Majumder's 1996 study, women were found to earn 66 per cent of male earnings.

11. Fatema's husband in the village had objected to her entering garment work on the grounds that she had no experience working with electric machines and might get

Along with gender segregation by task, the factories also observed segregation along spatial lines. In some factories, even male and female machinists worked in separate 'lines'. In most factories, the cutting and finishing sections occupied a more clearly demarcated space: either on a separate floor, or a separate room or in an area of the same room. Once this gender division of tasks and space had been established, they took on the character of a norm. This was poignantly illustrated by Rupbon, one the few women we found working in the ironing section, who spoke of her embarrassment in finding herself on the male side of the task divide: 'When people ask me what I do, I don't tell them I iron because it is men's work and I feel embarrassed about it. I tell them that I stitch buttons. I feel so ashamed every month when they call out "Rupbon, iron-man!" at paytime. Those who have machining skills can go any-where and get higher pay. I could get a higher wage elsewhere but I don't go out of embarrassment because I would have to give an interview as an ironman in front of everybody.'

The organisation of labour on the factory floor also reproduced a class hierarchy. Women who came from better-off backgrounds had usually completed at least secondary education, tended to dress more smartly and generally had a different trajectory within the factory. Those who had no prior machining skills were hired as 'trainee operators' rather than helpers. Alternatively, depending on their education, they were hired straight into positions as floor or line supervisors and quality controllers. Education, partly as signifier of class, was the key factor explaining women's promotion prospects: women without any could only hope to achieve the next grade up as machinists. As management correctly recognised, class-based hierarchies could be mobilised in the interests of factory discipline, along with gender-based ones, since women from poorer backgrounds, who made up the majority of their machinists, were as likely to defer to women they deemed to be from a much higher status, as they were to men.

The social hierarchies of the wider community thus tended to be reproduced in microcosm within the factory. This was not

---

electrocuted. She did not allow it to stop her: 'If I have that written in my fate, then that is how I have to die.'

necessarily a conscious strategy on the part of all employers, but a reflection of the particular worldview they tended to subscribe to, and the model of gender propriety which it embodied. Nevertheless, it served to maintain discipline on the factory floor and to reassure the workers, their families, the general public and the employers themselves that the garment industry upheld the same values and norms as the rest of society and consequently represented a 'safe' environment for the women who worked in them.

## Who were the garment workers: a brief description

Finally, since much of the analysis in this section of the book relies on our qualitative interviews with women workers, and given that the sample of women interviewed for the study was small, let me conclude this chapter by describing some of the key characteristics of the women working in the garment industry which have been documented by studies which relied on larger-scale quantitative data. This literature tells us that the women who came into the garment industry in Dhaka conformed in some, but not in every, way to the stereotype of the Third World woman worker noted in Chapter 1. Many were indeed young (Lily, 1985; Hossain et al., 1988). Zohir and Paul-Majumder (1996) found the average age of female garment workers to be 19, with 80 per cent less than 25 years old. However, in economic and other terms, they were a more heterogeneous group than suggested by the prevailing stereotype. There is little evidence, for instance, that the majority of them were single. Estimates of percentages of single women vary between 40 and 55 per cent, while estimates of married women in the garment industry vary between 36–45 per cent (BUP, 1990; Zohir and Paul-Majumder, 1996). The rest of the women were divorced, separated or widowed. The most recent available survey carried out in 1997, suggests that percentages of single women have not increased (Newby, 1998).

If education is used as a crude indicator of economic status, there is also little evidence that the women were uniformly poor. Feldman (1993) found on the basis of her survey that 89 per cent of women workers had some education and 56 per cent had at least completed primary schooling. According to their survey, Zohir and Paul-Majumder (1996) found that 26 per cent of women in the industry had never attended school and 32 per cent had only basic primary education. However, 32 per cent had attended secondary education while 10 per cent had gone into higher education. There appeared to be more women with secondary or higher levels of education in the garment industry than in the formal urban manufacturing sector in general and employers were reported to be finding it difficult to find educated women to fill some of the supervisory positions.

However, there is some support for the possibility that a significant proportion of women in the garment industry were rural migrants. Zohir and Paul-Majumder found that 70 per cent of women and 83 per cent of men in the garment industry they surveyed in 1990 had come from the countryside. Sixty-five per cent of the female migrants were unmarried compared to 60 per cent of male migrants and 17 per cent of women who had migrated had done so on their own compared to 40 per cent of men. Newby found that 87 per cent of women in her survey were migrants into Dhaka: 64 per cent said they had migrated in search of work and 63 per cent had entered work within a year of arriving in the city. Women were most likely to say that they had migrated in search of work if they had migrated with siblings and other relatives, i.e. 'individually' rather than in association with parents and husbands. Although much lower than those of men, the rates of individual migration by women are nevertheless remarkably high for a country where women have traditionally migrated in association with their families.

Not surprisingly, most of the women who described themselves as migrants came from the districts of Mymmensingh, Barisal, Comilla and Faridpur: these are the districts with higher population densities which have supplied much of the male migrant population into Dhaka city as well (Newby, 1998). Very few migrants came from moderate density districts such as Sylhet and Rajshahi. Feldman (1993) found that 45 per cent of female garment workers in her sample compared to 9 per cent of male came from landless families; less than 7 per cent of women came from surplus producing households compared to 30 per cent of men. In other words, female migration into the cities appears to be far more closely linked to poverty than male.

Let me turn now to some of the characteristics of the women interviewed for the Dhaka component of this study. Appendix 2 contains a statistical summary of their main characteristics along with their responses to the key questions of the research. It shows that women workers in our sample were aged between 16 (our lower cut-off point) and 37, with the majority in their twenties. Twenty-one of the workers described themselves as illiterate, while 35 had completed primary schooling. Only 12 women had gone as far as Matric (Class 10) or IA (Intermediate) levels of education. Garment employment was the first experience of paid work for around 15 of the women in the sample. However, the majority of those who had worked before had been engaged in some form of home-based earning activity, including home-based cultivation and livestock rearing, and handicrafts. Around nine women had worked as domestic servants. In addition, a few women had participated in work outside the home, mainly in other factories or as government family planning/health visitors. Only one woman described herself as a prostitute.

Because of the focus on 'household decision making' in this study, it was clearly important to get a sense of who constituted household membership for the women taking part. However, this did not always prove to be an easy undertaking. Many of the women in our sample were relatively recent migrants into Dhaka; about half had arrived within the last ten years. While married women had generally come with, or joined, their husbands rather than specifically in search of work, almost all the unmarried migrants had come, either on their own or with siblings or 'fictive' kin, to find jobs, often explicitly in response to information about the possibility of employment in the garment industry. The presence of young, single women migrating on their own into the city had created a wide variety of householding forms which were impossible to capture with any exactitude. Some of the young migrant women lived with relatives, sometimes very close relatives (e.g. a married sister and her family) and sometimes a more distant relative ('a second cousin from my father's side').

With close relatives, pooling of expenses was a common practice.

With more distant relatives, the women lived as boarders, contributing part of their wages towards rent and food, using some for their own expenses and sending some home to their parents. Two young women were boarding with a distant relative while their fathers, who had also migrated, lived separately in a 'mess' arrangement. Others lived in a 'mess' arrangement with women from their village, or with non-related women from the same neighbourhood, sharing the rent of a room and perhaps having common eating arrangements.

Consequently, there was a high proportion of households in our sample which were not only female-headed but made up entirely of young women. Thirteen of the women workers described themselves as heads of their own households while an additional six described a sister or mother as head of their household. Of the forty-three ever-married women in our sample (some currently married, others divorced, separated or widowed), eleven had not had any children. All the rest had at least one or two children. Only seven women had more than three children. The median age of the youngest child was just over five while the median age of the oldest was around nine.

A variety of arrangements were reported for the care of young children. Where there were other female family members who did not work, there was no problem; where there were not, the child or children might be left behind in the village with a grandmother or a sister. In some cases, a young sister or niece was brought into the village from the city to help out with child care or with domestic work in general. In still others, older children looked after younger children or else the child was left to play with children of other tenants. In one or two cases, women explicitly paid a neighbour to look after the child.

Large-scale statistical surveys are likely to miss out on this diversity of living arrangements adopted by the garment workers if they are not alert to the variations possible. For instance, based on a 1990 survey, Zohir and Paul-Majumder estimated that 80 per cent of factory workers live with their families, 10 per cent with relatives and 8 per cent in 'mess' arrangements. However, our more in-depth analysis suggests that they may have imposed a far greater homogeneity on residential arrangements than was the case. It was clear that migrant workers, or those who found themselves on their own in the city, sought to overcome their social isolation there through the creation of fictive kinship networks (see Islam, 1998, for a perceptive analysis of these strategies). It was often extremely difficult to establish precisely what relationship the different members of an apparent household had to each other because of women's tendency to describe in kinship terms people who then transpired to be acquaintances. Thus, someone referred to in an interview as 'my sister' turned out to be someone 'who is like my sister', an 'aunt' became 'someone I call my *khala*' and the 'guardian' transpired to be the landlord, because 'he acts as my guardian'. Newby's study (1998), which differentiates women workers living with a husband or parent(s) from those living with other relatives or non-relatives or alone, does manage to capture some of this diversity. She found that around 40 per cent of garment workers lived in these 'unconventional' households.

It was particularly difficult to establish a 'fixed' definition of who made the households of women who had 'migrated on their own' leaving most of their families behind in the village, since members of their family often came to stay with them in Dhaka for extended periods at a time, or as members from the domestic unit in the city went off to spend long periods in the village. Household boundaries were therefore clearly far more fluid than is normally allowed for in statistical surveys. In place of the conventional definition of a group of people who shared a common residence and budget, many of the women described households which were based on 'affective' definitions. They might live away from other members of their families for much of the year (thus invalidating the residential definition); they might not send or receive remittances from them (invalidating the common budget definition); they might not eat with them for most of the year (the common cooking pot definition). Nevertheless, in analysing women's labour supply decisions, it became very clear which group of people 'counted' as far as the outcomes of such decisions were concerned. It was this group then that constituted 'the household' for the purposes of our analysis.

## Conclusion

In this chapter, we have noted some of the major economic and social changes that have been occurring in Bangladesh in the course of the past century and their impact on gender relations. Despite these changes, women's labour force participation in Bangladesh appears to have remained extremely low and unchanging for much of this century, and largely confined to home-based forms of economic activity. In a country where tailoring is traditionally a male occupation, where women are confined to the domestic domain by norms of seclusion, where men have been defined as primary breadwinners, and where there is a large pool of male unemployment, the speed with which women responded to the new opportunities offered by the export-oriented garment industry which emerged in the early 1980s obviously requires an explanation. From the employers' perspective, lower female productivity was more than outweighed by women's docility on the factory floor, their reluctance to challenge the harsh conditions of work which prevailed within the industry. However, as I noted at the outset, patterns of employment cannot be explained simply in terms of employers' preferences. In the next chapter, I want to turn to women's reasons for responding to these opportunities.

# 4

# Renegotiating purdah:
# women workers and labour market
# decision making in Dhaka

There is no doubt that women's entry into factory employment represented a radical departure from the long-established norms of female seclusion in Bangladesh. This was evident in the great deal of public attention, usually not very favourable, that it evoked. There were lurid commentaries in the media, dwelling on this strange new phenomenon of large numbers of young, 'unaccompanied' women on the streets of Dhaka every day on their way to and from work:

> A group of girls . . . with faces in cheap makeup, gaudy ribbons adorning their oily braids and draped in psychedelic coloured sarees with tiffin carriers in their hands are a common sight [these] days during the morning and evening hours. These are the garment workers, [a] new class of employees. (*New Nation*, 22 December 1986)

Public disfavour was also expressed in the moral denunciations of the religious community to the breakdown of the 'natural' principle of sexually-segregated spheres. Islamic economists devoted learned treatises to this question (see, for instance, Islamic Economics Research Bureau, 1980) and concluded that not only did such employment take away work from men, the natural breadwinners of the family, but it represented a threat to the very fabric of the moral order:

> Men and Women sit in the same working place face to face. Whatever liberal arguments are put forward in favour of this arrangement, in reality

the close proximity of opposite sexes arouses lust and love for each other which on many occasions lead to immoral and scandalous affairs between them. (Hossain, 1980, p. 270)

Religious meetings were frequently organised within the vicinity of the factories, often lasting for two or three days and nights, during which time various mullahs used loudspeakers to denounce the behaviour of the 'bold' garment women who moved around the streets of Dhaka unaccompanied by any male guardian. For those who may have missed the message, the speeches were recorded in cassette form for wider circulation.

Women workers also had to deal with the unwelcome attentions of the men they passed on the streets on their way to and from work, attentions which ranged from leering, suggestive comments and abusive catcalls to more direct sexual overtures. Women coming home late at night after extended overtime were particularly fearful because, in addition to the 'normal' quotient of harassment they experienced on the streets, they could also be picked up by police for whom any woman on the streets after dark was automatically labelled a prostitute.[1] For women in a culture which expressly forbade their public appearance, and especially for those for whom the daily foray into the public domain was still a new and uncomfortable experience, these encounters served as a constant face-to-face reminder that they were transgressing 'male' space and had consequently laid themselves open to harassment by any passing male.

The view that the women who worked in the garment industry were of loose moral character was so widely held that even the epithet of 'garment girls' had come to assume a perjorative meaning within local discourse. As Kaneez told us: 'People say that the garment girls are bad. When we come out of the factory in a group, the men say, "Here come the garment girls, pick the one you want."' Mumtaz emphasised how their overtime hours fed people's suspicions: 'People talk, they see the women renting homes in this area, they think, what does she do, she is just like a, you know . . .

---

1. Any woman out on the streets after dark was assumed to be a prostitute. A number of factories had issued their workers with identity cards with photographs which they could use to prove that they had legitimate reasons for being on the streets after dark.

[prostitute] . . . coming home at ten o'clock at night, sometimes she doesn't come home all night, so they start having doubts.' Asma told us how reluctant she was to disclose to people outside her family that she worked in a garment factory because of the reaction this invoked: 'I don't even admit I work in garment factories because even uttering that word shames me. People always make nasty comments and say, "Oh, she works in a *garment* factory! Hmmm . . ." They imply so many things.'

This general disapproval was constantly fuelled by rumours about 'incidents' of a sexual nature relating to garment girls, spread by word-of-mouth or reported in newspaper articles, and often assuming a very exaggerated form:

> I can't remember the name of this factory – it was in Narayanganj – but I heard that one hundred and fifty girls were found to be pregnant. Can you imagine that, *one hundred and fifty girls pregnant*! That is why people say such terrible things about garment factories. I heard this from a girl who lives next door to us. I am not sure I believe it, of course. I don't think I believe it. But one of those girls told me, 'It doesn't matter if you believe it or not, it's the truth. I've seen it with my own eyes! 'She used to work in that factory, you know. After this happened, she gave up working in garments.

In the past, it had generally been assumed that only extreme economic distress could have explained women's presence in forms of employment which exposed them to such public opprobrium. However, the economic diversity of the female work force that we noted in the previous chapter suggests that poverty did not suffice as an explanation. In this chapter, I want to use women's testimonies on their labour supply decision to explore how and why this apparent break with purdah could occur. For analytical purposes, the decision to enter garment factory employment can be disaggregated into a number of distinct, but closely related, sub-decisions, each involving a range of alternative considerations. First and foremost, it entailed the basic decision to earn. Secondly, it entailed the decision to work outside the home and hence go against long-established norms of female seclusion. And thirdly, it entailed the specific choice of garment employment over alternative forms of outside employment.

I will be using women's testimonies on these different aspects of their labour market decision to find out about their own 'preferences' regarding these various options. I will then widen the analysis to take account of the preferences of other members of their households in order to establish how the decision was actually made; whether it was arrived at consensually in deference to a shared vision of joint household welfare; whether it entailed a process of negotiation over divergent preferences; or whether the outcome was a conflictual one, a case of one set of preferences within the household overriding others. In the final section of this chapter, I want to use this analysis to revisit some of the theoretical questions raised in Chapter 2. To what extent did the processes of decision making described by the women workers bear out a rational choice calculus, as predicted by neo-classical economics, and to what extent did they represent a response to economic desperation, as suggested by those who emphasise the resilience of patriarchal constraint? And if it did conform to rational choice considerations, how were women able to 'take on' what have long been described in the Bangladesh literature as the unchanging/unchangeable structures of purdah and patriarchy?

## Deconstructing the decision to work: why work?

Let me start with the question 'why work?'. This is not generally a meaningful one to ask men in Bangladesh, or indeed in much of the world, and tends not to be included in surveys of men's work patterns (Dex, 1985; Morris, 1990). It is taken for granted that men work because they are the primary breadwinners. It is, however, considered a meaningful question to ask women because of the widespread assumption that they are generally supported by a male breadwinner and do not need to work. The decision to work is therefore considered to have an element of choice and calculation.

The reasons given by the women in our sample for wanting to take up paid work could be summarised in fairly conventional economic terms as a response to certain needs and preferences (see Appendix 2). What differentiated their accounts was the relative weight given to need versus preference. For instance, women who came from very poor households had very little discretion as to whether or not they would work. Many had already been earning long before the arrival of the garment industry in domestic service or in small workshops or factory units. The other group of women in our sample who also had very little discretion in the matter were those who had taken up paid work in response to some specific adversity: the death of the main breadwinner, abandonment or divorce by a husband, loss of land or the collapse of the family business. This was a more economically diverse group than the first, differentiated not only by their current economic circumstances but also by the extent to which the crisis was seen as an irreversible decline in their fortunes or a temporary setback.

A third group of women entered employment as a way of improving the family's living standards or their children's prospects. These women had a degree of choice. They were from better-off households and sought additional income as a way of bringing about a 'fit' between the aspirations of their social class and their family's material circumstances. Finally, there was a fourth group of women, unmarried and often living with their parents, who explained their entry into the factory primarily in terms of earning for their own needs and preferences. Some sought to earn in order to have money for personal consumption, some sought to save in order to defray the costs of their dowry for their parents and some simply in order to have some savings of their own.

It will be seen from this preliminary discussion that the reasons that women gave for their decision to take up paid work could all be accommodated within a rational choice framework. However, the varying degrees of urgency which characterised their decision introduced variations in the extent to which the decision was experienced as an act of agency on their part, or one that had been imposed on them by their circumstances. Women from the poorest backgrounds as well as those who had taken up paid work in response to some misfortune in their lives were the ones most likely to have been forced into the distress sale of labour. Others, however, had made the decision to take up paid work from a position of some economic strength and could presumably have opted to stay at home rather than endure the public disapproval that such employment attracted. The testimonies of this group, more than the others, offered important insights into some of the factors and motivations which lay behind women's apparent willingness to break with purdah norms, the second dimension of the labour supply decision we want to consider.

## The decision to work outside

Women's explanations for why they opted to work outside helped to uncover the multiplicity of meanings embodied in what has often been represented in the academic literature as well as in popular understandings as a monolithic cultural rule. These different meanings related to different levels of experience. At a primary and deeply personal level, purdah defined women's sense of propriety or of virtue, of what constituted the 'right' way for women to behave, where 'right' could be defined in religious or in cultural terms. At another level, it was a matter of family prestige: conformity to purdah norms signalled the ability of its guardians to protect and provide for women in their family and for women to concentrate on their primary domestic obligations. Finally, at a more impersonal level, purdah was experienced as a form of social control, imposed on women by dominant interests within the wider community.

The community which featured in women's accounts was made up of various groups of people, some 'given', some 'chosen', with whom the garment workers had varying degrees of personal contact. There were those they knew personally, such as members of their families, of their kinship networks and of the village communities from which most of them originated. These were 'given' groups, but they were operated to a greater or lesser extent as 'chosen' groups, depending on the extent to which women valued membership of these groups and sought to strengthen or expand them. There were acquaintances and neighbours, also people with whom they had some personal contact, but whose opinions mattered less to them. Then there were the male strangers they encountered on their journeys to and from work. And finally, there was the more diffuse and amorphous *samaj*, made up of religious and other influential figures, who had no contact with the women personally, but who were the self-declared arbiters of the social order and took it upon themselves to define its rules.

Women were clearly aware of the negative views of this wider community. By taking up outside employment, they were effectively accepting the cultural costs such employment entailed. However, the meanings that they themselves ascribed to purdah, how transgressive they viewed their decision to be, and the extent to which they were supported in their views by members of their immediate family, played an important role in determining how painful these costs were. Women who were most likely to experience factory employment as a painful choice were those who subscribed to a narrow version of purdah which proscribed any form of outside work for women:

> No man, other than my husband, should see even the hair of my head. Even my sons become 'other men' when they reach adolescence. All this is in the Hadith-Koran. Allah does not want women to mix with men. He asks us to remain within four walls, wear a *dosh-hather* [ten foot long] sari and a burkah if we have to go outside.

Clearly, women who subscribed to such definitions were most likely to experience outside employment as morally transgressive behaviour and hence to pay a painful price in taking it up:

> I am in need, that is why I have come to work, otherwise I would have stayed at home, done *namaaz-roza* [prayer and fasting]. I feel bad, but what else can I do, I have to live somehow . . . But we are being sinful because it is a sin if other men see you. That I walk through the streets is a sin.

However, this orthodox view of purdah was no longer seen as particularly relevant to the lives of most of the women we spoke to. Some allowed for the possibility that their behaviour might be violating official precepts, but took a pragmatic view of the matter:

> I know it is bad to be working in a factory but I am here, because we can't all be saints.

> The Koran says that if a woman's hair is seen by a stranger or her hands, then it is a sin. But only one-quarter of the old rules remain; three-quarters have gone.

Others argued that the norms of purdah were conditional, rather than absolute, and could be waived in the face of 'exceptional need'. Many drew directly on the authority of the Koran to back up their arguments:

> Islam forbids women to work but Allah won't do anything for me if I just sit at home. I have to try and and help myself, only then Allah will help me . . . If I have to support my family . . . is it a *faraz* to work or to sit at home?

> The Koran says it is one's duty to preserve oneself. So even if we are breaking the Koran by coming outside to work, we are not breaking it fully . . . It is said in the Koran that when one's survival is at stake, one can eat anything, even that food which is forbidden by the Koran.

Still others pointed to the weakening of traditional family ties and community safety nets as a source of support in times of need and the contradictions this set up between the old ways and new imperatives. Many spoke bitterly of the hypocrisy of those who publicly denounced their break with purdah, but failed to provide them with the protection and provision which had enabled women to conform to the dictates of purdah in the past. Aleya, for instance, challenged what she saw as the attempt of the mullahs to exercise power without responsibility: 'The *maulvis* object to garment work because they say we come into contact with strange men but we say to them, "Can you feed us? If you want to object, then you have to feed us." ' And Hena questioned the moral logic behind community censure: 'People say that the garments have made girls shameless. But they have the wrong idea. The girls are helping their families by working there. That is courage, not shamelessness.'

For some, their bitterness with the community at large was linked with their more personal experience of the failure of their extended family networks to assist them in times of economic need. Saleha, for instance, had been deserted five years previously by her husband. She worked to support herself and her two young sons since there was no one else to do it:

> The elders from the family said, why should a woman from this family be working. I used to feel bad but I have to survive somehow . . . Circumstances are not the same for everyone, I have two sons to bring up. I know people will help me for one or two days, but not forever. I will have to bring them up on my own.

In the case of Afifa, who had taken up employment to help out her
father, bitterness with her prosperous uncles, who had done little
to assist them in their time of need, underpinned her reaction to
community censure:

> My uncle has a six-storey house, but he doesn't let us live in it, so who is
> he to object? People are very good at criticizing. But there are many who
> are even worse off than me, who are disabled, blind or destitute, does
> *shamaj* take *them* in and provide for them? Instead of starving, if a person
> is working for her living, why should *shamaj* criticize her?

Rabeya's husband had been a violent man and an irresponsible
breadwinner who finally divorced her after three years, blaming
her for not having any children.[2] Although Rabeya had two
brothers, neither was prepared to take responsibility for her or for
their ageing mother. Asked if anyone had objected to her taking
up factory employment, she replied:

> No one objected. Who would object? Does anyone feed me, has anyone
> given me shelter? If they had, if someone had become my guardian and
> taken responsibility for me and said, 'Don't do this kind of work, you can
> come and stay with us', then I would have listened. They won't feed me or
> support me, how can they object?

What these various observations suggest is that orthodox notions of
purdah, while promoted actively by the more conservative sections
of the moral community, were no longer viewed as economically
sustainable by most of the women workers. They put forward in its
place an alternative and, for them, more consistent version of
purdah, one based on a *practical* morality, in which the defining
emphasis was shifted from formal compliance with community
norms to the substantive intent of behaviour, from social control to
individual responsibility. Many poured scorn on the idea that
confinement to the home guaranteed a woman's virtue:

> One can maintain purdah anywhere, even in an open field. And one who
> cannot maintain it will not be able to do so even within four walls.

2. Although, as Rabeya pointed out, he had already been married twice before and
there were no children from those marriages either.

I believe that if you are an immoral person, then even keeping you under lock and key will not change your character. In fact, letting you mix with four or five virtuous women may even help to improve it. But if you are good, then mixing with five or six women who are not virtuous will not take away your virtue.

The emphasis on individual responsibility was also expressed through the idea of 'the purdah of the mind', the view that by her modest deportment, lowered eyes, sombre mien and covered head, 'every woman carried her purdah with her'. This elaboration evoked the image of purdah as a kind of invisible corridor which stretched elastically from the threshold of women's homes to the factory gates to protect their virtue:

Even if I am wearing a burkah and have to get on a crowded bus, I have to push past men. Wearing a burkah won't change that. The best purdah is the burkah within oneself, the burkah of the mind.

I feel if my heart is good, if I keep my faith, if I say my prayers and follow my religion, I can still have a job. I can mix with anyone and know that my mind is purer than yours. People say things and one should not listen. One should rely on what one's heart says. And my heart says that I am pure.

As long as I maintain my modesty, my purdah is not at risk. There are some women who, when their dupatta slips down and leaves them exposed, will not cover themselves immediately. That is the difference between maintaining decency and failing to do so. You see, if I keep my fingers closed into a fist, you cannot open my hands, can you? Even if you try, it will take you such a long time, it will not be worth your while. Similarly, if I maintain my purdah, no one can take it away from me.

And finally, there were those who challenged the idea that responsibility for upholding moral standards lay with women alone. As the following comment by Angura suggests, they were arguing for a more 'equitable' reallocation of the burden of responsibility for the maintenance of women's virtue, on the grounds that purdah was as much about the 'eye' of the beholder as it was about the behaviour of 'the beheld':

If anyone says anything to me on the streets, or follows me, then it is not my sin and God will deal with them. A woman only breaks purdah if she is walking down the street in a flimsy saree, with her head uncovered, so everyone can see her and think what is this girl doing, what kind of clothes is she wearing.

As we can see, these attempts by women workers to contest the official discourses around purdah were not a rejection of purdah itself. They had little to gain from direct confrontations over the long-established cultural norms, norms that had taken deep roots in their own definitions of self-hood. Rather it was an attempt to reinterpret it, to use the core idea of purdah to establish a more consistent and authentic notion of morality which recognised the practical imperatives of everyday life. Nevertheless, these attempts to renegotiate the meaning of purdah were also attempts to rene-gotiate the boundaries of permissible behaviour, to expand their sphere of agency and choice. They consequently had practical implications: struggles over meanings were, as Berry (1988) put it, simultaneously struggles over material access.

## The decision to work in garment factories

Changing notions of purdah explained why it was no longer only 'destitute women', women without male support, who were pre-pared to consider the possibility of work outside the shelter of the home. What I want to look at next is what made the women in our sample opt for factory employment over alternative possibilities of outside employment. The advantages and problems of factory work mentioned by the women are summarised in Appendix 2. Here I will be elaborating on how they rationalised their choices. Women's testimonies on this question suggested that the conventional con-siderations of skills, qualifications and relative returns highlighted by neo-classical analysis were important considerations in their decisions, but only after a prior, often unconscious, demarcation of their 'preference possibility sets', which separated out admissable forms of employment from inadmissable ones. This demarcation related to cultural considerations which do not normally figure in neo-classical notions of 'employment opportunity sets'. Cultural context was in this sense endogenous to preference formation.

Gender was one aspect of the demarcation process, delineating male and female occupations within the labour market and confining women to certain limited segments. Class differentiated these segments further. It divided our sample of workers very loosely into those for whom garment employment was their preferred option and those for whom it was a default one. For women from poorer households, many of whom had already been working for a living before they joined the factories, garment employment was preferable to the other forms of employment available to women of their class. This was partly on straightforward economic grounds, such as pay and working conditions, and partly on more intangible grounds, such as the self-respect, dignity and status attached to such jobs compared to the alternatives available to women of their class.

Women from better-off households were less happy about their employment choices. They would have preferred some form of government employment, partly because of the greater security of such jobs, but also the greater respectability and prestige associated with them. Having failed to secure such jobs, which needed not only the appropriate educational qualifications, but also money to pay for bribes or else influential contacts to secure an interview, garment employment was a next-best option, but they remained uncomfortable about a form of employment which fell short of their status aspirations.

In addition, however, whatever factors might have facilitated the first wave of women workers into the garment industry, the resulting female-intensiveness of factory employment had an independent 'frequency-dependent effect' in inducing other women to join. The larger the proportion of women in the industry, the more acceptable a form of employment it became for those who were still wavering about their decision. The observed predominance of women in the garment labour force transmitted two kinds of signals which promoted this effect: that these jobs were available for women and that they were suitable for women. The informal social networks through which women workers had acquired information about this new industry – relatives, acquaintances, friends of the family, fictive kin, neighbours – facilitated this simultaneous interweaving of factual and evaluative information. This process of diffusion-by-example was illustrated in the case of Delowara. She heard about the factories while she was still living in the village from cousins who were working in one and had come back to their village on a visit. Her conversations with them about what factory work was like, and how many women like herself were now working in them, gave her the idea of taking up such work herself: 'It was the knowledge that they worked in a factory that made me determined to get a job for myself. If they could do it, why couldn't I?'

For Mumtaz, the key source of information had been garment workers living near her house:

> The garment workers used to tell me, 'We sew clothes, we are machine operators.' I couldn't understand what machine operations were. I used to think, 'What are they talking about?' The tenants who used to live next door used to tell me all this. I would sit outside our house and listen to them. My brother would say, 'Why are you listening to them?' If my brother came, I would move away, but I used to think that I will find out what this 'garment' business is.

The importance of informal social networks in disseminating information about factory employment pointed to the role played by women workers' own representations of their jobs in legitimising the possibility of such work for other prospective workers. They provided an alternative discourse about such work to the more negative ones which prevailed in the wider community and helped to contest widely-held public views of the garment factories as hotbeds of scandal and sexual impropriety. Although most workers acknowledged that there were some women who 'who liked to flirt' and 'behave like lovers', they were portrayed as 'bad apples', an atypical minority whose behaviour tarnished the reputations of the virtuous majority who were in the factories 'to earn a living, not for romance'. As Delowara argued passionately, it was unfair to lump all garment women together as 'loose women':

> The majority of people are very critical of women who work in garment factories, they say those women are bad, they have no character. That is what people have said to us. So we said, 'Don't say *women*. If one woman has done something bad, then say *woman*, don't say *women*! You can't judge a whole group of people by one woman's misconduct.' They say, 'Where

there is one bad, ten more will go bad.' We reply 'Never. You can never hang a whole group of people on the basis of what one person has done.'

Women's discussions about the nature of garment employment threw up examples of some of the metaphors and analogies through which they sought to 'feminise' and normalise factory work, to transform it from the public perception of a *haram* (forbidden) to a *halal* (accepted) form of work. The 'inside/ outside' dichotomy was a recurring theme in their descriptions, along with other contrasts between 'huge' and 'little', 'heavy' and 'light', 'clean' and 'dirty'.

> People from our village say, you work so late, we are asleep by then. We tell them, you work in the fields all day long, you work like donkeys . . . We stay clean and work in an office.

> Men can labour out in public in front of everyone. Women can't, they can't work in hotels and restaurants, for instance. But uneducated men, they can pour water, hand out plates to other men, women can't do that sort of work. A poor man can drive a rickshaw, or a baby taxi. Women can't push carts.

> We cannot do what men do. Men can work in the open, but we cannot work in front of a crowd of people, we must hide inside the factory or within the home . . . The jute mills are for men . . . women should not go there. Mills are different. Factory work is little work, it suits women. Those are mills, huge workshops, huge machines, they may have to carry huge machinery around, those are men's jobs.

The fact that the factory gates were frequently locked and guarded strengthened the image of a protected environment. We found frequent contrasts drawn between the orderly reality of the world inside and the lurid imagination and ignorance of those on the outside:

> People outside say so many things about garments . . . They have never seen the inside of a factory, they have no idea of what really goes on inside or what it is like.

> Of all the income earning activities, if there is one that is *halal*, it is garment work. People outside never come inside the factories, they think

that girls come here, laugh freely, mix freely. If they could only understand
what it was really like, they would give us more value.

As we noted in the previous chapter, it was in the employers'
interests to protect the reputation of their factories and they did so
by introducing various rules and regulations to maintain discipline
on the factory floor. Many of the women workers drew on these
rule-bound aspects of work organisation to counter the image of
sexual freedom and impropriety which featured so frequently in
the popular imagination.

> Garments is like a college, a school. Factory XXX even has a uniform.
> They tell you the rules at the interview: 'You have a responsibility and you
> must work accordingly. Never do anything to spoil the name of the factory,
> when we tell you what your duty for the day is, you have to do it, whether
> it means working till four or all night.'

> About the rules of the office, I was told that we would have to be careful
> to make sure that we conducted ourselves decently in office, that we got
> on with our work, that we didn't talk when we were supposed to be
> working ... When they said that we had to be careful about how we
> conducted ourselves, they meant that if someone approached me in the
> road, I shouldn't talk to them. Someone might insult me, I should not
> retaliate, I shouldn't get involved with discussions with anyone. I should
> just concentrate on my work.

The fact that most factories were usually located in residential
areas, rather than industrial estates, and occupied premises that
might previously have served as home or office, also facilitated
their representation in some of the testimonies as a *domestic* space:

> This place appears safe to me. It is like the home. We work in one of the
> rooms, the gates are closed when we come in and then, we go back home
> straight after work.

The 'domestication' of factory life was also echoed in the use of
familial metaphors to describe relationships on the factory floor.
The terminology of fictive kinship is by no means unique to factory
life. We noted examples of such use in the context of women's
residential relationships and neighbourhood networks (see also

Islam, 1998). In a culture where the family and family-based relationships remain pivotal to a variety of socio-economic networks, the construction of unofficial kinship relations can serve many different purposes: to make claims on others, to reconstitute forms of hierarchy or to disguise essentially exploitative relationships. In the context of the factory floor, the use of gender-related kinship terminology helped to de-sexualise encounters between non-related men and women:

> It doesn't matter whether there are men or women in the factory if you think of them as your brother or sister. What is wrong with working together, don't we work as brother and sister?

> People outside have the wrong impression about garments. If anyone asks me, I say that the atmosphere is very good and that men and women work like brothers and sisters.

Finally, many of the workers stressed the sheer demands of the production process itself, in which each stage of the process depended on the efficient and timely completion of the previous one, in creating highly regulated interactions in the work place. The idea that workers could engage in flirtatious behaviour within the factory floor was dismissed impatiently since, it was pointed out, anyone who chose to engage in idle chit-chat would be immediately identifiable through hold-ups in production.

> How can we get up to anything, there is no time to talk. If we do, there would be a pile-up in the process. Anyway, we cannot even hear each other speaking. And when work is over, we are too tired to do anything, but go straight home.

> I don't believe our purdah is spoilt by coming into the factory. We are kept so busy. I may be in love with someone, but inside the factory, no matter what time it is, they don't give us five minutes to ourselves. If I have something important to say to you, I will have to save it till tiffin. There's no time for idle chat.

In sum, what these testimonies help to spell out is the role, and power, of discourse in the 'making of a woman's occupation'. While the rationalisations of individual women for taking up a form of employment which appeared to go against the grain of gender propriety may not have added up to a great deal individually, collectively they helped to constitute an alternative and more positive discourse about such work to the one promoted by sections of the media and the religious community. Employers' preferences for 'docile' female labour, and women's need for work, may have provided the material conditions in which this process took place, but it was the meanings invested in such employment by those already within it which helped to transform it into a possible option for other women who might in the past have excluded it from their admissible opportunity sets.

However, it was also precisely these meanings that made employment in the garment factories a far less attractive proposition for men. I should add that the obverse side of the widespread perception of garment employment as 'women's work' was the discomfort expressed by some of the male workers we interviewed at finding themselves in an industry dominated by women. This partly reflected status considerations about the kinds of women who worked in the factories, but also a certain amount of sexual unease at the unaccustomed proximity to so many women. Kalam, who had a Secondary School Certificate (SSC), had tried, but failed, to get a job as a clerk in a government ministry. He now worked in the cutting section of a garment factory. He had not yet informed his parents in the village about his job:

> I felt very small. I had studied and yet this was all I could get. The situation being what it is here, I just didn't feel very good about myself . . . what with the girls and all . . . it is not inconvenience that is the problem, but that some of them ruin our reputation. Within the factory, our reputation is impeccable, the Administration sees to that, but I see girls who are working outside go out of the gate and stand in the road talking all kinds of things with boys from outside.

Malek came from a poorer background. He had no education and had previously run a tailoring business from his home. It had not proved particularly profitable and he had joined the industry as a band-machine operator. He was convinced that people outside the industry, particularly those who were 'Allah-conscious', regarded those who worked in the factories through 'eyes which are disgusted' by their sexual impropriety. As an 'Allah-conscious' man himself, he explained the source of his discomfort:

> These girls do not maintain purdah and we work alongside them. The way they carry on these days with cosmetics and so on, it is a great injustice to the boys who work here . . . You see, girls are like a flame around boys who are like wax. When they move around in front of the boys, then the boys melt just like wax. When the boys' eyes fall on them, then later, when they go to sleep, their imagination brings back that image. Then these boys dream a sin and this sin does them great harm.

## Deconstructing the decision to work: consensus, conflict and negotiation within the household

I have so far focused on women's own motivations for working, their reasons for opting for factory work and the rationalisations through which they sought to reconcile their decision to work outside the home with dominant cultural notions about women's position. Questions of choice and agency clearly played some role in most of their decisions because such employment required women to go against the grain of established behaviour. Not all the women we interviewed were able to reconcile the 'cognitive dissonance' this entailed so that the extent to which they perceived their entry into factory employment as an active choice varied.

However, as we have seen above, gender ideologies are not only about women. They also simultaneously define what it means to be a man in the public, as well as in the private, domain. Given the power of prevailing ideologies about the role of men in protecting and providing for women in their family, women's desire to take up factory employment could be taken to constitute a very public statement about men's ability to fulfil these roles. Consequently, if factory employment entailed certain forms of cognitive dissonance for women, it raised other forms of dissonance for the men in their families. And since the majority of women made the decision to take up factory employment in consultation with other family members, rather than on their own, there was clearly a very real possibility that their assessments of the costs and benefits associated with factory work diverged from those of other family members.

This is what I want to focus on in the next sections of this chapter: the decision making processes behind women's entry into factory employment, taking account of both their own preferences in the matter as well as the preferences of other relevant members of their households. I have placed the processes they described into a number of categories on the basis of a simple, two-way classification of the kinds of 'agency' that they ascribed to themselves in the decision to take up factory work and the extent to which these processes were characterised by conflict or consensus. While the more immediate source of differences between women workers on these issues reflected whether they had been motivated in their decision by adversity or opportunity, this difference was itself a reflection of the underlying intersections of class and gender in their lives.

Their class positions helped to explain the economic motivations which led to their entry into the labour market, the urgency of such motivations as well as the range of occupations perceived to be available to them. However, their position within the family, and the specific gender roles associated with these positions, affected how they experienced their choices and the probability that they would encounter resistance from other family members. Marital status was a particularly significant dimension of this so that women from similar class backgrounds often offered very contrasting testimonies on the processes by which they entered factory employment, depending on whether they were married, were hoping to be marrried, had ever been married, had given up on marriage or what was happening within their marriage. This will become evident in the discussion which follows.

### Reluctant agency, uncontested decision making

We noted earlier that a number of women had come into the factories as a result of some specific adversity in their lives. Within this larger group, there was a distinct sub-group of women for whom the adversity in question had been the loss of their husbands through death, divorce or abandonment and the absence of an alternative adult male in the family to take on the headship role.

There were around seven women in the Dhaka sample who fell into this category. The absence of opposition to their decision to take up factory work reflected the fact that they were seen, both by themselves and by others, to have very little choice in the matter. The fact that it was the loss of husbands that was the common factor in this group is significant. In a society where women spend their lives under the social protection of men, the loss of any male guardian is likely to be experienced as a period of heightened insecurity. However, whatever the depth of immediate personal loss associated with each event, not all have the same longer term implications. In the normal course of events, the death of a father tends to occur after guardianship has already passed from father to husband or very soon before.[3] The loss of a husband, on the other hand, cannot easily be accommodated if the woman has no son old enough to step into his place.

These were the women whose entry into factory employment most closely conformed to the idea of distress sale of labour, although they were not necessarily the poorest women in our sample. Regardless of differences in class background, they experienced their entry into garment employment as a contraction, rather than an expansion, of choice. Razia Sultana was an example of this group. She had been precipitated by the death of her husband from a situation where she was comfortably provided for to one where she found herself the sole breadwinner for four stepchildren from his first marriage[4] and two children from her own marriage with him. While she recognised that the availability of garment employment had saved her from having to choose between descending into ever-deepening poverty or dependence on the charity of relatives, it was not a choice she had ever expected to make and she continued to mourn her loss of security:

3. Women whose fathers had died when they were very young also described a great deal of insecurity in their lives, but it had generally happened too long ago to show up as an influence in their current work decisions.

4. Razia Sultana's husband had previously been married to her older sister with whom he had had the four children. When she died, Razia Sultana's mother urged her to marry the widower because she did not want to lose contact with her grandsons. Consequently, since Razia Sultana's stepsons were also her nephews, responsibility for them passed to her when her husband died.

Before my husband's death, I never had to worry about work, we had servants, I knew I was cherished. I never moved alone. I used to wonder how garment workers worked all day and then came home and did the housework while people like us stayed at home all day and yet needed servants to do the housework . . . Now suddenly I have to worry about how to survive.

Khatun also began work because of circumstances beyond her control. Her personal history was closely intertwined with, and bore the marks of, the political instability and economic underdevelopment which characterised Bangladesh's own history:

During the [1971] troubles, my husband and father were murdered by the *razakars* . . . My son was just over a year old then. We never found their bodies . . . My mother and sister died of illness. I had two brothers, one drowned and the other died of illness. All of them are dead. I have a stepbrother in Khulna but he takes no news of me. My brother is buried in Azimpur graveyard. I have no one left. I don't talk to anyone. I have a lot of grief inside, that is why I don't talk to anyone.

When Khatun's husband and father were killed, and she found that she would have to fend for herself, she began working as a domestic servant. She put her son to work as well when he was eight years old and he has worked ever since. Although she recognised that garment factories had provided a lifeline to women like herself, she had been brought up with very different expectations about the life she would lead: 'I never thought that I would have to work but it was in my fate. If I had known earlier, I would have taken poison and killed myself.' She now looked forward to the day her son would qualify as a driver and she would be able to retire from garment work and return to domesticity.

Rahela had walked out on her husband when he brought home another woman with whom he was clearly having an affair. Her parents acted on her behalf in getting a divorce, waiving her entitlement to *din mohr* (a form of alimony) from him on condition she retained custody of her young son and daughter. She returned to her parental home and had resolved never to marry again – her experience with her husband had given her 'a hatred for all that'. She had decided to find work in order to contribute towards her children's expenses, but had not been able to find employment suitable to a woman from her class background. Her account expressed the hopelessness felt by women who had been brought up to believe in marriage as the fulfilment of women's destiny and found themselves having to deal with a very different reality:

> I work in garments because . . . what else can I do? I don't see any other options available. What I would have liked best is to be a housewife. My husband would have worked and I would have stayed at home, looking after the family. Occasionally we would have gone out visiting. But the way things worked out, this was not possible. And things might not be better for my daughter. It is possible that she might have to work. I doubt her fate is likely to be any better than mine.

Renu's entry into factory employment also exemplified a reluctant agency in that she was literally driven into it by the violence of her husband. Her father had died when she was very young and she had been married off at a young age to a man from a neighbouring village who turned out to be an irresponsible breadwinner and an abusive husband. She had stayed on with him nevertheless in the hope that he might have a change of heart once they had a child, but it proved to be futile:

> He would work well for two days, digging earth, and then he would sleep for two days . . . I wasn't working then so I sometimes ate for two days and then I starved for the rest of the week. He used to give me a hard time, he used to beat me . . . I wanted to leave my husband many times but I thought I have had one son but he died, now I am going to have another and things will be better, our marriage will last. But when my daughter was born, I saw nothing changed and my heart broke and I came away.

## Active agency, uncontested decision making

There was a second category of women who were also bereft of male support and had also entered unopposed into factory employment, but differed from the first in that they described the decision to take up factory employment as an active choice on their part. There were eighteen women in this category. Most came from very poor backgrounds and many had already been earning a living before the emergence of the garment industry. This group viewed the availability of garment employment as an improvement, as well as an expansion, of their job opportunity sets. Not only did it offer higher returns than most of their previous employment options, it also offered them an identity as workers that they valued. For many, it rescued them from the far more demeaning occupations they might otherwise have had to enter. Angura's mother had brought up her two daughters on her own, after her husband had died, by working as a domestic servant, but refused to let her daughters become servants because:

> She told me that if I worked in other people's houses, I would have to wash their dirty clothes and that the bad food they would give me to eat would make me ill. She couldn't bear that I should have to do that. She said she would rather keep me next to her and let me die than have me work in other people's homes.

Angura supplemented her mother's income as soon as she was old enough by doing home-based tailoring for people within their locality. When a garment factory opened in a nearby neighbourhood, she joined it:

> We can earn much more money now because these factories have opened. When we sewed from home, we could not earn enough to survive. Sometimes I did not even get 100 takas in a week, sometimes it was 150/- or 250. That was not a proper job, now I have a *chakri*.

Monawara had been married off at the age of thirteen. Her husband began to show signs of mental instability very soon after their marriage, unable to hold a job down and frequently beating her. She left him, taking her young son with her, and returned to her brother's household. But relations soured because her sister-in-law began to resent having to feed her. She moved into domestic service so that she would no longer have to live in her brother's home. When factory employment became available, she left domestic service and took up a factory job. No one contested any of her decisions since no one wanted to take her on as their responsibility.

Factory employment initially left her worse off than domestic service. Living in her employer's house had saved her rent and in addition she earned 100/- a month, food, oil, soap as well as clothes. Her starting salary in the factory was low (although it improved with her productivity) and she now had to pay rent. However, as a domestic servant, there were no limits to the demands on her time and she was literally at her employer's beck and call at all times of the day or night. Her assessment of domestic service versus garment employment spelt out graphically what she valued about her new identity as a factory worker:

> I left their employment because I couldn't go out without their permission. If I wanted to go to my own house, I would have to ask them first, if they said no, I couldn't go. Here in the factory, I work from 8 to 5, I get one hour lunch break and I can do overtime. If you do overtime, they give you tiffin and money and you are earning more. You get time off on Fridays. You have your freedom. I finish at the factory at 5 and go home and cook . . . It's my own house and my own bed. It's not like that working in people's houses. In other people's houses, you have to obey all their orders and can't go to sleep before 12 o'clock at night and you have to get up in the morning before them . . . There is no such thing as overtime pay.

Shefali was the only woman in our sample who admitted to having been a prostitute before she entered factory employment. Her mother had committed suicide when her father had deserted her to marry again. Shefali had been a small child then. She and her two younger brothers had been brought up by their maternal uncle and aunt, but the children had to return to their father when their uncle died. Her father married Shefali off as soon as he could to a widower with three children, but the marriage did not last long and she returned home.[5] Her father kept taunting her with the failure of her marriage: 'He said, you could not keep your husband, you are no good at anything . . . you might as well sell yourself.' In the end, she decided to migrate to Khulna: 'I thought if I have to listen to all this from my father, I might as well sell myself.' No one protested when she had left because no one cared.

In Khulna, she earned her living through a variety of means. She

5. Shefali told us that she could not reconcile herself to the fact that his wife had committed suicide like her mother and that he might therefore turn out to be like the man her father was.

worked the day shift in a jute mill. In the evenings, she cooked for a group of male mill workers who lived on a mess basis. She also worked for a while for a jatra company as a singing girl. She began to slide into casual prostitution, sleeping with some of the mill workers in return for money or clothes or cosmetics. One of the men at the mill became obsessed with her. Despite her protestations – 'I told him, I am a street woman, I have nothing in the world, I am all I have, I can give you nothing' – he proposed to her through her landlord and she finally accepted.

Marriage promised the start of a new and better life for her, a return to respectability. However, within two months, his obsession with her had passed and he told her to return to her home because his family did not approve of him marrying a jatra girl. However, she could not return to her family since her father had disowned her: 'He says he has no daughter, only five sons.' Instead, she made her way to Dhaka. When we met her, she was working all day in the factory and in the evenings as a domestic servant in her landlord's house. Comparing her present occupation to her past, she said:

> I used to dress better before, but you know something about my character. I used to be bad that way. Someone would call me to him and give me something and I would do what he wanted. But I prefer the way I live now to the way I did then. If I can't eat properly, or if I only eat one meal a day, I would still prefer to live this way.

### Active agency, consensual decision making

A third category of women was made up of those who had made an active choice to take up factory employment, and for whom the absence of opposition to the decision reflected consensus within their household about the value of their wage contributions rather than poverty or indifference. Fourteen women in our sample fell into this category. Some, like Afia, were unmarried daughters living with parents. She was the eldest of five children and had joined the factory after her matriculation in order to help out her father, the sole breadwinner, who managed a small shop. She said that since she had no older brother who could have shared the responsibility for looking after the family with her father, she had decided to earn:

> My father is getting older and he cannot manage alone. My younger brothers and sisters are studying and they need support . . . No one suggested I take the job and no one objected. I gave up the studies myself. If I had wanted to continue my studies, my parents would have begged or borrowed to help me.

She ignored the reservations expressed by sections of their extended family on the grounds that their reservations were not backed up with the kind of support which would render her economic contribution redundant:

> Our well-to-do relatives, like my maternal uncles, were not happy when they found out that I had taken up this job. But after they heard from me that I worked with mainly women, they did not say any more. Even if they had objected, I would not listen to them . . . Our rich relatives will not give us money every month, why should I listen to them?

Mumtaz also made the decision to contribute to the family budget when she realised that her family could not survive on the earnings of a single breadwinner. She was eighteen years old and had been forced to give up her studies when her father abandoned them after a long period of illness and mental instability. They had initially gone to stay with her mother's brother, but were made to feel the objects of charity. Her brother, who had been preparing for his MSc., began to give private tuition as a means of earning but it was clear that his income was not enough and Mumtaz decided to seek employment as well: 'I saw the pressure on my brother, I saw the hardship that our family was going through, that my *mama* and *chacha* were neglecting us, they had not been around to see us or find out how we were.'

Her brother explained why none of the family had objected to Mumtaz's decision:

> We have relatives . . . They are reasonably well-off, but we don't want to ask for help and make ourselves small. We want to try and stand on our own feet . . . The idea to work came from Mumtaz. She saw other girls doing it

and thought she could do it as well. When she suggested it to us, we had no objections . . . When this kind of tragedy occurs, many people fall apart with worrying: What will happen, what will we do, how will we eat? We didn't respond like that, we pulled through together.

A number of married women also described their entry into the factory in terms which could be called a 'joint welfare maximising' consensus. Jahanara exemplified this category. She and her husband had come to Dhaka after a drought-related crop failure had forced him to sell his land. They both agreed that a second income was needed if they were to be able to pay high rents in the city and send their four children to school. Jahanara's parents were grieved by the fact that they had married off their daughter only to have her take up waged employment, but Jahanara pointed out that it was in their grandchildren's interests: 'I told them that I did not work before, but now they have four grandchildren who have to be educated so it is necessary for me to work.'

Shahnaz Nur was one of the women who had taken up employment because of family adversity. She had been married to an educated man and they had initially lived with his parents. However, he failed to find regular employment in the village and was forced to take up manual waged jobs, in a mill and even, for a few days, as an agricultural labourer. His parents offered very little financial support and after the birth of their first child, asked them to live separately because his mother in particular resented the idea of having to support their family. Shahnaz began to work for a local non-governmental organisation, making jute handicrafts from home which the NGO then marketed. She thus became the main breadwinner for their family. Her husband helped her out with the jute work. He told us how he had felt about his situation:

I felt bad that I was unemployed. I had no interest in 'business' because it does not bring a steady income. I wanted a regular income. Although I was unemployed, I was helping my wife with her work so I was also working. So no one could say I was unemployed.

Finally, his brother-in-law got him a job in the cantonment in Dhaka and they came away from the village to live next door to her

father on the outskirts of the city. Within a year of their arrival,
Shahnaz joined a garment factory:

> One person's income is not enough for the whole family. We could not
> buy clothes. My job has helped to improve the living standards of the
> family. We would have found it difficult to educate the girls. . . . My
> husband had no objections. My father was upset, but he said, I got you
> married, I am no longer responsible for you, it is up to your husband.

The women described so far all explained their decision primarily
as a response to family need, although the 'need' in question
ranged from basic living standards to children's education. There
were other, albeit less frequent, examples of women who entered
work from a position of some economic privilege and for more
personal reasons. Nazneen was twenty-five years old and single.
Her mother had died in 1975 and her father married again three
years later. Her family were well-off and highly educated. Her
older sister was a qualified doctor, practising in a private clinic in
the city. Her younger siblings were all still students at the
university.

Nazneen herself had not gone beyond Matric, but displayed a
strong entrepreneurial spirit from an early age. She had taken
diplomas in various crafts which she then taught on a private basis
to other girls from her neighbourhood. Joining the garment factory
was a logical next step. She could see other girls in her area, many
less educated than her, were joining and it clearly paid more than
what she had been earning through her private efforts: 'I thought,
if they can do it, so can I.' Her stepmother, who we interviewed,
said she was aware that people around might say that had she been
Nazneen's real mother, she would not have let her work, but that
both she and Nazneen's father had full confidence in Nazneen's
judgement and had no reason to put any obstacles in front of her:
'If all the girls in Bangladesh were like my Nazneen, there would
be no unhappiness among women in this country.'

## Active agency, negotiated decision making

Having focused on women who, for various reasons, had not
encountered any opposition to their desire to take up factory
employment, I want to now turn to those who did and who
consequently had to negotiate with family members before they
could enter such employment. There were ten women who fell into
this category. They generally came from families for whom basic
survival needs were assured, so that concerns about gender propriety and family reputation carried greater weight in how other
family members defined 'household welfare'. However, the forms
of resistance that the women encountered, and who it was offered
by, generally varied according to marital status, as did the rationales
they used to overcome resistance.

For young, unmarried women, resistance came from parents and
the wider kinship network. The challenge they faced was to persuade their guardians that factory work would not compromise
their reputations and hence their marriage prospects. Delowara
was the young woman mentioned earlier in this chapter who heard
about garment employment from visiting cousins who had taken
up factory work. Her father had fallen on hard times and it was no
longer possible for Delowara to continue her education. Her own
reason for wanting to earn was simple: 'If I worked, at least I would
be earning some money, I would be able to feed myself and I would
be able to buy some of the things that I wanted. There would be
one less mouth to feed at home. If I stayed in the village, I would
have to depend on my family.'

However, her parents were adamantly opposed to the idea of her
going off to the city on her own to work and she described the
fairly protracted process of negotiation by which she got them to
agree. Firstly, she got her cousins to intercede with them on her
behalf, but they failed:

> My father said no, so did my mother. I said, 'If my cousins can do these
> jobs, why can't I?' But my parents were against it because of what people
> might say, they were afraid I might go off and fall in love with someone, or
> do something like that. I said, it is better than me just sitting around here.

I might be able to earn something. My father talked about loss of honour and chastity so I said to him 'Abba, if I am going to throw away my chastity, I can do that sitting right here. And if I am not going to do it, I can take care of myself even if I do go out to work.'

She then persuaded her brother to plead her case:

I told my brother, you explain things to our father and I will explain it to our mother . . . I then explained to my mother . . . 'If (my cousins) can do these jobs, why can't I?' My brother said to my father, 'You can see that Halima and the others have gone there to work, so what is wrong with Apa going there as well?'

She also mobilised her cousin's wife to further intercede on her behalf:

I pointed out to her, 'If I decide to do something so terrible that my parents lose face in our society, if I decide to have a love affair with someone, I can do that even while I am living at home . . . can't I? I don't need to go there in order to do so. But I am not so silly that I would do something like that to them.' So I explained things to her and she spoke to them and . . . finally they agreed. They were mostly worried about my getting involved with some man. There were other things as well. For example, I had never been into town before. I might not be able to look after myself in this new environment. I had never been to Dhaka, so they worried about that as well. They said, 'These are not good times, you don't know what might happen. It might not be safe. Something bad might happen to you.'

Having finally won her parents' consent, Delowara migrated to Dhaka with her cousins and they helped her to find a 'mess' arrangement with two other girls from her village. But members of her extended family in the village continued to worry:

When we go home to visit, our grandmothers say to us: 'Take care about how you behave. Make sure that you don't do anything bad. Don't fool around with anyone. Don't give people a chance to make comments about you. Don't let your family down . . .' and so on.

In the case of married women, objections to the idea of factory employment were obviously more likely to come from husbands than from fathers. A common element in women's strategies to overcome resistance in such cases was to invoke the welfare of their children. This was the strategy used by Kohinoor. She wanted to work because she felt her husband's income did not stretch far enough to cover their own needs as well as his obligations to his widowed mother and unmarried sister. However, first she had to deal with her husband's anxieties about the aspersions this cast on his adequacy as a breadwinner. Kohinoor described how she overcame his reservations:

> My husband asked me why I wanted to work, was it because he couldn't feed me. I said, 'I could stay at home, but we would suffer. If I work, I will bring in money, people will respect us.' If one's husband can't provide, does one go around saying one is working for money? It is between us. I made him understand. So he said, 'Alright, go, but when I start earning enough, then you must give up work.' His elder brother said to him, 'Why have you let your wife work?' My husband told him, 'Now everyone works.' But even now he still says, 'With the money I get, you don't have to work, just look after the children.' I say, 'The children will have to be educated, that is the problem, I must go on working.'

Jorina had initially gone to the garment factory simply to accompany a neighbour who wanted to apply for a job but had ended up being offered a job as well. For the next few days, she concealed her employment from her husband, going to the factory after he left for work and returning home before him. She knew her husband would object on the grounds that it was a demeaning occupation for someone from their social background. The tactic she used to win his agreement, when she finally informed him about what she had done, was to invoke their shared concerns with their children's educational prospects:

> In the beginning, my husband was angry when I told him that I had found a job because it was in 'garments'. He himself has a 'bhodro' job as a clerk in the university and he was worried about our family prestige. He would not have been angry if it had been a government job. It's not that he thinks that women who work in factories are of a 'different' sort but there have been incidents. He asked me why I had joined, where was the need? I told him, we have four children, they have their whole future ahead of them. If they are to get a decent education, to move in good company, you

need money. I was just sitting at home doing nothing when we need money for the children's clothes and books. Now I am using my time profitably.

However, not all the women in this category described motives for wanting to work which were bound up with family need or maternal altruism. Some also had other more personal reasons for doing so. Morgina had already been working in a garment factory when she got married. She said that she decided to continue working, despite her husband's misgivings, because she too, like Kohinoor, felt his financial obligations to his elderly parents in the village rendered his earnings inadequate: 'He has two families to support and only one income'. However, behind this economic rationale, she also had another simpler personal motivation which was that she enjoyed the opportunity of being outside the house:

> I have been working for three years and I like it. I don't like it at home. In the factory, everyone is working and even if there is no conversation, the day passes quite well. At home there is nothing, no hard work, only cooking and cleaning so I don't like it there. It is quiet and lonely at home. In the factory there are more people and we are all working together.

### Active agency, conflictual decision making

Our final category was made up of women who, like those in the preceding category, had also encountered opposition to their desire to take up factory work, but unlike the preceding group, had decided to take up such employment in spite of this opposition. There were eleven such women in our sample. Such conflictual outcomes occurred almost invariably in the context of marriage. In some cases, the conflict was resolved as a result of the husband succeeding in wearing down his wife's resistance. Rupban's husband, who had left his first wife, played on her insecurities as a woman who had been abandoned by her first husband and who was herself her husband's second wife: 'Everybody in his family knows I am his second wife but he says that there is no problem if I fast and pray and take care of him.' He had been taking her to religious meetings in their area where women factory workers were denounced as little better than prostitutes. By the time we interviewed her, she had succumbed to his pressures and decided to leave her job within the year.

However, in other cases, it was the wife who managed to wear down her husband's opposition. This was the case with Banesa. She described her husband as a good man: 'He never looks at another woman, he prays five times a day and never complains' – but also as a bit of a simpleton who was easily influenced by the neighbourhood gossip: 'They told him if you keep this wife, you will not have a peaceful household.' Her husband worked at a biscuit factory where he earned 900/- a month while she tried to supplement their income, raising poultry at home. However, they had frequent quarrels about money and she finally decided to find a factory job after he had hit her during one such quarrel. She learnt to sew at a local tailoring shop and then applied for a factory job. When he found out, her husband was so angry that he locked her out of the house. Because Banesa had initially concealed the fact of her employment from her parents who lived in another part of Dhaka, she could not return home, but slept on the verandah with their youngest child. However, her secret was given away by a distant uncle who told her parents that he thought that Banesa was seeing too many films: her factory was located in the same building as a cinema hall.

She encountered a storm of opposition when she was found out, but managed to persuade her brother to visit her factory and see how respectable it all was. For a while she moved in with her parents, but by the time we interviewed her, her husband had also come round to the idea of her job, partly, as he explained, because he saw the economic sense of it:

> I was opposed to her working because when a women earns, it doesn't look good. People say that she is feeding herself. People think this is bad, I thought so too. Where did she go, what did she do? I forbade her to work, but she went anyway. I used to get angry, but she went anyway. Now I don't feel so bad about it. What harm can come of it if we behave decently? The country prospers, we get by as well.

Hanufa used to sew quilts at home to supplement her husband's increasingly irregular earnings from petty trade. She had remonstrated with him to find more regular employment but he responded with violence: 'When she talks out of line like that, I cannot control myself. She's scared to hit me back. No man will tolerate that sort of behaviour from his wife. I shouldn't beat her, but she should realise that just because I am unemployed, she can't say whatever she wants. If women realised this, then no one would beat them.' When their daughter was a year old, Hanufa decided to find a job, despite her husband's violent opposition. As she explained: 'I saw that women who are working can run the family better . . . I decided myself, my husband did not agree, he used to tell me to cope on his income and get by with sacrifices . . . But I have a daughter, she has a future ahead.'

In the context of already conflictual marriages, a wife's decision to enter garment employment was often associated with a radical shift in the marital relationship. In some cases, it signalled the end of the marriage. In Kaneez's case, the birth of her baby was the immediate event which precipitated her entry into garment work, but behind it was the history of a relationship which had began as a 'love marriage', but had deteriorated into a violent and unhappy one. Her husband turned out to be an unreliable drifter who could not hold down a job down for more than a few months at a time. They had moved in with Kaneez's family after he had quarrelled with his own parents, but he continued to drift, living off Kaneez's family as well as handouts from his own family.

Their relationship soon deteriorated into violence. Kaneez explained her decision to enter the garment factory when her baby was born, despite her husband's violent objections, in straightforward terms: 'I came here because of need. If there had been no need, I would not have come.' However, her mother gave us a brief history of how the moment of need arose:

Kaneez went into the factory after her baby was born. It was a caesarian delivery so that Kaneez had no breast milk and the baby was in bad shape. Kaneez just walked to the XX garment factory which was the nearest one to us and got herself a job there . . . She felt that with the money she would be able to save her baby. Her husband was opposed to it because he felt that girls from 'good' families did not work in garment factories. But he could not stop her. She had a big fight with him about it, saying that if she did not take this job, she would not be able to buy milk for her baby. And what was she supposed to do then? Feed the baby rice starch?

Kaneez told us that her mother used to weep at the idea of her daughter having to work in the factory, but accepted that she had no choice. Her husband, however, left Kaneez soon after she joined the factory and by the time we interviewed her, she had heard that he was going to marry again.

Violence was also a feature of Aleya's marriage and indeed the reason behind her decision to leave her marriage. Her husband was blind and much older than her. He worked in the second-hand clothes business with the help of a son from a previous marriage. He had in fact been married six times before and, according to Aleya, each of his previous wives had left him because of his violence. She heard about the garment factories while she had been living in the village and had used her small savings from her poultry raising to train in machining with a local NGO. She then left her husband and came away with her twelve-year-old daughter to Dhaka. She lived initially with her brother and his wife and worked as a domestic servant while she searched for a factory job. By this time, her husband had followed her to Dhaka. He objected to her entry into factory work because it would bring her into constant contact with other men, preferring her to remain in domestic service:

> My husband told me not to work in a factory because he thought I might leave him for another man. When I worked in people's houses, he did not object. He wanted me to work inside a house because there would be no men. He heard that garments were not good, in the papers it said that some garment girls had become pregnant.

Aleya, however, had suffered enough at his hands: 'I went into the factory anyway. I told him, "I would rather work and earn my own living than sit and listen to your lectures." ' She herself was very clear that she preferred factory work to domestic service for reasons similar to those we came across earlier. As a servant, she had earned 300 takas a month. When she found a factory job, she joined as a 'helper' on 150/- a month. In domestic service, pay increases were dependent largely on the whim of the employer whereas in the factory, she fully expected to receive productivity-related pay increments as her machine control improved. Furthermore, while overtime work was compulsory in garment employment, it was also officially recognised and remunerated. As a domestic servant, the concept of overtime did not arise because there were no contractually agreed hours of work: she worked as long as her employers wanted her to work. Finally, she also valued the self-respect which came with a 'proper' job: 'Although every job is valuable, being a servant has no prestige or self-respect. Self-respect is more important than food. If you work in a house, you are just a servant.'

## Revisiting theories of choice:
## unified and bargaining models of the household

In so far as the majority of the women we interviewed took up factory work for economic reasons, their decisions can be seen to be consonant with economic theories of choice. However, we have also seen how social rules, norms and values also played an important role in their decision making processes, shaping not only their ability to choose, but also how they constructed their choices. In this section, I want to return to the question of preferences as a starting point for exploring in greater detail what these testimonies tell us about the interactions between structure and agency in women's labour market decisions. As we noted in Chapter 2, economists use the concept of preferences as a short-hand for 'what people want and how much, the dimensions of desire' (Folbre, 1994). In other words, for the motivations which give human behaviour its purposive character. However, they have little interest in what determines these preferences, generally treating them as exogenous to their models and focusing their attention on those aspects of behaviour which can be explained by variations in prices and incomes.

The women's testimonies, by contrast, suggest that if we *investigate* their preferences rather than inferring them from observed behaviour, we find that they play a far more important role in explaining decisions than economists are prepared to concede. Decisions about the allocation of the time of different household members to alternative activities were not merely a matter of comparing their marginal productivities. They were also influenced by prevailing ideologies about gender roles which created widespread social expectations that men would take up paid work and that women would stay at home and look after the family and children. Such expectations were incorporated as meta-preferences by individuals and translated into particular allocations of family labour in which gender played a more significant role than productivity in determining decisions about who did what.

At the same time, however, these social expectations did not translate mechanistically into a uniform set of individual preferences, but were mediated by individual histories and experiences. In some cases, variations in the preferences reported by women workers could be boiled down to subjective differences in their interpretations of these gender ideologies: some women were more creative in their interpretations, others were more timid. In some cases, variations reflected differences in their class backgrounds. As we saw, women who had grown up largely fending for themselves were more likely to view factory employment as a welcome addition to their opportunity set. By contrast, for those who had grown up taking the idea of lifelong male provision for granted, the prospect of working in a garment factory clearly entailed a painful degree of 'cognitive dissonance'.

In some cases, such dissonance began to shrink as meta-preferences began to change. Thus, many women in our sample reported starting out with reservations about the propriety of factory employment, but changing their minds in the light of the observed presence of other women *like themselves* within the factories. Their preferences thus shifted, not merely in response to the availability of new opportunities, but also in response to the social meanings which came to be clustered around these opportunities over time. Nevertheless, there were also women in our sample, particularly those who had suffered the loss of a male breadwinner, for whom the problem of cognitive dissonance persisted. They did not perceive their entry into factory employment as an active choice because they remained firmly wedded to a meta-preference ordering which gave value to a more traditional domestic role. They had come into the factories, because they had to, not because they wanted to.

Thus one set of insights provided by women's testimonies into household decision making processes related to differences in women's own preferences and what they implied for women's agency in relation to their labour supply decision. It suggests that what might be viewed by neo-classical economists as a similar set of labour market outcomes, 'revealing' similar underlying preferences, in reality embodied very different orders of preferences and different degrees of responsiveness to economic signals. As I will be arguing in the next chapter, these differences in the motivations and preferences which brought women into factory employment had important implications for the transformatory potential of such choices. For the rest of this chapter, however, I want to explore a second set of the insights into the nature of women's choices and labour supply decisions provided by our analysis, those which come into view when account is taken of the role of preferences other than women's own in decisions relating to the allocation of women's labour.

As we have seen, most women made their labour market decision in consultation with their families. The interactions between women's own preferences and those of other family members gave rise to rather different processes of decision making, some apparently co-operative and others conflictual, sometimes violently so. Co-operative forms of decision making could be further unpacked into those which reflected an absence of opposition and those which were the result of an active consensus. The absence of opposition from other family members tended to signify poverty or indifference. Among poorer women, the absence of opposition signified the poverty of other family members and the social isolation that this imposed on them. Among women from more middle class backgrounds, the absence of opposition was generally associated with the loss of the male breadwinner, and the unwillingness of any member of the wider family network to take economic responsibility for them.

Decision making on the basis of active consensus, on other hand, drew attention to some of the shared concerns which formed the basis of household co-operation. Whether it was based on agreed definitions of what constituted a necessary standard of living, or on agreed priorities about children's future or on unified efforts to deal with family adversity, this category of households exemplified the gains from co-operation, described in bargaining models as well as the interdependency of utility functions posited by unified preference models. Such active consensus about women's work preferences was also associated with shared views about the irrelevance of orthodox views of purdah and a united front to the religious community that sought to exercise power without responsibility in relation to women's behaviour.

However, the limitations of neo-classical theory, and its lack of a theory of power, become glaringly evident when we consider the cases of women who encountered conflicts over their labour market preferences. Unified preference models rule out the possibility of power and conflict altogether, so they are unlikely to have a great deal to contribute to our understanding of such processes. Bargaining models, on the other hand, do allow for the possibility of conflicting preferences, but restrict themselves to the analysis of differentials in bargaining power in order to predict whose preferences are most likely to prevail in such situations. Like the rest of neo-classical economics, they have no interest in how preferences are formed and hence no explanation for why such conflicts might occur. At most, conflicts are seen to express subjective differences of opinion, to be expected between any group of individuals living together, but without any great social import.

Our analysis, on the other hand, threw up certain systematic gender dimensions to the conflicts in preferences reported by the women workers, which suggested that much more than a difference of opinion appeared to be involved. Such conflicts were more likely to occur over women's labour supply decisions than men's; resistance to women's employment preferences was most often expressed by male, rather than female, household members; and it was most frequent, and most intense, in the context of a particular set of gender relationships within the family, those of marriage. In other words, women's desire to take up factory employment clearly touched an important 'nerve point' in gender relations within the family. A more detailed analysis of the nature of these conflicts, and how they were, or were not, resolved, is consequently likely to shed considerable light on the nature of the relationship between gender, power and conflict within the family.

## Identity, interests and the question of power

Shanu's household is a good starting point for this discussion. It not only provided an example of male resistance to women's employment preferences, but it also illustrated how male resistance varied according to the specific family relationships involved. Shanu's husband, Shamsul Alam, had six daughters from a previous marriage as well as a baby daughter with Shanu. The income from his trading activities fluctuated from month to month and the idea of his older daughters taking up factory employment appeared to be one solution to the family's financial problems. The decision was not taken unilaterally by Shamsul Alam, but discussed with members of his extended family whose approval he clearly valued. According to Shamsul Alam, he received active encouragement all round:

> Nobody in the family objected to the girls working. I went to see one of my senior relatives . . . I told him I had come to ask his advice and he told me to come and see him after office hours. So I went to his house and his wife, she works in the National Hospital Institute, they are very respectable people, she said, 'What's wrong with working? We all work. Now they will work as well.' . . . Then I discussed it with my sister and brother-in-law as well and they were all in favour. So was my uncle. They said, 'They'll be working with other girls. What's the harm?'

However, when Shanu subsequently expressed her desire to also take up garment employment, the reaction from her husband, and according to him, from the extended family, was very different:

> They all objected to Shanu working. They pointed out that the child was still young, a year and a half, and still being breastfed. The family wouldn't be looked after properly . . . She might be on duty till nine at night. We wouldn't eat regularly. We would have to eat stale food. The children would cry. There might not be enough food in the house some days.

Shanu's own reason for wanting to work was that she was being taunted by her stepdaughters for sitting idly in the house, 'eating' from their wages. Negotiations on this matter went on for several

months with neither Shanu nor Shamsul Alam prepared to concede. In fact, according to Shamsul Alam, he found out from his
daughters that Shanu had gone to a number of factories in his
absence despite his express disapproval. Shanu finally managed to
overcome his resistance, principally by assuring him that she would
complete all her housework before she went to work and that the
welfare of the family would not be neglected.

'Paternal altruism' thus merged smoothly with self-interest for
husbands like Shamsul Alam, in the kind of officialising strategies
referred to in Chapter 2. Concerns about their own welfare were
not just expressed by husbands who had opposed their wives' desire
to work. It was evident also in the case of husbands who had made
the decision jointly with their wives. As Jahanara's husband put it:
'I do not like the idea of my wife working. Her working affects me
in that she cannot give me any time or look after me. I put up with
the inconvenience because we need the money badly.'

A related source of resistance to women's work reflected concerns about the possible ramifications of their labour market
participation for gender roles within the household. Not all men
were equally resistant to the renegotiation of housework in the face
of women's new responsibilities. We did come across examples of
husbands and brothers who took on extra domestic chores in
response to women's additional work burdens – tidying the house,
helping with the cooking, giving children tuition in the evenings or
looking after them if they were unemployed.[6] Salma Akther's
husband, who decided to take on a greater share of housework
when he saw how hard she was working, was one example of this:

> She told me not to, but I do as much as I can. I do the shopping and
> sometimes cook the rice. I wash my own clothes most of the time. Even if
> my friends tease me, I ignore them. They say to me, you have sent your
> wife to work in the garments and now you are doing the housework. I tell

6. According to Zohir and Paul-Majumder (1996), over half of 160 married women
they interviewed reported some help from their husbands with domestic work, with the
hours of work husbands put in increasing with the hours of work women spent in factories
and their earnings from factory work. Estimates from the 1990/91 Labour Force Survey
also support this point in that husbands of garment workers were found to do more
housework than husbands of non-working women (Zohir, 1998).

them it does not offend me to do my own cleaning. If she were not here, I would have to do it myself. I don't listen to them.

Nevertheless, by and large, women's new responsibilities in the market place had not led to any radical renegotiation of gender roles in domestic labour. Where possible, women workers shared their domestic workload with other female family members, older daughters, mothers, sisters or sisters-in-law. In some cases, they hired domestic help. Where these possibilities were not available, they adopted Shanu's strategy of organising their domestic obligations around their working day: they woke up earlier than male members of their households, went to bed later and devoted their weekly holiday to completing the remaining housework.[7] Men's freedom from domestic chores was the other side of the coin to men's obligation to provide for the family and it was not always possible to separate out the extent to which women saw their continued responsibility for housework as the proper response on their part and the extent to which, like Shanu, they treated it as a bargaining tool for gaining consent for their desire to work. In fact, it is likely to have varied according to the degree of harmony – or its absence – in the relationship involved. For instance, Anwara did not see any reason why her husband should have taken on additional domestic responsibilities. Instead, it was her mother and sister who lived on the same premises who stepped in when she started work:

> I cook in the morning and my mother cooks in the afternoon. My mother and sister clean the house. I wash everybody's clothes on Friday. I wash my husband's clothes. Even if other people's husbands wash their own clothes, I wouldn't let him, that would be an injustice. Just because I am working, why should my husband have to suffer? And what else can I do with my days off?

7. According to estimates based on the 1990/91 Labour Force Survey (LFS), Zohir (1998) found that men working in the garment industry worked an average of 60 hours a week on income-earning activities as well as household chores (mainly doing the bazaar) while women working in the garment industry worked an average of 80 hours a week, with cooking as their main domestic chore. Other members of their households, both male and female, worked roughly equal number of hours – about 45 a week.

On other hand, Sahara, who had a fairly conflictual relationship with her husband, clearly had no choice in the matter of housework:

> My husband is a nightguard; he goes for duty at eleven at night and comes back at six in the morning. He gives us no help with the housework, just sleeps all day. And while we eat left-over rice from the previous night in the morning, he wants freshly cooked food or else he will go to the local shop and spend 10 takas for his breakfast. So after cleaning the house and feeding the children, I cook him rice in the early morning before I go to work.

The refusal by men like Sahara's husband to help in any way in the housework may have reflected their reluctance to allow any encroachment on their own leisure time. However, it also reflected symbolic considerations in that for many men, their sense of their own identity was bound up with a view of gender roles within the household, which placed it beyond question or renegotiation, a matter of doxa. This view was given explicit articulation by Kamal, a male garment worker, in the course of explaining why he had refused to let his wife go out to work:

> I don't think men should have to do household chores like cooking, cleaning and looking after children. That's not their job. The jobs have already been divided up. Domestic chores are the responsibility of women and the men are supposed to go out into the world and work. If both of them work, they should hire a maid. If a man helps a woman with some of her domestic chores, it can be done as a matter of co-operation. For example, if a woman works, her husband prepares the food if she is going to return late ... Men are doing it in such cases because they have to. Asking why those men help with this work is like asking why I eat. I eat because I have to survive. Those men do it because they have to.

Male gender identity also appeared to be at stake in a third set of reasons which underpinned men's objections to the idea of women's paid work. This related to the unease experienced by some men about accepting money from those who, by convention, they should have been supporting. The presence of a working woman within their family was seen to reflect poorly on their own capacity to fulfil their breadwinning role, particularly when the work in question was such a public one. This unease was evident in some of the comments with which husbands greeted their wives' desire to take up factory work: Kohinoor's husband had asked her 'Am I not feeding you properly?'; Banesa's husband explained that 'when a women earns, it doesn't look good: people say that she is feeding herself'; Amina's husband declared: 'I am her husband, why should I eat her food?'

This discomfort with accepting money from a female member of the family was not confined to husbands, but also experienced by other male members who were designated family breadwinners. Shilu's father told her that he would rather have begged to feed his family than let his daughters work. Delowara's father refused to 'eat' from the money she sent home to the village every month, putting it aside for her instead. Mumtaz's brother expressed some unease about 'eating from his sister's money' although he recognised that it was no longer practical for families in their situations to hold on to old views about women's place: 'When people are struggling to survive, it is no longer logical or practical to give consideration to purdah.'

A fourth source of resistance to women's desire to take up factory employment related to the question of family honour. Again, such resistance was not confined to husbands, or even to male family members; it also came from parents, from siblings as well as the larger extended family. Nevertheless, concerns about women's reputations took a particularly intense form in the context of marital relations, because here anxieties about propriety were shot through with sexual jealousies and fears about wives' infidelity. For instance, we noted earlier that Shanu's husband explained his reluctance to let Shanu work in terms of his concern for the household's welfare. Shanu herself, however, told us that his main fear was that she might get involved with other men. In fact, in the first few months of her job, he used to go to fetch her from the factory every evening and, even now, he would get very angry when she came home late.

In Hanufa's case, one of the reasons for her husband's violent opposition to her entry into the factory was his anxiety that she would get involved with other men. When he saw that she was adamant, he bought her a burkah to wear to and from work and came to fetch her at the factory gate every evening to ensure that he knew her movements. That his sexual insecurities had not been diminished with the passage of time was demonstrated when he beat Hanufa up when she came home one day with a new sari which she had been awarded as a productivity bonus. Unfamiliar with this practice, he was convinced that it was the result of a liaison with some man in the factory. In Banesa's case, her husband's jealousies were aroused by neighbourhood gossip and she told us how the first day or two when she started to go for training on the machine at the nearby tailor's shop, he had her followed by a friend to find out what she was up to.

Lutfa's husband's refusal to accede to his wife's desire to enter the garment factory precisely was also a product of his sexual anxieties. Although they needed the money – he worked in a factory all day and then pulled a rickshaw evenings – he had not at first been prepared to let her work in the factory. As he put it,

> She first said she wanted to work in a garment factory 8 years ago, her khala was working in one as a helper for 90/-. At that time I was scared, I had just got married and I was more suspicious. I said, a man can spend 90/- on cigarettes, why should you work every month for 90/-? . . . But I allowed her later, my doubts had gone.

According to Lutfa, it was the birth of her first child that led him to change his mind. He felt that her sexuality had been muted by motherhood and he was now prepared to trust her.

When we consider these various reasons for men's resistance to the idea of women taking up paid work, and the sheer strength, sometimes bordering on violence, of some of the resistance reported, the idea of conflicting preferences does not appear to fully capture what the conflicts were about. Rather than a subjective difference of opinion between individuals, what appeared to be at stake was a much more fundamental conflict about the kinds of changes that men and women were prepared to tolerate to the culturally-sanctioned division of roles and responsibilities within the household, and by extension, outside it. As we saw, this was partly related to gender identities. The fact that social constructions of gender identity simultaneously defined male as well as female identities explained why men's resistance to women's desire to work was so often rationalised using the same discourse of norms and values about gender roles as did women's rationalisation for wanting to work. While it may have been the case that some of these definitions, and the behaviours which went with them, could be adjusted with relative ease to accommodate aspects of change in the household's circumstances, others appeared to come close to, or even to constitute, the very core of individual gender identity and were hence most resistant to renegotiation. Clearly, ideas about the appropriate use of women's labour belonged in this latter category.

However, the question of identity clearly does not tell the whole story since what emerges very strikingly from the testimonies in this chapter is that women and men appeared to have rather differing levels of tolerance to changes in these 'core' beliefs and practices. In other words, men's sense of what constituted proper behaviour for women in their family appeared to be far more threatened by women's outside employment than women's sense of what constituted proper behaviour for themselves. Gender asymmetry in adherence to conventional understandings of the domestic division of roles and responsibilities makes more sense once it is recognised that these understandings also underwrite a particular, and asymmetrical, distribution of power and privilege within the family. Men were able to claim a variety of material privileges on the basis of these conventional understandings of gender roles: control over household resources, exemption from domestic chores, expectations that their comforts would be given priority as well as the respect and authority due to the household head and breadwinner. Consequently, while women explained their desire to work in terms of material gains to the family, men saw it as a threat to their material privileges within the family.

In addition, our analysis also suggests that marriage crystallised these conflicts of identities and interests in a particularly intense form. Male privilege appeared to be simultaneously greater, but also less secure, in the context of marriage than in other gender relationships within the family. Being a husband entitled men to expect a level of attention to their personal comforts from their wives to an extent that did not appear to occur in any other family relationship.[8] Men's identity as breadwinners appeared more threatened by women's work in the context of marriage than it did in other relationships and while concerns about women's reputations cut across the family, sexual jealousy in relation to women's outside employment was specific to marital relationships. Finally, the exercise of male authority and its corollary, female deference, appeared to be far more critical to men's sense of their own masculinity in the context of marriage than in any other family relationship. Fathers could expect deference from their daughters and older brothers from younger sisters, but male *power* was not involved in quite the same way as it appeared to be in the relationship between husband and wife. This is evident in the vehemence of the views expressed by some of the male garment workers in our study to the idea of women working:

> They want the same rights as men so when both husband and wife earn, there is discord in the house. Women begin to feel that as they are earning on their own, they no longer depend on their husbands to feed them and they often say so. That is why they are becoming a little too free. When I marry, I will not let my wife work. Then she will have to obey my wishes because she will be dependent on me.

> I haven't let my wife work. Women have to stay at home and look after the family's needs. Some of these girls who are earning their own income are becoming too free to the point where they are not paying attention to their husbands anymore. Suppose their husband tells them something, they will reply that they earn their own money and do not have to eat their husband's food. And if a husband is not earning enough to run his household, he feels belittled. When some girls get freedom, they don't know where to stop.

These responses were to a general question about the implications of women working and it is revealing that the question was largely interpreted in terms of the threat to male authority within marriage. It is unlikely that the discourse of power which was so transparently expressed in these responses would have figured in quite the same way in the context of any other relationship within

---

8. It could be said that children were likely to have such expectations of their mothers, but of course did not have the authority to enforce it.

the family. Furthermore, not all the male workers who expressed views such as these were married, so that it can be taken that they were articulating a 'common sense' view of marriage, and the implications of a working wife, rather than one derived from their own experiences.

## Bargaining and the limits of economism

The views expressed by the male workers echo, in many ways, the 'resource-based' notion of power expressed in bargaining models of the household, with the workers in our sample spelling out in greater detail than such models usually do, the consequences they feared would result from any shift in the economics of the marital relationship: wives disobeying their husbands, demanding equal rights in the home, neglecting their domestic duties, wanting to pay their own way, becoming 'too free' and easy, starting to 'talk back', abandoning their 'soft and pleasing' voices and engaging in various other forms of 'insubordination' which would make men feel 'belittled'.

However, economic theories of bargaining do little to illuminate a basic conundrum thrown up by some of the testimonies reported in this chapter. The conundrum is this: bargaining models concern themselves with the relative resource positions of different household members, including their potential earnings in the market place, in order to explain whose preferences are likely to prevail in situations of conflict. What we have in the present context is a situation in which a number of subordinate female members have sucessfully managed to 'bargain' with the dominant male members of their households to secure access to an economic resource which both economic theorists, as well as many of the men we interviewed, believed would have the effect of increasing women's bargaining power relative to men's.

The processes through which this conundrum was resolved gives empirical substance to our understanding of bargaining as well as providing some important insights into the particularities of power in the context of family relationships. First of all, the fact that women felt the need to obtain the consent of household heads to take up factory work, that they invested a great deal of effort in persuading household heads to give this consent if it was not immediately forthcoming, and that they did not simply go ahead and take up the employment, with or without the head's consent, suggests either that they were so cowed by male authority that they were incapable of acting on their own initiative or that the perceived economic gains from factory work had to be balanced against the consequences of insisting on their preferences in the face of his resistance. Given the very active agency displayed by women in dealing with male resistance, let us turn to the second explanation as the more plausible.

The implications of open defiance were twofold: symbolic and material. As we have noted, a key aspect of familial contracts was men's responsibility to protect and provide for women within the family by virtue of their role as fathers, husbands, brothers and sons and women's commensurate obligation to defer to male authority in important family matters. For women to have insisted on their preferences in the face of male resistance would have constituted a fundamental violation of the claims and obligations which bound members of the family together as a family. It would also have been seen as undermining men's sense of self-esteem. In addition, a related implication of open defiance is that it would have put women's continued membership of the family into jeopardy and, with it, the material benefits which they derived from such membership. The fact that most women appeared to be prepared to defer to male authority within the family suggests that, for most women, the benefits of male provision and male protection outweighed the perceived advantages of paid work which had motivated them to seek it in the first place.

Two 'exceptional' categories in the decision making processes described earlier help to provide indirect support for this interpretation. The first category was made up of women who had entered factory employment in open defiance of male authority within the family. Their testimonies make the point that male authority was not absolute, but conditional on men fulfilling their obligations to those dependent on them. The defiance in question was by wives of husbands who had forfeited their claims to their wives' deference by failing to fulfil their contractual obligations as husbands. In the majority of the cases, this entailed the abdication by men of their responsibilities as primary breadwinners. While irresponsibility was often accompanied by violence, it was generally the irresponsibility rather than the violence that drove women to defy their husbands' wishes, particularly when such irresponsibility began to impinge on the welfare of their children. This was evident in Monowara's account of why she left her husband, taking their child with her:

> He used to beat me before, but only to punish me, only when he was angry, but he always used to give me food and clothes. But then I began suffering in every way, I didn't have any oil, soap, food and clothes, there wasn't any income coming in. I found it impossible when he began to beat me on top of that . . . I wrote a letter to my brother telling him how bad my situation was and asking him to come and get me.

The second 'exceptional' category was made up of women who described their entry into factory work as a reluctant choice forced on them by the loss of male, usually husbands', support. Their testimonies helped to explain the strength of most women's stake in achieving outcomes which did not jeopardise such support in any way by spelling out what it was about the consequences of such loss that made women fear it so much. As we saw, none of these women had encountered any objections to their entry into factory employment because no one cared enough, or could afford to care enough, to raise such an objection. They were effectively on their own and they knew it. It was this sense of 'aloneness', of helplessness in a world that they had not been equipped to deal with on their own which helped to explain what the loss of male protection signified for women in general.

It featured prominently in Razia Sultana's account as she mourned her fall in status from cherished wife to bereft widow: 'Before my husband's death, I never had to worry about work, we had servants, I knew I was cherished. I never moved alone.' Khatun, who lost her husband in the 1971 war and had struggled to bring up her son on her own, also spoke of how different her life had turned out to the one that she had been brought up to expect and how hopeless her future had appeared: 'I never thought that I would have to work for my living, but it was in my fate. If I had

known earlier, I would have taken poison and killed myself.'
However, it was Renu, who had finally been driven out of her home
by her husband's economic irresponsibility and male violence, who
expressed most clearly the fear and anxiety that accompanied a
woman on her own in a society where the absence of male
protection signified extreme vulnerability and where even a violent
husband offered some degree of protection:

> I would not have had to work if I had a father or a husband. When I was
> married, even if I was not earning, at least I was with him. No one could
> say anything to me. Now, even if they say nothing, I feel afraid, I feel they
> might. That fear is always there. Don't all women have this fear inside
> them. I am a woman on my own; I have to go to the bazaar, I have to go
> here, I have to go there; men stare at me, they pass comments. Don't I feel
> the shame? What if someone lies about me, makes things up, what response
> can I make? If I lived with my parents, then no one could say anything. I
> am alone; wherever I go, I go alone. If someone kills me, no one will know.
> My mother and brothers will get to hear of it, but by then I will be dead. If
> I could, I would have gone to the village; no one talks to women like that
> in the village. In the village, they only talk about the village.

This fear, 'the fear that women have', of being alone, bereft of
male protection, signalled the continued relevance of 'patriarchal
risk' in shaping women's ability to make choices. As long as they
remained dependent on men, not only for their economic needs,
but also for social protection so that the loss of male guardianship
was associated, not simply with a possible decline in their economic
status, but also heightened social vulnerability, women were
unlikely to engage in forms of behaviour which might alienate
male support. Consequently, while women did seek to negotiate
with male family members, when they encountered resistance to
their desire to take up outside employment, their negotiations were
generally aimed at achieving a consensual solution.

A study of actual processes of household bargaining in situations
of conflict thus traces some of the reasons for the persistence of
co-operation within the household to women's unwillingness to
push conflict to the point of breakdown. However, the co-operative
nature of the household in turn helps to explain why, despite their
weaker material position, women were able to achieve decision

making outcomes which favoured their own preferences. In other words, it tells us why bargaining outcomes within the household were not determined by material advantage alone. As we have seen, a great deal of men's resistance to women's employment preferences reflected their anxieties about its implications for their own privileges within the family and for their self – as well as public – image as family breadwinners and guardians. However, the intimate nature of family relationships meant that women tacitly understood, and often empathised with, male anxieties and fears, an understanding that they were able to put to effective use in their negotiating strategies. The essence of these strategies consisted of discursive and practical efforts to allay male anxieties and achieve a workable compromise.

The discursive aspect of their strategies derived from the fact that, although men were materially advantaged in the bargaining process by the asymmetrical terms of the patriarchal contract, they did not generally express their opposition to women's employment preferences through the use of force or material threats, but rather in terms of its implications for household welfare or for women's reputations or for family honour, concerns which were sometimes genuine and sometimes examples of officialising strategies. Women were able to engage in the bargaining process at this discursive level by seeking to contest these interpretations, to provide counter definitions of household welfare and gender propriety. Conflict resolution therefore took the form of negotiations at the normative level, as 'who ought to get what' or 'who ought to do what' rather than as the naked interplay of command and resistance over 'who gets what' or 'who does what'. In this context, women's appeals to the shared household goals, and particularly to shared interests in children's welfare, were clearly difficult for men in their capacity as family guardians and fathers to counter, particularly when they could see the legitimacy as well as material validity of these appeals.

In addition, women undertook a series of practical accommodations to achieve their goals, what Villareal (1990) terms a policy of 'yielding and wielding'[9] in which concessions were made in certain

9. Villareal uses this phrase to describe very similar strategies adopted by women in relation to male family members in the context of rural Mexico.

areas in order to win concessions in others. Thus, we noted the effort that women made to ensure that men's domestic comforts were not affected in any way by their entry into factory work. Where they could, they devolved domestic chores to other female family members. Where they could not, some hired domestic help, while others completed their chores before they went to work in the mornings, after they came home from work in the evenings and on the weekly holiday. In addition, we noted how they sought to defuse the implications of their mobility in the public domain: coming home straight after work, never 'loitering' at the factory after hours; only going out outside working hours when they were accompanied by their husband or their children. As Kohinoor told us, 'I never go anywhere without telling him. After all, because I work, it doesn't mean I can go everywhere without his permission, he would think I was putting him down because I was earning. I always ask his permission, I give him respect.'

However, as a footnote to this section of the analysis, it is worth pointing out that the strong hostility expressed by the male workers in our sample to the idea of their wives working, and evidence that at least two of the women in our sample were giving up work under pressure from their husbands, suggests that any sample of garment workers, however randomly selected, would have a particular bias built into it. It would represent only those women who had not encountered any objections to their work preferences from other family members, those who had encountered objections but managed to surmount them and those who had simply bypassed these objections. It would not, however, be representative of those women who had been prevented from taking, or even seeking, employment in the garment factories by dominant family members, despite their own preferences.

'Second-generation' economic models of women's labour supply do recognise that working women may not be fully representative of all prospective female workers but their explanations of sample bias retain the voluntaristic underpinnings of neo-classical economics. Prospective women workers are seen to have decided against the idea of working because they have failed to attract a high enough wage in the market to offset the value of the work forgone at home (Sapsford and Tzannatos, 1993, p. 60). The analysis here

highlights the relevance of male power and 'suppressed preferences' for understanding sample bias.[10] Economists are right to
surmise that the observed presence of women in the garment
factories reveals something important about their preferences, even
if they are not always correct about what it reveals. Our analysis
suggests, however, that observed outcomes do not tell us the full
story about the exercise of choice. An analysis of the testimonies of
women who were prevented from taking up factory employment
would have given us a more complete picture about power, preferences and negotiation in the context of women's labour supply
decisions.

## Revisiting structural constraint:
## the significance of time and place

We have examined in some detail the various motivations which
led women to seek paid work, the reasons why they opted for
garment employment over other alternative forms of employment
and the various strategies they deployed to win the support of their
families. However, this focus on the exercise of individual agency
to renegotiate cultural norms should not be taken to imply that
these norms had somehow vanished. The continued relevance of
social constraint explains the continuing resistance that women met
with in the wider community, the harassment they encountered

10. Unfortunately, by focusing only on women factory workers, we have not been able
to provide any insights into these processes of 'preference suppression'. However, Islam's
study of poor urban women in the informal sector (1998) includes the following revealing
testimony from Zahanara, a married woman who worked in home-based piecework, on
the factors embodied in her apparent 'choice' to work at home:

> I think our primary responsibility is to make our home. I think women should not
> work like men, then they will not be able to do the household work properly, their
> health will suffer, the children will not be trained and they may lose their husbands as
> well. After all, husbands will never consider our paid work as important as theirs. I got
> beaten so many times for doing paid work, remember? Last week, I had a bruise just
> under my right eye, remember? I was a little late for serving him lunch, he snatched
> away the (work) from me and threw that wooden seat towards me. I don't know how
> Allah saved me that time, it could have made me blind. Do you think this man will ever
> allow me to work outside?

in the streets and the rumours, gossip and moral denunciations that characterised public response.

The process of 'taking on culture' had clearly not been a cost-less one and women's willingness and ability to pay it had not materialised overnight in response to employers' recruitment strategies. Instead, it has to be seen in relation to the larger socio-economic changes which were occurring in Bangladesh over this period and their implications for the structure of constraints facing women. In this concluding section of the chapter, I want to draw together the interactions of 'time' and 'space' in creating the social conditions under which women were willing to take on some of these larger structures of constraint, the process of 'restructuring structures'.

In terms of historical time, we have already described the major socioeconomic transformations of the past decades in the previous chapter: the growing landlessness and impoverishment and the increased diversification of livelihoods out of agriculture. The 1970s were highlighted as a period of particular instability when floods, war, drought, famine, political assassinations and military coups followed each other in rapid succession leading to massive political and economic dislocations. All of these transformations combined to undermine women's traditional economic roles without providing them with access to any new alternatives. The emergence of 'demand' dowry was explained as both a symptom of the growing devaluation of women as well as an additional cause of it.

Thus, the material conditions under which women might have been willing to consider taking up outside employment had been in existence some years before the advent of the garment industry – but their ability to do so remained constrained by the continued resilience of social norms in curtailing the demand for their labour. Women from all classes were affected by a growing vulnerability to 'patriarchal risk', although women from poorer households were at a particular disadvantage. Poverty had the effect of eroding men's material ability and social obligation to provide for family dependants, but the resilience of purdah norms, and the resistance of the community, prevented women from such families from being able to provide for themselves.

The question of 'space' came into the picture because of the significance of the wider *locale*[11] of decision making in mediating the effects of social norms. We noted earlier in this chapter that the women workers showed a great deal of understanding and empathy with the reasons given by family members to their outside employment and indeed invested a great deal of effort in putting their anxieties to rest. However, their attitudes towards the objections of the wider community were very different, and often characterised by resentment, hostility and bitterness. While they were well aware of the attempts of the religious community to police their behaviour, most saw this as empty posturing by the self-appointed guardians of the social order whose claims to moral authority had become detached from any grounding in material or social responsibility. Their attitudes to the claims of this community were summed up pithily by Aleya: 'If they want to object, then they have to feed us.'

In challenging the rights of this wider community to regulate their behaviour, women workers were also questioning the continued relevance of social norms which they believed belonged to a different time or a different place when the notion of community itself had a very different meaning. This had been the face-to-face 'moral community' of rural society, whose ability to regulate the conduct of its members had been effectively backed up by the power to distribute and to withhold resources. However, this notion of community had been gradually undermined by the social changes of the past decades, even in rural society. And it had certainly not been carried over intact into the urban context in which the garment workers were now located.

While there might have been concern on the part of some of the workers about their reputations in their mohallas, or neighbourhoods, others, like Afifa Sultana, emphasised the fact that 'society' counted for little in their decisions:

> We do not receive any help from anyone outside the family and we help no one. Society does not give us any financial help, therefore it has no right to object to our working in garments ... The people in my

11. The term comes from Giddens (1979) and connotes the use of space as a setting for interaction where the physical environment is one of the elements mobilised in the interaction (p. 207).

neighbourhood sometimes pass comments about my working in my garments but I do not think them to be of any consequence.

The irrelevance of the notion of community in the old sense of the word was summarised in the words of the father of one of the women workers who told us: 'Who is *shamaj*? *Shamaj* is people who are educated, who own houses and cars and work in government jobs. *Shamaj* is people like you, not people like us.'

From the point of women seeking employment, the urban locale therefore had a dual significance. First of all, it represented greater employment opportunities for women, just as it did for men, than did the rural economy. As we pointed out in the previous chapter, migration by women into towns in search of work had begun even prior to the advent of the garment industry, so female labour force participation rates in the cities, while low, were still higher than those in the countryside. However, the urban *locale* of garment employment had another, more gender-specific significance in that it represented a relative freedom from the 'fettering restrictions of shailish and samaj' (Adnan, 1988) that had constrained women's agency in the rural areas. Many women had made the decision to migrate to the cities precisely to circumvent the most restrictive aspects of the 'moral community' of the village and escape into the relative anonymity of urban life, where they could take up whatever livelihood they could find without incurring the censure of their community or bringing shame on their kin (Kabeer, 1988). The pattern of migrant settlement in the city facilitated this quest for anonymity. As Islam and Zeitlin (1989) noted, migrants into Dhaka city did not necessarily settle according to their geographical origins, so that different slum settlements were made of a regionally heterogeneous mixture of people.

The social significance of urban space often occurred in women's testimonies in terms of its contrast with village life. Daisy, for instance, had grown up in the village and had first attempted to take up employment as a family planning worker when her father ran into debt, but the ensuing gossip put an end to it. When her father died, she decided to migrate to the city to earn her living: 'If a girl in the village remains unmarried, people say bad things, that is why it is better to stay far away, nobody sees anything, hears anything, or says anything.' For Razia Sultana, the city offered a widow left to fend for herself the scope to earn a living without shaming her extended family: 'What can you do if you return to the village? In the town, at least you can go to the market if you need to buy something . . . and my village is after all in Noakhali district where women observe purdah very strictly, they are not allowed to move around freely.' Rabeya believed that the city offered greater anonymity to women like her to earn a living: 'What can I do, if I went to my husband's village and worked, his parents would become small in the eyes of other people. Although I am working in Dhaka, nobody sees me or knows me.' And as Shahnaz Nur's husband testified, the city made it easier for men to accept unconventional behaviour on the part of the women in their family. His wife had supported the family, even when they had been living in the village, because he had been unable find steady employment, and she continued to work after he found a job in the city. He told us why he found it so much easier to live with the idea of his wife working in the city than he had in the village:

> I felt bad when I was unemployed and my wife had to work. I used to feel that if I had a job with good pay, she would not have to work. Now I do not feel so bad. The environment in Dhaka is different. Women can work. Everybody in the village, relatives as well outsiders, criticize the idea of women working. This makes one feel guilty about allowing one's wife to work. It is not so in the city. People in the city do not ask you direct questions about why your wife is working. That is not the custom in the city.

## Conclusion

The garment factories came to Bangladesh at a critical juncture in its history. The events of the preceding decades, and particularly of the crisis-ridden 1970s, had brought home to women in a very stark way that they could no longer rely on male protection in times of crisis and, increasingly, not even in course of the more 'everyday' processes of impoverishment. The intersection of individual biographies with these larger historical changes helped to create the willingness on their part to take on community norms: changes in the locale of decision making made it more possible. The garment workers we talked to were representative of many of the trends documented at the national level and their testimonies bore witness to their effects. They were some of the individuals behind the statistics.

The crises of the 1970s were manifest in their personal tragedies in the form of the loss of a father or a husband, which had marked the beginning of working lives of many of the women who would later seek employment in the garment factories. In other cases, drought, loss of land, lack of jobs had led their families to migrate to Dhaka in search of employment as a part of the greater wave of rural–urban employment we noted earlier. We noted the effects of the changing face of marriage in bringing women into the factories: wives who had been left by husbands because dowry had not been paid or because they wanted to marry again for dowry, as well as young unmarried daughters seeking to contribute to the escalating costs of dowry. We noted also the increasing acceptance by male breadwinners that the family could not survive on their incomes alone.

It is in this perceived erosion of the patriarchal contract, and the increasing inability of men to sustain the model of the male bread-winner, that the genesis of women's entry into factory employment has to be understood. It made it possible, and necessary, for them to abandon old ways of behaving as passive occupants of predestined roles and to find new forms of agency which would allow them to anticipate the consequences of patriarchal risk and to take full advantage of the opportunities that came their way. However, there was an interesting class-related difference in how 'time' featured in women's accounts, suggesting that their view of the social changes which had given rise to the willingness of women to come out of the home in search of work was very much linked to the circumstances of their own lives.

For women from poorer families, like Shamsunahar, who worked in response to basic need, this willingness had existed for some time and it was the emergence of the opportunity which explained why so many women had entered the garment industry:

> They couldn't work before because there were no factories. If factories had existed then, then of course they would have gone there for work. Without

that option, women had to engage in different tasks, whatever they could find. God determines where you will go and what you will do with your life. He decided the factories would be set up at this stage and therefore the women came to work here.

Jorina, on the other hand, had experienced a more protected upbringing, and had entered factory work primarily to save for her children's education. In her opinion, women had entered the factories as a result of a generalised increase in their sense of uncertainty about their lives, but she saw this as a relatively recent phenomenon:

> If the garment factories had opened up fifteen years ago, I don't think so many girls would have come forward. Girls were not so *chaloo* [smart] then; they would not think 'Let me work; let me save; I am going to need the money. Who knows what the future holds?' Now we know that husbands do not last forever. Every girl with any sense wants to secure her future. Many things have happened in Bangladesh, each event is overturning more of the old ways. That is why the girls are becoming more *chaloo*. That is why when the garment factories chose to employ women, the women were prepared.

# 5

# Individualised entitlements: factory wages and intra-household power relations

In the previous chapter, we established that the decision to take up factory work was largely initiated by the women themselves, often in the face of considerable resistance from other family members. It was clear that this resistance reflected a belief on the part of these family members, and husbands in particular, that women's access to an income of their own would not only adversely affect the household's welfare or standing within the community, but also their own privileged status. It was equally clear that women hoped to gain something important enough from their access to wages to have accepted the compromises that many had to make in order to defuse this resistance. In this chapter I want to explore the impact of women's access to wages on various aspects of their lives in order to establish what these gains might have been and the extent to which they bore out male anxieties about their likely impact on intra-household relations.

Factory wages had certain of the characteristics that some of the social scientists discussed in Chapter 2 consider to be necessary, and even sufficient, for women's access to employment to have a transformatory effect on their lives. They were literally visible in that they were earned in the public domain in contrast to more hidden, home-based earning opportunities previously available to women. They were economically visible in that they took the form of cash; they constituted a significant share of household income in some of the households in our sample. Their regularity was particularly valued in households where male earners were engaged in forms of self-employment which yielded fluctuating income streams, while their magnitude made a particular difference to households where income from other sources was either absent or negligible.[1]

However, the objective potential of waged employment to bring about a shift in intra-household relations cannot be taken to constitute evidence that such a potential was always actualised. Research into this question has consquently moved beyond the question of simple *access*, the mere availability of waged income, to a focus on *control*, the extent to which women have a say in its disposal.[2] This will also constitute the starting point of our analysis. However, it is important to bear in mind that disposal decisions are unlikely to be one-off events. In their attempt to track the process by which incomes entering the household were assigned to various uses, Beneria and Roldan point to the existence of a number of potential 'control' points, points at which the ability to influence decision making had important implications for the exercise of allocative power within the household. Pahl's work (1983) suggests a hierarchy of such points, distinguishing in particular between what she calls the 'control' or policy function, decisions relating to the allocation of income and the 'management' function, which refers to the implementation of these allocative decisions.

In this chapter I will be exploring more direct evidence of the impact of women's wages, tracking them from their point of entry into the household to their 'exit', as it were, in the form of various immediate or postponed expenditures and transfers, paying particular attention along the way to these potential control points. I will start out by examining how these wages were managed and the relationship between various forms of income management systems and women's ability to exercise control over their wages. Were the wages merged, literally or notionally, into a common pool under the allocative management of a 'benevolent dictator' to be redistributed according to the Beckerian welfare maximising principle?

1. About 27 of the male breadwinners were reported to have irregular incomes while 14 of the women in our sample said that they had taken up paid work because the male income was not sufficient.

2. A useful discussion of this literature is to be found in Morris (1990).

Were they appropriated by a malevolent patriarch and allocated according to his own selfish interests? Or were women able to exercise full or partial control over them, the precondition stressed in many studies as necessary to improvements in their bargaining position?

On the basis of this analysis, I will be arguing that the conventional focus on who 'controls' women's wages is not necessarily a particularly helpful way of exploring the transformatory implications of women's earning capacity, directing as it does our attention to questions about direct financial decision making. Instead, we need to expand the focus of the analysis to take account of the broader issue of *choice*, to ask what kinds of choices were made possible for women as a result of their new status as economic actors within the family. And we may also wish to consider some of the unintended ways in which women's access to wage-earning opportunities transformed the wider structures of patriarchal constraint.

## Ideology and co-operation in the management of women's wages

An obvious place to start the enquiry would be to ascertain what happened to women's wages once they entered the household. Twenty-nine out of the 60 women interviewed said that their income was pooled. In 15 of these cases, it was pooled under the management of the male household head, either a husband or a father, while in 12, it was pooled under the management of the garment worker herself. Three women reported 'partial pooling', contributing part of their wages to the household pool and keeping a part back. Ten women said they kept their incomes separately from other income flows into the household. Finally, there were 18 households where women workers reported being the sole income managers. These tended to be the 'unconventional' domestic units, either headed by the garment worker and entirely reliant on her income or made up of young single women who had migrated on their own into the city and managed their own budgets, whether they lived as boarders or in a mess arrangement. The important question for our analysis, however, is not how income was managed, but whether there was any relationship between systems of management and the exercise of control.

There are intuitive grounds for assuming, and it generally proved to be the case, that women who managed some, or all of their earnings, were more likely to have exercised a say in its disposal than women who did not have any such managerial function. At the same time, the relationship between 'management' and 'control' was by no means cut and dry. For instance, male and female management of pooled household income did not have symmetrical implications for the exercise of allocative control. Male management tended to be associated with a greater degree of unilateral decision making, female management with greater likelihood of consultation with male family members. In addition, while information on allocative decision making told us something about the exercise of power within the household, even more revealing perhaps were some of the rationales given by the women for the adoption of particular patterns of allocative decision making, their explanations for 'the decision about decision making'.

For instance, the rationale for male control over household finances would appear at first sight to be self-explanatory. As household heads, responsible for the collective welfare of its members, it made sense that men would also make the policy decisions on household finances. Certainly, a number of the women workers reported handing over their wages to their husbands, or fathers, in terms which suggested that they regarded it as routine and unexceptional, in no need of any further explanation. At the same time, there were a number of women who placed an emphatic stress on *surrendering* control over their wages, making it clear that it was intended to reassert the symbolic authority of the household head. This strategic emphasis on relinquishing control over their wages cropped up, not unexpectedly, most frequently in the testimonies of wives in relation to husbands, particularly those wives who had initially encountered resistance to their desire to take up factory work. Their actions can be thus seen as a further aspect of the 'yielding' dimension of the strategies discussed in the previous chapter, women's attempts to defuse the threat that their newly-employed status might appear to pose to male authority in order to retain family support for their decision.

Jorina, for instance, who had met with initial resistance from her husband to the idea of her job, explained why she handed her entire wages every month over to her husband: 'As it is, he is letting me work, how would he feel if I also kept the money.' She saw their incomes as completely merged, with no distinction as to how each was spent. Morgina brushed off her husband's continued expressions of reservation about her factory employment, but nevertheless handed her wages over to him every month. Her rationale for doing so was similar to Jorina's: 'My husband thinks people will think ill of him for letting his wife work. I tell him he shouldn't listen to them. But I give him my salary; whether he spends it or not, it makes him happy. I give him the money and he spends it as he needs to.' However, concern about the feelings of household heads was not reported only in the context of marriage. Sathi Akhtar, who lived with her aunt and uncle and their daughters, explained why neither she, nor her working cousin, kept back any of their wages in similar terms: 'We just hand over the money to my aunt or uncle and they buy what is needed. If we bought things, they would say, just because these girls are earning, they behave this way with us. To prevent them from saying this, we immediately hand over the money.'

Given that the idea of women working for a living was itself still an anomaly for so many households, it was not surprising that many women relinquished their wages to those who were regarded as household heads, whether they did so on strategic grounds or as an unquestioned norm. However, less expectedly, ideologies of the male breadwinner also served to rationalise a very different form of income management, one in which women kept back their own wages and managed them separately from other income flows within the household. These were households where men refused to accept women's earnings, precisely on the grounds that they were the family breadwinners and it is indicative of the fluidity of the relationship between norms and practice that the same norm could be used to rationalise quite different practices. In general, men's reluctance to accept women's wages because of its reflection on their breadwinning capacity was more common to middle class households than poorer ones, and expressed more often in the context of father–daughter than marital relationships.[3]

Nazneen, for instance, who kept back her entire income, said: 'I spend very little on household expenses. My father says about his daughters, my girls earn, that is enough for me.' Delowara's father had been reluctant to let her take up factory employment and had clearly agreed on the understanding that she was working towards future dowry costs. Although Delowara sent home a monthly remittance, this was put aside for her, her parents refused to 'eat' out of it themselves or even accept gifts from her:

> Sometimes, when I feel like it, I buy things for my parents, mostly things like clothes. But when I buy them things, they get angry, they say, 'Why have you spent your money buying us these things? Don't you think we can buy things for ourselves if we need them? Why are you spending money on us unnecessarily from your salary?' So I say, 'I bought them for you because I wanted to. If I was a boy, it would be alright for me to buy you things, wouldn't it? So just pretend I am a boy.'

However, there were also examples where husbands refused to 'eat' from their wives' incomes because they felt that it compromised their dignity as the family breadwinner. This was the case with Kohinoor's husband: 'When I get my wages, I tell him what I have got. He never takes money from me. Often I give it. He says why should I take money from a woman, don't I earn enough?' In some households, the adoption of 'partial pooling' of women's wages represented a compromise solution, embodying simultaneous recognition of male responsibility as well as female entitlement. In these cases, women would hand their regular salaries to their husbands but keep back overtime earnings: 'The salary is for the household, the overtime is mine.'

Aside from the complexities introduced into the relationship between decision making and power within the household by the underlying ideological justifications determining who would exercise allocative authority over women's wages, a focus on 'formal' decision making as an indicator of the control function also gave a misleading picture of how control was actually exercised.

3. This pattern is also noted by Kibria (1995).

Regardless of the particular model of income management adopted, the 'jointness' of household welfare inevitably entailed members in various forms of interdependency so that formal 'control' frequently diverged from actual decision making. Jointness was manifested in the common practice of 'earmarking' a portion of income for particular collective expenditures, thereby removing that portion of income from the arena of active decision making and 'control'. In some cases, earmarking took an ideological form, creating a notional separation of income that was physically pooled: 'My wages go on the children; his go on our necessities.'

In other cases, earmarking reflected more practical considerations. In households where male wages were irregular, the monthly lump sum character of women's wages led to its earmarking for 'lumpy' monthly expenditures, such as rents or electricity bills, or the bulk purchase of non-perishable staple food items. Mabia's household typified this practice. Her husband worked as a mechanic on a contract basis, earning different amounts of money each month. He kept back some of his earning for conveyance and pocket expenses; the rest was pooled under her management. The different timings of their income flows determined how their incomes were allocated:

> My income comes in regularly every month. It goes on the monthly bazaar, things we buy in bulk such as rice, lentils and so on – and what we need if guests arrive . . . Daily food and requirements – fresh vegetables, meat, spices, oil and soap – my husband buys these as we need them.

Interdependencies between household members also explained instabilities in systems of income management reported by women like Kohinoor. She lived with her husband and his unmarried sister and had decided to work, despite his reservations, because she felt his income was being stretched too thin. They kept separate accounts, but divided up responsibility for joint expenditures between them so that she paid the rent and electricity bills while he was responsible for daily and monthly bazaar. However, this separation of management was only nominal and the interdependencies showed through in her account:

He never takes my money. But for a while I gave it for the monthly bazaar and he was able to buy a machine out of his income to improve his business . . . His money is also spent on his sister and his mother. I don't give my family anything – they don't need it. We bought a cassette player – well, he bought it but he couldn't have done it without my earnings.


## Information, conflict and the management of women's wages

One common factor in the income management systems described above is that they were largely made on the basis of consensual decision making. In fact, according to Rabia, as long as men observed their responsibilities to their households, women would consider the issue of who 'controlled' their wages to be largely irrelevant: 'Some women give their wages to their husbands and some keep it themselves. If a husband looks after his wife and gives her what she needs, then there is nothing wrong with giving him her wages. But if he drinks and gambles with her money, then it is better for her to keep the money and spend it herself.' Our interviews confirmed that the question of control over their incomes only became significant for women in situations of conflict, almost invariably in the situations of marital conflict. Here the fact that women were the direct recipients of their wages was a critical factor. Just as it allowed them to hand control over their wages to the household head, so too it gave them the option of withholding such control.

Sometimes women asserted independent control over their wages in open defiance of their husbands. Hanufa, whose husband refused to earn a regular living, kept control of her own earnings in order to make sure that the rent was paid and that priority was given to her daughter's welfare and educational expenses. Kaneez had taken up work when her daughter was born because it was clear that her husband had no intention of making any regular contribution. Her practice of handing over her wages to her mother began when they were still married as a way of keeping it out of his hands. In response to his demands for the money, she told him:

This is my hard earned money, I can't just hand it over to you. You are a man, you should be earning, or if you can't do that, go and pick pockets. I have my own future to think about. How can I depend on your earnings, when they are so irregular? You work for three months and then you sit around for six. You don't earn anything, you don't give me any money – how are we supposed to manage?

In addition to these examples of overt assertion of control over their own wages, there was also evidence that in some households, women sought to exercise covert control over some part of their incomes. As Asma put it, 'Some women lie to their husbands while others distract him from thinking about any money they might be handling themselves.' As a result, the formal income management practices they reported for their households were frequently subverted by a more shadowy, unofficial set of practices, based on the strategic management of information by the women workers in question. Rather than pooling their incomes, and by extension information about their incomes, under the management and control of their husbands, these women withheld information about their earnings as a way of retaining unofficial control over them. Six women in our sample reported such practices.

Studies of income management within the household have highlighted how men in contexts as varied as a Mexico City slum (Beneria and Roldan, 1987) and the 'gentrified' borough of Islington in London (Wilson, 1991), frequently withhold information about their incomes from their wives as a way of retaining control over its disposal. In Bangladesh too, men often refuse outright to share any information about their earnings with their wives or else share only partial information. Women have also withheld information from men: there is a long standing tradition in rural Bangladesh among women who had no earnings of their own of keeping aside *ak musthi chaal*, a handful of rice each day as a form of saving. However, men's and women's ability to withhold information is not symmetrical. Men can withhold information about the resources at their disposal quite openly, since there is no ideological pressure on them to disclose such information. Women, on the other hand, generally tend to resort to secrecy, 'the weapon of the weak'(Scott, 1985), since the ideological space for their personal control over resources is far more curtailed.

In one sense, therefore, the women in our sample who secretly withheld information about their earnings were following an older tradition. What differentiated them was the magnitude of the sums involved. There were a number of aspects to factory life which contributed to their ability to engage in these clandestine forms of control. Its internal procedures and practices were still relatively new and unfamiliar to the general public. Factories were also closed off to outsiders so that knowledge about them was more difficult to acquire than it had been in more established female activities, especially those carried out within the home. Finally, the fluctuations introduced into women's monthly earnings by their overtime earnings offered them some room for manoeuvre as to how much information to disclose to their husbands.

Sahara's husband wasted a considerable proportion of the household income on his gambling and drinking habits. She handed over her monthly wages to him at his insistence, but lied to her husband about her overtime, 'stealing' it every month and saving it with her sister as her insurance for the future. Hanufa, as we saw, openly kept back her own wages which she spent on collective household expenses, given her husband's failure to make any regular contribution. However, she kept the fact of her overtime earnings secret from her husband, putting them into a separate savings account in her daughter's name. Rupban had not only withheld the fact of overtime earnings from her husband, but also lied about the magnitude of her regular wage. She was able to withhold information in this way because the distance between her home and work location[4] placed her working life outside the easy surveillance of her husband. This distance had its costs, literally financial ones, and Rupban calculated that it only made economic sense to make the journey into work every day because she evaded paying train fares:

> In the beginning the ticket collector used to catch us. Then I used to pay. But now he knows us and doesn't ask for the fare. Now and then we give him two or four takas. I know I have to answer to God for not paying the

4. Rupban lived in Tongi, an industrial satellite town just outside Dhaka and commuted into work every day.

train fares but if I paid, it would cost Tk. 360 every month and I would
have no money left to take home.

## Beyond management and control: the question of choice

The question of what happens to women's earnings once they enter
the household has been one way in which the implications of their
access to employment opportunities for the distribution of power
within the household has been investigated. Our discussion of this
question has pointed to some critical intervention points at which
the ability to influence decisions had important repercussions for
how women's access to income translated into allocative control
over it: decisions regarding the management of different income
flows into the household, the extent to which women withheld or
shared information about their earnings and the formal and informal exercise of allocative authority in relation to their earnings.

Different systems of income management clearly had a role to
play in mediating the extent to which women were able to exercise
some voice in the disposal of their wages. Inasmuch as the transformatory potential of wages for intra-household power relations is
frequently equated with the question of who 'controls' these wages,
the study of allocative decision making tends to be the terminus of
many explorations of the relationship between women's wages and
the distribution of power within the household. However, our
discussion has also highlighted how elusive the concept of control
is, particularly in the context of households organised around
ideologies of 'jointness'. There was no one-to-one relationship
between management and control. Women's ability to exercise
control over their own wages reflected a range of different situations, including situations where they had negotiated such control
with the household head, refused to relinquish control to the
household head as well as where there was no male to act as
household head.

Even where *formal* control was clearly centralised in the person
of the household head, *actual* control was less easily attributable to
any single individual or decision, but rather distributed among
household members in ways which were frequently disguised by the

fluidity of the discourses and practices used to effect that distribution. Formal 'control' over income could disguise the absence of discretionary power in many areas of household expenditure, regardless of who had been authorised to make key allocative decisions. A focus on formal control also missed out on the informal slippages which occurred as a result of the interdependencies between household members and the illicit forms of control exercised by women who sought to withhold full information about their earning capacity from their husbands. Consequently, it is not clear how useful a focus on women's control over their wages is in capturing the transformatory potential of these wages.

I would therefore like to push the discussion beyond the question of control to focus on the question of *choice:* in other words, to ask what *difference* women's wages made to their lives, what kinds of options became possible as a result of their new earning status. This will also allow us to address some important questions about the relationship between control, choice and power. For instance, is 'control' necessary for women to exercise 'choice' or is it possible for women to achieve their goals, regardless of who controlled their wages? And if so, under what circumstances? Moreover, in situations where women were found to be exercising enhanced choice as a result of their earning status, we would also want to assess the larger implications of the choices they made. Did they serve in some way to destabilise or subvert male power within the household, and women's subordinate status within the wider community, or did they merely reproduce the status quo, leaving these asymmetries largely intact?

Bearing these qualifications in mind, I will be re-analysing the testimonies provided by the women workers, but this time from the standpoint of 'choice'. I will be focusing in particular on two aspects of their testimonies. One aspect relates to information of a factual nature: how were women's wages actually utilised and to what extent did this reflect their allocative priorities? The second aspect is an evaluative one: what were the meanings and values that women attached to the allocative uses to which their wages were put and to their wage-earning capacity in general? As I hope to show, factual information on the utilisation of women's wages is important, but does not suffice to establish its transformatory potential. The subjective meanings which women invested in these uses are also critical because they help us to establish the extent to which women believed that they were making choices and the extent to which these choices were seen as transformatory. An important pattern which emerged out of this analysis, and one which links it to the analysis in Chapter 4, is that the circumstances which had led women to seek employment in the first place, the motivations behind their labour market choices, shaped in important ways how they perceived their access to wages and how this access translated into impact. Consequently, we will be organising our analysis of these questions loosely around the categories established in the last chapter.

## Economic need and 'optionless' choice

Women who had entered factory employment in response to the loss of male support, particularly the loss of husbands' support, were, as we noted earlier, also least likely to experience their access to wages as an expansion of choice. This is despite the fact that these women were also usually likely to exercise full control of their wages. There were about ten women who fell into this category. Economics had something to do with this outcome. For women like Renu, who were barely able to meet their basic survival needs, the disposal of their wages was so dominated by survival imperatives that there was little scope for exercising a meaningful choice. As we saw in the previous chapter, she had been driven out of her marriage by her husband's violence and his failure as a breadwinner. At the time of the interview, she had left her little daughter in her mother's care in their village and was earning a wage of Tk. 630 a month, with another Tk. 100 if she did overtime. She sent Tk. 100 for her daughter's expenses and paid Tk. 250 as rent. Here is her assessment of her job: 'Do I like the work? What is there not to like? Hard work never killed anyone. But if I don't work, I don't eat. Everything has to be paid for, even water has to be paid for. If I don't pay, I won't even have water and how can one live without water?'

Fatema's first husband had died, leaving her with a one-year-old daughter. She married again and had a son, but her second husband had left her three years ago. She initially lived with her brother, but he was too poor to take responsibility for her and suggested that she find herself a factory job. She now lived with her mother and two children in one room in which they slept and cooked. She saw little economic change in her life as a result of her employment and indeed felt that their hardships had increased since leaving her brother's house. Nor had she experienced any change in other aspects of her life: 'What rights do I have? I do everything on my own. I have to do my own bazaar since I have no husband. When I went to rent a house, the landlord would not consider me because I don't have a husband. Even if I am virtuous, they call me loose, because I don't have a husband.'

However, the failure to experience access to waged employment as an expansion of real choice was not a matter of economics alone. There were others in this group who had also been forced into the labour market by the loss of the male breadwinner, but for whom basic survival needs were not at stake in the same way as they were for Renu and Fatema. These were women we discussed earlier as having been brought up with the expectation of the lifelong support and protection of a male breadwinner. They had not expected or wanted to earn their own living. They consequently experienced their entry into the labour market in terms of need rather than choice, even if the need in question was not as desperate as it was for women like Renu and Fatima. The fact that many of them came from better-off families, for whom factory work had low status connotations, deepened their sense of apathy towards their jobs.

We have noted the case of Razia Sultana who had been forced to take up paid employment after the death of her husband in order to provide for herself and her children. Her economic situation was not desperate. Her brother was currently 'eating' with her and contributing to household expenses while her husband's family helped out with the children's education. Nevertheless, her entry into factory employment was symbolic of her decline in status from cherished and socially secure wife to bereft and socially vulnerable widow. She worried about her future because she could save nothing from her salary. Above all, she worried about being left on her own, particularly as her brother had recently married and it was likely that their joint residential arrangements would soon come to an end. She was the main provider for her family, she controlled her own earnings but it had not enhanced her status in her own eyes: 'Garment work may be hard work, but it doesn't mean you eat better than anyone else. We tend to give more to the men in the house. My brother is older, he is a man, we have to give him more. If a woman eats less, it doesn't look so bad. If I don't get enough to eat, I wouldn't complain. But if he doesn't, it looks bad to me.'

Rahela had walked out on her husband when he brought another woman home. She had returned to her parents' house with her children. She handled her own salary and spent it largely on her children and on her younger brothers and sisters but she did not appear to attach a great deal of importance to her new purchasing power: 'At first I felt very bad, but then I thought how long could I go on like this. I could not even give my children anything. My parents look after me and my children, but I could not do anything for them. Now I can buy a few little things for the children and myself – clips, cream – and fruits for the house.' As her wages increased, she began to make more of a contribution to the children's expenses – their clothing and tutor's fees. She might have been happier working if she had managed to get a more 'respectable' job but she knew she did not have the relevant qualifications. For a while, she had kept up the pretence with her extended family that she had a job at Dhaka art college, but her late hours of work gave her away. This was her assessment of what her wages meant to her:

> I don't think my value has increased since I started working. The only difference is that now I can buy a few things for my children independently. But nothing has changed for me within the family. I was in need of a job but not a job like this. If I had studied further then I could have got a better job. I don't have any satisfaction from the job but I have no other alternatives.

Shefali's testimony illustrated very poignantly the precarious autonomy of a woman who was more literally on her own than any other woman in our sample. While she was economically vulnerable, it was not the economics of her situation which defined her sense of hopelessness, but her social isolation. She had fended for herself since leaving her father's house after a failed marriage and had turned to casual prostitution to supplement her earnings as a mill worker and part-time domestic. When one of her co-workers in the mill proposed to her, despite knowing about her past, she hoped that the marriage would rescue her from the rootlessness of the existence. However, as we saw, this hope proved futile. Her husband sent her away within two months of their marriage, saying that he had been taken over by madness in marrying a *jatra* girl and had now come to his senses. When we interviewed her, she worked all day as a machinist in the factory and all evening as a domestic for her landlord's family in exchange for shelter and food. She consequently had to maintain a punishing schedule to keep up both jobs. She worked in the factory from about 7 in the morning to 6 in the evening, cleaned and cooked till midnight and then woke at 4.30 in the morning to finish off her domestic chores before setting out once again for the factory.[5]

While she preferred her present mode of livelihood to the casual prostitution she had engaged in previously, it had not freed her from the insecurities of being a woman on her own. What was particularly striking about her account of her life was the utter absence of any conventional social relationships. She found jobs, accommodation, information through chance encounters, the kindness of strangers, someone she had met on the streets or on a bus, someone who knew someone she knew. She believed passionately that the the vagaries of her life could be traced to the absence of any 'normal' love in it:

> It is because I have never had the love of a mother or father that I became bad, that I took to the streets. People are forced to sell themselves to survive. To get by in the world, you need certain things, the love of a mother and father, the protection of a husband, to be a mother to your own children, to take care of a home, to exchange affectionate words with

5. Although it should be said that many of the married women in our sample described similar working days.

your brothers and sisters, wander around all day carefree with your friends. I never got these things when I needed them, I still don't have them today.

Her present too was shaped by this sense of isolation. Her reason for continuing to work as a domestic, despite the impossible hours she had to work, was not simply to extend her income but because it offered some hope of protection and, more importantly, some sense of emotional connection with the family that employed her:

> The woman I work for, I call her my sister, but I am not free in my mind with her. They give me food, they talk to me, but all the time, I am asking myself why I was put on this earth. What offence did I give to God, that after all this suffering . . . there is still no end in sight. Being able to stay with this family, it was only after I begged them to keep me on . . . I try to avoid any trouble with them, who knows over what matter they might speak harshly to me and it would cause me such pain. I go out of my way for them to make sure that this does not happen. Every month I give my factory wages to the mistress to look after for me, I have bought nothing for myself from them. With this month's wages, I have bought a shawl for her and socks for the child. All the time I am wondering to myself, how can I make them love me? This love is all I want. If you have some love, then nothing can hurt you. This is my greatest sorrow, not lack of food, nor clothes, nothing like that. It would just please me that everyone should love me . . . People find happiness one way or the other, either with their parents or with their husband and children. But I did not get this happiness from anywhere.

## Contributions, claims and joint welfare maximisation

In contrast to this group of women for whom factory work was simply a way to survive, there were others who described the decision to take up factory employment in terms of their desire to contribute to the collective welfare of their families. Some were married women whose earnings contributed directly to household welfare; others were unmarried daughters whose ability to earn lessened demands on the household budget. These were all women who had described themselves as exercising an active agency in their labour market decisions. They did not report uniform income management patterns: some handed their wages over to the household head, others retained full or partial control. They all came from households supported by a male breadwinner and all were sufficiently economically secure to have opted to stay at home. Nevertheless, it was clear from their accounts, and from testimonies of other family members, that their earnings had made a discernible economic difference to their households' collective welfare function.

In some cases, it contributed to improvements in the household's standard of living: in the standard and diversity of household diet; in the quality of hospitality offered to guests; in the quality of housing. Some reported the purchase of consumer durables as a result of their earnings. In other cases, their earnings had put the household on a more secure footing: debts could be paid off or avoided in the future; money was set aside for emergencies; productive assets, including capital for the husband's business or land in the family village, could be purchased or saved for. The ability to save was frequently cited to signify the difference that their wages had made. In yet other cases, women's wages were used specifically for their children's welfare, particularly education and private tuition. Indeed, as we saw in the previous chapter, child-related expenditure was given by many women as a major rationale for their entry into waged work.

The assignment of their wages to collective household expenditures reflected the ideology, as well as the reality, of the corporate organisation of household relations in Bangladesh. It should be noted that male breadwinners also generally contributed a major portion of their incomes to household welfare. Discourses about the disposal of household income, regardless of who had earned it, tended to reflect this co-operative ideology. Whether these collective needs were met through the ear-marking of separate income streams for collective needs or through pooled arrangements, the question of 'control' over household income flows was often a formality in households where there appeared to be little conflict over priorities.

This appearance of consensus would appear to render the issue of power irrelevant. However, there was evidence that power was still a factor in such households, but that it operated through more hidden routes than would be revealed if the enquiry was confined to questions of who managed or who controlled their incomes. It was primarily evident in areas of 'inertness' or 'non-decision making' in household behaviour, areas which testified to persistence of certain unquestioned asymmetries between men and women. One such asymmetry, and one that has been noted in other studies as well, related to personal expenditures. This was considered a more legitimate category for men than women. Men were much more likely to report recreational activities generally denied to women: smoking, tea shops, gambling, cinema, eating outside, having friends over. As far as women were concerned, their attitudes were often exemplified by that of Jorina: 'As long as I have clothes to wear, a roof over my head and my children are happy, I am happy.' Their main personal expenditures were clothes and gold jewellery. These were sometimes described as gifts from their husbands, and hence not their own choice, or else as a work-related requirement. Many of the women pointed out, for instance, that their clothes requirements had increased since taking up factory jobs, since they had to maintain a smart appearance.

In addition, patterns of investment in wider social networks revealed other persistent forms of asymmetry. When married women described expenditures on guests, the beneficiaries of this hospitality were almost always friends and relatives of the husband. Similarly, when they talked of looking after relatives or sending them remittances, it was generally relatives of the husband who were the main beneficiaries of this support, not their own. The practices of marital exogamy and patrilocal residence in Bangladesh meant that women were generally cut off from their own families and their childhood friends after marriage. They were incorporated into their husband's family and social networks and, given their economic dependence, had neither the material wherewithal nor the cultural sanction to offer any assistance to their own families. Consequently, men were the most direct beneficiaries of investments of household income in the maintenance of social and familial networks. Women benefited, but indirectly, as dependants of men rather than in their own right.

However, despite evidence of these asymmetries in the allocation of household resources, the fact that women were now making a contribution to household income, and a sizeable one at that, did not go unacknowledged. Women themselves tended to describe this acknowledgement in symbolic rather than material terms, in terms of 'respect' rather than 'entitlement': 'When you contribute to the family, they love you more, they give you respect.' However, recognition was also manifested at the level of practice. Zohra may have handed over her entire salary to her husband, but as she pointed out, he could not spend it as he wanted. She had justified her decision to take up factory work in terms of the need to meet their children's educational expenses and that was what her income was largely used for. She also pointed to another important change in her relations with her husband. In the past, she had always had to provide an account for any requests for money that she made. This was no longer the case: 'When I want to buy something, I just ask for it – it may be his income or mine. He never asks why I need it. Nor would he spend without asking me.'

## Patriarchal constraint and strategic gender needs

A third group of women, about fourteen of our sample, used their wages to meet certain strategic gender needs. I should explain my use of the term 'strategic gender needs' since it differs from the usage popularised by Moser (1989) in the context of her approach to gender training. I have elsewhere discussed why I find her usage problematic (see discussion in Kabeer, 1994, Chapter 10). I am using the concept here because it appears to capture what I am trying to describe. I use the term 'strategic' because the uses to which the women in question put their income reflected certain underlying structural shortfalls rather than individual preferences; I use the term 'gender' because these structural shortfalls were rooted in the asymmetries of the patriarchal contract; and I use the term 'need' to signify the fact that these uses reflected, and served to confirm, women in their status as dependants, rather than a willingness on their part to act on these asymmetries in order to transform them.

We saw from the previous chapter that women in the family were likely to invest far more effort than male members in achieving co-operative outcomes in situations of conflict because they had more to lose from the breakdown of family relations. However, these investments could not guarantee the stability of family relationships, particularly marital relationships, which continued to break down, often for reasons that were beyond the woman's control. The various examples of strategic gender needs to which the women in this category allocated their income reflected their sense of vulnerability as women, and the pivotal role that marriage continued to play in their lives, despite widespread evidence of its increasing instability.

A perennial source of insecurity for many of the married women in our sample was their fear that, through no fault of their own, they would fail to live up to their side of the patriarchal bargain, thus providing their husbands with the justification for leaving them. For a number of the women in the sample, their worst fears appeared to have been realised and they used their wages to postpone, or mitigate, its consequences as long as possible. These precautions were rarely taken openly for fear of risking the very outcomes they had been undertaken to avoid. Instead, they often took the form of the half-truths and outright deceptions through which we noted that some of the women in our sample sought to retain a degree of unofficial control over their wages.

In the case of Salma, the fear in question stemmed from her childlessness, a condition generally blamed on women in the Bangladesh context and regarded as sufficient grounds for divorce. She had married into a well-to-do household and appeared to have an extremely loving husband.[6] Nevertheless, after eight years of marriage, they were still childless. She spoke of the role that she felt children played in cementing the bonds of marriage and of her fear of the fate that her failure to bear children had condemned her to:

> I worry about the future. Men don't always feel the same; he treats me well now but what will happen if God does not give me any children . . . What will become of me if he decides to remarry? Sometimes I worry so much, I

6. I should point out that when we interviewed her husband, he expressed his affection for her, did not appear to blame her in any way for their childlessness, was aware of her anxieties but puzzled by them: 'If we don't have children, we will adopt a child, that is what I think.'

stop eating, my throat dries up. Everyone is affectionate with me – my husband, my in-laws. They love me; my husband loves me but I worry that it won't last if I don't have a child. He tells me off for worrying so much but if I don't have a child I will not be able to show my face.

She valued her employment status because it gave her a fragile sense of security and a respite from her worries: 'I often tell myself that I have a job and that I should not worry. I try to have confidence. I tell myself, I have no worries. I have no children so if my husband leaves, no one will cry for me, I will manage on my own ... When I come here and chat, I enjoy myself a little and forget.' Every month she made a point of handing over her salary to her husband but in recent months she had started keeping back some of it to put into a clandestine bank account which she had opened in her own name: 'I want to save because I need to think of my own future. Suppose he dies, how will I manage? I don't have any children so I can't live with his parents. If you don't have children, you are not valued.'

Hasina had also joined the factory because of her childless condition but her situation was further complicated by her highly conflictual marital relationship. Hers had been a 'love' marriage and she described the very passionate sexual relationship that she had had with her husband at the beginning. However, her feelings towards him began to change when she found out that he already had a wife and children living in another neighbourhood. Their relationship became increasingly unhappy and violent as her trust in him was eroded:

The thing that keeps going around in my mind is 'He has married twice. I have no way of knowing that he will provide for my future.' I have no faith in him, basically. What I think is that any man who is so addicted to women, who drinks so much, who can marry again when he already has a family and children of his own can never be trusted. I don't trust him.

Her husband began to visit his first wife and children for a day each week, but Hasina was able to use his continued sexual infatuation with her to ensure that their home remained his primary one because she could not face the prospect of being on her own. And to some extent, she was still in love with him. The idea of earning her own living came to her because, after four years of marriage, she had not had any children and anxieties about her future set in:

> The idea came to me that I could use a skill and get myself a job. I don't know where the realisation came from, but it came from within my mind. I think it partly came when I realised what having a co-wife meant. She can't stand for me to have anything nice to eat or wear. She hates me because my husband lives here and only visits them for one day each week . . . It is also true that initially I had thought I would have children of my own and I could rely on them. But now that I haven't had any children, I have realised that I have to make my plans for my future myself. Nobody can afford to rely on anyone else, you have to do things for yourself. I know I have a co-wife, so I have to make arrangements accordingly. Or if, God forbid, my husband leaves me, what will I do then?

She was very open in her refusal to hand over any of her wages to her husband, saving it instead in a bank account and with her brother. This led to considerable conflict with her husband but she remained adamant:

> My husband knows that I save it all. He also knows about the money that I have kept with my brother. He has a lot to say about it, he says, 'You eat my salt and yet you save your money with your brother' so I say, 'Why shouldn't I? Since I work so hard, why shouldn't I save my money?' . . . If I spend my own money on everything for the household, then he wouldn't spend anything, would he? In any case, there are many things he refuses to buy. Because he says he has children and another wife, there would be problems about where he should keep those things . . .

For Amena, anxieties about her marriage stemmed from the fact that she had five daughters and no sons.[7] She knew that her mother-in-law had been urging her husband to find another wife who could give him sons. She joined the factory because she

---

7. It is, of course, not possible to generalise from the small and purposively selected sample in this study but 'reproductive failures' of various kinds did appear to feature disproportionately as a factor in bringing women into the factories. Two of the 43 ever-married women in our sample of 60, had not had any children while 14 had only had daughters. Like Amena, the need to save for their daughters' dowry, as well as their anxieties about their own future, often featured in their testimonies as a reason for working.

calculated that the financial burden of dowries for five daughters would feel less onerous for her husband if she was able to contribute. Her role as manager of household income gave her a certain degree of discretion as to the information she shared with her husband regarding the allocation of household income. She had started up two deposit accounts in the bank, one in her husband's name which he knew about, and one in her own name, which he did not. Every month she scrupulously paid an equal amount of money into both.

Rupban used her access to wages to try and mitigate the consequences of the painful trade-off that she, in common with a number of other women in our sample, had been forced to make when her marriage broke down. Under Islamic law, the claims of the biological father are prior to those of the mother and it is the father who is given ultimate custody in the event of marital breakdown. Women are allowed custody when the children are young or longer, of course, if the father does not claim them. However, if they want to remarry, their children have to be returned to the biological father or left behind with other relatives. Few men are willing to accept responsibility for the biological offspring of another man, although they often expected their own offspring from a previous marriage to be cared for by a subsequent wife.

Rupban had kept custody of her children when her first marriage broke down and she had returned to her brother's house. But her brother began to put pressure on her to remarry as he could not afford to take long-term responsibility for feeding her and Rupban had to choose between her love for her children and the security of a second marriage. She opted for the latter, leaving behind her children to be cared for by her brother, in order to marry a man who had left his first wife but had retained custody of their four children. Rupban did not seek to question the justice of this arrangement, but she missed her own children desperately:

> When I go home to my own village, sometimes I meet my children. My husband does not know about it. He does not know to this day that I cry for my children and that I think about them all the time. I can never feel the same way about his children the way I do for my own. I can't help it, it is the way the world is.

As we noted earlier, she used the distance between her home and her work place to conceal the magnitude of her earnings and her overtime money from her husband. She sent what she saved to her brother for the children's upkeep, hoping that this would guarantee that they were well cared for. However, by the time we interviewed her, she had decided to give in to her husband's pressure to give up her job in case it jeopardised her marriage: 'Since he does not want me to work, I have told him I will give it up by next January. God will have to look after my children.'

A final example of a strategic gender need for which women used their wages related to dowry costs. This was a need which had brought many of the young unmarried women in our sample into the factories. Najma Akhter was one: 'This job is not because of any particular hardship, but out of a particular financial need ... Parents who cannot afford to marry off their daughters are able to do so if the girls have some money of their own ...' Like many other women, she was not happy about the practice – 'everyone cannot afford dowry, what will happen to girls who cannot afford dowries?' – but felt that it was the unavoidable cost of getting married. Her aunt, with whom she stayed, told us:

> It takes a lot of money to get a girl married these days. One has to give a lot of things to the groom, like a watch, a ring, cassette player, and other demands. Her father does not have the means to give 10,000 takas to the groom or sometimes they ask for 15–20,000 takas. So the girl works, then her money can be kept as savings and utilised at the time of her marriage to pay for the dowry or meet other demands.

By and large, we have discussed the allocational priorities expressed by the women in this section as 'needs' rather than 'preferences' because they were rarely experienced, or talked about, as a *choice* by the women in question, but rather as a necessity imposed on them by the fact of their gender. That they often entailed the clandestine use of their wages was indicative of the vulnerability of their position. While the use of their wages to address these needs helped to mitigate some of the insecurities engendered by the asymmetries of the patriarchal contract, it did little to challenge or transform the terms of the contract.

## Transformative choices and strategic gender interests

I want to now turn to the testimonies of those women who used their economic opportunities in ways which appeared to have transformatory implications, sometimes in terms of their own sense of self-hood, sometimes in their relationships within the family and sometimes in their position in the wider community. Twenty-two women in our sample fell into this category. It was not that they used their incomes in ways that were necessarily radically different from some of those we have been discussing so far, but rather that they invested often similar choices with very different meanings and motivations. Like the women in the previous category, their choices also reflected the structural asymmetries of the patriarchal contract but, unlike them, their choices acted against the grain of asymmetries, often pushing back the pre-existing limits on their capacity to exercise choice. Strategic life choices around marriage were a critical aspect of this and cropped up repeatedly in their testimonies, although the form these took clearly varied according to whether women were speaking as daughters, as wives or as mothers. We will consider each group in turn.

## The transformatory potential of women's wages: daughters' perspective

As we noted in Chapter 3, daughters in Bangladesh have come to be increasingly regarded as economic liabilities by their parents. They make little, or no, economic contribution while they are growing up; they offer even less by way of support after marriage; and in recent decades, the emergence and inflation of dowry demands accompanying the marriage of daughters has plunged many parents into debt and impoverishment. However, the expansion of wage-earning opportunities for young women, in which the garment industry had clearly played an important role, was beginning to alter this relationship between daughters and parents.

One aspect of this change was evident in daughters' perceptions of themselves. Dilu, who had taken up employment to support the

family when her father fell ill, told us how access to waged employment had transformed her sense of self-worth and agency: 'We now
know we can survive and support ourselves, that we can feed and
clothe ourselves. We are not a burden on our parents. We have
arms and legs and we can make use of them.' Having become used
to her earning status, Nazneen expressed her reluctance to become
a dependant after she got married:

> I like working better than the usual housework women have to do. I want
> to go on working after marriage. What can one do sitting at home?
> Pushing utensils around, is that all women are good for? If I earn more
> and my husband doesn't like it, then I will have to make him understand
> that there is nothing wrong with a wife earning more.

A second set of changes related to women's relationship with their
parents. They valued their ability to contribute to the collective
upkeep of the family and spoke of their satisfaction in being able
to repay some of their parents' efforts, and in some cases, considerable self-sacrifice on their children's behalf. Angura's mother had
the option of remarrying after the death of her first husband, since
her brothers were keen to arrange it, but she would have had to
leave her two daughters behind with them. Instead, she migrated
to Dhaka where she took up work as a domestic servant to feed
herself and her children. Angura felt that her mother had sacrificed
her own chances for a better life in order to take care of her
daughters:

> My mother wanted to keep her two daughters with her. If she had married
> again, she could not have done that. She would have been selling herself.
> She would have left us with her brother's family and they would not have
> looked after us. Another's child is not the same as one's own . . .

Angura was twenty-four years old when we met her and, although
she was under pressure from her extended family to marry, she
had decided that she would only marry if she found a husband who
would accept responsibility for her mother:

> People tell my mother to marry me off and she would also like it. But my
> mother has suffered a great deal in her life and now I want her to have

some peace ... A lot of proposals come but I have only one mother. Suppose I get married and have to leave her alone, she will grieve and think that if only she had a son, he would have looked after her for the rest of her life, but because she had only daughters, they have gone off to another house and she is left alone to suffer ... My mother has looked after me and now I want to look after her.

A third set of changes related to increased willingness of some young women to refuse to acquiesce to unsatisfactory marriages. Afifa knew her family had fallen on hard times and that the kind of dowry that would be demanded for her to be able to marry a man from her class was beyond their means. She was determined to hold out against marriage until she found a man who would be prepared to marry her without making any demand for dowry:

> They say, if you change your house and move to a pucca building, we can get better proposals for your daughter. I told my father, if we have to change our house for me to get married, I will not marry that person. He is not marrying the house, what does the house matter? I will not marry anyone who demands a dowry even if it means not getting married at all. He will be marrying my dowry then. When the dowry finishes, my value finishes.

Her description of what she wanted from life suggested that she was keenly aware of the wider injustices of women's situation and was determined that she would not capitulate to the social pressures that led women to settle for whatever fate had in store for them:

> I don't have any special person in mind. But I will have to marry someone who will marry me for myself, not for my family. I am 20 but I do not feel like getting married now ... I do not approve of girls getting married young. They are not mature enough to understand everything. They are helpless when their husbands leave them. They do not know what to do or how to hold on to their marriage. Their husbands take advantage and do whatever they like. They leave them at whim and many girls in the village are suffering this way. Then they come to the cities to work. I know of many girls in the garment factory who have suffered like this. Seeing them I wonder what is the point of getting married.

While some of the women workers, like Afifa, had made the decision not to concede to dowry demands because of their contempt for men who used it as a route to self-enrichment, there was also evidence of a reduction in the incidence of dowry demands as a result of forces which had little to do with the intended agency of any individual woman. According to Asma:

> If a woman is earning her own living, then often the question of dowry is less important. I have seen marriages where the men got nothing out of it but the girl. In Garment B, where I was before, I saw a number of cases like that. The men didn't ask for dowry. They just went to the court and had a registry marriage.

The suggestion that dowry is being waived in the case of women who are regarded as economically productive is a plausible one, given that the practice of dowry in Bangladesh does not have the sanction of religion or long-established custom,[8] but rather has arisen relatively recently. If it was indeed a reflection of the declining value of women's economic role in the latter half of this century, as was argued in Chapter 3, then logic dictates a reversal would occur when women's economic value starts to rise. As Hawa's testimony suggested, there were various ways to interpret this willingness on the part of men to waive dowry. One would be to see it as yet more evidence of male greed:

> There are so many women working in the garment factories now . . . this has brought about some social changes. These women have managed to save some money. Now you will see, even a rickshawallah wants to marry one of the garment women. Even the rickshawallah thinks, 'The girl is working in a garment factory. She has money of her own. I should marry this girl.' Then he will be able to live off his wife's earnings. He might earn some money and his wife might earn some money. Then he might give up driving his rickshaw and live off what his wife earns. That is how these men behave.

However, putting to one side the behaviour of 'rickshawallahs' who, for Hawa, was the archetypical 'uncouth' man, other parts of her testimony pointed to both women's greater economic value to prospective husbands as well as their greater ability to rely on themselves:

8. As it does among the Brahmin castes in India.

Because women can work and earn money, they are being given some recognition. Now all the men think that they are worth something. Look at me, for instance. I am earning Tk 600 a month. Won't the man who marries me think I am doing well now? Of course, he will! Because I'll take my wages and put it in his hands! Well, I would have to, otherwise how is he going to know I am worth anything? Well, perhaps I won't hand over *all* my money. I will give him some and I'll keep the rest myself, for my own future. If that man goes off and dies somewhere, then at least I will have that saving. I will need that money to eat.

Given the pragmatic, rather than romantic, view of marriage taken by many of the women in our sample, the waiving of dowry was seen as the logical outcome of women's transition from economic liability to economic asset.[9] As Dilu pointed out: 'If a woman is earning something, the man's family is interested in her. The more she earns, the more interested they are. They aren't interested if she is poor. The difference is that rather than asking for a huge dowry, they may be willing to just take the girl.' Or, as another worker announced with some pride, 'How can they ask for dowry to marry us? *We* are the dowry.'

## The transformatory potential of women's wages: the wives' perspective

Married women acted on the possibilities opened up to them by their access to waged employment in ways which reflected the quality of their relationships with their husbands. In harmonious marriages, they were more likely to hand over their wages to their husbands, in symbolic recognition of their role as family bread-winner and household head. As we noted from Jorina's testimony, this often led to subtle changes in household decision making

9. A similar logic appears to be at work in rural areas (Kabeer, 1998; Begum, 1988). A young unmarried village woman interviewed by Begum explained why she gave greater priority to finding a job in the garment factory than to finding a husband: 'You never know, after marriage my husband may abscond with my dowry money or divorce me after some time. So what's the use of spending so much money on dowry incurring great debt in the process? It is better I work and stand on my own feet first . . . If I can earn, there will be no shortage of men willing to marry me.' (1987, p. 120)

processes, in acknowledgement of their greater contribution to the household budget. Other women described this change in more explicit terms. For Shanu, her economic contribution had resulted in a greater entitlement to be heard in household decision making. We noted how she had been pushed into seeking work by her step-daughters' taunts that she was 'eating' from their wages and had engaged in protracted negotiations with her husband to overcome his resistance. However, having won the right to work, she expressed little interest in controlling her own income: 'I give it to my husband because we have hardship in the family. Moreover it is not wise for the wife to take on the responsibility for the family.' Despite this, it was clear that there had been a discernible shift in how decisions were taken in her household. Her husband told us that he gave much greater weight to her priorities in recognition of her contribution:

> I manage the household finances . . . But the money she earns is very useful. She gives the entire amount to me. To give her credit, she doesn't waste a penny. But when she brings me the money, I have to buy her whatever she wants. She may want a new sari or she may say that the children need something, this daughter needs a book . . .

Shanu put the change more forcefully:

> We couldn't say a word before we started working. If I had not been working, my husband would have ordered me to look after his children and see to their needs . . . If one works, one has different rights. If you are at home and do not earn, then the man is more powerful.

Other married women chose to retain some form of control over their earnings in order to start savings of their own, either opening separate bank accounts or keeping their funds with a trusted relative. In some cases, the savings were undertaken with the husband's knowledge; in others, they either lied or simply failed to inform them. Their desire to save was a response to the enhanced awareness of 'patriarchal risk' that we have commented on in earlier discussion, a widespread conviction on the part of many women that marriage was no longer a guarantee of lifelong security:

The husband is the biggest asset for a woman, but only if he is an ideal person. Otherwise one should save separately. Because one cannot depend on men these days.

Even if the husband won't allow it, women will still save in the bank because he might leave them and they will then need the money for the family. There are many women who earn 800 takas but say that they only got 300 or 400 and save the rest in the bank or with her own family.

I have classified the decision to save on these grounds as having a potentially transformatory impact, because they represented a pro-active agency on the part of women to strengthen their overall fall-back position in the event of marital crisis. In this, they differed from women in the previous category, whose decision to save was a more defensive reaction, a response to their own perceived failure to live up to the terms of the patriarchal contract.

In the context of some of the less satisfactory marital relation-ships reported by women workers, access to wages allowed them to act to improve the quality of their lives. The discussion in the previous chapter has already pointed to evidence of domestic violence in women's lives: in fact, 14 out of the 43 women in our sample who were, or had been, married, reported such violence. Others had been deceived or humiliated or else found themselves going hungry because their husbands refused to provide for them. Some of these women sought to renegotiate the terms of their relationships with their husbands, using the more credible threat of exit provided by their new financial self-reliance to extract concessions.

Others, like Aleya, chose to actualise the 'exit' option. She was the woman who had been married off when she was very young to a blind man who had himself been married several times before and who had a long history of wife-beating. She heard about the garment factories while still living with her husband in the village and had used her small savings to acquire machining skills from a local NGO. She then left her husband, taking her young twelve-year-old daughter with her. The two had taken up work in a garment factory in Dhaka. Her husband followed her there and, although she took him back, she described him as 'less angry' than he used to be. However, she did not let him forget the fact of her newly-earned independence: 'I remind him all the time that I don't eat from his money any more, I work for my own living and I feed myself. He is afraid that I will leave him because he is old and blind and I can stand on my own feet.'

The shift in the balance of power was graphically symbolised for Aleya not only by the cessation of his violence, but also by the fact that he now handed over his earnings to her: 'He gives whatever he gets, he doesn't keep any back.' It could be argued that the special circumstances of her husband's blindness meant that the distribution of bargaining power within the household was not so heavily loaded against Aleya. Nevertheless, it was her ability to earn her own living, rather than her husband's age and disability, that helped her to finally stand up to him and put an end to his violence: 'It is less miserable now. He used to beat me before, he doesn't beat me anymore. I stayed with him for my children, what else could I do. Who will give me work with 2 children?'

Sahara also made a clear connection between her new earning power and the lessening of her husband's violence: 'As I am earning now, our financial condition is better. So he does not beat me like before ... There are less quarrels; now there are days when, even when I speak up to him, he does not argue with me because I am helping with the money.' Along with her new status as earner, she believed that the widening of her networks and horizons, as a result of her employment, had helped to give her the courage to stand up to him: 'I was a fool before. After I joined the garments, I have become smarter. One mixes with ten or more people and learns about life. I could not speak like this before and would only sit in the house. But now I can speak up and answer my husband.'

We have cited Hanufa's marriage as an example of a highly conflictual marriage, punctuated by outbreaks of violence on the part of her husband. After one such episode, she decided to throw him out of the rented room in which they lived. She was able to do so because it was her wages which paid for the rent and she had the support of her landlord and his family. Her employer also threatened her husband with the police if he ever harmed her again. Although she took her husband back after a period of time, her point had been made. She had shown that she could manage without him and that she had alternative 'guardians' who had her interests at heart. When we interviewed Hanufa's husband, he was contemplating finding a more regularly paid employment, perhaps in a garment factory: 'I never thought of garments before. But since I don't earn much, I am thinking about it.' It is unlikely that Hanufa would ever have been able to throw out her husband, even temporarily, if she had not been financially self-reliant and her testimony bore this out:

> Garments have been very good for women, even for me. I have become more courageous . . . Now I feel I have rights, I can survive . . . Suppose my husband says something, I won't care because I can feed myself. If any relatives say anything, I won't bother, I will think that I don't need to go to their house. I can earn and survive – I have got the courage.

Sathi Akhter's life history exemplified in many respects the costs that women paid for their dependence on male support. She described the process by which she had moved from an attitude of passive acquiescence to her fate as a woman – 'There is no difference between a woman's fate and a prisoner's fate and it is no different for the daughter of a prime minister . . .' – to taking active control over her life. Her own mother had died when she was eleven years old and her father had married again soon afterwards. Sathi was married off a few years later to a man chosen by her father. She had acquiesced to his choice because she, like many of the women we interviewed, believed that this would give her a continued claim on her father's support, should anything go wrong with her marriage.

Something did go wrong with her marriage: she found out within the first month that her husband was already married and had a child by his first wife. 'When I found out,' she said, 'something happened to me. I thought if he can deceive me about a thing like that, what else is he capable of, he could easily turn around and beat me.' She returned to her father's house, but was not made welcome. Her stepmother, in particular, did not hide her resentment at having an extra mouth to feed and her comments – 'What is the point of having a daughter around, they don't work and they don't feed you when you are old' – had the desired effect. Sathi left her father's house, resolved to become self-reliant:

That was when I decided to get into garments and look after myself. I realised that even when you marry according to your guardian's wishes, you can still have tragedy ahead of you. I entered the factory because of what my guardians said. If someone hurts you and then gives you food, that food is *haram*. If you hear things said about you, and you have any sense of dignity, you will not wish to stay around. So I swore I would eat from my own income. I will never again eat at my father's expense. If I can feed myself, I will eat or I will not eat at all.

She now lived with her uncle and his family. Since her wages were pooled with the rest of the household, her personal living standards had not benefited particularly from her earning status. But she valued the more intangible gains that her job had given her: 'My greatest satisfaction today is that I do not have to put up with anyone's gibes. I earn my own way.'

Sathi's response to her unhappy experience of marriage had turned her against the whole idea: 'The idea of marriage gives me the creeps. The thought of the future no longer troubles me. Marriage proposals come but I just say I am already married.' Other women who had also had unfortunate marriages had not necesssarily ruled out the possibility of marrying again, given the continued importance of marriage as the accepted status for women, but were more prepared to lay down conditions than they had been able to the first time round. Husne Ara's relationship with her first husband broke down because of continued dowry demands by her parents-in-law:

I thought it would have been one thing to give more dowry if I was happy with him, but since I wasn't, what was the point? For example, his sister and his father always argued with me and he never stood up for me. I thought if the person that I am supposed to live with until I die doesn't protect me, what is the point of giving more dowry? . . . My parents arranged my marriage, they gave a dowry, they gave money, but the marriage did not last. Now I had to make arrangements for my own life. My life was broken but I had to do something about it. That is why I came here to work.

She returned to her parents' house and took up garment work. A line supervisor in the factory became interested in her and sent a marriage proposal to her parents. When we interviewed her, she was in the process of making up her mind. These were the conditions she had put to him before she would consider his proposal:

> I have told him I would not leave my job, that I would only marry somebody who would let me work, that I would rather give up the man, but not the job. He has accepted this. I have also told him that I would not give a *paisa* of my earnings to him if I didn't want to; and if I wanted to, I would. He has said that he wouldn't be depending on my earnings, he didn't want to run his household on his wife's earnings, and he would have his own pocket money. Then I told him that as long as my parents were alive, I would send them money, no one could stop me. He told me that I could do whatever I like with my money, he would never stop me, my parents had brought me up, they had suffered so many hardships, there was no question of my not giving them money. I believed him, but I did not accept what he said straightaway. I only believed him after I got to know him better . . . I think that after all that he has promised, if he takes my money from me and does not let me send some to my parents and brothers and sisters, then it is better to starve rather than eat his food . . .

However, although he had agreed to these conditions, there had been a sudden – and unexpected – demand for dowry. Husne Ara had been reconciled to the idea of her parents paying *some* dowry, given that it had become the norm, but she wanted the payment to be voluntary on their part rather than a 'demand' from her prospective in-laws. She had given her suitor an ultimatum:

> He has to decide by the 10th of next month. His father and brother want to come and discuss it with my parents . . . I don't know what my decision will be. He asked for dowry, for 16,000 takas, but I have told him I will not give him two *paisas*. I have told my parents this as well. If they want to give dowry, it should be with a happy mind. But now he says he doesn't want anything. . . . I didn't like his demand for dowry. I wrote a reply to him saying that he only wanted dowry, not me. He should have said that he only wanted me. I had already thought I would have given dowry and made his side happy in any way I could. His friends must have told him that nowadays marriages are not possible without dowry demands and that if he made a love marriage without dowry, then he would be cheated.

Husne Ara's testimony highlights the new models of marriage that were being bargained for by women who had paid, and were no longer prepared to pay, the bitter price of economic dependency within marriage. As far as she was concerned, women's ability to earn their own living was critical to their ability to hold out for greater dignity within marriage:

> Some women think that they can't do anything if they are married. They think that their husbands have turned them into beggars. Some women are afraid that they will never find a husband so that he becomes more important than money. But other women think there is no reason to live with a husband if he makes you suffer. That it is better to live on your own . . . I think that it is good for women of our country to work, to educate themselves and to stand on their own two feet. They can marry after that. If I marry again, I would not give up my job. For me, work is beneficial. Only with work can I stand on my own feet.

### The transformatory potential of women's wages: the mothers' perspective

We have already seen in the previous chapter that for many women, their reason for taking up employment was linked to their children's welfare, particularly to their children's educational prospects. In this section, I want to consider a particular set of choices made by women, in their capacity as mothers, which had important transformatory potential for the life chances of the next generation of young women. Momta was an example of a phenomenon which appeared to be occurring among many of the women in our sample: the growing determination that their daughters would not pay the price of economic dependency that their mothers had paid. Momta had been married off to a man that she felt no affection for. When she gave birth to a daughter, the negative reactions of her husband and his family made her decide to leave the marriage and return to her own family. Her mother had wanted her to return to her husband, but her older brother agreed to take her in. However, when he married, his wife began to express her resentment at the additional financial burden of supporting Momta and her child. Her brother offered to arrange a marriage for her but, as we have seen in other cases, this would have required

Momta to give up her daughter. Instead Momta came away with her daughter to Dhaka and found work in a garment factory.

Her explanation of how she saw her choices provided a moving example of the way in which maternal altruism and the search for economic security meshed seamlessly together in women's lives.

> I would not get married again, I would have had to give my child up to her father and he has married again. A stepmother will never love someone else's child . . . The day that my brother says to me, 'Come back with your daughter, I will take responsibility for her and I will not give her back to her father', that is the day I will be ready to return. Today I just work to support my daughter and myself. It is hard work. But when I come home and take my child in my lap, when I go to sleep with her, all my misery seems to go away. I don't feel tired anymore. I have a lot of dreams for her, but I don't know if they will come true. I want to put her in a hostel as a cadet but you need 40,000 takas so it is not possible. I want her to pass her MA and when she is grown up, she will know her mother gave her life for her. Then maybe she will give me respect. If I am lucky, she will look after me. If she is educated, if she becomes a doctor, she will work with the poor and understand their hardships and realize that she was like that once. But uneducated, she will not.

Momta had effectively sacrificed her chances of marrying again – with the concomitant security and respectability that it might have brought – in order to keep her daughter with her. She worked for her daughter and dreamt of a better life for her than the one that her parents had prepared for her. In return, she hoped to win her daughter's love and respect, some recognition of her efforts and 'if she was lucky', some security in her old age. It was in such explanations of women's desire to make a better life for their children that the complex, and inseparable, interweaving of love, altruism, tenderness, self-sacrifice and material self-interest that is the defining feature of familial relationships was at its most revealing.

But Momta's comments revealed something else as well, something which recurred in a number of other accounts: the re-valuing of girl children and the greater willingness on the part of mothers to invest in their education. Daughters, as I pointed out earlier, have always occupied second place to sons in Bangladeshi culture and, as the values and practices of one generation were transmitted to the next, with mothers often a primary transmitting agent, it was difficult to see how this situation would change. Yet a change does seem to be under way. The loss of faith in the traditional patriarchal family to safeguard women's interests and to secure their future expressed by many of the women workers appears to be part of a much more widespread anxiety and bitterness expressed by women in Bangladesh.[10] Statistical estimates of divorce, male abandonment, marital instability and female-headed households do not come close to capturing how widespread this loss of faith appears to be. With the manifest failure, or inability, on the part of so many men to 'deliver' their side of the patriarchal bargain, it is not surprising that so many women were looking back on the choices that their parents had made on their behalf, on the life chances which these choices had given them and questioning whether it had been enough.

Women who had been married off 'too young to be able to evaluate their own benefits and losses', as one woman worker put it, and then paid the price for their parents' lack of judgement in choosing a husband, did not want the same thing to happen to their daughters. Neither did women who were married off so early that 'they were having babies when they were still babies themselves'. Neither did women who, when deprived of male support, found themselves having to compete in a labour market for which they were ill equipped. Whatever their individual rationale, these were all women who felt let down by the deal that their society had given them. Denied the opportunity to make something of their own lives, they wanted fiercely that their daughters' lives should not be similarly circumscribed. In the phrase used by many, 'Our lives are over, but our daughters have a future.'

Kaneez, for instance, had been prepared to tolerate her husband's beatings and economic irresponsibility as long as she was the only one affected by his behaviour. But when her daughter was born and it was it was clear that his irresponsibility was now going to impinge on her child's welfare, she decided to defy her husband

10. I found similar sentiments being expressed by many rural women I interviewed in 1997 (see Kabeer, 1998).

and take up a factory job, even though she knew it would jeopardise her already shaky marriage. When he left, and she later heard that he married again, she was deeply upset both for herself and for her daughter. She was determined that she would only think of marrying her daughter off when the girl was old enough to understand the implications of her choice and to speak on her own behalf:

> It is my daughter I feel sorry for . . . she cannot understand anything. I just want my daughter to grow up properly before she marries. I will first bring her to adulthood and then marry her off. If she has anything to say, she will be old enough to be able to say it. Her father says, when the girl is older, she will search me out, she will come to me. But right now, she wants to kill him for never coming to visit.

However, although she had not expected to have to work for her own living and knew that it grieved her family that she had been forced into what they saw as a low-status and unrewarding job, she also saw the positive side of what she was doing:

> Even though I slave the whole month, the smile comes back to my face when I get my wage packet. If I had not been working, I think my husband would have misbehaved more. He would have thought, 'She can't work, she isn't educated, she will only get value from people when I give her value'. When I began earning, I got more courage, I could speak up, I could survive on my own.

For many of these women, education held out the promise of a better future for their daughters. While the importance of education has traditionally been recognised for sons, the value that women were now investing in their daughters' education presented a marked contrast to the low value given to their own education by the preceding generation of parents.[11] The reasons they gave for valuing daughters' education varied. Some saw it in terms which did little to challenge patriarchal values, but made the process of accommodating to these values somewhat easier; it was believed,

---

11. Evidence from the World Bank (1995) and from Kabeer (1998) suggest that mothers appeared to attach greater value to their daughters' education than did fathers. The gender gap in education was smaller in households where mothers had some access to economic resources.

for instance, that education would improve the likelihood of getting a 'good' husband, would reduce the amount of dowry that had to be paid or would teach their daughters how to conduct themselves in 'good' society.

However, there were other women who saw education as a means of strengthening their daughters' fall-back position, allowing them to stand on their own feet, giving them access to better job opportunities than they themselves had been able to aspire to. Dilu, who had left her husband when she realised he was already married with children, pointed out: 'It is important for girls to get an education. They can do many things if they are educated. Above all, it gives them something to rely on. It is an advantage, an asset.' Kohinoor resisted her husband's pressures to give up work because she wanted to ensure that her two daughters went into higher education:

> I want to educate them because I have had to earn my own living. If something happens in their family, they will also be able to earn. I don't want them to have to earn their own living, but if they have to, I don't want them to say, my mother did not educate me so I have to do lowly work (*choto kaj*). I feel ashamed of garment work, for educated people, this is lowly work.

Jahanara's reasons for stressing education for her girls touched on the generalised loss of faith in marriage as a source of security for women:

> Nowadays, girls have no secure future. Even if one gets them married, one cannot feel at peace. Anything can happen . . . We can no longer afford to spend what is needed to marry them off so it is better to spend whatever we can on their education. If there should be any trouble or if their husbands leave them, then they will be able to stand on their own feet.

And along with these various practical reasons for wanting to educate their children, a number also invested education with an emancipatory potential. They saw it as the precondition for becoming *manush* (human), for exercising their critical faculties and control over their own destinies rather than being subject to the arbitrary whims and commands of others. Hanufa, for instance, saw education as one way of helping her daughter to understand her choices and perhaps escape the confining parameters of her own life:

> If I had known before, I would not have got married. So many girls of my age have not got married or have got married at a later age. I do not want my daughter to suffer ... If she is educated, then she can read, write and understand. I could not understand anything. I want my daughter to be educated so that she can work and does not have to struggle ... I want her to get married when she has the capacity for understanding and deciding what is good for her future ... Sometimes I feel if my father had not arranged this marriage, I would not have suffered so much. I don't want her to blame anyone else for her life. She should make her own choices.

Whatever the particular meanings attached to education by different women, the decision to invest in girls' education has a longer term transformatory potential. It addressed a significant and long-standing form of gender inequality in Bangladesh, giving the next generation of young women in Bangladesh an economic capability which the previous generation of women had been denied. And if the mothers were right, and there is some empirical evidence to suggest that they may have been,[12] it offered a resource which would improve the terms on which their daughters conducted their own bargains with patriarchy.

## Assessing the impact of women's wages: the larger picture

The various impacts discussed so far were based on an analysis of women's testimonies on how their wages were spent and what their jobs had meant to them. Our interviews with them also included two questions relating explicitly to this aspect of their testimony, one asking them to list the positive and/or negative changes they perceived to have occurred in their own lives as a result of their

12. For instance, there are studies from Bangladesh to suggest that educated women are less likely to suffer domestic violence (Schuler et al., 1996); more likely to have some role in household decision making (Newell, 1998); and from South Asia, in general, to suggest that they are less likely to discriminate against their own daughters (Dreze and Sen, 1995).

earning status and the other asking them to list the changes they
believed may have occurred in the lives of women in general as a
result of their access to waged employment. Given the general
tenor of the discussion in this chapter, it is not surprising that most
women were very positive in terms of the changes in their own
lives. Out of the 60 interviewed, 44 gave unqualified positive
responses, 11 gave a mixed response and 5 gave largely negative
responses, where the reasons for mixed and negative responses can
be found in some of the disadvantages associated with factory work,
summarised in Appendix 2.

However, in terms of the social impact for women of access to
waged employment in the garment industry, the responses were far
more ambivalent. Only 34 offered unqualified positive evaluations,
16 were mixed in their opinion while 10 gave negative evaluations.
The positive social impacts reported by women workers echoed in
aggregated form the individual impacts we have been discussing.
One set of responses stressed the importance of garment employment in poverty terms, referring to some of the more demeaning
jobs that women had been driven to take up in the past as a result
of economic distress and to the stresses within the family brought
about by scarcity:

> Many are able to help themselves and live on their own, even those who
> have been abandoned. They would have starved or been unable to bring
> up their children.

> I think it has provided opportunities to many women. Even women who
> were on the streets, moving about as fallen women, have had a chance of
> earning their livelihood, they have become decent.

> It has reduced the abuse of women . . . when a family lives on one salary,
> there is usually friction. If one person is earning, he brings home two seers
> of rice but many people want to eat that rice, everyone gets a small portion.
> If two people bring home rice, then everyone has a larger share and things
> are better. Where there is hunger, there is conflict.

Some stressed the importance of some degree of economic self-
reliance at a time when women's traditional sources of security had
been eroded and when dowry demands had inflated the costs of
dependent daughters to parents:

Before, when one had only daughters, one could not feed or educate them. You could not pay their dowries so they suffered. Now the girls can work in garments, the rules have changed a little bit. The value of women has increased. Parents are happy when girls can help to support them.

People like us, poor people, we have benefited. If our father dies, we can work in garments. If our husband dies, we can work in garments. Even if they are alive, we can still contribute.

If garments had not come to Bangladesh, so many women would have had to eat by sacrificing their honour or eating off their brothers. Without these factories, they would have had no honour. Now their value has risen. Daughters whose parents used to curse them, even they get respect now. If husbands die, or don't look after their wives or bring in co-wives, the woman can come here to work. The garments have saved so many lives.

And others emphasised the strengthened position of women, their ability to stand up for themselves, particularly in the context of increasingly fragile marriages:

There has been a great deal of advance. Before women had to be like slaves, work like slaves, they could not say anything. Now they have more courage. Since they have started working, society is giving them greater value. The law is on their side. If their husband misbehaves, they can take him to court and the court will settle the matter.

A girl's value increases when she works, everyone values a girl who has money, it increases in the family too. In my mother's time . . . women had to tolerate more suffering because they did not have the means to become independent, they are better off now, they know about the world, they have been given education, they can work and stand on their own feet. They have more freedom.

However, if the positive evaluations pointed to some of the important changes which were seen to have occurred as a result of the garment industry, the negative ones were a reminder of what had not changed. One factor which featured frequently in the negative evaluations related to status-related social values. In a society where the idea that women would be protected and provided for by male guardians still retained a powerful hold, the presence of women in factory employment was seen to reflect badly on her as well as on her family. Moreover, by bringing together women from very different class backgrounds, the garment factories were seen to reduce all their workers to the same lowest common denominator. The awareness of the persistence of public opinions which associated the garment factories with various forms of sexual impropriety further devalued the work in the eyes of some of the women:

> It is natural that people look down on garment work, it is a lowly job, people from the bustees work here, people from good families work here, everyone is forced here through need. They take anyone, old, young, married, unmarried, you don't need an education. Some people take their wages with a thumb print, some can barely sign their names.

> Women's value has not gone up by coming into garments, it has gone down. They call out to us in the streets, that brings down our value. When illiterate women and educated women are all working together, their value becomes the same.

One of the male workers put the matter bluntly: 'Their value may have gone up but their status has gone down.' In addition, the negative social evaluations also provided a reminder of the persisting asymmetries of the patriarchal contract in Bangladesh, the vulnerabilities it generated for all women, but particularly for women without male support. Access to waged opportunities had not been sufficient to eradicate these inequalities because such inequalities were only partly economic.

> Some people come into garments out of greed, some out of need. No one wants to sacrifice their pride but it has meant a loss of prestige. In social terms, nothing much has changed. A husband is a husband, you cannot be his equal. Even if I were to earn one lakh takas, I could never be anything other than a girl. We can never be equal. That is the way it is and that is the way it should be.

> The women who are respected now are the ones who were respected before. Why should anything change just because they work? ... What respect can a woman have if she has no husband and is struggling for her children to survive? Women are valued when they have a husband and children and come from rich families, it has nothing to do with them working. Even if women earn more than men, they have fewer rights, men have more value than women. If someone asks me who I am, I tell them my father's name, nobody would know my mother's name.

One of the striking features of gender subordination in Bangladesh is the importance of male *protection*, even more than male *provision*, in women's lives. Without male support, women were not only at risk of economic free-fall, but they were also socially vulnerable, denied respect (and accommodation, as Fatema cited earlier in this chapter, was) and in danger of various forms of sexual harassment. As these comments suggest, this was one aspect of patriarchal structures which had not been radically altered by women's access to wages and it influenced how women experienced, and assessed, the impact of their wages.

As we argued in the previous chapter, the resulting generalised insecurity on the part of women, *the fear that women have*, explained their reluctance to engage in open confrontation with their families over their desire to take up paid employment. The analysis in this chapter reinforces this point. It explains why in so many of the cases we have examined, women chose not to exercise control over their own incomes, or when they did, to very consciously utilise them in ways which did not threaten established norms and practices of male privilege within the household. On the contrary, there were far more examples of the discursive and practical efforts that women made to deny that their wages had made any difference to the balance of power within the household. Monowara summarised this strategy succinctly: 'The woman who understands won't show her power; the one who doesn't, will.' It also explains the reluctance of so many women to leave unsatisfactory marriages, even when they entailed extremely violent relationships. While Renu did finally walk out on her abusive husband, it was his failure as breadwinner, rather than his violence, which drove her to this decision. The bleakness of the choices that many women felt they faced was summed up in Rumi's comment, 'What is the harm if your own husband beats you up, at least you are not being beaten by an outsider.'

### Necessary, sufficient or irrelevant?
### Summarising the impact of women's wages

The analysis in this chapter suggests that the impact of women's access to waged work was not a uniform one, because the women themselves were not a uniform category, defined solely or even primarily by their gender. Rather, they were differentiated by class, age and marital status, by their past histories and their current circumstances. They consequently responded to new opportunities from very different material and experiential standpoints and utilised these opportunities very differently. Those who had been propelled into it by circumstances beyond their control were least likely to have experienced it as an expansion of their choices. They tended to attach very little significance to their wage earning capacity beyond its immediate economic implications and were most likely to report negative impacts at both individual as well as on a social level. In individual terms, they regretted that they were no longer able to remain within the norms of cultural propriety, that they had to work in a job with little social standing in the community at large, or at least for women of their class and that they were having to fend for themselves without the support and protection of a male guardian. At the social level, they saw the fact of women having to seek paid work outside the shelter of the home as symbolic of the increasing fragility of women's position in society, a mirror at the social level of the breakdown of the patriarchal contract in their own lives.

However, our analysis has also suggested that, despite their ambivalence about the *social* impact of garment employment on women's lives, the vast majority were largely positive about its implications in their own lives. Most had chosen to take up such employment, entering the labour market for the first time, often migrating into the city on their own to do so. However, what was particularly remarkable about their accounts was not simply that they had initiated the decision to enter the garment industry, but that they had done so in the face of considerable opposition from more powerful members of their families. In that sense, an import-ant decision had already been negotiated in women's favour at a stage which is not generally taken into account in various social science attempts to analyse the relationship between women's wages and intra-household bargaining. Such attempts seek to explore the exercise of decision making authority in relation to the disposal of women's wages, but not in relation to the decision to take up waged employment in the first place. Yet, if we return to the idea of 'control points' as a way of exploring power and agency within the household, then negotiations over women's desire to seek factory employment in a context where they had hitherto been denied such opportunities clearly constituted a first, and very critical, point in the process by which access to waged employment was translated into an impact on women's lives. Once the decision to work had been negotiated in women's favour, all the potentials associated with earning wages became part of the expanded possibilities open to women, *an expansion which they themselves had initiated*, whether or not they then actualised their full potential.

How individual women chose to act subsequently reflected how they were positioned within their families, the quality of their relationships with other family members and their own subjective evaluations of their options, needs and interests. Some sought to achieve objectives which did little to challenge the overall structures of constraint, but went some way towards easing the costs. Others sought to expand their ability to make choices, but in ways which avoided open confrontation, opting instead for private renegotiations which left the public face of male authority intact. Only a few used their wages to bring about an overt, discernible change in intra-household relationships. However, despite this absence of a widespread and dramatic challenge to patriarchy by the women workers, their testimonies pointed to important ways in which their access to waged employment had made a difference to their lives.

It offered them a new sense of identity and self-worth. For poorer women who were accustomed to fending for themselves, factory employment offered higher returns, better working conditions and greater dignity than they had obtained from personalised, isolated and menial forms of employment previously available to them. For women who had never worked before, the key transformation was in their status from economic dependants to economic actors. Their increased sense of self-worth was evident in the way that they stressed that they were standing on their own feet, that they were no longer dependants, that they could buy what they needed when they needed it, and that they did not have to be constant supplicants from husbands, brothers or other family members.

The difference was also manifest in the greater value given to women workers by other household members: the 'perceived value' factor. Regardless of whether their wages were relinquished into a common pool, appropriated by the household head or retained under their own management, it had been earned by their individual efforts and their contribution to the collective welfare of the household was undeniable. While most women did not speak of a straightforward relationship between earnings and claims – intrahousehold allocational processes rarely work so crudely – there were sufficient references to feeling valued, loved and respected as a result of their hard work to suggest that, along with an increase in the collective standard of living, women's own well-being was also being given its due.

Finally, the difference was manifest in the strengthening of women's fall-back position in a variety of ways. In some cases, this strengthening was an intended consequence of their actions. For instance, we noted the precautions that individual women had taken against the breakdown of their marriages: opening their own bank accounts, saving with trusted relatives, the purchase of jewellery and so on. However, women's fall-back position was also strengthened as an unintended consequence of broader changes associated with the emergence of factory employment itself rather than as a result of specific individual actions: the alteration of the economic relationship between parents and daughters; the more routine presence of women in the public arena; the evidence of waiving of dowry demands for working women; the rise in the age of marriage, making the pressure to marry less urgent.

At the same time, we have argued in the course of this chapter that the continued resilience of many aspects of patriarchal constraint, and the specific kinds of risks they generated for women, meant that their search for greater control over their own lives rarely took the form of direct challenge to male authority within the household or of open conflict over intra-household allocations. Rather it was more likely to operate through frequently hidden

expansion of possibilities and potentials, through the quiet renegotiations of allocational priorities and through the disguised
strengthening of their fall-back position. Nevertheless, there were
sufficient numbers of them in our sample who sought to make
choices that went against the grain of long-established custom,
using their strengthened fall-back positions to bargain for a better
deal for themselves, to suggest that their positions had genuinely
been strengthened.

We have noted some examples of these more strategic life
choices in the course of the chapter. Some women used their
greater sense of self-reliance to take a stand against dowry, determined not to marry unless they found a husband who was prepared
to value them for themselves. Some demanded the right to continue to provide financial assistance to their parents after marriage
as *their* precondition for marrying. There were also those divorced
women who were able to take responsibility for themselves and
their children rather than abandon them for the uninviting security
of a second marriage. There were women whose husbands had
beaten, abused, deceived or neglected them who used the
improved credibility of their exit option to renegotiate the terms of
their relationships – and in some cases, to exercise the exit option.
And finally, we noted the greater determination, backed by their
greater financial ability, of women to give their daughters a better
chance in life than they themselves had been given.

## Conclusion

As Renu's description of *the fear that women have* eloquently illustrated, women's ability to exercise agency and make choices in
Bangladesh are not circumscribed by economics alone, but by their
social vulnerability. If they appeared to be prepared to put up with
violence at the hands of more powerful members, to accept the
abuse or neglect meted out to them as the subordinate members,
to remain in degrading relationships regardless of what it might
entail for their well-being and dignity, it was because they feared
the alternative of going it alone far more. The women who actualised the transformatory potential of waged employment and

challenged patriarchal constraint head on were thus a minority in our sample and probably in the total work force. However, they can be seen as pioneers of new social possibilities for women in Bangladesh, the beginning of a trend. They may not have fully freed themselves from the debilitating 'fear that women have', but the transformative nature of some of their actions have made it more likely that the fear will be lessened for succeeding generations of women in Bangladesh who decide to follow in their footsteps and step into the unknown. Social transformation, after all, does not occur as a single discrete moment of rupture with the past, but as a gradual diffusion of new possibilities. As more individuals are prepared to take risks and challenge the old ways of doing things, the risks associated with such behaviour begin to diminish and others find it easier to follow their example. Jorina's husband offered the following succinct summary of the model of social change at work in Bangladesh:

> Women came into this work out of need, the need of the stomach, otherwise they would not have come in such a wave. Shamaj has also understood that there is such a need. Perhaps in the beginning, people used to despise these girls, they saw their behaviour as anti-social, people's minds were suspicious. But that is changing. In this country, we are seeing that wherever there are constraints and rules, as there are with women, when women begin to gradually challenge it, when they become established in this challenge, that rule starts to disappear, people's minds begin to change.

# 6

# Across seven seas and thirteen rivers:[1]
# background to the London study

Let me now turn to the London component of the study. In this introductory chapter I will be providing some background information on the women and families who were interviewed in this second phase of the research. I will be tracing the trajectory through which a large community of Bangladeshis came to be settled in the East End of London in the course of the second half of this century. I will also be examining the historical development of the clothing industry in Britain in order to find out what it was about industry's demand for labour which explained the large involvement of the Bangladeshi community within it. And finally, I will be investigating some of the reasons for the silence on the working conditions of Bangladeshi workers in the debates about exploited labour recounted in Chapter 1.

## The Bangladeshi community and migration to Britain

Like other South Asians, Bangladeshis have been involved in overseas migration to Britain for several hundred years. Historical records show the presence of lascars, as Indian seamen were called, on board the ships of the East India Company from its earliest days (Adams, 1987; Gardner, 1995; Visram, 1986). While those recruited

1. This phrase comes from a collection of Bengali children's stories called Thakur Ma-er Jhuli. It is the way that a lot of stories which deal with distant lands with a mythical quality begin: Once there was a prince who lived in a far off land, 'seven seas and thirteen rivers' away.

from the port of Calcutta came from all over Bengal, there always was a disproportionate flow from the eastern districts of Chittagong, Noakhali and Sylhet. By the mid-twentieth century, however, the main flow of Bangladeshi migration into the UK originated in Sylhet. At the time of the study, Sylhetis were estimated to form 95 per cent of the Bangladeshi population in the UK (House of Commons Report, 1986–87). Mr Ashraf Hussein, one of the older members of the community in London, offered the following explanation for this highly selective process of migration in an interview with Caroline Adams:

> Why did Sylhetis become seamen, although they live so far from the sea? This is what I think. Because Sylhet was not affected by the Permanent Settlement, so that the landholdings remained invested in those who worked them, therefore there was a class of relatively well off small landowners. They were petty bourgeois in the village context, and they had a lot of pride, because they were landowners, and also because they were descended from saints, and not the original sons of the soil. This meant that they were not willing to do manual work there, where they would be seen and shamed, so they went away to a foreign place, where nobody would see them. It was not that they were afraid of hard work, here in England they would do anything, but they did not want to be seen by known people. The reason the farmers needed to go away and work was partly because their lands were subdivided between brothers and also because the economic situation was ruining them. They couldn't get a proper price for their rice and sometimes the merchants cheated them so that they didn't get paid at all. They had to sell their rice at harvest time, when there was plenty of rice and the price was low and then the merchants would keep it and sell it in time of shortage for a high price. Some of the families were quite desperate, and of course, they weren't educated enough to get office jobs, even if there were any, so the ships were the only thing. (cited in Adams, 1987, p. 12)

The different elements in Mr Hussein's explanation are worth considering in some detail. The reference to 'descent from saints' is based on the belief of many Sylhetis that they are descended from holy Arab missionaries and that it was consequently demeaning for them to work as waged labour for others. It is certainly true, as we noted in Chapter 3, that the east of the country, the districts making up the Chittagong division, experienced earlier and more pervasive Islamic penetration as a result of contact with the Arab traders who came to the port of Chittagong. Even today, the inhabitants of Chittagong division, which includes the district of Sylhet, are generally considered to be more conservative in their outlook than the rest of the country. There is some statistical support for this belief. The 1989 Bangladesh Fertility Survey (Cleland et al., 1994) found that 59 per cent of those interviewed from Chittagong division claimed to pray daily compared to 35 per cent in the rest of Bangladesh while 27 per cent claimed 'strict' observance of religious precepts compared to 18 per cent of the rest of the country. Districts in the Chittagong division also had higher levels of fertility and lower percentage of women in paid activity than elsewhere. However, earlier exposure to Arab influence, and higher current levels of religiosity have not resulted in similar migration patterns in these other districts, despite the fact that both Chittagong and Noakhali are coastal districts, while Sylhet is not.

The second element in Mr Hussein's explanation refers to processes of impoverishment and land fragmentation which were creating an increased competition for jobs in a situation of shrinking employment opportunities. On its own, this explanation is not sufficient since these processes were not unique to Sylhet. Indeed, they may have been less severe in Sylhet than in some other districts in Bangladesh. Sylhet had, and still has, a lower density of population than many other districts in Bangladesh and has long been an area of net in-migration, receiving migrant labour from Orissa and other nearby states during the British era to work on its tea estates and, more recently, labourers from the more densely populated neighbouring districts of Mymmensingh and Comilla. It is also worth pointing out that only 0.80 per cent of women migrants into the garment industry in Dhaka came from the district of Sylhet compared to 20 per cent, 23 per cent and 14 per cent from the more densely populated districts of Mymmensingh, Barisal and Comilla respectively (Newby, 1998, Table 4.9).

However, processes of land fragmentation and impoverishment juxtaposed with the third element in Mr Hussein's explanation – the distinctiveness of Sylheti landholding patterns – may provide a more plausible explanation for the district's distinctive migration pattern. Sylhet was transferred from Bengal to Assam by the British in 1874[2] and its land tenure system reformed as part of the Assamese Revenue system. This gave it a very different landholding pattern to the rest of Bengal (Gardner, 1995). Whereas the rest of Bengal was made up of a few large estates which were divided up by their landlords or zamindars to be sublet to numerous tiers of tenant cultivators and sharecroppers, Sylhet was made up of large numbers of independent cultivators. Although few of these cultivators were particularly rich, and some holdings were exceedingly small, they were nevertheless independent farmers.

Ownership of land not only made Sylhetis more reluctant to undertake demeaning manual work for others 'within the sight of known people', but it also allowed them to take the kinds of risks that poorer, landless households generally could not. As land fragmentation reduced the size of farm holdings, migration out in search of work was an obvious option open to some of these families, but their lack of education limited their choice of occupation: 'the ships were the only thing'. Throughout this century, therefore, a steady stream of men left their villages in Sylhet for Calcutta where they sought employment with the Navy or with British-owned shipping lines. As Carey and Shukur have pointed out, those who migrated to the UK out of Sylhet did not come from the poorest sections of the population but from small landowning families who could afford the cost of sea passage.[3] Estimates suggest that only 14 per cent of migrants overseas came from landless families (Gardner, 1995). Tracing the geographical distribution of the 'sending' villages, Gardner has pointed out that Sylhet's main river, the Kusiyara, is characterised by a heavy traffic in people and trade with Calcutta. Some of the main stops for these cargo ships within Sylhet district were Markhuli, Enatganj, Sherpur, Maulvi Bazaar, Baliganj and Fenchuganj. All of these, with the exception of Markhuli, were the main 'Londoni' areas from which the Bangladeshi community in London originates.

2. It was re-assimilated into Bengal after a public referendum in 1947.

3. This was also the pattern among Pakistani migrants to Britain who were disproportionately drawn from small landowning groups and among Indian Punjabi families where richer caste groups, largely owner-occupiers, dominated international migration streams (Ballard, 1983; Kessinger, 1979).

It was the connection with shipping that explained the early concentration of the Bangladeshi community near the docklands of East London. A small Sylheti community had, in fact, settled in East London from the days of the East India Company, but it began to grow in the mid-1930s as Bengali seamen jumped ship and made their way to East London, no matter where their ship had docked, because they knew that they would find help and guidance about work, accommodation and loans from their compatriots. There were then no immigration laws to prevent them coming into Britain, and as members of the Commonwealth, they were entitled to stay and work in the UK as long as they wanted, once they had obtained an identity card. The need to 'jump' reflected the fact that they were breaking their contract with their shipping company which had a two-year warrant to find them. Even so, numbers remained small, confined to unaccompanied men who intended to earn enough money to support their families in Bangladesh with a view to ultimately returning there.

This changed with the introduction of the Commonwealth Immigrants Bill in 1962. In response to the increasing attention being given to the 'race problem' in the media and in parliamentary debates, the bill introduced a voucher system whereby only those citizens of the Commonwealth with Ministry of Labour vouchers would be permitted to come into the UK as primary migrants. As Gardner (1995) points out, although intended to curb immigration, the bill had the opposite effect, as the prospect of earning higher wages combined with the fear of further restrictions led to a rush for permits. However, the 'race' problem began to take on ever-more alarmist proportions; Enoch Powell's 'rivers of blood' speech was symptomatic of the time. In 1965, the government introduced restrictions on the number of vouchers to be issued each year so that they fell from 30,130 in 1963 to about 8500 after the restrictions. The second Commonwealth Immigrants Act of 1968 introduced yet further restrictions, this time very explictly aimed at curbing 'New Commonwealth immigration', as it was euphemistically put. By the 1970s, all new immigration had stopped and only dependants of those already resident were permitted entry into Britain.

The voucher system helped to reinforce the pre-existing Sylheti

predominance in migration streams from Bangladesh since those
with kinsmen and fellow-villagers stood a much higher chance of
being sponsored than those without any prior links in Britain.
Networks thus continued to play an important role in facilitating
migration. Immigrants from the 'Londoni' areas in Sylhet, who had
settled in the UK earlier on, now acted as brokers in assisting others
from the village to obtain vouchers and to provide contacts and
information once they arrived in the UK. The Bangladeshis who
emigrated during the late 1950s and early 1960s had taken jobs
wherever they could find them. Many settled in the Spitalfields
ward of the Tower Hamlets borough in East London, not far from
the docklands where Bangladeshi seamen had jumped ship in the
early years. Others, however, went further afield to other towns and
cities where work was available. Jobs varied from place to place, but
were usually in unskilled or semi-skilled manual labour: cotton
mills in Oldham, steel in Sheffield and Scunthorpe, heavy engineering and foundries in Leeds. As a House of Commons report noted
in 1986: 'Sometimes the main reason for the present existence of a
town's Bangladeshi community is a single factory, such as the
Birmid factory in Smethwick, now closed' (HMSO, 1986, p. v).

Like the Pakistani community, Bangladeshis who came to the UK
had started out as 'sojourners' rather than 'settlers', hoping to
make their fortune in the UK and to return home as rich men of
high status (Carey and Shukur, 1985). By the late 1960s, these
hopes had begun to fade. They could only find jobs as unskilled
labour, wages which were not sufficient to finance the dream of
return, nor had the economic situation improved sufficiently at
home to entice them back. They began to bring their wives and
children over to join them in the UK. However, the process was a
slow one due to a variety of factors, including the high costs of
travel, the dearth of suitable housing, harsh application of already
cumbersome immigration procedures, growing racial harassment,
the concern of men about the exposure of their women to Western
values and influence (Carey and Shukur, 1985). Many of the
women joined their men in the UK in the 1980s, many years after
the latter had first come to Britain. According to the 1981 census,
there were around 2 men to every woman in the Bangladeshi
community in Tower Hamlets, compared to the borough equiva-

lent of 1 woman to every 0.98 men. By 1985, there were about 100,000 Bangladeshis in Britain, according to the British government and 160,000 according to the Bangladeshi government (see HMSO 1986). Recent research supports the figure of 162,835 in 1991 (Paul Barker, *Guardian*, 4 August). It is estimated that around 50,000 live in East London (Hilary Clarke, *Independent on Sunday*, 1998).

The community always retained its links with the East End of London, with the degree of concentration becoming greater rather than less over time as the result of a steady influx of Bangladeshi workers laid off from manufacturing industry in the Midlands and the North during the recession in the 1970s (Carey and Shukur, 1985). The borough of Tower Hamlets alone accounted for a fifth of all Britain's Bangladeshis, while the Bangladeshi population in Tower Hamlets accounted for about 9 per cent of the borough's population. In other London boroughs, it rarely exceeded 1.5 per cent of the population. Estimates by members of the community put the total Bangladeshi population in the borough at about 26,000. As with other areas with high concentrations of South Asians, an infrastructure of groceries, halal butchers, sari shops, travel agents and mini cab companies, centred around Brick Lane, Cannon Street Road and Hessel Street, developed over time to cater to the needs of the community.

However, the bulk of Bangladeshi men were employed in just three sectors: catering, retail and manufacturing, primarily clothing. The Bangladeshi dominance of 'Indian' restaurants in the UK was a response to the apparently insatiable British taste for 'curry' but its origins can be traced to their migration history: 'Sylhetis gained something of a monopoly of work as cooks and galley hands aboard British ships and many of them continued in this speciality when they came ashore, establishing tea houses and cafes along the waterfront' (Ballard and Ballard, 1977 cited in Carey and Shukur, 1985, p. 409). However, it was their involvement in the clothing industry which is of particular concern in this book and I want to interrupt our account of the community in London with a brief historical account of the industry in the British context. I have drawn particularly heavily on Morris (1986), as well as Phizacklea (1990), for this. As we will see, the picture that emerges bears out

Phizacklea's point that the conditions which led to the involvement
of an immigrant group like the Bangladeshis in London's rag trade
were not so much an echo of the past, as a continuity with it.

## Echoes of the past:
### women, immigrants and the clothing industry

Before the Industrial Revolution, tailoring was a handicraft occupation in Britain carried out by men working on their own, making
up cloth which they or their customer had bought, often travelling
from house to house, village to village. The early eighteenth
century saw the emergence of a system of master tailors/shopkeep-
ers who bought material and employed journeymen tailors on a
waged basis to work on the production of garments for sale, thus
laying the foundations for a market in 'ready-made' clothing, where
one pattern was used to cut out multiple garments rather than a
single garment being made to measure for a particular customer.
The journeymen tailors were still skilled craftsmen responsible for
making most of the garment, but they now sometimes gave over
simple finishing tasks like buttons and buttonholing to women in
their families. As the market for ready-made clothing expanded, a
system of subcontracting began to develop. Journeymen tailors
subcontracted work from master tailors on an 'outwork' basis,
making the garments in their own workshops or from their homes.

The sewing machine was invented in 1851, followed in 1858 by
the invention of the band knife which allowed several garments to
be cut at the same time. The mechanisation of production led to a
further expansion of the market in ready-made clothes and the
possibility of the greater subdivision of the production process into
a series of increasingly simpler tasks. Certain distinct categories of
workers began to be increasingly associated with the clothing
industry as these various changes occurred. Their presence was
linked to certain features of the industry pointed to by contemporary investigations. One was the marked fluctuation in the demand
for certain types of clothing, so that periods of overwork were often
accompanied by periods when there was no work available. The
second was the rise in the practice of subcontracting, with the

increasing possibility of contracting out increasing stages of production to middlemen who would then contract out the work even further. This allowed for a degree of flexibility to be built into the process to allow for fluctuations in demand. The third feature, which followed from the first two, was the 'sweated labour' conditions which prevailed in the industry, consisting of low wages, long hours and insanitary work conditions. 'Sweating' was not unique to the tailoring trade, but closely associated with it in the public mind from very early on because of early research carried out by *The Lancet*, the journal of the British Medical Association, in 1887 into the 'sweated' conditions in the tailoring trade (cited in Morris, 1986, p. 80).

As the industry began to move away from craft production, where the tailor made the garment almost throughout, to a stage where it became possible to subdivide the production process into a series of simpler tasks, mainly carried out within small workshops or from the home, more women and girls began to be drawn into its labour force. The dilution of skills and the casualisation of employment associated with the new forms of organisation led to a fragmentation of the production process to such an extent that the worker responsible for carrying out these activities had to accept whatever remuneration they were offered. There were various reasons why women constituted a cheaper and more vulnerable labour force than men, and hence the ones who were drawn into this form of work. The British counterpart of the twin ideologies of male breadwinner/female dependant, and the reality of women's greater responsibility for domestic work and child care served, in the first instance, to differentiate the terms on which women and men entered the labour market.[4] It was generally assumed that men worked to earn the 'family wage' while women worked to simply

4. Although female labour force participation has been on the rise throughout this century, from 27 per cent of total employees in 1881, to 34 per cent in 1948, to 42 per cent in 1980 (Dex, 1985), women remain overwhelmingly concentrated in specific areas of the labour market and in a narrow range of less well-paid jobs. Between 1841 and still in 1911, 75 per cent of working women in Britain were concentrated in domestic service, textiles and clothing (Scott and Tilly, 1980). Even in the 1970s, 5 out of 27 industries in the UK accounted for around 70 per cent of women workers (Chiplin and Sloane, 1976).

supplement it. In addition, the increasing possibility of subcontracting out parts of the work, such as button sewing and plain machining, to the home, allowed employers to take advantage of even cheaper captive segments of the female work force: 'the elderly, the sick, and the young mother tied to her home by growing children' (Morris, 1986, p. 40).

However, also important in contributing to women's status as exploited workers in the labour market was the role of the trade unions. As in every industry where there was skilled and well-paid work, the craft unions in the clothing industry fought to ensure that their privileges were not eroded through competition with cheaper labour. Skilled tailors were among the first to organise in defence of their privileged status, constituting themselves as 'closed groups' in order to exclude unskilled and female workers from their ranks. Access to the status of skilled workmen was strictly controlled by the apprenticeship system and was not open to women who were identified as the major route through which male skills could be diluted and wages lowered. Although the unions resisted most attempts to legislate for the condition of male workers, believing this to be a matter of negotiation between union and employer, they gave strong support to any measure which restricted the hours, conditions and extent of female labour. However, because it proved impractical to seek the total prohibition of female labour, they concentrated their demands on the introduction of protective legislation, with the aim of abolishing homeworking entirely and seeking to place restrictions on the employment of married women. Sometimes this protectionism was defended in blunt terms, as in this letter from an English worker to *Trades Newspaper* of 16 October 1825:

> The labouring men of this country . . . should return to the good old plan of subsisting their wives and wages of their *own* labour, and they should demand wages high enough for this purpose . . . By doing this, the capitalist will be obliged to give the same wages to men alone which they now give to men, women and children . . . I recommend my fellow labourers, in preference to every other means of limiting the number of those who work for wages, to prevent their wives and children from competing with them in the market, and beating down the price of labour. (cited in Humphries, 1980, p. 157)

More often, however, trade unionists were able to mobilise discourses about family, motherhood and the moral fibre of the nation which converged with those of various social reformers in support of their demands. George Shipton, Secretary of the London Trades Council told the Royal Commission on Labour that his objections to an increase in the number of women in waged work was based on his anxiety about the 'wholesale degenerating influence' which occurred when men allowed their wives and children to go to work instead of acting as the responsible breadwinner and keeping them at home. Henry Broadhurst, Secretary of the TUC's Parliamentary Committee argued that male trade unions had to think about the future of their children and of the country and 'that it was their duty as men and husbands to use their utmost efforts to bring about a condition of things, where their wives should be in their proper sphere at home, instead of being dragged into competition for livelihood against the great and strong men of the world' (cited Morris, 1986, p. 120).

Although much of the protective legislation was ostensibly aimed at married women, and explained why most of the female workforce until the early decades of this century were made up of young single women from the rural areas,[5] it served to define all women as a 'special' and subordinate category of worker in the market place. Not all women lost out as a result of these restrictions. Those belonging to the families of organised male labour benefited indirectly through the increased level of wages that their men were able to bring home. On the other hand, there were others who did not have access to this 'family wage'. Restrictions on their ability to compete in an open labour market served to concentrate them in low-paid, badly organised sectors of the economy, those most likely to be characterised by sweated conditions.[6] In this category were

5. In 1911, 69 per cent of all single women in Britain were in the workforce compared to only 10 per cent of married women (Scott and Tilly, 1980). Of all working women in Britain, 14 per cent were married in 1911, 43 per cent in 1951 and 59 per cent in 1970. Thus, the post-war rise in female labour force participation has been largely a rise in the participation of married women (Dex, 1985).

6. Between 1841 and still in 1911, 75 per cent of working women in Britain were concentrated in domestic service, textiles and clothing (Scott and Tilly, 1980; Morris, 1986).

'unsupported women' as well as the wives and children of the casual labourers who, in the London context, were made up of men thrown out of work in the declining industries as well as rural migrants.[7] The existence of this underemployed male labour force, eking out an existence in the building trades and on the docks, made it imperative for women from their families to seek out some form of work. By 1891, 60 per cent of workers in the tailoring trade in East London were women (Morris, 1986, p. 12).

The other social category with a sizeable presence in the clothing industry were immigrants, at that time, largely Jewish immigrants. A Jewish community was already in existence by the nineteenth century in some of the larger cities of Britain, particularly London, but also Leeds and Manchester. Prevented from becoming City freemen until 1832, they had set up a flourishing second-hand clothes business at the City limits which subsequently evolved into a wholesale business in ready-to-wear clothing. The wholesale clothier cut out cloth in stock sizes and gave it out to the lowest bidding 'sweater' who also acted as 'middleman'. His workshop was at home where his wife and children worked along with the wives and children from casual labouring families in the docks and building trades. When new waves of Jewish refugees fleeing from pogroms in Russia and Poland came into Britain between the 1880s and 1914, they gravitated naturally towards areas such as clothing, with an already established Jewish presence. As Phizacklea points out, not only did many of these immigrants come equipped with the necessary skills, having been tailors in their homelands, but faced with problems of language and anti-semitism, it was to be expected that friends, relatives and co-ethnics would enter an industry where their compatriots had already created a niche. Large numbers

---

7. Analysing 1901 Census returns, Bowley (1921) estimated that around 9 per cent of manual workers' households were dependent solely on a female breadwinner, 41 per cent which were solely dependent on a man's wage and 48 per cent were dependent on a combination of incomes from husband, wife, siblings and children. At the same time, a higher proportion of women in waged labour were sole breadwinners of their households compared to the percentage of such women in the population at large. Charles Booth (1902) pointed out that of 82,000 persons engaged in the clothing trades in 1891 who were classified as heads of households, 30,000 were women. This did not take account of households where men still appeared as heads, even if women were the sole breadwinners.

settled in East London so that by 1900, it was calculated that nearly one person in every three in Whitechapel, and one in every four in the parish of St George was Jewish.

As foreign immigrants, Jewish workers were targeted as the cause of various problems faced by the indigenous working class (Morris, 1986). There was widespread support in the TUC by the 1880s for restrictions on 'alien immigration' as it was felt that by cutting down on the number of unskilled Jewish workers coming into the country, conditions in the 'sweated trades' might be improved. Although 'sweated' labour had been a feature of the industry from the outset, it became closely associated in the public mind with foreign immigrants. Indeed, it was the starting assumption of the House of Lords Select Committee set up in 1888 to look into the problem of 'sweated labour'. However, the committee subsequently accepted that sweated conditions existed even in the absence of immigrants and turned its attention on the problems of homeworkers instead. There was also a widespread perception that Jews undercut English workers, forcing them into casual work. A London dock labourer giving evidence to the 1892 Royal Commission on Labour argued that 'the foreigners' were averse to the hard work and hence their gravitation towards 'easier' trades and the resulting displacement of the English workers:

> They go into shoe-making and tailoring and cabinet making. That is more easy and cleaner for them: and should a foreigner go in to do that to all intents and purposes an Englishman will have to to step out. It is the Englishman that comes to the dock. (quoted in Jones, 1971: 110, cited in Phizacklea, p. 26)

Despite the absence of conclusive evidence on this issue, hostility to foreign immigrants led to demands for immigration control which were incorporated into the Aliens Act of 1902.

## Gender and race in the London clothing industry

This disproportionate presence of women and immigrants has always been a particular characteristic of the London industry.

Historically, it was made up of two sections which have evolved somewhat differently: ladies' ready-made suits and coats and men's and boy's outerwear. Men's outerwear, particularly the cheaper ready-made end rather than the high class 'bespoke' end, is a reasonably standardised product and lent itself more easily to the subdivision of various operations so that semi-skilled machinists, mainly women, were recruited in increasing numbers very much earlier into this section of the industry. It was in this ready-made men's wear section that power-driven machines were first introduced, changing workshops into factories overnight, usually on the same location since new premises were neither sought nor available. Machinists in these large factories, employing around 300–500 workers, were both men and women, but men tended to be assigned to tasks classified as skilled, as defined by the London Tailor's Society in the mid-nineteenth century (Birnbaum, n.d.), while women were assigned to tasks defined as semi-skilled. However, the basis on which these definitions were made were extremely dubious. As Birnbaum pointed out, when women replaced men in tasks, the skill content of the task was seldom reduced, but the task was reclassified from skilled to semi-skilled.

The women's wear industry was largely centred in London. Women's suits and coats had originally been imported from Germany. Production was begun in Britain by Jewish refugees who came to settle in London, Leeds and Manchester from Russia and Poland (Morris, 1986). Women's wear then, as now, was a highly differentiated product, limiting the subdivision of tasks, and prone to seasonal fluctuations and changes in fashion, limiting the size of retail orders and hence the length of the production run. The women's wear industry in London was dominated by the Jewish community and the family unit was the main source of labour. Small Jewish-owned firms also played a key role in developing the subcontracting system in London. Jewish men who had been working on piece rates as tailors in workshops, or in their homes, for women's outerwear firms began taking on contracts for the production of clothing in bulk.

Factories tended to be small in this sector, seldom employing more than 150 workers. In contrast to men's wear, where machinists were mainly female and classified as semi-skilled, all the machinists in women's wear were male and classified as skilled. The rationale given for this discrepancy was that women's coats were of heavier weight, women's clothing was more complicated and hence required greater 'discretion' on the part of the machinist. The equation of masculinity with skill was evident in the practice of apprenticing a boy to the tailor. Women were generally employed as handworkers in the industry and were usually Jewish. The work force in a typical factory was around 60 per cent men.

The inter-war years saw a number of changes in the manufacture of clothing in Britain. Increased concentration in the retail sector allowed for longer runs and production planning. Larger firms, particularly in menswear which had fewer fashion fluctuations, could benefit from the possibility for further subdivisions of the machining stage of production into distinct stages so that instead of making the whole garment ('make through'), each machinist would only make one stage of it ('section work'). This period was marked by growth of larger manufacturing firms and also of mass unionisation. There was mass recruitment of women to lower-paid 'semi-skilled' machining jobs while the higher-paid skilled tasks of pattern-making and cutting remained in male hands. In tailored women's wear, similar changes brought non-Jewish women into this sector but with a less dramatic change in the sex ratio. Jewish male machinists continued to maintain a presence in the factories and to be classified as 'skilled'.

The clothing industry has undergone further restructuring in the period since the Second World War. Overcrowded factory premises, shortages of skilled labour and the high charges of the subcontracting firms in the traditional large urban centres led the larger manufacturers to move out to new development areas in places such as South Wales, where premises cost less and where the absence of alternative job opportunities for women assured a cheap and plentiful supply of trainable 'green' labour. Decentralisation was particularly rapid in London. Premises were costly and opportunities for women workers arising from the strength of other sectors of the London economy reduced the supply available at the wages on offer. The larger premises available in the new areas allowed factories to reorganise production methods, further fragmenting and 'sectionalising' tasks, while improvements in road transport allowed this decentralisation to occur without loss of contact with suppliers and buyers.

However, not all sectors of the industry had equal incentive to relocate. Instead, the post-war organisation of clothing production gave rise to a dual structure. Production of long runs of relatively standardised items of clothing, such as men's wear, which had been carried out in the larger firms, as well as of good quality dressmaking at competitive prices for multiple retailers such as M&S, BHS and Littlewoods, were the sections of the industry which had most to gain from the economies of scale offered by the new sites. They were the ones to relocate and to set up production in modern, well laid out medium-sized factories, using up-to-date machinery and a unionised work force. However, the main part of women's wear remained in London. The London industry has retained its comparative advantage for two very polarised segments of the clothing market: up market haute couture where proximity to designers, retailers and export buyers remains a crucial advantage, on the one hand, and down market production of short runs of fashion garments for small boutiques and street markets, and for filling in temporary shortages of low quality garments for the retail chains.

For London firms to retain their competitive edge in these sectors, they had to be able to turn orders around extremely rapidly and to respond to frequent changes in fashion. The key to their success lay in the malleability of their labour force, the ability to take on and lay off workers as orders fluctuate and to impose compulsory overtime to meet deadlines. The industry remained reliant on a dense network of subcontracting relationships. There were a few larger manufacturers who either had their own factory premises or simply acted on behalf of the retailers and wholesalers in finding contractors to take on production and taking responsibility for supply of the finished product. Cut-make-and-trim (CMT) or make-and-trim firms worked on a short-term contract basis for manufacturers who supplied materials, patterns and sometimes assisted with premises and machinery. They either completed the whole production process or else assembled pre-cut garments. They either had all their workers on-site ('indoor workers') or no on-site workers or a combination of on-site workers and outworkers ('outdoor workers'). Industrial outworkers worked on a subcontracted basis for manufacturers or contractors, either carrying out production on their own premises or contracting out yet further to homeworkers. Finally, at the end of the subcontracting chain were the domestic outworkers or homeworkers, individuals working from home on order supplied by outworkers or CMT firms.

The following description from Wray paints a picture of the post-war clothing industry in London:

> It is here that a large number of small, inconvenient and relatively badly equipped factories dating from pre-war days, continue to exist, and even to flourish. Many of them are outdoor factories and, although there was a tendency for firms to switch from outdoor to indoor production immediately after the war, the outdoor contractor seems to have regained much of his pre-war importance in London. There are acute labour difficulties in London (as in other pre-war clothing centres) but they have been met by utilising all available sources of labour, including the post-war influx of Cypriots (many of whom are trained tailors) and Jamaicans. There are few bars of race, creed or colour in the London clothing factories. Some manufacturers notably blouse makers make good use of home workers. (Wray, 1957, p. 63)

Thirty years on, Phizacklea suggests, many aspects of this description still hold. The dualism has persisted and become far more clear cut with the post-war immigration into the inner cities. However, there have also been some changes. The power of the multiple retailers to dictate their requirements increased considerably since the 1950s. The post-war shift into longer runs of standardised production in the new larger factories had been encouraged by those retailers who wanted good quality goods at competitive prices rather than high fashion. However, it was these retailers who by the 1960s were beginning to look towards the low-wage economies of Taiwan, South Korea and Hong Kong, where a highly disciplined and non-unionised labour force could produce the same quality goods at a fraction of the price.

The availability of cheap locations to source production had an undeniable impact on the British clothing industry, but it was not a straightforward one. First of all, as we saw in Chapter 1, the import threat was not entirely from cheap Third World economies, despite the widespread perception to this effect in Britain. While imports into Britain doubled between 1980–86, about half of the increase came from developed countries, largely within the EEC. Secondly, not all sectors were equally affected. Import penetration went much further in the production of standardised clothing such as men's shirts (75 per cent) than it did in unstandardised women's fashionwear (28 per cent). Technical innovation to increase labour productivity was one option for British industry to restore its competitive edge in the international markets. However, while there was some diffusion of the use of microelectronic equipment in the pre-assembly stages of grading, marking and cutting, the assembly stage, which represented 80 per cent of total labour costs and 30–40 per cent of total costs, remained untouched. The limpness of the material made mechanisation in the most labour-intensive stage extremely difficult and, as long as there was cheap labour available, uneconomical.

Instead, as Phizacklea points out, 'clothing manufacturers off-loaded their high-risk, unpredictable sectors of demand (fashion clothes) and maintained flexibility by increased subcontracting domestically to the many small inner-city firms dominated by ethnic entrepreneurs and labour' (p. 48). The vast majority of entrepreneurs as well as labour in the London clothing industry were of ethnic minority origin. According to the 1979 Labour Force Survey, 43 per cent of the 60,000 strong work force in the London garment industry was drawn from the ethnic minorities. This estimate did not include homeworkers who were largely unregistered and, hence, escaped official data-gathering exercises.

Still further changes occurred by the beginning of the 1980s. The share of imports in total sales had grown steadily from 8 per cent in 1954 to 32 per cent in 1979, so that domestic manufacturers had lost a sizeable share of their market to overseas suppliers. Against this background, the recession of 1979 had a drastic effect. It led to a price war between high-street retailers struggling to secure a share of the shrinking market and to a phenomenal rate of closure of factories in the inner cities. Manufacturers had to find a way of cutting their costs and of passing the reduction in their profits down the subcontracting chain. An increased reliance on subcontractors allowed them to pass on the risks of fashion change to the smaller units who were next in line. For the smaller units, survival depended on the ability to move in and out of open economy, evading legislation about workers' rights and taxation. As a 1984 GLC report (cited in Mitter, 1986, p. 50) noted:

> A common method used by contractors to deal with the financial problems is to liquidate the business and start up shortly afterwards under another name, thus avoiding creditors. This is often done with the same premises, same machinery and same workers. One group of clothing workers in London has been employed over the last five years by one employer operating through no less than eight different companies in succession.

A survey by Phizacklea in early 1985 suggested that retailers targeting the fashion-oriented, over-25-year-old market were now generally buying their clothing from factories outside London. There were only twenty-five large registered manufacturing firms employing over fifty workers left in London producing for this sector. They tended to be unionised and paid their workers above minimum wages. A second group, also manufacturers, were involved in more price competitive clothing for low-price retail chains, supermarkets and mail order firms such as C&A, Littlewoods, Tesco and Asda. These were far more heavily involved in subcontracting out work to outside contractors and to CMT firms. They paid their in-house workers at least the agreed minimum rates with holiday pay. The final group were the most numerous and also the most representative of the London industry. It was made up of 'manufacturers' who had no production facilities of their own, or else very skeletal staff for finishing garmernts as well as the great mass of CMT firms, often existing in highly precarious subcontractual positions. CMT firms were largely owned by ethnic minority entrepreneurs and many had ethnically homogeneous work forces. They produced high-fashion, medium-to-poor quality garments for the under-25-year-olds. A report by the National Union of Tailors and Garment Workers and the Hackney Trade Union Support Group provided a vivid description of this end of the London economy:

> The employers operate in a ruthlessly competitive market ... trying to make a living in a very insecure industry. They mainly do outwork for larger firms. Operations like design, marketing, forward planning, skills training just do not exist in these firms. The employers operate under very

tight margins and once they fail to fulfil an order, at the price, and in the time, demanded by the manufacturer they will lose future orders from that manufacturer. Many of the employers are quite ruthless, they operate on the backs of their workers ... they employ direct a small number of workers (often so-called 'self-employed' or 'off the book'), they do not deduct the proper tax and national insurance, they do not pay overtime or holiday pay, they do not abide by the employment and health and safety at work legislation. All these practices keep th employers' overheads to a minimum. The firms are in fact producing fashion garments for the major fashion multiples like British Home Stores, Chelsea Girl and Richard Shops. (NUTGW, 1983 cited in Phizacklea, 1990, p. 6)

## The Bangladeshi community and the London clothing industry

For the Bangladeshi community which settled in London's East End, the rag trade was a major source of employment and the pattern of economic activity within the community was closely bound up with the changing fortunes of the industry. From the early 1960s onwards, Bangladeshi men, emigrating largely on their own, had provided the bulk of the labour for the clothing trade in the East End of London where both the community and the industry were concentrated. Most of the larger manufacturing firms in the area were owned by Jewish and Cypriot entrepreneurs, while the smaller ones were owned by Indians and Pakistanis. Although some Bangladeshis had developed new areas of the garment trade, in suede and leather, they were less involved on the business side of the industry compared with members of some of the other South Asian communities. Instead, most Bangladeshis (about 70 per cent) worked as unskilled or semi-skilled manual workers. The London industry went from a situation when machinists in the women's wear sector were largely Jewish males to a 50:50 balance by 1950, to 60 per cent female machinists by the 1960s. By the 1970s, however, Bangladeshi men formed the largest single group of machinists in this sector and clothing provided 20 per cent of the available jobs in the Tower Hamlets area where most of them lived (Phizacklea, 1990; Carey and Shukur, 1985).

Bangladeshi workers were mainly concentrated in the small

factories and outdoor units where they formed the most casualised sections of the labour force. They tended to be paid in cash on a piece rate basis; this was 'clear money' which allowed both employer and employee to avoid tax and national insurance payments. A report by Duffy (1979, cited in Mitter, 1986) provides a graphic account of the organisation of labour in a white-owned clothing factory in 1979 and of the insecure position of Bangladeshi machinists within it:

> The factory was divided into three separate sections, each in its own building. One of these buildings was used as a cutting room, where there were six white cutters. The cutters were weekly paid. Another building, with perhaps 40 to 45 workers, performed the specialist machining, finishing, and top pressing functions, producing the racks of garments ready for dispatch. These workers were racially mixed, with perhaps half of them Bengalis. The employer said they were weekly paid.
>
> The third building, the 'machine room', was occupied by about 45 young Bengalis, all engaged in flat machining ready cut work from the cutting room, which was later passed to the finishing room. The premises belonged to the employer, the machines belong to the employer, the work belonged to the employer, but none of these Bengali machinists were actually employed by the firm.
>
> They were divided into several 'units', each with one of the Bengalis as a 'governor', who was responsible for negotiating for batches of the ready-cut work on a sub-contract basis from the cutting room. These machinists were paid on a piece-work basis, by their respective 'governors'. The 'employer' has no legal responsibility for any of these workers. Asked what happened when there was a shortage of work, the 'employer' replied that it was not his problem: 'that is up to them', he said. As they were not employed by him, he did not have to make them redundant. If there was no work, there was no employment. (Duffy, 1979: 36)

Duffy also records the attitudes of the white workers towards the Bangladeshis:

> . . . the white cutter complained that the Bengalis claimed tax allowance for their children in Bangladesh. Somewhat inconsistent with this remark was his further claim that 'they don't pay tax' . . . The man further contradicted himself when he remarked that 'they have accountants who come in . . . but they are Indians too'. (p. 37)

However, even these jobs began to be cut back by the beginning of the 1980s as more employers began 'putting out' work to the homeworking sector. As Mitter (1986) points out, in an economic environment where pressures on margins were intense, overhead costs on electricity or rental on machinery could be reduced through relegation to the homeworker. It was also easier to avoid the scrutiny of Inland Revenue and VAT officials, particularly given the intensified activities of the Inland Revenue Fraud Squad in 1981–82 to end the payment of 'clear wages' and tax evasions. Large numbers of factories began closing down as more and more work was 'put out' to homeworkers (Birnbaum et al., 1981). The effects were devastating for the Bangladeshi community, where levels of unemployment among men ranged between 60–70 per cent. With the rise in homeworking orders, Bangladeshi women had both the economic need and also the opportunity to increase their homeworking activity. Many became the primary earners for their families.

While the burgeoning of the 'ethnic economy' became the subject of academic research and media attention, its true size and rate of growth during this period went largely unacknowledged at the official level. The paradoxical finding, that, although investment in the clothing industry had fallen dramatically since 1974 and was at an all time low in 1982, there had not been any significant decline in productivity growth in the industry was attributed by a major study into the industry to a rise in labour productivity through the shedding of labour, increased scrapping of older plants and some investment in labour-saving technology (Hoffman and Rush, 1985). However, Mitter pointed out that this calculation attributed the entire output of the clothing industry to officially registered employees, a dubious assumption in an industry which had always operated in the 'twilight area between the regulated and unregulated economy' (p. 63). It took no account of the possibility that labour may have been shed from the officially registered economy in order to shift production to smaller, often illegal outdoor units, but also increasingly to homeworkers. Indeed, a smaller scale study of the Cypriot community in London suggested in the percentage of homeworkers in the total work force in clothing had risen from 40 per cent in 1979 to 60 per cent in 1984 (Mavrou, interview with Mitter, 1986, p. 59).

There were obvious reasons why Hoffman and Rush had failed to take account of the vast network of small firms which proliferated in the inner cities since, until 1985, the Business Statistics Office had not collected data on firms employing less than twenty people. Improvements in its data collection procedures allowed for a much more accurate picture to be obtained of the industry. Thus, as Phizacklea noted, under the old procedures it had been estimated that there were 1707 firms in women's and girls' light outerwear, lingerie and infant wear. Under the new procedures, it was found that there were 3172 firms with less than 10 employees in women's light outerwear alone in 1987 (Phizacklea, 1990, p. 54). Seventy-two per cent of units in the women's fashion wear sector employed less than 10 people in 1987. Focusing on this segment of the industry, Mitter (1986) calculated that a total of 13,100 jobs had been shifted out of the factories to create the equivalent of 17,030 jobs for the sweatshops and domestic outworkers between 1978 and 1983.

If the small firms and outdoor units which proliferated in the inner cities tended to be overlooked by researchers and official bodies, the homeworkers in the garment industry were even less visible. A trade union official from the industry was cited in the minutes of evidence to the House of Commons Select Committee on Employment, April, 1981 as declaring, 'We have no idea of the degree of homework, let alone who is participating in it' (quoted in Allen and Wolkowitz, 1987, p. 31). According to Department of Employment research on homeworking, manufacturing homework had become a relative rarity and had been overtaken in significance by white-collar homeworking based on the new information technology (Hakim, 1984) while in a later study, Hakim maintained that ethnic minorities were under-represented in the homeworking labour force (Hakim, 1987a). However, she subsequently acknowledged that the 1981 Homeworking Survey did not in fact provide any information on the proportion of home-based workers who were from ethnic minorities (Hakim, 1987b).

Phizacklea has pointed to some of the methodological flaws which gave rise to Hakim's conclusions. First of all, the 1981 Homeworking Survey, on which they were based, used a definition of homework which covered anyone who worked at home, including self-employed workers and independent contractors. A sample of homeworkers based on this definition would inevitably under-represent ethnic minorities who tended to be concentrated in manufacturing homework. Furthermore, it was collected on a random national basis, whereas manufacturing homeworkers were disproportionately concentrated in areas of the country associated with hosiery and clothing production. Finally, the studies had not taken into account factors particular to immigrant women engaged in homeworking which might militate against their inclusion in the sample: language barriers, the fear of many immigrant women to open their doors to strange interviewers and anxieties about the legality of what they are doing.

Official data collection methods probably continue to underesti-mate the level of economic activity among the ethnic minorities, given that many of them are likely to work in the 'twilight area between the regulated and unregulated economy'(Mitter, 1986). It almost certainly underestimates the extent of homeworking. It is worth pointing out, for instance, that although official estimates of female labour force participation rates among Bangladeshis and Pakistanis in 1977 was 17 per cent, a study of the Pakistani com-munity carried out by Anwar (1979) around that period found that the majority of its women were active in the homeworking sector which had been excluded from the official statistics. Consequently, a 1995 Labour Force Survey which found employment rates to be 20 per cent among Bangladeshi women is probably an underesti-mate, particularly given that none of the employed women were classified as working in the manufacturing sector (HMSO, 1996).

Returning to the discussion in Chapter 1, therefore, I would suggest that at least one reason for the deafening silence on the conditions of Bangladeshi homeworkers in the debates about pro-tection from 'unfair competition' related to this invisibility of homeworkers in general. However, I would also suggest a second reason which emerged in the course of the research carried out by Nick Chisolm and myself during the World Development Move-ment (WOM) campaign. This related to a more particular view of homeworking as a logical cultural choice for 'Asian' Muslim women and hence not necessarily a matter for public concern. Certainly, cultural explanations were to the forefront in the interviews that Nick Chisolm and I carried out with trade unionists and employers in the East End of London in 1985. There was little evidence that they linked the concentration of the Bangladeshi community in very narrow and specific niches in the labour market to their economic marginalistion. Rather they saw it as confirmation of the different culture of immigrants, their desire to stick together and indeed their *preference* for the kinds of jobs they had.

In the course of the research, I was struck by the very contrasting discourses of 'culture', on the one hand, and 'economics' on the other, which came into play in discussions about different categories of British workers. The notion of 'culture' rarely figured when the labour market behaviour of white workers, whether male or female, was under discussion. Instead, the discussion focused on such issues as relative skills, wage differentials, costs of child care, trade union membership and collective bargaining power. However, in conversations about Bangladeshi workers, and workers from other Asian communities within the UK, a highly racialised discourse of difference almost invariably crept into the conversation: '*they* always stick together', '*they* don't pay tax'; '*they* keep their women at home'.

White employers complained that they could not compete with Asian factory owners who employed people from their own communities and exploited them through various 'feudal' practices, such as paying a single wage for husband and wife, or by using unpaid family labour. The local media contributed to a general association in the public mind between the exploitative conditions which prevailed in the clothing industry and the predominance of the immigrant community within it. Shah pointed to headlines in the East London Advertiser about 'the Indo-Pakistani sweatshop system which is infuriating East London's tailoring industry' (June, 1973) and which put the blame for 'slave' conditions in the industry on immigrants. Trade unionists we interviewed put forward the view that Asian workers lacked class consciousness. As one trade unionist we interviewed put it: 'Overall the union is weaker than it used to be because the "traditional" worker, that is, the Jewish tailors, have left and no new union members are coming in. The younger people coming in are the "ethnic people", they are not interested in trade unions.'[8]

8. Field interviews: Nick Chisolm and Naila Kabeer, 1986.

Thus, the exploitative conditions in the East End clothing industry tended to be equated in the public mind with the cultural attitudes and practices of immigrants. Here is the account given to us by one trade unionist we interviewed as to why there were so many Bangladeshis involved in clothing:

> The larger unionised clothing factories began to close in the seventies, you began to lose the highly skilled workers, there is no way that that level of skill exists nowadays. The employers went for a change in the production process, to get the unskilled work done outside their particular firm so that the skilled workers they employed directly could concentrate on skilled work. This produced 'shell-making' on an outwork or homework basis. From about 1974 onwards, Bengali immigrants provided a pool of labour that could perform this function. So the Bengalis stepped in and provided the semi-skilled operations involved in shell-making. Factories began to farm out work to the Bengalis. This suited the Bengalis in that they prefer to be self-employed or work on an extended family basis or whatever. And they prefer their women to work from home. It suited the employers because it meant that they could bring the part-finished garments into their factories and have their skilled workers finish it and this helped them to keep their costs down, not by cheap labour but by organising their labour process more productively.[9]

Another, responding to a question about whether Bangladeshis were doing worse than others as a result of the deteriorating conditions in the industry, said:

> As regards the Bengalis, if you come into the industry at a time when it is declining, then you are bound to come off worse than other groups . . . What seems to be happening is a great deal of part-time work, where you turn up at 7 in the morning and if the employer wants you, you work. That situation is in some ways worse than it was in the 30s, but that is because there is no organisation. I think the point has to be made that for the Bengalis, self-employment suits them.

Given these beliefs, it was not surprising that there was such a silence on the issue of the working conditions of Bangladeshi women in the East End of London when there was such strong condemnation of their working conditions in Bangladesh to the

9. Field interviews: Nick Chisolm and Naila Kabeer, 1986.

extent of seeking to restrict the import of their products. The strength of the belief that immigrants had *chosen*, and were content, to work in badly-paid and casualised forms of employment led Shah to make the following disclaimer in his study of the clothing industry in the East End:

> The immigrant . . . neither has the luxury of a choice of employment, nor indeed is in a position to worry about the 'image' of an industry. She/he has merely entered a trade where there was a demand for labour and because of the nature of the skills, people of low skills and language difficulties could be easily accepted . . . Undoubtedly immigrant workers are prepared to tolerate poor working conditions more because they have to than because they have any affinity for them. These conditions are part of the urban fabric of the East End and the industry needs to be located there. To suggest that immigrants have generated these conditions is as fallacious now as it was when applied to the Jews of the nineteenth century. (Shah, 1981, p. 205)

## Gender, work and the ethnic economy

While there was, and still is, remarkably little research on the Bangladeshi community in the East End of London, there is even less into the lives of women within the community. Scattered references to them do exist, but tend to reproduce representations of 'Asian'[10] women in the more general literature as 'cultural dopes' whose actions were fully explicable by their religion and culture. A report on the East London clothing industry, for instance, attributed the predominance of homeworking among Bangladeshi women to such factors: 'In the predominantly Muslim community of Tower Hamlets, Bangladeshi women rarely seek mainstream employment opportunities outside the home. Powerful family expectations and social and religious customs tie them to the home as well as the pressures of child care.' A report on the Bangladeshi population of Tower Hamlets prepared by Patrick Duffy for the Commission for Racial Equality echoed the cultural theme (1981): 'Free mixing of the sexes is generally disapproved

10. 'Asian' is often used as a shorthand for immigrants from Bangladesh, India and Pakistan.

of in Islam, and the woman's role outside the home is severely restricted. This restraint on Bengali women contributes to their isolation and restricts their opportunities to learn English.'

This genre of analysis has been criticised for relying on, and helping to reproduce, common-sense stereotypes about the passivity of 'Asian' women, the patriarchal structure of the family and the power of religion: as Parmar (1982) pointed out, 'it becomes easy to blame cultural, religious and communal factors for the subordinate positions which Asian women occupy in the British social structure' (p. 238). She suggested that even if culture and religion did have a role to play in explaining the high incidence of homeworking among Muslim women, the neglect of other structural factors, such as young children, lack of access to child care facilities or indeed to alternative forms of employment, resulted in a crude, monocausal explanation which concealed the complexity which shaped these women's lives. In similar vein, Morokvasic (1983) had this to say about the limitations of the culturalist paradigm in studies of immigrant communities in general:

> It is a literature shaped by selecting a certain number of characteristics observed in a limited number of migrant women. These characteristics are usually attributed to the women's alleged 'cultural backgrounds' and commonly labelled 'tradition'. Needless to say the stereotypes operate for all migrant women irrespective of their specific national and cultural origins'. (p. 13)

A different approach is evident in some of the more recent literature on ethnic minority groups in Britain in its move away from a narrowly culturalist perspective to a consideration of some of the larger structural factors mentioned by Parmar as well as the more positive role of culture in such circumstances, as 'capital' rather than as pure constraint (see, for instance, contributions to Ward and Jenkins, 1984, particularly Ladbury; see also contributions to Westwood and Bhachu, 1988). It is evident for instance in the study by Phizacklea (1990), seeking to explain the much higher rates of self-employment among certain ethnic minority groups: 21–24 per cent among South Asians and Cypriots compared to 9 per cent among Afro-Caribbeans. She suggested that high rates of entrepreneurship in particular ethnic communities reflected a combination of racism and exclusionary practices which confined most ethnic groups to limited segments of the labour market as well as migration patterns which gave these particular groups access to family and community members, in particular to female labour. Ethnic minority employers have been able to mobilise ties of kinship and community to ensure the viability of a particular form of economic activity, labour-intensive enterprise, in which they have a comparative advantage.

Ladbury (1984) and Mitter (1986) have suggested that ethnic enterprise may have had particular attraction for communities who are keenly concerned with the honour ('izzat' or 'filotimo') of their women, as both South Asians and Cypriot communities are. The creation of community-based enterprises within the clothing industry offered the possibility for women to work at home or else in a 'safe' environment outside. Ethnic and family links keep wages low and workers non-unionised: 'in a hostile white world, many of the immigrant women are afraid to incur the wrath of their own men' (Mitter, 1986, p. 57). However, Mitter also stresses that the rise of sweatshops and homeworking in these communities cannot be attributed solely to patriarchal values. Racism in the labour markets which confine ethnic minority workers to the worst paid and least desirable occupations made the possibility of working within one's own community an attractive option. Her interviews with nine Bangladeshi homeworkers in the East End of London in 1982 revealed that men in the families were either unemployed or working on a casual basis in clothing or hotel/catering in which they earned no more than £100 a week. Her interview with one of the homeworkers highlighted the kinds of fears that might explain why women from the ethnic minorities often opted for homeworking:

> When you live in Newham, you have little choice, sister. Burning down of an Asian home does not make news any longer. It is accepted as a regular happening in the East End of London . . . How can I look for jobs outside my home in such a situation. I want to remain invisible, literally. Also, sister, I am a widow and I really do not know what my legal status is. If I apply for cards and things, I may be asked to leave the country. At the

moment, my uncle brings my machining work to my home. It works out to be 50 pence per hour, not great. But I earn and I feed my children somehow. Most of all, I do not have to deal with the fear of racist abuse in this white world. (1986, p. 130)

This genre of studies thus moves beyond the simplifications of narrowly culturalist and static approaches to the situation of ethnic minorities to asking broader and more dynamic questions about how the internal features of a community interact with the larger context in which it finds itself. It is this relationship between internal and external, between preference and constraint, that we need to address in attempting to explain labour market patterns among the Bangladeshi community in the UK, particularly those of its women. On the one hand, there is no doubt at all that the community faced enormous discrimination in the British context.[11] Here is how a House of Commons report summarised their situation in 1986:

> The Bangladeshis are the most recently arrived of Britain's major ethnic minorities and are considerably the most disadvantaged. Their problems generally differ in degree rather than in kind from those of other ethnic minorities, partly reflecting their recent arrival, but the difference of degree is sometimes substantial. They tend to occupy the worst and most overcrowded housing, their recorded unemployment rate is exceptionally high (although some will be obtaining income from commercial activities within the home), average earnings are lower than for any other ethnic minority, there is considerable under-achievement among their children at school, fewer than in other ethnic minorities have a reasonable command of English (the low proportion of men being able to speak English being especially distinctive), the language barrier and cultural factors restrict their access to health and social services and they appeared to be disproportionately affected by racial violence. (p. iv)

The report summarised the root causes of Bangladeshi disadvantage as three-fold. The first was their recent arrival from a rural peasant society to an industrial urban society in which they lacked the skills necessary to find well-paid jobs. The second was a poor

---

11. Some aspects of this disadvantage are evident in the statistics reported in Appendix 3.

command of English: in 1984 50 per cent of Bangladeshi men and 76 per cent of Bangladeshi women spoke English either 'slightly' or 'not at all' (see Appendix 3 for more recent estimates). And finally, of course, they faced racial discrimination.

However, to restrict the analysis of the community's involvement in the labour market purely to a chronicle of its disadvantage denies its members a history and identity of their own, any role as active subjects who bring their own aspirations, allegiances, values and resources to bear on their labour market decisions and their negotiations with discrimination. On the other hand, to explain their labour market position purely in terms of cultural identity and preferences would be to ignore the implications of the adverse wider conditions in which their choices were shaped. It would also be to produce a very monolithic account of the Bangladeshi community in the East End of London, ruling out the possibility that there might be contested views of 'culture' within the community and that different members might have different views of what it means to be a Bangladeshi in Britain. Finally, of course, it would take no account of the fact that cultural preferences have not proved a barrier to outside work for women in the Bangladesh context. Clearly, we need a more detailed analysis of the significance of these various factors in the lives of the Bangladeshi community in the East End of London in order to assess which particular configuration of 'internal' and 'external' factors best help to explain the particular pattern of female labour force participation which characterised it. However, before undertaking such an analysis, I would like to provide a brief overview of the homeworkers in our sample and of their families by way of background.

### Who were the homeworkers? A brief description

There was, as stated earlier, very little information on the Bangladeshi homeworkers so it was difficult to provide the kind of statistical information on them comparable to what we were able to compile for the women workers in the Dhaka sample. Appendix 3 contains what we were able to find on manufacturing homework in the UK context and on the Bangladeshi community. It also provides a profile of the homeworkers from our sample along with frequency counts of their responses to the key questions of the research. In this concluding section of the chapter, I will simply draw attention to some aspects of this data which are relevant to the analysis which follows.

As Ballard (1983) has pointed out, the migration process characterising the Bangladeshi and Pakistani communities differed from that of most other ethnic communities, including those from other parts of the Indian sub-continent. While most groups chose the 'family reunion' option, so that, for instance, Sikh wives had begun joining their husbands in the late 1950s, Bangladeshis opted to become 'international commuters', working in Britain, saving as much as possible, and making long visits home. This pattern was repeated several times and it was only in the early 1980s that their wives and children began to join them in Britain. As the national data compiled in Appendix 3 shows, only 40 per cent of Bangladeshis in the mid-1990s had been born in Britain compared to 60 per cent of Caribbeans. Consequently, a much lower percentage of them spoke English than any of the other ethnic minority groups, although differentials were less marked among the younger generation.

The Bangladeshi community has a larger household size compared to the rest of the population: around five members per household compared to around two in the white population and four in the Indian. A much higher percentage of the population was married: 67 per cent of the age group 16–64 compared to 57 per cent of the white population and 33 per cent of the black. The majority of households were made up of married couples with dependent children; there were very few lone mothers.

Unemployment rates were (and have remained) high among the Bangladeshi community (Spitalfields Working Party, 1983). According to national statistics, only 66 per cent of Bangladeshi men were employed in 1995, the lowest activity rate for any community (HMSO, 1996). They were more likely to be found in part-time or temporary employment than men from the other ethnic communities and also had the highest rates of self-employment: 22 per cent compared to just over 10 per cent in the white community. They were also largely found in skilled and semi-skilled manual work: as we have seen, this was largely in clothing, retail and catering. Bangladeshi women also had lower rates of employment than women from the other ethnic minority, as well as majority, groups: only 20 per cent of Bangladeshi women were officially registered as employed compared to around 70 per cent of white and Afro-Caribbean women. They were overwhelmingly concentrated in the occupational category 'public administration, education and health'. However, given that these employment figures do not include *any* Bangladeshi women in manufacturing, it is clear that the official statistics continue to exclude employment in the unregistered economy, including homeworking.

The interviews with both the homeworkers in our sample, as well as with the male clothing workers, echoed many aspects of this wider picture. Most of the male workers interviewed, as well as the husbands and fathers of the women workers, had arrived in Britain several years before the women. They had come on their own, although often with the help of family, kin or co-villagers already resident in the UK. Many had started out working in mills and foundries in the Midlands until they had been laid off in the recession of the 1970s. They had lived in boarding houses, or in 'mess' arrangements, sending as much money home to their families in Bangladesh. Some had come to the UK unmarried and returned home to marry. Others had already been married, but left their wives behind in Bangladesh as well as their children. They would return to Sylhet for a few months or a year to be with their families and then came back to Britain. Families were thus apart for several years at a time and, as Gardner points out, could be considered as 'settled' in both Bangladesh and Britain simultaneously. The boundaries of the household, whose elasticity we noted in connection with migration into Dhaka city, were now stretched through international migration to accommodate a membership which was separated by 'seven seas and thirteen rivers'.

The women in our sample had arrived far more recently. Only three of the fifty-three women we interviewed had been born in Britain. The rest had been born and brought up in the Sylhet district of Bangladesh, mainly in its rural areas. Forty-three of the women had migrated to join husbands, while seven had migrated to join their fathers. Twelve women had migrated within the five years previous to the interview, while thirty-three had migrated with the previous ten years. Only twenty-seven said that they could speak any English.

There were certain demographic contrasts with the women workers we interviewed in Dhaka. Since a lower cut-off age of sixteen was used in selecting women in both components of the study, neither sample included women younger than this. However, there was no upper cut-off point. This resulted in many more older women in the London sample than we found in our Dhaka sample: forty-six of the women were twenty-five or older. Clearly, homeworking allowed for a much wider age distribution of women compared to the far more youthful work force hired by the garment factories in Dhaka.

The majority of women (forty-four) in our sample were currently married. In terms of the national statistics as well, it should be noted that the Bangladeshi community had a higher incidence of marriage (and a lower incidence of divorce and separation) than other ethnic groups and it also reported a younger age of marriage for its women. The high prevalence of married women in our sample also reflected the process of female migration into Britain, in that most of the women came to join their husbands rather than their fathers. None had come as independent migrants (the Caribbean pattern). Nationally, households within the Bangladeshi community tended to be made up of nuclear families, mainly married couples with dependent children. The community had a higher child dependency ratio than any other ethnic group. Echoing the national picture, most of the women we interviewed lived in nuclear families and the majority of the ever-married women in our sample had young children. The median age of the youngest child was between two and three years. Households also tended to be large by British standards: most had five or more members, compared to an average of two members in white households.

Our sample also mirrored the very limited occupational profile of the Bangladeshi community, particularly women, to be found in the national data. The majority of homeworkers had only ever done homework, over half of them for five or more years. Some had known how to handle a sewing machine beforehand, others had learnt from relatives, usually husbands, in the industry or else from neighbours who were already doing homework. They mainly did 'flat' machining on linings and sleeves of coats and jackets. However, there was a small minority of women in our sample who had also done other kinds of work, some outside the home.

The occupational profile of the men in the community was somewhat more varied, particularly those who had been in the country for two or three decades. As already pointed out, they had started out working in heavy industry in other parts of Britain or in the docklands of London. However, as recession wiped out these jobs, these men either remained unemployed or had gone into a variety of entrepreneurial activities as well as waged labour in the clothing and catering industry. Those men who had migrated in more recent times either started out in the East London leather industry (a job which was considered far more unpleasant than clothing because of the stench of leather) or else began and remained in clothing. Ten of the homeworkers in our sample reported a male earner in the garment industry; eleven reported earners in catering while six reported earners who were, or had been, employed in other factories, mainly in the Midlands. Nineteen of the male household heads were currently unemployed.

All the male workers we interviewed were, by virtue of our selection criteria, involved in the clothing industry. The majority worked as machinists in small factories or outdoor units of around 20–25 other workers, sometimes female workers of different nationalities or else in entirely Bangladeshi outdoor units. Only one or two workers mentioned ever having seen a Bangladeshi woman working in a clothing factory and they surmised that the woman in question was probably a widow. Most of them worked on heavier items, such as woollen coats for ladies, as well as gentlemen, but some had also made jackets and skirts. It should be pointed out that, like the homeworkers, most of the men in the clothing industry had not started out with machining skills. They generally either joined as a helper, cutting threads and keeping the floor tidy, and taught themselves 'machine control' or else joined as 'trainee' machinists.

## Conclusion

The predominance of women, and of immigrant communities, in the UK clothing industry, particularly its London sector, is a long-standing one. Bangladeshis were simply the most recent significant ethnic group to have been drawn into the industry in East London. This chapter has reviewed some of the general literature on the industry which helps to explain this association, but I was unable to find any studies which explored in any detail why, in an industry which relies, and has always relied, so heavily on female labour, Bangladeshi women were overwhelmingly concentrated in the homeworking sector. However, the wider literature on the 'Asian' community did throw up some competing hypotheses as to what the reasons might have been.

One set of explanations drew attention to the culture of the community and to the restrictions it placed on the mobility of its women. A second set of explanations pointed to ethnic disadvantage in the wider labour market, and the constraints it placed on the choices of members of the ethnic minorities, forcing them into particular labour market niches in order to survive.

The analytical challenge for the study is two-fold. As Ballard and Ballard (1977) pointed out, we have to recognise that these external constraints are, in a sense, prior to the internal preferences of different ethnic minorities. They set the limits within which these groups must operate. However, different groups have arrived in Britain through different trajectories, bringing with them different resources, different constraints and different cultural aspirations. The particular behaviour of these groups, and of different categories of individuals within them, has to be explained in terms of the choices that they are able to make within these limits and the various strategies that they are able to draw on to circumvent, modify, challenge or transform these limits. To set this in the context of the questions that this book has set out to address, we would need to move beyond generalisations about the position of Asian women in the British context which are 'read' off from a fairly simplified representation of a shared set of restrictions to a more situated understanding of the Bangladeshi com-

munity. It is within this more situated understanding of the
opportunities and constraints facing the community as a whole
that the labour market decisions of its female members will begin
to make more sense.

# 7

# Reconstituting structure: homeworkers and labour market decision making in London

This chapter focuses on Bangladeshi women's decision to enter paid work in the London context. It will explore why they opted to work in home-based piecework rather than following men from their community, and women from other ethnic minority groups, into other sectors of the garment industry or into the wider labour market. The structure of the chapter is similar to that adopted in Chapter 4. The analysis is organised around the constituent elements of the decision in question: the decision to take up paid work; the decision to work from home rather than outside; attitudes to outside work in general and to work in the garment factories in particular. As in Chapter 4, I will start out by considering women's own perspectives on these questions before going on to consider the preferences of other family members on their decision. I will conclude with some reflections on what the London side of our story adds to our understanding of the interaction of structure and agency in women's labour market choices.

## Deconstructing the decision to work: why work?

The first point to note is that the existence of a state-guaranteed social safety net in London made it, at a very basic level, a very different decision making environment from that prevailing in Dhaka. Even when a household had no employed members, it could still cover its basic needs for food, shelter and clothing through various forms of state assistance, including unemployment benefit, income support, child benefits, housing benefit and state-subsidised health and education. As a result, the decision to take up paid work by the women in the London sample was not motivated by basic survival imperatives in the literal sense that some of the women workers in Dhaka were. Nor were they motivated by the need to pay for their children's education.

In addition, dowry-related saving, which had featured frequently as a primary, or secondary, motivation for women's decision to take up paid work in Dhaka did not feature in the testimonies of the women in London. While there were fewer unmarried women (the group for whom it featured most often as a motivation in Dhaka) in the London sample, the absence of any reference to the need to save for their daughters' dowries in the testimonies of mothers interviewed in London suggested that dowry itself was not particularly widespread among the community in London. Morever, although most of the married women in the London sample had been born, brought up and married in Bangladesh, none of them reported dowry payments in connection with their marriage. Certainly there was exchange of gifts between the families of the bride and groom but no evidence of the 'demand' by the groom's side for the kind of commodities or cash that characterised such demands in the testimonies of the Dhaka workers and in the Bangladesh literature in general. The most likely explanation is that dowry had not been as widely adopted in Sylhet district as it had in other parts of the country. Dowry, as we have noted already, is not a practice associated with Islam but one that has emerged in response to the changing economics of gender in Bangladesh. As one of the more religious and conservative districts in the country, it may have been slower to spread to Sylhet. A reading of Gardner's study of marriage practices in rural areas of Sylhet district around the time of this study suggests that 'demand' dowry of the kind to be found in most parts of Bangladesh had only very recently begun to emerge in the district.

Consequently, neither basic survival imperatives, children's educational expenses nor the need to accumulate dowry-related savings, important motivations in the Dhaka context, featured in the testimonies of the London workers. Nevertheless, what constituted an acceptable standard of living in London was generally higher than could be provided by reliance on state benefits alone. In households with no male member in employment or those headed by women themselves, women's homeworking activities made a critical difference to the standard of living. There were around sixteen such households in the sample. The motivations for working reported by other homeworkers included the desire to save, to increase their purchasing power, to improve the household's standard of living and to buy things for their children. Some variation therefore did exist in the economic significance of women's earnings to their households, but clearly not to the extent that characterised the Dhaka sample.

## The decision to do homework

The reasons that women gave for taking up homeworking could generally be accommodated within an orthodox economic model of labour supply decision making viz. the absence of the necessary human capital qualifications, child care and domestic obligations and 'cultural constraints'. These reasons were not mutually exclusive and some women gave more than one. Ten women explained their homeworking decision in primarily cultural terms, often resting on a strict definition of purdah which ruled out the consideration of any form of work outside the home: 'The gaze of any man over the age of 12, be he Bengali, or Jamaican or English, violates a woman's purdah.' For this group, the decision to do homework could be seen as an explicit rejection of outside work and a positive and long-term preference for homework.

A second, and more widely advanced explanation, related to perceived 'human capital' deficits. Outside work was seen as requiring education and language skills – the two were frequently bracketed together in their testimonies – which many of the women did not possess. Sixteen of the women mentioned language as the main problem while six mentioned education.

> I don't have any education so I have never looked for outside work. Whatever job you look for, you need to be able to read and write.

I haven't tried to work outside the house or in a factory because I wouldn't be able to speak or understand people nor could I travel around.

I didn't try and work outside because I couldn't make people understand or travel around by myself.

As the quotes suggest, the inability to communicate fluently with people outside their community constituted a major obstacle for women, not only in relation to outside employment, but also in the possibility of more routine interactions with people outside the community. Nevertheless, lack of education and linguistic skills were not necessarily disqualifications for outside employment for all members of the community. Many of the male garment workers we interviewed also had very low levels of education and in fact put forward their *lack* of educational qualifications as the reason they were working in garment factories:

When I got here, my landlord's son told me I would get work in garment factories because they do not ask for educational qualifications.

We go for these jobs because we have very little education.

Many Bengali people are working in the garment industry. That is because if you don't have educational qualifications, then you have to do jobs which require only manual labour.

Nor was the inability to speak English restricted just to the women in the community. As we saw from the previous chapter, among South Asians, the largest ethnic group in Britain for whom English was not a first language, Bangladeshis, men as well as women, were least likely to be able to speak it. However, while many of the male workers in our sample reported that they had arrived in the UK without prior knowledge of English, it had not prevented them from finding outside employment. Some worked in situations which hired largely Bangladeshi workers so that their lack of English did not constitute a major problem. Others had acquired proficiency in English usually informally over time through frequent exposure to conversations in racially-mixed environments:

When I came here, I learnt to speak English through trial and error.

After my arrival, I started to attend 'English as a second language' classes, but I had to stop shortly after. I could not write and study at the same time. Instead I learnt by listening to other people and trying to reply when spoken to.

Finally, the third reason, and the one most widely cited, related to the demands of women's domestic roles. Around twenty-nine women referred specifically to their child care responsibilities:

> If you go to the office or factory, who will look after the children, that is the problem, isn't it? It's alright for single people or for people with one child in nursery school. I think that the people who work in factories must be single, otherwise how can they work with small children?

> If you work at home, the biggest advantage is that you can look after children at the same time and they will always feel assured that their mother is at home. Children feel better when their mother is at home. Of course, it is hard to work at home with the children, that is why I don't do it full time.

Twenty women also referred to more general domestic responsibilities to explain why they were in homeworking. As Mrs Riju reported: 'I have to attend to my husband when he comes home from work, he has to wash and I have to find his towel or sandals and get him tea and something to eat. He doesn't know how to machine, but he helps when we have guests and I have to cook for them.' Her comments draw attention to an additional factor which cropped up in several of the homeworkers' testimonies. As with other South Asian communities, the Bangladeshis have brought with them a strong tradition of hospitality: visiting and receiving friends and relatives made up a major part of their social life. Women's labour was central to the sustenance of this social life since they were primarily responsible for preparing tea, snacks and meals for their guests and attending to them. This combination of child care responsibilities, caring for the family, doing the housework and discharging the obligations of hospitality clearly had a constraining effect on women's choices:

> I have never looked for outside work. I have two children, who would look after them? I have to look after the children, look after the house and attend to our guest.

I can't do regular work. I have to cook for the children by 12. And I am
often interrupted by our visitors. Then I have to make my husband's tea.

Some of the rationales that women gave for their homeworking
decision were thus specific to the community: their lack of linguistic
skills and purdah considerations, for instance. Others, however,
were more general. The compatibility of homeworking with
women's obligations was a rationale that the women in our sample
shared with women in general in the UK. Thus an early study by
Hope et al. of an ethnically diverse, but predominantly English,
group of homeworkers in London concluded: 'Any explanation of
why it is mainly women who do homework . . . cannot ignore the
family roles of these women . . . All the women in our sample
considered housework and child care to be their responsibility and
regarded help from their husbands as a generous concession'
(Hope, Kennedy and de Winter, 1976, pp. 98–9). A similar conclusion was reached by another study, again of mainly English
homeworkers in Yorkshire: 'The explanatory emphasis put on the
care of young children obscures what is a life-long experience of
women, namely that of servicing others on an unwaged basis' (Allen
and Wolkowitz, 1987, p. 79). A more recent study published by the
National Group for Homeworking found that 95 per cent of the
homeworkers they interviewed were women, 40 per cent were Asian
women, and 75 per cent had school-age children (*Home Truths*,
cited in the *Guardian*, 13 September 1994).

However, Allen and Wolkowitz point to interesting differences in
the way in which women from different ethnic groups formulated
what appeared to be a similar point about their domestic obligations. While the white women in their sample were more likely to
say that their husbands 'preferred' them to work at home, the
Pakistani women tended to say that their husbands would not
'allow' them to take outside employment (p. 82). Whether this
reflected minor differences in language use or major differences in
perceptions of male authority, the authors note that the influence
of husbands' wishes had the identical effect of constraining
women's work options.

## Attitudes to outside work

As we have noted, only a very small minority of women adhered to notions of purdah which would totally preclude any possibility of outside work. The majority, while accepting that notions of gender propriety should shape women's work preferences, rejected the stricter version of purdah put forward by some sections of the community in London. Their understanding of purdah was one which recognised the the different reality of life in Britain:

> If I keep my own purdah, even when there are a thousand people around, nobody can do anything ... If a man wants his wife to stay within the home in this country, and keep purdah, there is no point to bringing her here. In that case he should have left her in Bangladesh.

> I wore *burkas* in Bangladesh. Here we have cardigans, coats and jumpers, they serve the same purpose as burkah. There aren't coats and jackets in Bangladesh, that is why they need to wear the burkah. There is one purdah, but people have created many branches of it. For many people, it is believing in God in your heart. But you have read what is written: according to that version, we are breaking purdah even though we may work at home, because we still have to go to the doctor and shopping ... I agree with what I have read, but in this age it is not possible to maintain those standards. We have never observed purdah the way it was in the very beginning. It is the heart that matters.

Such reformulations of purdah expressed views about the acceptability of outside work which closely echoed those put forward by the women workers in Dhaka in which the emphasis was on individual responsibility for morality and on conformity to the spirit, rather than to the letter, of purdah:

> There is no reason why my purdah would be spoilt if I went out to work. My purdah is in my mind.

> How can purdah be spoilt going to work ... everything depends on the mind. If you put on a burkah and see a man on the street and think about how handsome he is, your purdah is affected. But if your eyes fall on him like a brother or father, then your your purdah is not spoilt.

> Purdah isn't the clothes you wear, but what is inside your heart. You can work outside and still retain your purdah.

In fact, not only were the majority of homeworkers in principle willing to consider outside work, but a few had already had experience of outside work, or were actively seeking it. However, norms about gender propriety had not been abandoned and remained evident in the kinds of outside employment for which women expressed a preference. The 'respectability' of the job, and its compatibility with their child care obligations, were key factors in explaining the pattern of employment preferences which emerged in their testimonies.

> If I got a job in a creche, I could take the children with me . . . If I got that kind of job, I would do it, but I can't get anything. I want to do any kind of work, apart from factories. And I don't want to work in shops, I don't like that. If there are men in the creche work, I don't mind, they won't be looking at me, they'll just be managers or officers.

> I would work in a saree shop, that would be suitable for women like me, or teaching our children Bengali or babysitting. The salary would have to be very good. I would have to earn at least £80–100 a week after deductions to make it worth my while to work outside. I once put my name down at the new women's organisation at Whitechapel, I wanted to teach Bengali children and women.

> I'd quite like to work in a nursery school as a teacher, I hope I do that when the children are older . . . I am interested in it because it is with children, you play with them and look after them. People from outside don't come in and it won't be necessary for me to go out anywhere, I can have my own children there as well. I wouldn't like to work in a shop, you have to stand behind the counter and serve customers.

It will be seen that both respectability and child care considerations led to a degree of convergence in the kinds of jobs preferred: creches, nurseries, schools, clinics and perhaps saree shops, all based within 'the community'. In addition, however, there was also a small minority of women whose preferences extended beyond the narrow range of work options mentioned so far. For these women, the pay or prestige associated with a job appeared to be a more important consideration in determining their preferences. They tended to be younger women with relatively high levels of education who were more self-confident about finding their way around: 'I am doing college to improve written English; I want to work in an office.'

## Attitudes towards garment factory work

It is clear from the preceding discussion that women's actual employment preferences were more wide-ranging than would be suggested by an examination of their 'revealed' preferences alone. However, employment in the clothing factories or outdoor units which made up the London industry, was almost unanimously rejected by all the women interviewed. The reasons that they gave for their reluctance suggested that such employment crystallised various anxieties related to the boundaries of gender, culture and class. For some women, the anxiety stemmed from the presence of men and women from other cultural groups on the factory floor, their anxieties about the breakdown of gender segregation and about the possible threat to cultural identity:

> I wouldn't work in a factory, there are all kinds of men, I don't like the idea of working there. It's not very Islamic, it would be outside purdah to work in a factory. It's alright if you can work and keep your purdah, but there are many women who mix with English women and behave like them, they change their own culture. It's like Bangladesh, people in the villages behave one way and those in the town behave another. Bengali and English culture is different, to mix with them, you lose your own culture and accept theirs . . . I don't mind if other people behave like that, but I don't like it.

> I couldn't work with men . . . It is forbidden by our religion and also there are many people in this community who like to spread bad stories. Also there are many bad women and men. I have heard many incidents from people about this boy falling in love with that girl or saying some bad thing to that girl . . . Even if you are a virtuous woman and are seen talking to a virtuous man, people will say bad things about you, they will blame you. I would feel ashamed if that happened to me.

For a second group of women, the problem lay not in the presence of men or women from other cultures, but in the presence of large numbers of *Bengali* men within the factories. Their reluctance to take up factory jobs had less to do with religious or cultural strictures and more to do with the attitudes they anticipated from Bangladeshi men in the work place and with the gossip that might be generated within the community. It was also evident from the women's testimonies that these anxieties were shared by other members of their families, particularly male members, who were concerned about its implications for their image as family bread-winners and guardians:

> I don't want to work in the factories . . . there are English and Bengali men working in them. I would feel ashamed, purdah is spoilt for Muslim women and it is a sin . . . The English men may ignore you, but however good you are, men from our community will spread scandal about you. They won't say it in front of you, but they will go somewhere else and say it. I don't know about this area so much, but you must know what it is like in Bangladesh as well, they just make things up.

> Some women would feel ashamed, they would think how can I work in front of everybody? They feel ashamed because they didn't go out in front of men in Bangladesh and here they would have to go out in front of strangers . . . But the other problem is that some men will say I won't let my wife go out in front of other people . . . They feel ashamed in front of other Bengalis because they will say he's sent his wife and his daughter out to work because he can't support them himself, that is how people think. If I go out to work, they will think he can't feed his wife, that is why he has sent her to a factory.

> We couldn't go to the factory, even to pick up orders, there are thousands of Bengalis there, women can't go there, it would be shameful. The men would say, they can't fill their stomachs. They'd say, in Bangladesh, one person's earnings could feed ten, but here even though the husband is working, the wife has come out to work as well, she can't fill her stomach. They'll say so many things. Nobody else will say them, only our people. And there aren't any English factories without Bengali men. There might be four that are good, but there will be two who will say, Look, she's here, she can't fill her stomach. I am not afraid of men, I am afraid for my reputation.

Finally, there was a third group of women for whom objections to factory work had a straightforward status dimension. As Shona explained, 'Some women won't go out and work in factories because they don't want to, they say, did I come to London to work in a factory?' Status considerations were also implicated in their reluctance to work alongside Bengali men in the factories. Those who came from families with some social standing in the village community that they had come from in Bangladesh, sought to preserve this standing within the East End community:

> I don't want to work in garment factories. Too many different kinds of Bengali men there. After all, we are not all the same. There is too much mixing in the factories. There are all kinds of men from our community there. If a man is only used to driving rickshaws and has never held a book in his hand, he will not know how to behave anywhere. That is the type of man who seems bad, it is not his fault, he did not get any education. Many of the Bengali boys here don't know how to behave around us; they have not been to college and they have grown up according to the culture of this country.

It is instructive here to note that the explanations offered by the male clothing workers who were interviewed during the research gave explanations for the absence of Bangladeshi women from such work which closely echoed those of the women. While it was true, as one of the men pointed out, that 'there are many reasons why so few Bengali women work in the factories, every Bengali family has its own reasons as to why they do not let their women go out to work in factories', nevertheless, many of their testimonies referred to the same norms of gender propriety referred to by the women and confirmed women's anxieties about the kinds of moral judgements that would be made about them were they to take up factory jobs:

> There are many reasons why Bengali women don't work in factories. Their husbands don't want it and even if they did, our community would not allow it. Our people think it is shameful for women to work in factories – because they are full of men. People say bad things about women working in factories. Friends and relatives will dislike such women. Our society and culture keeps our women away from work. It is best for Bengali women to work at home; the money is a little less, but they will have privacy. Or they can work in play groups with children; they can also become dinner ladies if they want to.

> I have only ever once seen a Bengali woman in a factory and she was a widow trying to make ends meet. Our women do not like to work in

factories because of our religion and culture. Our religion does not allow women to work with men; neither does our culture, particularly where there is a large group of men. People think badly of such women. Husbands and fathers will not allow this to happen. Anyway, our women have to look after the children and do all the housework, they have too much to do at home.

In all my working years I have never seen a Bengali woman working in a factory. This is probably because they are too shy to go out to work although there is now a trend for them to get educational qualifications and then get a job. They still don't like to go into the factories. It is true that husbands and fathers don't allow them to work. This is because we say bad things about women who go out to work. So parents and husbands feel ashamed and don't let the women go out. I have nothing against women going out to work, in this country all women try to work.

In addition, a number of men also expressed anxiety that mixing with women from other cultures with different moral standards might have an undesirable influence on women from their community:

There are some African, Indian and Irish women working in my factory. Their culture is very different from ours, they don't think it is bad for women to go out to work. But our culture is very much against this. If my wife goes out to work, we lose our family prestige. It is not religion that stops our women. Purdah is not ruined as long as women keep their hair and bodies well-covered. Our religion is not against this, but our culture is.

It is best our women don't work in these factories because men and women work together, mix freely, talk and laugh. Our women do not like these things. The Turkish women are Muslims, but very different, very westernised.

To sum up, therefore, it would appear that factory employment in the clothing industry was constructed very differently in the London context than it was in Dhaka and hence carried very different connotations for Bangladeshi women in London. Women's antipathy to such work in the London context focused largely on the perceived impropriety of working alongside men, particularly men from their own community, and anxieties about the potentially corrupting influence of other cultures. In addition, weaving through most of these testimonies was a recurring theme: a concern with

what 'people' in the community might say about women taking up
such work. In other words, the factories were not perceived as
impersonal working environments inhabited by fellow workers, but
as an extension of the community and inhabited by its representatives. Bangladeshi women would be literally under the gaze of the
community, and as an overwhelmingly male gaze, their social
discomfort would be compounded by sexual unease.

## Deconstructing the decision to work: consensus, conflict and negotiation within the household

Having explored some of the reasons that women gave for taking
up homeworking, their attitudes to outside forms of employment,
and to garment employment in particular, let me turn now to their
accounts of the processes which underpinned their decision to take
up homework. I have categorised these processes, as I did those of
the factory workers in Dhaka, on the basis of the kinds of agency
that women brought to bear on their decisions and the extent to
which the decision making outcomes embodied conflict or consensus within the household. However, ascertaining the nature of the
agency involved in women's labour supply decisions was a far more
complex task when the decision in question resonated with cultural
prescriptions governing women's behaviour, as it did in the London context, than when it entailed them going against the cultural
grain, as it had done in Dhaka. I explain why in the next section.

## Passive agency, consensual decision making

Around six of the women in the London sample described the
decision to do homework in terms which suggested a 'passive' form
of agency, because they appeared to have so thoroughly assimilated
the preferences of others that 'choice' and 'constraint' became
indistinguishable in their testimonies. Sometimes, the 'others' in
question referred to the community in general. These were women
who explained the decision to do homework in terms of 'meta-
preferences' which embodied cultural/religious norms and values,

as with the woman who had talked about the gaze of *any* man over the age of twelve violating a woman's purdah. In other cases, the 'others' in question were dominant family members. In such cases, the women appeared to have assimilated the preferences of those in authority over them so thoroughly that 'choice' and 'constraint' appeared simultaneously as the reason for their decision. Thus, when a woman said, 'I don't want to work outside, and anyway, my husband wouldn't allow me to', it was impossible to work out which had come first: her preference or his constraint. Was she expressing her own active antipathy to outside work, with her husband's wishes merely reinforcing it, or had she adapted her preferences to the certain knowledge that her husband would not permit her to take up outside work?

I have described these decisions as 'passive' on the grounds that they entailed a qualitatively different form of choice to those made by women due to their child care obligations, their lack of proper qualifications or even their own subjective preferences. The key difference is that in the first case, women's work choices had been predefined by cultural norm or dominant family preferences to exclude, even hypothetically, any consideration of paid work options, apart from those based at home, while in the second, the possibility of working outside had in principle been entertained before being refrained from.

## Suppressed agency, conflictual decision making

The question of agency was easier to ascertain in the case of women who declared that they themselves were not in principle opposed to outside work, but who had opted for homeworking in deference to dominant preferences within the household. There were around thirteen cases of conflicting preferences reported, but they varied considerably in how conflict was dealt with. In five of the cases, conflict remained hidden. One example was that of Mariam Bibi. Her husband had come to Britain over twenty-five years ago, soon after they got married, and had worked in the steel mills in the north of England before they closed down. She was forty-five years old and had come to the UK to join her husband from Bangladesh around seven years ago. They now lived in London with his brother's family. Finding it difficult to make ends meet, her husband had suggested that Mariam Bibi follow his brother's wife's example and take up homeworking. However, when she described how the decision was made, it was clear that she herself would have been prepared to consider the option of outside work, but had not even raised it as a possibility because she knew what her family's reaction would have been.

> My husband's family haven't actually forbidden me to go out to work but yet in a way they have. They don't like their women going out to work. It would be shameful for them because the woman's purdah would be spoilt. I don't think purdah is broken just by going out, purdah is only spoilt by what you do. I don't know why they forbid it. I don't know what jobs are available outside. Anyway, I don't want to go out to work, my thoughts haven't gone that way . . . I'll do some work at home as long as I can . . . I can only go to work if my husband lets me, if he doesn't I won't go.

Mariam Bibi's testimony manifested some of the slippage between 'choice' and 'constraint' noted in the testimonies of the earlier group, but she differed from the women in this group in that her decision to work within the home was based on her acquiescence to the dominant preference against outside work within her family, rather than on her own antipathy to such work.

The dominance of other preferences in women's labour supply decisions was more clearly in evidence in the case of Mrs Miah. She had been married for twenty-two years, but had only joined her husband in the UK in the last two years. She was now forty. It was clear from her testimony that her husband had very strong views about any form of activity that would take his wife out of the house on a regular basis:

> My husband doesn't let me go out too much, he thinks I'll learn bad things. He says to me, why should you go out, you will be seen by 10 people going to the market, you should behave like you behaved in Bangladesh, there are more Bengali than English people in this area, they'll say, I saw so-and-so's wife walking on the street.

Her own view of purdah was less restrictive:

Purdah is up to me, if I am good, my world is good, if I'm bad, my world is
bad. You can spoil your purdah inside as well as outside the house. The
person who is bad will be without purdah wherever they go. Not everybody
becomes bad if they go out, the five fingers on your hand are not the
same, are they?

Nevertheless, she had little choice but to abide by her husband's
injunctions. His restrictions on her movements left her with a great
deal of time on her hands and her desire to take up homework was
partly fuelled by boredom:

I don't have anything to do at home apart from the cooking. I have never
looked for work outside, my husband doesn't let me, how can I go out? I
got the idea because wherever I go, I see people machining, everybody has
a machine at home, I thought if I get a machine, I can do some work. It
was my own decision, I got bored just sitting around the house.

Her stepdaughter, who lived next door and also took in homework,
taught her to use the machine and made the necessary delivery
arrangements. Her husband bought her a machine but cautioned
her not to neglect her domestic duties: 'He said if I wanted to do
homework, it was up to me. But he didn't like it, he said it was
difficult to look after the children and the house and work at the
same time. He has got used to it now, although he still says things
occasionally.'

Mrs Islam reported far more overt conflict over her work
decision, a symptom of the more generally conflictual nature of
her marriage. Like Mr Miah, her husband had also ruled out
activities which might expose her to corrupting influences, initially
agreeing to let her attend English classes and then withdrawing his
permission 'in case she became bad'. He forbade her to seek
outside employment on the same grounds. She found herself with
time on her hands and decided to take up homeworking: 'I don't
have any children and apart from cooking, I don't have anything
else to do. I felt that if I worked, then I kept myself occupied and
earned some money to buy the things I want. I had to use my time
somehow, I can't always go visiting other people.' She got the idea
of homework from the landlady in their house who taught her how
to handle the sewing machine. Her husband agreed to the idea on

condition that it did not take her out of the house: 'I'm a married woman and my husband says, If I can't feed you, I'll bring you work that you can do at home.' Initially, he had arranged for the delivery of orders to be undertaken by a sub-contractor friend of his, but this arrangement had to come to an end when they moved house. He then took over the responsibility himself.

In Rabia's case, it was parental preferences which had shaped her homeworking decision. Her father had migrated to the UK nearly thirty years ago, but had left his wife and children behind in Bangladesh, visiting them whenever he could. They had finally joined him two years before our study. Rabia was sixteen years old by then. The fact that her village had its own high school allowed her to complete her Matric before she came to Britain. She had hoped to continue her education so as to improve her chances of landing a decent job, but her parents were firmly against it:

> I wanted to go to a language centre to learn English so that I could get a good job ... I want to do a job that requires academic qualifications, people respect those kinds of jobs, but my parents refuse their permission. I think that they fear that I will become uncontrollable.

Instead, she was encouraged by the rest of her family to help her mother out with her homeworking orders on the grounds that it would help her to pass her time. Rabia, however, was quite clear that her employment preferences lay elsewhere:

> I don't like machining, I am not interested in working in a factory or a shop. I wanted to do a course at our local college but my parents won't let me go as there is no one to accompany me. I had found out about the course on my own initiative and I asked my parents for permission, but they have taken no notice. They ask who is going to take me there? My father doesn't like me machining, he thinks that it is not necessary for me to do so much work at such a young age, but he won't let me go to college either.

However, although parental authority was the immediate constraint on Rabia's ability to make choices about her work options, she recognised that her parents were themselves acting in response to constraints imposed by the extended family and the wider community:

> My parents might have been willing to send me to a college or a language centre, but we have older relatives and people from our village here who have told them that girls who go out to school become wild, run away with boys and forget their religion. My parents gave in to the pressure because they think that I am grown up now and so they worry. But they don't trust me. If they did, they would let me go to college.

## Negotiated agency, conflictual decision making

The examples of conflictual decision making I have been discussing so far all refer to women who had opted for homework in deference to dominant opinion within the family. A different category of conflict was reported by a few women who had encountered objections, not only to the idea of outside employment, but also to the idea of homeworking itself. While most women found it difficult to contest family objections to outside employment, acknowledging the validity of the concerns underpinning these objections, even if they did not always share them, objections to homeworking, which invariably came from husbands, were seen to have less legitimacy and therefore more likely to be contested. In most cases, husbands' objections related to the fear that their wives would neglect their domestic responsibilities: 'My husband doesn't want me to work outside, he is even reluctant to let me work at home. He thinks I should look after the children, help them with their education and keep the house clean.' Women were generally able to counter these objections by assuring their husbands that their domestic responsibilities would take priority over their homeworking: 'My husband was worried I would neglect the children and not feed them on time, but I showed him I could manage. It is not difficult to look after the children, clean the house, do the cooking and earn money homeworking, is it? [laughs].'

This conditional support for women's desire to do homework was echoed in the comment of one of the husbands who was present during the latter part of an interview: 'My wife's sewing does not interfere with the housework or the cooking. My house is clean, as you can see.'

Tahmina, however, adopted a very different course to deal with her husband's resistance to her desire to take up homeworking. She and her husband had arrived in Britain soon after their marriage and within a year of each other. She got the idea of homeworking when she saw how many women in their neighbourhood were doing it, but her husband was actively against the idea, feeling that there was no need for his wife to be doing such work, just because everybody else was doing it. Tahmina's strategy was to simply ignore his objections, relying on her own initiative to implement her preferences:

> Initially, my husband didn't want me to work, he refused to get me a machine or to telephone the factory so I had to do it myself . . . I never went to language classes, I learnt English just by listening to other people . . . And then I rented a machine for £2 or £3 a week. My husband can't machine so I had to get used to the machine by myself by practising on scraps . . . Eventually my machining became even better than my friends'. My first employers were Greek and Jewish, I also made dresses for an English factory. I phoned them up when necessary and opened the door for them. I didn't have any communication difficulties and after the first week or so, I was on good terms with them.

Her tactics paid off in the end. Her husband did not only get used to the idea of her homeworking, but had also withdrawn his earlier objections to the idea of her employment outside. When we interviewed her, she had begun looking for outside employment.

Masuda reported a less happy outcome. Her first preference would have been to work outside: 'There is nothing wrong with working outside. Purdah isn't the clothes you wear but what is in your heart. You can work outside and still keep your purdah. My own opinion is work is good for the health and gives you some economic security.' In fact, she had once briefly and surreptitiously taken up factory work: 'People have many reasons for not working outside, but I will tell you my own experience. I wanted to work in a factory but my husband wouldn't let me. But I once went and worked in a factory for three days without telling anybody. I didn't even know the work then.' After this incident, her husband agreed to let her take up homeworking and had bought her a sewing machine. She did the rest herself, practising on the machine till she became good at it, buying the *Hackney Gazette* where homeworking possibilities were advertised on a weekly basis and then ringing up the factories in question. However, a few months before we talked to Masuda, her husband had decided that she was not being able to combine her domestic work and her homeworking in a satisfactory fashion and therefore the homeworking had to stop. He had just sold her machine by the time we interviewed her.

## Active agency, consensual decision making

A final category of decision making evident in the homeworkers' testimonies was that based on an active consensus among family members as to how women could best use their time. There were around thirty-four women in our sample who fell into this category. In some cases, the consensus reflected the absence of a male household head and hence women's ability to make unilateral decisions about their own time allocation. In Zaheda's case, it reflected not so much the absence of a male head, but her primary responsibility as breadwinner. She was forty-three years old when we interviewed her. Her father had emigrated to the UK thirty years ago, but she herself had lived most of her life in Bangladesh. She had married in Bangladesh and borne a child, but systematic mistreatment at her husband's hands led to the dissolution of her marriage. Her father then arranged a second marriage for her to an acquaintance of his who had lived in Britain for seventeen years and was thirty years older than Zaheda. She had been reluctant to leave Bangladesh because she could not take her daughter with her, but had succumbed in the end to family pressure. She had joined her husband in the UK twelve years ago.

Her husband's age and illness meant that Zaheda increasingly took on the main breadwinning responsibilities for the entire family: 'I started tailoring work because we found out that we could not cover the rent, the rates and other expenses . . . It was the need for money that led me to this job.' However, her job possibilities were constrained by her difficulties with English, despite her efforts

to learn. Combined with the burden of looking after an elderly
husband, and his four children from a previous marriage, the
question of outside work did not arise:

> I have never tried to work outside the house or in a factory because I
> wouldn't be able to make people understand me nor could I travel around.
> I also have to look after my husband and give him tea and so forth. He is
> not a well man . . . once he was on a machine for several days. It is only by
> the grace of God, he is alive. So how can I go out?

However, while she had effectively taken on the role of household
head and breadwinner, it was a role that had been forced on her
by her husband's condition rather than actively sought, and her
testimony was pervaded by her sense of resignation: 'Although my
husband was over sixty when we got married and is now over eighty,
I don't have any complaints or regrets to tell you of − I tell
everything to God. My life is based on the practice of patience, that
is probably my fate.'

In other cases, women exercised a more positive agency in
making their decisions, opting for homework on practical grounds
with the support of the family. Tahera Banu's husband, who was
himself a machinist at a local garment factory, had not merely
supported her homework decision, but had actively assisted her in
getting started when she came up with the idea. He had bought
her a sewing machine and taught her how to use it. She gave up
for a while because her machining had brought complaints from
their previous neighbours. They had then moved into the Tower
Hamlets area and she took it up again, explaining it as a response
to the fact that her children were now older and entailed additional
expenses:

> The point is before our family was small and one person's earnings were
> enough. But now the family has grown, the children are older and their
> expenses have increased. A pair of trousers or shoes won't last more than
> two weeks. If I buy them shoes, I have to get two or three pairs for each
> one, because they wear them out within two or three days. And I have to
> spend a lot of money on their clothes, they won't wear anything cheap,
> they only want expensive clothes. One person's earnings are not enough.

Her husband continued to work in a garment factory and helped out by picking up her orders on his way home from the factory and then delivering the completed work. Neither she nor her husband had any objections in principle with the idea of her working outside. Indeed, she was quite favourably disposed to it since it would bring in more money. Her main constraint, as far as she was concerned, was her 'human capital' deficit:

> I don't know any English and I don't have qualifications for teaching Bengali either. If I had passed my Matric or studied further I might have given private tuition or even taught in schools, but I have never thought of these jobs because I don't have the qualifications. If I knew English and I had found an outside job, I would have taken it and my husband wouldn't have objected. It would be something to be pleased about. I'd like to work outside but you need English wherever you go. I would have earned more money and someone like me could certainly do with more money.

### Moving out of homework: exceptions who proved the rule?

Women's testimonies as to their motivations in taking up home-working, and the varying degrees of conflict or consensus they encountered from other family members, tell us that, rather than being a uniform response to purdah-related constraints on female behaviour, their decision represented a variety of different considerations and had been arrived at through a range of different decision making processes. This heterogeneity was further emphasised by the fact that not only were many of the women interviewed favourably disposed in principle to the idea of outside work, but some of the women had actually done, or were currently engaged in, outside work and others were actively seeking it at the time of the interview.

As we noted in Chapter 6, 7 per cent of women in the Bangladeshi/Pakistani community were reported to be 'unemployed' by official estimates, suggesting that these women were actively seeking work. We also noted that a small minority of employed women within the community included in the official statistics appeared to work largely in occupations classified as 'public administration, education and health'. Based on the preferences expressed by the

women in our sample, these jobs were likely to have been
community-based social service jobs (see Appendix 3). It is worth
investigating the testimonies of women who had taken up outside
employment, or were actively seeking it, to find out whether there
was something exceptional about these women which led them to
make different choices from the rest of the women in their community, or whether the culture of the community was more flexible
than it was often portrayed.

We can distinguish broadly between two groups of women in this
category. The first group were those who were responding to the
incapacitation or loss of the male breadwinner. The absence of a
male breadwinner gave them the economic incentive to seek better
paid outside work, but it was also indicative of the absence of a
significant source of constraint on their ability to do so. Zohra
Khanum was forty-five years old and had no children. Since both
her husband and stepson worked in garment factories and could
bring her orders, she had drifted into homework about fifteen
years ago:

> I started machining because I didn't have anything to fill my time with, I
> thought I would be able to stay at home and still be able to save money . . .
> I heard other people talking about homework. I did not have any children
> so people suggested that I buy myself a machine and do some work to
> occupy myself. I learnt machine control from a woman who lived some
> distance from here.

She had not enjoyed the work but felt that at that time there were
few options, not only because there were fewer 'community' jobs
around for Bangladeshis, but also because of the greater fear of
racist violence at that time: 'There weren't so many Bengalis in this
area before or facilities for training . . . Homeworking helped me
pass the time. I didn't like it, but the main thing was that I didn't
want to just sit at home alone without doing anything. There was a
greater fear of going out then, people used to get beaten up
regularly.'

A year prior to our interview, her husband had returned to
Bangladesh and it was clear to her that he had no plans to come
back. She decided to train as a creche worker and had put down

her name for work in a number of local schools. She explained her reasons for wanting to give up homeworking, partly in terms of its practical disadvantages, but also in terms of her own loneliness:

> I stopped machining because my body can't stand it anymore, also the work is so irregular. It doesn't matter if I earn more or less working in a creche. I'll be around children all the time and since I don't have any of my own, I feel sad when I am at home on my own. If I work with children, my mind is refreshed, my time is used up and my body gets some fresh air and exercise. I think it will be good for my health if I work outside. And I will be paying tax and national insurance to the government so when I have to go to the DHSS or to the doctor I will feel proud of myself.

In Fatema Begum's case too, her husband's departure to Bangladesh had provided the impetus behind her decision to take up outside work. She was in her early fifties and had nine children, five girls and four boys. Four of her daughters and one son were married; the younger ones lived with her and were still at school. She had spent most of her married life in her husband's village, living with his parents, but had finally joined him around ten years ago. Her husband was disabled and got an allowance from the government, but was afraid that it might be withdrawn one day, so she had taken up homeworking as an additional source of security. Her husband had acted as her middleman. However, a few years earlier, he left her and returned to Bangladesh. For a while she relied on her children to phone the factories and fetch the work. Then she took up a job as a minder in a local school, but did not manage to keep it for long.

Feeling isolated in London, she decided to return to her village in Bangladesh with her younger children and had admitted them into the local primary school. However, they would not settle into what was for them a new and unfamiliar culture:

> I wanted to see if they liked it, but they became crazy, they would keep calling for a rickshaw and asking to be taken home to London. If we went somewhere by rickshaw and got off at a house, they would call it back and ask to be taken to our house in Aldgate East, the rickshawallah didn't understand what they were talking about. They wanted to come back here, they wouldn't attend classes, they said that they would come back to

> England by themselves . . . so I came back. A mother has to think of her children's happiness.

She took up homeworking again, but as sole breadwinner, found the earnings too irregular to support her family. Consequently, she decided to find outside work and became a machinist in a largely female garment unit in the locality. However, she was the only Bangladeshi woman in it, her English was poor and she found herself isolated from the other workers and the brunt of their hostility:

> They would all sit together and chat and I couldn't mix with them, I was older than the rest of them and I had different worries: if you haven't been bitten by a snake, how will you understand the pain of a snakebite? I had a fire inside me. Even though the children's father had left them, I couldn't leave them as long as I was in this world, they had to think of me as both mother and father. I haven't yet explained to the children why I am so sad, they are too young to understand.

In the end she gave up her job, unable to comprehend or deal with the hostility of her co-workers and unable to explain herself to them:

> What I didn't understand was the English girl beside me was competing with me. They used to have tea and chat but I would never get off the machine because I had other things on my mind. I would do 30 trousers a day, and I would be paid for that. But in her mind she was competing with me and couldn't beat me. In the end, she accused me of something and everyone sided with her. I thought the whole world was full of trickery, that there was no justice for me . . . So I got up quietly and left and never went back again . . . What could I do, they have too much speaking power, everybody in this country has speaking power. They didn't speak openly with me once. People share their thoughts, don't they? But there wasn't any of that, they didn't even think of me as a human being. If I am not treated as a human being, how can my children grow up as human beings?

She had continued to look for work for a while, but in the past year one of her married daughters returned to live with her when her husband went to Bangladesh. When we interviewed Fatema Begum, she had gone back to homeworking so she could look after her grandchild at home while her daughter worked in a pharmacy.

In Mehrun's case, the decision to take up outside work occurred in the context of an extremely conflictual marriage which ultimately ended in divorce. She had come to the UK with her parents, over thirteen or fourteen years ago, when she was about twelve years old and spoke English well. Early on in the marriage, her husband had gone for a visit to Bangladesh and she heard rumours that he was planning to marry again. She was expecting her first child at the time and took the precaution of registering the house assigned to her by a local housing association in her own name. In order to pay her rates and bills, she took on part-time work in a small, all-women outdoor unit:

> I knew the people next door owned a factory, I used to call the owner Dada (grandfather). I used to tell him about my problems and the unpaid bills that were piling up. He told me that my husband probably wanted me to lose the house, then it would all be over for me. But I didn't want to lose it. I have never had anything before in my life of my own except that the house and my two children. The house was the only security I had.

Her husband had not raised any objections to her factory work on his return from Bangladesh since it paid their rent. She gave it up when she had her baby. However, by the time she had her second child, their marriage had begun to deteriorate. Her husband's contributions to the household became increasingly erratic. Unable to manage on child support, she expressed the need to find outside work but this time, he was adamantly opposed. The marriage continued to deteriorate and in the end, she gave in to his demands for a divorce. She began homeworking again, but only to tide her over while she looked for a better job: 'I don't want to do homework anymore. It is boring and I find it hard to concentrate on working at home when I have to look after the children, cook, feed them, take them to school, wash the clothes, there is so much housework to be done. It's hard enough doing all that without having to do machining on top of it.'

## Moving out of homework: exceptions to the rule?

However, along with women who began to seek outside work in response to the absence of male support, there was a second category of women who demonstrated an active preference for such work, notwithstanding the availability of male support. One of the distinguishing characteristics of this group of women was the absence of child care constraints. They were either unmarried or they had no children of their own or else their children had reached school-going age. Their willingness to search for outside employment suggested that community norms were by no means uniformly interpreted or enforced. While the imprint of these norms were still discernible in the 'community-based' nature of the employment they sought, the experiences of the few who had sought jobs outside the boundaries of the community provided a reminder of the relevance of racist discrimination as a further constraint on their labour market choices.

Talia was thirty-six years old and had lived in the UK for fifteen years. Her husband had come to Britain over thirty years ago to study engineering. He was now working in a car factory. According to Talia, he had been unable to get a job commensurate with his qualifications for a very simple reason: 'He can't get a good job because employers discriminate against black people, he has applied to so many factories for a better job but he has never succeeded.' She herself had taken up homework eight years ago, partly to earn some extra money and partly out of boredom: 'I had to teach myself. I started because I was bored with being a house-wife, the children went to school and my husband was at work all day. I thought it would help with the housekeeping because it is a struggle trying to support the family on one person's income. My husband didn't object as long as I could cope with the housework and the children as well.' However, like some of the other women we interviewed, she too became dissatisfied with being cooped up in the house all day long and, encouraged by the fact that other women were taking up jobs outside, she decided to look for alternative work.

I enjoyed homework in the beginning but I am fed up now. I had never looked for outside work before, but nowadays so many women have jobs outside that for the last seven months I have been looking for outside work because I would prefer it to homeworking. I told an uncle a long time ago that I was bored with housework and wanted a job ... My husband supported me because he knew I was really bored, the children were grown up as well.

Her willingness to consider work outside the boundaries of the community were thwarted by what she perceived to be racially-motivated limits on her labour market options: 'I did an interview once for a food packing job but they said my English was not good enough. I couldn't see why you needed good English for a simple job like that. I think they were just racist and did not want to employ black people.' She was subsequently offered a job as a helper in a local school, where she would earn £20 a week, which she had been delighted to take on: 'I really enjoy this work, it helps me pass the time and earn a bit of money. I also learn a lot of different things. Mixing with English people improves your English. Working outside is good for your health, all that travelling keeps you fit. I am gradually cutting down on homework because I have the job at the school.'

Morgina and her husband were among the more educated couples in our sample, both having completed their higher education before coming to the UK. He had arrived twenty years ago while she joined him eight years ago. As long as the children were young, she had homeworking on a casual basis, taking on the extra work which her neighbour could not handle. However, she attended English classes after she arrived because she was keen to move out of homework partly because of its disadvantages – 'There is too much headache in homework and it's not right to work in a council flat either ... And your house gets in a state with thread everywhere ...' – and partly in response to the perceived advantages of outside work: 'I like working outside but I have some difficulties with my language, that is why I go to language classes, I want to learn the language properly ... I like outside work because you use up your time, I don't like sitting at home by myself and when I go out, I play with the children and pass the time.'

She was also open to the idea of acquiring further qualifications in order to expand her job options. New networks of information had opened for her when her children began to attend school: 'A teacher at their school suggested that I do voluntary work there but I told him I had to think about it ... I hadn't thought about working outside before but he gave me the idea. I didn't think about it before, my children didn't go to school, and I didn't know anything.' Then she received a letter from the school informing parents about the possibility of attending courses to train women for nursery work which she had responded to:

> We have done the course for mother and toddler group for six weeks, but they didn't give us any certificates. We told them there is no use in that, if we went somewhere else for work, we wouldn't get it without a certificate. We'll do more classes again in September and they'll give certificates to those they think are good ... I have discussed all this with my husband and he told me to go ahead ... If you go out to work, you get qualifications and a good record for anything you want to do in future.

Ameena was thirty years old and had come to the UK over a decade ago to join her husband who had his own outdoor clothing unit. She started out doing homework, but it had not been her preferred option:

> I don't want to sit at home because everybody in this country works, we've never wanted to claim unemployment benefit. Those who were not claiming did homework, and those who were claiming said homeworking wasn't worth the money. My husband encouraged me to work, he didn't have any objections ... I found a community work job and the chance to teach Bengali language in a school, but I couldn't do it because of the children. They are small and I don't have anyone in this country who can look after them.

As the children grew up, she decided she wanted to explore other work options. She attended an English language and community work course for two years at the City and East London College: 'I was very interested in learning English, your husband can't go with you everywhere, can he, you have to know the language. I wanted to do something, if you know English, you can do everything.' She began looking for a job in community work or a nursery after completing her course, but found that the qualifications were no guarantee of a job. When we interviewed her, she was still doing some homeworking, but had started taking driving lessons to improve her employment prospects:

> If I can drive, I will be able to do something. I had three small children before, but they are growing up now, my eldest son is ten, they can come and go to school by themselves, only one is left still at home. I am confident now I will be able to do something. I know my English isn't that good, I've just learnt enough to get around. But I could do a community job or a nursery job. If I wanted to go to a factory, I could go to ours, there is nothing to stop me. But I don't want to go on machining for the rest of my life. I want to do something else. It would be better than sitting at home.

Given the views of conservative sections of the community on the question of women's outside employment, and the gossip that it generated, it could be said that women who sought outside employment in response to the incapacitation or loss of the male breadwinner were the 'exceptions' who proved the rule, since male support was the norm on which women's domestic role was premised. However, evidence that there were also other women prepared to take up such employment, notwithstanding the support of a male breadwinner, suggests that community norms were not as inflexible as the conservative elements in the community would have liked, as outside observers believed and as the official statistics indicated. Nor were they interpreted in uniform ways by all sections of the community. Ameena's spirited defiance of the disapproval of the community of any behaviour on the part of women which appeared out of the ordinary was a case in point:

> I don't know why our women do not go out to work. It is partly a personal choice. It is also to do with Bengali society. Because I'm taking driving lessons, many women will say all kinds of things. If I go to Bengali grocery shops, people make comments. If I get a job outside today, some people will approve of it and some will not, they will say a Muslim woman is disobeying the *Shariat*. But I am working for my children and for my own happiness. If I work within my own purdah, I'm not breaking any laws, but if I do something wrong at home, nobody will see, but it's inside the home

that many bad things happen. But Bengali people think this way, they don't want to understand. If they are so virtuous, why did they come to London?

In addition, our discussion points to the importance of life-cycle variations in women's economic activity rates, neglect of which may exaggerate women's unwillingness to engage in outside work. It suggests that younger unmarried women, women without children or with no young children and women whose children were now old enough to do without the full-time care of their mothers were most likely to consider taking up outside work, while women with pre-school age children were least likely. This appears to be partly corroborated by official data on female labour force participation in Britain. According to the 1991 Labour Force Survey (cited in HMSO, 1996, Table 4.4), economic activity rates were highest among young, unmarried women (aged 18–34) in all ethnic groups. Although among Bangladeshi women in this age category, it was a remarkable 85 per cent, it was still nevertheless lower than women in the equivalent age/ marital category in all other ethnic groups. Moreover, given that women married at a much younger age in the Bangladeshi community than in any other – their average of marriage in the UK was twenty-one – there were likely to be a much smaller percentage of women in this category compared to other ethnic groups. We are consequently talking about a very small minority of women in the community in this category.

Where Bangladeshi women's economic activity patterns diverged most sharply from women in all the other ethnic groups[1] was at marriage. Whereas, in all other ethnic groups, there was little change in economic rates among married women in the 18–34 age group who had no children – for instance, it remained at 95 per cent for white women – it plummeted to 20 per cent among Bangladeshi women. The presence of a child under the age of five did make a difference for other ethnic groups – activity rates among white women fell to 46 per cent – but was more marked among Bangladeshi women whose activity rates fell further to 9 per cent.

1. With the exception of women from the Pakistani community, the other major Muslim group from South Asia, whose female labour force patterns were somewhat similar to those from the Bangladeshi community.

Activity rates began to rise for all married women as their children grew older: to 30 per cent among Bangladeshi women whose oldest child was over ten years old and to 76 per cent among white women. Finally, again corroborating the evidence presented in this chapter, economic rates were relatively high at 36 per cent among older women (aged 35–60) who had no dependent children (or presumably no children) in the Bangladeshi community. This increase was not evident among white women in this category of whom 67 per cent were economically active. All of this suggests that while child care responsibilities were a constraint on women's labour force participation for all groups of women in Britain, marriage constituted an additional, and indeed prior, constraint from women from South Asian Muslim communities, the Pakistanis and Bangladeshis.

## Revisiting theories of choice: unified and bargaining models of the household

When we consider the various categories of decision making processes which underpinned women's choice of homeworking, we find many echoes of the factors which featured in the decision making processes described by the women workers in Dhaka – as well as some important differences. The normative considerations which came into play in the decision making processes in London were very similar to those expressed in the Dhaka context. This is not surprising since both groups of households subscribed to similar cultural models about gender roles within the family and, hence, appropriate forms of behaviour for women and men. In addition, the decision making processes we described in London, like those in Dhaka, were characterised by varying degrees of agency and passivity, consensus and conflict. Some of them could be easily accommodated in a joint welfare maximising model of the household, based on unified preferences, where the unity of preferences reflected shared assessments of the relative returns to women's time in alternative possible uses.[2] However, there were

2. It is worth pointing out, however, that cultural constraints do complicate neoclassi-

other decision making processes that were better captured by a
bargaining approach in that they entailed conflicting preferences
within the household. The grounds on which these conflicts
occurred varied and, as in the Dhaka context, it was not always easy
to disentangle altruistic motivations from self-interest.

In the case of husbands, for instance, objections to outside work,
and in some cases, to homeworking itself, often took the form of
concern for children's welfare or the mothers' health.[3] However, it
was clear from many of the testimonies that men's own welfare was
also at stake in their objections and we have noted the various ways
in which husbands gained very directly from their wives' devotion
to their comforts. Consequently, a more cynical interpretation to
these objections would be men's fear of the likely consequences of
women's work for their own welfare: it may explain why economic
activity rates among Bangladeshi women plummeted most sharply
after marriage rather than after the first child. The 'conjugal
contract' which underpinned husbands' ability to made these
demands on their wives was graphically spelt out by Husna Khanam,
whose husband refused to help out with housework and had tried
to dissuade her from taking up homeworking in case it interfered
with her domestic responsibilities. He clearly saw her contributions
to his domestic comforts as the quid pro quo for his contributions
as family breadwinner: 'He can't do any housework, he doesn't
know how to. Of course he should help but he is not used to it, he
doesn't even wash his plate after he has eaten. I have to do it. I
have told him so many times but he won't do it. He says, What do I
feed you for?'

However, beyond the practical considerations underpinning

---

cal notions of rational choice, premised on well-behaved preference orderings over
different utility-bearing 'goods'. A preference function which entailed a preference for
working at home on grounds of purdah, in apparent indifference to the amount of
income forgone as a result, is hardly 'well-behaved', although it may be rational from
the household's point of view. It could be argued that the decision would be recon-
sidered if outside work offered a sufficiently large remuneration, but 'lexicographic
preference functions' nevertheless represent a challenge to the predictive power of
rational choice theory.

3. However, in at least one case where altruism took the form of concern for the
woman's own health, the concern appeared to be partly motivated by the husband's
anxiety that he might then end up having to look after her!

men's objections to women's desire to earn, there was evidence of symbolic considerations of the kind that featured in the testimonies of the Dhaka workers. For many husbands, women's outside work cast aspersions on their ability to fulfil their breadwinning roles in the eyes of the community. Again, Husna Khanam stated this very clearly in her account: 'Most women don't try to work outside, and their husbands don't encourage them. Their husbands will say, If you go out to work, other people will say, her husband can't feed her and my status as a man will go down.' Objections to women earning an income from inside the home were less vociferous than to outside employment, because of the greater privacy of the arrangement and its subsumption within women's domestic role. The other factor in husbands' objections to their wives' outside employment appeared to be related to sexual anxiety, often expressed as a fear that 'they would learn bad ways' and the implications of this for their standing within the community. As Sufia put it, 'The Bengali community sanctions women who go out to work by gossiping about them, they say that so-and-so's wife is working with men, she must be bad, eventually the husband is affected.'

Parental opposition to their daughters' desire to take up outside work – there were no cases of parents objecting to the idea of homework – was generally expressed as a concern for their daughters' reputation within the community and, by extension, their own. Once again, the question of women's reputation was frequently bound up with questions of sexuality. According to Sufia, 'People criticise parents who let their teenage daughters go out to work, they think that they will run away with men. It is an embarrassment for parents. If they work at home, the parents can keep an eye on them.' However, while parents believed that they were acting in the interests of the family by curtailing daughters' choices, not all daughters agreed. Many attached far less weight to community opinion than did their parents. Ruxana's testimony made this clear. She attributed her ability to move out of homework into part-time youth work to the fact that her marriage had moved her from the more conservative authority of her parents to the more flexible authority of her husband: 'When I lived with my parents, I could not go out very much because they would not allow me to. But

after my marriage, I was free and my husband . . . has encouraged
me to do any work I can.'

She blamed the strictness of parental authority in relation to
daughters on a culture in which a woman's marriage prospects
were defined in terms of her reputation:

> I think the reason why girls from other countries who come here are able
> to work outside is because their parents have brought them up that way
> and they have the freedom. But in our community, parents don't allow
> girls to go out to work because they think the girl will become spoilt and it
> would be difficult to get her married. But if you can trust your daughter,
> then it is alright. If the girl wants to work outside, let her. The real point is
> trust – whether as a parent, you trust your daughter.

She regretted that the cultural values of her community, and the
lack of trust it bred in parents towards daughters, had closed off
the opportunity for her to acquire any marketable skills, aside from
machining: 'I never got the opportunity at my parents' house. But
I could have learnt other things apart from machining. My parents
wouldn't let me, what could I do? They don't trust girls or
something.'

However, as in the Dhaka context, a narrowly economistic version
of bargaining would fail to capture some of the factors at work in
shaping these decision making processes. In particular, it would fail
to capture the extent to which struggles over material access within
the household often took the form of struggles over meanings. It
was clear that a great deal of the conflict reported by women in
relation to their work options revolved around notions of family
honour and reputation within the community. While the behaviour
of all family members affected its social standing, the testimonies
in this chapter echo the finding from the Dhaka context that
women's presence and behaviour in the public domain constituted
a particular threat to family honour that men's did not. The
conflicts reported in this chapter over women's work preferences
consequently took the form of conflicting evaluations of the extent
to which women's outside work did indeed threaten family honour.

As in Dhaka, there was a clear hierarchy of interpretive power
within the household so that some interpretations of household

welfare and family honour carried more weight than others. Because Bangladeshi family hierarchies tend to coalesce along lines of age, gender and lifecycle, it was most frequently men as a category who occupied positions of authority over women and it was women who had to negotiate consent from more powerful male members before they were able to act on their preferences. Interpretive privilege derived partly from men's material advantages, but both were in turn embedded in the socially-sanctioned claims and obligations which defined relationships between family members. Privilege and responsibility were closely bound up with each other so that male responsibility for family welfare carried with it the authority to define the collective welfare of the family. This was evident in the testimony of one of the male workers explaining why he did not let his wife go out to work:

> I don't like women who go out to work. I think women should stay at home and look after the children and do the housework. If they go out to work, who would look after the children and the home? Anyway, women change if they start working. They try to dominate their husbands. This is very bad. Women should only go out to work if their family is in financial difficulties. In that case, they can go out to work wearing a burkah.

Those in authority within the household were thus in a position to define its 'joint welfare function' in terms which not only prioritised their own interests, but also dissipated competing definitions which might threaten these interests. Thus, husbands who felt threatened by any attempt on the part of their wives to depart from the pre-existing division of labour and responsibility were able to draw on their interpretive authority so as to define the collective interests of the household in terms which precluded such choices for their wives. The accepted authority of some household members to pre-empt the choices of others, through the exercise of interpretive privilege, resulted in a form of power which operated through the tacit understandings among family members about acceptable and unacceptable choices rather than through open conflict. This more implicit operation of power is evident in Mariam Bibi's statement cited earlier, 'My husband's family haven't actually forbidden me to go out to work but yet in a way they have.' It also explains why, despite the fact that she herself did not subscribe fully to the dominant view of purdah within her family, she did not raise the possibility of outside work with her in-laws, anticipating in advance what their response would be.

Thus, we can see that there is a great deal of overlap in the kinds of considerations which featured in women's labour supply decision making in the Dhaka and in the London context. Similar discourses about family roles and gender propriety operated amongst Bangladeshi households in both contexts and women in both contexts put a great deal of store by obtaining family consensus on their labour supply decisions. However, there is still an unexplained dimension to the story. Despite the similarities in familial and gender ideologies which informed Bangladeshi women's labour supply decisions in the two contexts, these ideologies appeared to define a far more restrictive set of labour market options in the London context than they had in Dhaka. While we can understand why women in London rejected the idea of working in clothing factories, given the predominance of Bangladesh men in their work force, it was striking that far fewer women in London expressed a preference for outside work than did in Dhaka, that many of the women in London who did express a preference for outside employment not only encountered considerable resistance from other household members, but that it was usually preferences other than their own which dominated the final decision making outcome. This was in contrast to the Dhaka context where it was women's own preferences which tended to prevail in the final outcomes.

Of course, just as the Dhaka sample was biased against women who had failed to win consent to do outside work, it could also be argued that by focusing only on women homeworkers in the London context, our sample was biased against women who had succeeded in overcoming familial resistance to outside employment. However, unlike the Dhaka context, where there was likely to be a large, but unknown, proportion of women engaged in home-based forms of paid work, official statistics in the UK suggests that the percentage of women from the Bangladeshi community who took part in outside employment was indeed small, with only 12 per cent in full-time work. We are, I would suggest, looking at real differences in either preferences or constraints in the two contexts, rather than at an artefact of sample definition.

To understand what might explain these differences, I want to re-analyse some of the homeworkers' testimonies to find out what they might reveal about the London context to explain women's greater apparent preference for home-based work, men's greater resistance to the idea of women from their families taking up outside employment and the lesser likelihood of women challenging male authority in situations of conflict. I would like to suggest that an important component of the answer lies in the very different weight given to 'the community' in shaping women's behaviour and choices in the two contexts, not only in situations of conflict but also in more consensual processes of decision making. As we saw in the Dhaka context, while women workers were well aware of community disapproval towards their participation in factory employment, their attitude was one of indifference, resentment and even hostility, attitudes which were often shared by other family members. By contrast, 'the community' and its norms and beliefs figured as a very real presence in the testimonies of the homeworkers in London, to be clearly taken into account, both by them and by their family members.

It is not immediately self-evident that the community should loom so much larger in the accounts of the women and their families in London than they did in Dhaka. International migration is, after all, a potentially centrifugal process, offering migrants the opportunity to renegotiate the 'rules' of the place they are leaving in the light of the very different 'rules' of the place they have migrated to.[4] For Bangladeshi women, migration to London involved the movement from a society with strict controls over their mobility in the public domain, and very low levels of participation in paid work, to one where women had considerable freedom in the public domain and a long tradition of paid work outside the home. Yet it appears that for the Bangladeshi community,

4. This is, for instance, the substance of a quote from Germaine Greer, speaking presumably as a female Australian immigrant, cited in an article by Isobel Hilton: 'Migrants are special people who have the courage to venture into the unknown in order to beat the systems of inequality and limitation into which they were born in the old country.' (*Independent on Sunday*, 17 October 1993)

migration entailed a reconstitution of the 'old' rules in the new environment, with all the restrictions that these implied on women's ability to take up public employment. In order to understand what it was about 'the community' that was significant in the London context, I want to shift the analytical focus from a concern with household decision making processes to the broader context in which these decisions were being made. I want to draw attention in particular to how factors of 'time' and 'place' helped to construct London as a very different configuration of constraints and opportunities, and hence a very different decision making environment, to that which prevailed in Dhaka.

## Time and place in the making of the community

First of all, there was the question of 'time'. It is important to bear in mind that the men and women who featured in our London sample were first-generation immigrants. We see evidence in the London testimonies of some of the stresses involved in making the adjustment from a slow-moving, rural society in one of the poorest countries in the world to the fast-paced urban life in one of the richer ones. The normal process of transition involved in international migration was made immeasurably more difficult by the shock of contrast between two very differing cultural milieus. It is also important to remember that the immigrant community also came from a district which is considered to be among the most religious and conservative in Bangladesh. Many had spent their formative years in Bangladesh, a period when the norms and values absorbed are often a powerful influence on definitions of self and others in later life and are likely to have been carried over by both women and men when they settled into their new environment.

Secondly, we need to take account of how gender differentiated the migration process. While many of the men in the community had migrated to Britain a decade or more ago, most of the women in the community, and in our sample, had arrived far more recently, some in the last five years. Like other South Asian immigrant women, they came to Britain, defined as 'family dependants' under the voucher system: they were 'sent' or 'sent for' rather than, as the migrant women in the Dhaka sample had often done, arriving on their own initiative. Many had left behind the families and social networks they had grown up with in order to join husbands or fathers with whom their contact had been non-existent or very minimal. While the practice of marital exogamy and patrilocal residence has traditionally cut Bangladeshi women off from their natal family networks and childhood friends after marriage, this isolation obviously took on a particularly stark form when marriage entailed resettlement in a distant country, 'seven oceans and thirteen rivers away', rather than in a not too distant village.

Turning to the 'question of place' in the decision-making processes considered in this chapter, I would point, first of all, to the role played by the particular nature of the migration process through which Bangladeshis had entered Britain in explaining the geography of their settlement patterns. We have noted already that the vast majority of Bangladeshis in the UK not only originated from a particular district in Bangladesh but also from particular villages in this district, villages clustered around the major landing points for river transport between Sylhet and Calcutta. We noted too the role played by the voucher system in reinforcing the selective nature of this migration to the kin and community of those who had already settled. This shipping link was a major reason why so many Bangladeshis settled in the East End of London, close to its docklands. 'Path-dependence' in settlement patterns led to an increase, rather than a decrease, in the geographical concentration of the community over time. As Bangladeshi workers were laid off from factories in other parts of Britain during the recession of the late 1970s, they made their way to their compatriots in East London.

The geographical cohesiveness of the community, both in terms of its origins and in its subsequent settlement patterns, has meant that Bangladeshis reconstituted themselves in the London context as a highly localised community, clustered in a few boroughs in its East End. These boroughs thus approximated what Giddens (1979) calls the *locale* of their operations, a space which was physically demarcated and where the presence of known others was a major factor influencing all encounters of social life. The anonymity associated with migration into Dhaka from different districts in

Bangladesh into geographically dispersed settlements scattered around the city was not a feature of migration into London where it has led to the construction of a geographically concentrated 'face-to-face' community linked by personal networks which extend to their communities of origin back in Sylhet.

However, the other important factor contributing to the centripetal character of the settlement process has been the invidious discrimination and outright racism that Bangladeshis, along with other black and Asian groups, encountered in the UK, and which has led to their concentration in the deprived inner city areas of the country. The Bangladeshi community in the UK is not simply concentrated in the Tower Hamlets borough of the East End of London, but also largely around the area of their initial settlement, Spitalfields and the neighbouring wards of St Mary's, St Katherine's and Shadwell. The majority of Bangladeshis also live in council housing in 'safe' neighbourhoods in these areas rather than in the more racially antagonistic, white owner-occupied housing estates (see Appendix 3). In 1994, about 60 per cent of Bangladeshis lived in council housing compared to 10 per cent of the white community (Office for National Statistics, 1996). Many of the white estates have been effectively no-go areas for Bangladeshis: Carey and Shukur (1985) noted that on one such estate, seven out of nine Bangladeshi families had to be evacuated to safer accommodation in 1984 after a year of constant and severe harassment by local youths.[5]

During this period, the National Front was particularly active in the borough. While it polled around 2–4 per cent of votes in the three wards of Tower Hamlets with the highest Bangladeshi concentration, it polled between 9 and 19 per cent in the surrounding eleven wards. The community thus found itself hemmed into a small area within the borough. To move east or north of this area was to venture into National Front territory. The few who had

5. According to the British Crime Survey, nearly half of the South Asians who had been victims of crime, or the threat of a crime (assaults, threats, vandalism and theft) believed it to have been racially motivated compared to under a third of black victims. Thirty-six per cent of Bangladeshis interviewed by the Survey feared racial attacks compared to thirty-nine per cent Indians, twenty-eight per cent blacks and seven per cent whites (Office for National Statistics, 1996).

moved away from Tower Hamlets in search of better accommo-
dation have tended to seek it in 'safe' areas like East Ham and
Upton Park where there were high concentrations of other South
Asians.

Aside from the hard-core racism of the Far Right organisations,
there was also the more hidden and less publicly acknowledged
racism entrenched within the institutions of the labour market and
public sector services. We have already pointed out how employment opportunities for Bangladeshis were largely confined to clothing and catering where they generally worked for Bangladeshi or
other South Asian employers. The borough is also believed to have
some of the poorest social services in the country. While, as we
noted, many more Bangladeshis lived on council estates/low
income areas than other ethnic groups in the area, 67 per cent of
Bangladeshi families were judged to be living in overcrowded
housing compared to less than 10 per cent of the rest of the
population in Tower Hamlets (HMSO, 1986). Local schools, like
most schools in poorer inner cities, had a reputation for very poor
educational standards. These disadvantages were exacerbated by
the highly discriminatory character of local housing policy adopted
by a Liberal-led council in the area in the early 1990s, the explicit
aim of which was to exclude members of the community from
access to council housing. Liberal attitudes to housing proved to
be one of the most racially explosive issues in the area, and in 1993
helped to catapult a member of the Fascist Far Right British
National Party onto the local council for the first time in the area's
history.

The intersection of these acute forms of racial exclusion produced a community that was thrown back on its own economic and
social resources, the Bangladeshi version of the 'ethnic economy'.
The importance of the social networks of the community surfaced
continuously in the accounts of both the women and the men. It
was through relatives and acquaintances already resident in London that newly arrived immigrants obtained the information and
sponsorship that made their journey possible. They relied on these
networks to find them lodgings when they first arrived, to help
them make contact with local social services and to direct them
towards employment possibilities. Furthermore, these support

networks continued after the initial critical period of settling in to provide access to information, contacts and opportunities. Thus the majority of the male garment workers we interviewed were working in units owned by a Bangladeshi subcontractor or had heard of factory jobs through Bangladeshi informants in the factories or through the community grapevine. In the words of one of the male workers:

> It is only possible to move from one job to another with the help of a friend or a relative. It is only through them that you learn about new openings. You can't get a job just by asking the owner of the factory to give you one. You must go with a reference from someone inside. That is how many Bengalis find jobs in Turkish or Greek factories.

Community cohesion offered valued symbolic as well as material resources. In the face of exclusion from the mainstream of the economy and society by a hostile ethnic majority, the community drew on its own religion, norms and customs to reaffirm its cultural identity, effectively transforming their 'given' group identity into a 'chosen' one. The local mosque played an important role in the community's social and political life. Cultural events were organised by local entrepreneurs who brought over well-known artistes from Bangladesh while local community organisations regularly put on musical shows and dramas (Carey and Shukur, 1985). Where lesser antagonism from ethnic majority groups might have led to greater mutual exploration of cultural difference, what occurred instead was a sharper definition of difference, of discourses based on 'them' and 'us'. As Carey and Shukur (1985, p. 416) pointed out at the time, 'even young Bangladeshi children, whose command of English is indistinguishable from that of their white peers, and whose leisure patterns have absorbed elements from the local white (and black) working-class youth cultures, have found that skin colour and negative stereotypes about "Asians" have erected formidable barriers to interaction'.

The realities of 'skin colour and negative stereotypes' surfaced in the testimonies of both the women and men that we interviewed, but in somewhat gender-differentiated forms. Although national statistics show that around a third of women in the Bangladeshi/

Pakistani community said that they felt unsafe out alone after dark, compared to a fifth of women in the other ethnic groups, only a small minority of the women in our sample cited direct experience of racist attitudes as the reason for their anxiety and these generally did not take a violent form:

> The other day I went to ask an English girl about the buses. I walked towards her and said 'excuse me' when I was 5 or 6 steps away from her. As soon as I said that, she turned around and walked away! She didn't want to talk to me because I am a black person. It is upsetting that someone should walk away from me when I am trying to talk to them.

> I have never been mugged or anything although once in 1982 or 1983, a white boy snatched my bag from my hand in Aldgate. Once when I was on the bus, the white driver called me a 'bloody black'. I was a woman and on my own so I did not say anything. But when I was getting off the bus, I muttered, 'Bloody National Front'. I learnt this from the TV and that they assault black people.

Many more women expressed a more generalised anxiety about the possibility of racism towards members of their family or community:

> When an English person goes out, the thought never enters their minds that a Bengali person might attack them. They stay out till two or three in the morning but never think that a Bengali person might beat them up. But if our son or relative stays out, we worry that something has happened to them.

> Some of the English don't like us, otherwise they would not subject us to abuse when we go out. I see it happen before me, they spit and swear and call us 'Paki'. My son often tells me English children call him names at school.

> The older English people are alright with us because they know what happened in the past, about our histories, but the younger ones say, why have you come here to study, aren't there schools in your country, we don't go to other countries so why are you here? The girls at my daughter's school say these things to her.

By and large, women's fears for *themselves*, as opposed to members of their family or community, centred on dealing with unknown situations, with sexual harassment on the streets, or fear of

mugging cropping up as frequently as did the possibility of encountering racist violence.

> I get scared at night but not in the evening. I am a girl and I fear
> something might happen. I fear for my reputation. I'm scared of the
> National Front, they might start on me because I am Asian. They ask you
> for money and beat you up, that is what I have heard. I am scared in quiet
> streets in the day time, I'm scared of young men. I fear the Bengali men
> because they harass you on the streets, make comments, and the English
> ones in case they beat you up or ask for money.

> I have never been scared outside, although I have heard things from other
> people. But I don't go out often enough for anything to happen. People
> can only behave badly towards you if they find you on your own in a dark
> alley.

One reason why women may have been protected from direct
experiences of racist violence are the restrictions on their movements that we have been discussing in this chapter, both in terms
of how far they ventured beyond their immediate neighbourhood
on their own, as well as how late in the day they were likely to be
out on the streets. This protection was not available to the men
from the community since their need to work, their dealings with
local authorities and their greater participation in the public life of
the community all combined to take them out on the streets on a
more routine basis and later into the evening. A striking feature of
men's accounts was consequently how much more frequently they
referred to both direct and indirect encounters with often violent
forms of racism at work, in schools and on the streets:

> Nowadays the majority of English people are racist, the minority is neutral.
> I can say this from my personal experience. In 1979, my father and I were
> attacked in Poplar. They called us racist names and beat us up. The police
> do nothing if you report a racist attack.

> About ten years ago, I was attacked in a road off Brick Lane. It was 9 in the
> evening and I was returning home after visiting a relative's house. 10 or 15
> English youths jumped on me. They punched and kicked me many times.
> I was too frightened and alone to fight back. When people came out from
> nearby shops and houses to find out what all the noise was about, they
> released me and ran away. I went back later that evening with some friends
> but we could not find them.

In 1980 when I was still at school, the white schoolboys would bully Asian boys. They were usually skinheads. Whenever those white skinheads got a chance, they used to beat up Asian boys. They found a Bengali boy alone in a school toilet and beat him up really badly. It is different now. We are more alert and stand up for ourselves. Many white people in the area are OK, but some are really bad and there are still a lot of attacks.

I always return home by 9 o'clock in the evening. I have never been attacked because I never stay out late at night. Most attacks happen late at night. Last year, my friend was badly beaten up at midnight. He was in hospital for many days. He has recovered from his wounds, but mentally he will never recover from the experience. He is now unbalanced by his fear. It is frightening what is happening to our people.

Sometimes I have to work till late in the evening. I have often heard of Bengalis being attacked. One night I was returning home on the underground. Three white men got on the train and beat me up very badly. I don't like white people because they hate us.

I have been attacked twice. This first time was at a bus stop. A white English youth attacked me with a glass bottle. It wasn't for the money. It was a racial attack. The white people in this country are racist, they may not always say it but it is always in their minds.

## The community as bearer of rules and resources

I have spelt out in some detail the threat of racial violence which operated as a daily backdrop against which the women and men of the Bangladeshi community in London lived their lives because it helps to explain why 'the community' took on such significance as a source of strength, safety and solidarity for its members. As a number of the women told us, they did not worry about moving around in the neighbourhood because it was a predominantly Bengali area. Women who had arrived much earlier in the settlement process, when the community itself was smaller in size, testified that their movements in the public domain had been correspondingly more constrained. Zohra Khanam, who had first arrived in the UK in the mid-1970s, reported how fear of racist violence and the absence of community support had restricted her movements outside the home in the early years. Her rationale for

taking up homework echoes the rationale cited by the woman
interviewed by Mitter (1986) and cited in the previous chapter:

> I didn't look for any outside work when I first arrived here. I was scared at
> that time because there were not many Bangladeshi women around. There
> weren't so many people before or facilities for training. Homeworking
> helped to pass the time . . . I didn't want to sit at home without doing
> anything. There was a greater fear of going out then, people used to get
> beaten up.

However, the routine social encounters and economic exchanges
through which valued resources were distributed within the community also helped to reconstitute it as a bearer of rules and norms.
Gender was a crucial aspect of this process of reconstitution since
conformity to gender norms was a key marker of a family's social
standing within the community. However, as we have demonstrated
in some detail, gender norms were not neutral; they entailed
markedly greater restrictions of women's choices than of men's. In
some cases, women had sufficiently internalised social codes of
conduct for these restrictions to be experienced as 'choice'. In
others, however, the constant references to 'what people might
say', the concerns about the damage that could be inflicted by
gossip and rumours within a closely-knit community, testified that
it exercised considerable power in enforcing conformity by women
and their families to accepted codes of gender propriety.

Women, like Mehrun, who had, however, through no fault of
their own breached the accepted code, were well acquainted with
the more negative aspects of community life. As a divorced woman,
she knew that she was the object of local gossip. While her response
was one of defiance, she would have liked to have moved out of
the neighbourhood and out of the orbit of the community's
surveillance:

> They say that I don't observe purdah because I go out. Because I don't
> have a husband, I have to buy my own groceries, do my own shopping,
> take the children to school and go to the doctor and the post office on my
> own. Everything is up to me, I have to rely on myself. People say they want
> to help but that is just talk, no one does anything . . . I don't want too
> many things, but my dream is to own my own house. I have this house

from the association and I live in it in peace but I want to move out of this area.

The community was a constraining factor in women's lives in other more everyday ways. While its physical presence enabled them to enjoy a greater degree of security in the public domain than they might otherwise have done, it also ensured that this mobility took a highly gender-specific form. There were the extreme versions of this, such as Mrs Miah's husband who imposed such severe restrictions on her movements that if she needed to go out for something, she did it without letting him know. But we also came across less extreme examples of these gender-specific constraints in women's tendency to avoid locations where men from the community were likely to congregate in large numbers. References to the discomfort invoked in them by the 'male gaze' of their community cropped up frequently when women explained why they preferred the 'neutral' environment of large supermarkets like Sainsbury's compared to the local Bangladeshi grocery stores, where men from the community went to pick up their weekly provisions:

> I don't go into grocery shops in this area because they are all owned by men from our community. I feel embarrassed in those shops. If you go into them, the men look at you. If one of them says something, how can you protect your reputation. I prefer to go to Sainsbury's, no one looks at you.

> My husband does the shopping, not me. I don't go for groceries, those shops are full of Bengali men, and though we are from the same country, our norm is not to go in front of men. I still feel the same. I don't feel embarrassed in front of English people, they don't look at you twice. But some people in our community spread gossip without reason. I know because I hear them talking about other people; if you can do that, they can talk about me as well. I don't mind the saree shops, because there are more women there.

Anxieties about community opinion served not only to curtail women's physical mobility, but also their access to economic opportunities. As we saw earlier in the chapter, it had curtailed Rabia's ability to continue with her education after she came to Britain, despite her own desire to equip herself for a well-paid secretarial job. Her references to the influence of extended family and 'other people' in influencing her parents' decision have already been noted. They were backed up by her mother whose explanation for halting Rabia's education reflected concerns for her reputation and anxiety about what 'people' might say:

> We have not sent our daughter to school because she has grown up. We want to get her married. Some people told us that as she was 16 years old, it would be difficult to get her admitted into any school. Besides we are also apprehensive about her going to school alone. People advised us that it was not proper to send grown-up girls to school in this country. Some of our relatives said that she was not going to work in an office, it was not necessary for her to study. Because we fear for our family honour, we would not let our daughter go to school alone. If she had some friends she could go to school with, we might have reconsidered the matter. But a girl's honour and respect can be lost in a matter of minutes and we cannot take the risk by letting her go to school alone. Every mother with a grown-up daughter has these fears . . . There are many ways in which a girl can become spoiled, I will not elaborate on that, you can use your own imagination. Girls in this country go out with any man and men make lewd remarks as girls go by.

Finally, in relation to the central concern of this chapter, the norms of the community also had the effect of reproducing a specific gender division of roles and responsibilities within the home and thereby reproducing a specific division of labour market opportunities. Women explained the homeworking decision in terms of their primary responsibility for child care and domestic chores, their lack of education and language skills as well as deference to the preferences of dominant household members. In addition, the desire to conform to generalised ideas about purdah and propriety also explained why women either preferred to work at home or else within a fairly limited set of occupations within the boundaries of community life. The reluctance to consider a wider range of outside occupations partly reflected their belief that they did not have the necessary qualifications. However, as their discussions about the idea of factory employment demonstrated graphically, it also reflected anxieties on the part of women, and of their families, about their exposure to unwelcome influences, unfamiliar ways, hostile attitudes.

Whatever the combination of factors explaining women's concentration in the homeworking sector, it had the practical effect of precluding them from direct competition with men from their community in one of the few sectors where the latter were able to find employment. It also had the effect of reproducing a gender hierarchy of skills within the sector. Although conditions in the clothing industry are considered among the least favourable by the general white population (Shah, 1975), the Bangladeshi men we spoke to did not have many other choices. Indeed, many preferred conditions in the clothing factories to those prevailing in some of the other jobs available to them. Those who had worked in factories making leather garments spoke of the unpleasantness of the job: 'The smell of leather was awful. The whole factory smelt awful. I always felt sick and went off my food for many days.' Nor was work in the catering industry considered particularly desirable. It involved work late into the night and usually at least one day of the weekend. Moreover, it often involved very menial forms of labour.

By contrast, clothing factories offered better wages, more regular hours and the status attached to skilled work. Indeed, men and women often spoke of their differential involvement in clothing in terms of gender differentials in skills. Here is how Gulam Miah who had joined the industry as a trainee machinist in the mid-1960s described his skills as a 'top' machinist after several years in the industry:

> A top machinist has to know all the different techniques in making a coat. He has to be able to make many different coats from beginning to end. There is usually a 'side' machinist and a 'lining' machinist but if they are absent for any reason, he has to be able to do their job, thus making a coat from beginning to end all by himself. So the job has many responsibilities . . . most important of all, his work must be faultless.

The skills of the experienced machinist were compared unfavourably to the kind of tasks that women generally did. Nurul Amin had been working as a machinist on ladies' coats and jackets since 1981.

He explained his views on women's work in the clothing factories he had worked in:

> None of the women were machinists. They weren't taught how to work a sewing machine because they didn't want to learn. They preferred to do other work, such as sewing on buttons. It is not easy to work an industrial sewing machine. They just wouldn't be able to do this type of work and even if they could, it would be a waste of time. By this, I mean that they are slow workers. By the time a woman makes four coats, a man has made ten. The work is too difficult for women. The women in our factory did 'finishing' work, they have special machines to make button holes. They could make a button-hole but they could not sew a coat from beginning to end. There is a lot of work involved in making a coat, but it is easy to make a button-hole or sew on a button.

Homeworking, which usually entailed simple, 'flat' machining of linings and belts, was also seen as unskilled work and as women's work. It was clear from the testimonies of some of the male workers that the idea of taking up homework, despite the insecurity of their own employment, was considered out of the question on grounds which had echoes of the 'inside/outside' divide which featured in the Dhaka testimonies. As another of the male machinists told us:

> My factory has no orders at the moment, it will probably get some during August and September. I might be out of work after Christmas. Some friends advise me to work as a home machinist. But it's impossible for a man to sit at home doing sewing work all day. It is not possible because I am used to working outside the home. How can I work at home? I won't be able to do it.

Abeda Sultana, one of the homeworkers, agreed with this viewpoint: 'Bangladeshi men don't work at home, how can they? They are men, they have to work outside.'

The gendered incorporation of the Bangladeshi community into the clothing industry, with men occupying the more visible and better paid roles as middlemen or workers in the factories and outdoor units, while women remained in the more hidden and less well-paid homeworking sector, thus served to preserve a division of labour which reproduced customary gender hierarchies within the family and in the wider community. Despite the various forms of discrimination that Bangladeshi men faced in the labour market, and the limitations placed on their employment options, they were able to enjoy certain privileges in the context of their own community by virtue of their position as men: As Husna put it:

> Men have to have higher wages, they won't work unless they are paid properly – £80, 100 or 150 a week. They won't work for less. They sew coats, there is no pay in linings, it's harder and the money is less. But people still say if a woman can earn £5 a day homeworking, she can buy something for the children and save the husband money. My husband makes coats in the factory, he doesn't do linings. He makes coats for £1 or £2 and can make good money if he makes 10 but for him to do linings for 10p, it's a waste of time and effort.

Men's privileged access to the few labour market opportunities available to the Bangladeshi community as a whole had an important symbolic value, upholding their identity as male breadwinners in a context where masculine identity was constantly threatened and undermined by racist violence on the streets, exclusion from mainstream labour market opportunities and discrimination in public services. In this, the labour market practices of the Bangladeshi community echo in some ways those documented in Birnbaum's account of the terms on which women and men from the Jewish community were drawn into the clothing industry in the early decades of this century, a time when it was a socially isolated group, 'with little hope, or desire, of finding alternative employment outside the community' (p. 7). There was no technical reason for the classification of male machinists as skilled and female as semi-skilled that was adopted during this time. Instead 'it arose out of the struggle of men workers from the Russian, Jewish and Polish communities to retain their social status within the family, even when excluded by their position as immigrants from the "skilled" jobs they might otherwise have done. Forced as they were to take on machining work usually done by women as "semi-skilled", they fought to preserve their masculinity by defining their machining as skilled labour' (cited in Phillips and Taylor, 1980, p. 85). As Birnbaum points out, the family unit played a key role in the industry 'and it would have been socially difficult for large differentials in skill and earnings to exist within one family' (p. 7).

## Conclusion

The gender inequalities inscribed in Bangladeshi culture have been reproduced within the British context, partly because of gender asymmetries in the migration process itself, but also because of the nature of the wider environment in which the community found itself. The women in my sample were mainly first-generation immigrants trying to adjust to a new and different life. The loneliness and isolation that women often experience in Bangladesh as a result of the cultural practice of marrying outside their own kinship and village had been compounded in their situation by the move from a rural peasant society to a hostile urban culture 'seven seas and thirteen rivers' away. Officially classified for immigration purposes as dependants of male members of their family, they were also in reality far more dependent on their immediate family networks than the women in Dhaka had been. Their homeworking labour was mobilised through kinship and community networks on the basis of ideologies which emphasised their role in the home as mothers, wives and bearers of the family honour (Westwood and Bhachu, 1988, p. 5). Although they frequently expressed their antagonism to the more constraining aspects of community life, very few sought to seriously contest official interpretations of community norms because they gained a great deal from acceptance within the community and paid a high price if they attracted its censure.

My reading of the accounts given by the women workers – and supported by those of the men interviewed – leads me to conclude that the preferences which influenced their labour market decisions operated at a number of different levels. It would clearly go against the grain of the accounts presented here to suggest that their concentration in the homeworking sector of the London garment industry invariably 'revealed' freely chosen preferences. In some cases, it *could* be regarded as a voluntary choice, based on meta-preferences about 'appropriate' work for women or on more practical considerations of child care responsibilities. In some cases, it was a negotiated outcome, a compromise based on women's assurances to their husbands that they would give priority to their domestic responsibilities. But in other cases, it reflected the exercise of overt power by dominant family members who considered outside work impermissable for women in their families.

However, it was also evident from the testimonies of both women and men that the preferences of dominant family members were themselves shaped by larger structural factors. Men might have had a disproportionate influence in shaping women's labour supply behaviour, but their own preferences were shaped by the defensive social relations of a community responding to the racism of British culture and practice. In particular, their exclusion from the mainstream sectors of the labour market and their resulting confinement to a few limited segments gave them a strong stake in excluding women, from their community, from these jobs so that they did not find themselves in direct competition. Had Bangladeshi immigrants found themselves in a more open and hospitable society, with many more avenues of employment for them to choose from, it is likely that the women from their community might also have been able to exercise more choice in the labour market as well.

# 8

# Mediated entitlements: home-based piecework and intra-household power relations

My aim in this chapter is to explore the impact of women's earnings from home-based piecework on their relationships within the household. Similar questions will be asked here as were asked in Chapter 5 in relation to the impact of women's factory wages. As in Chapter 5, I will be tracking women's earnings from their entry into the household as piece-rate payments to their assignment to different uses in order to explore issues of access, management, control and choice. I will be paying particular attention to critical intervention points in this process where the ability to influence decisions was likely to have important ramifications for the control exercised over the disposal of women's earnings. And I will be considering the kinds of choices that women's ability to earn from homeworking might have made possible for them.

Let me start by pointing to some very obvious objective differences between women's factory wages and their earnings from homework which are likely to have affected how these different types of income-earning opportunities may have been experienced. As I noted in Chapter 5, factory employment displayed many of the features that social scientists have considered necessary for women's access to paid work to have a tranformatory impact on their lives. It was located outside the home, giving it a high level of social visibility, and it yielded earnings of sufficient magnitude and regularity to give it an undeniable economic significance in the household economy.

Homeworking was a very different kind of activity. First of all, it was carried out within the seclusion of the home: indeed, it was the 'veiled' character of homework which explained its appeal to some of the homeworkers and their families. Secondly, returns from homeworking tended to be both irregular and often very low. As we shall see, these two characteristics were not unrelated. The home-based nature of the activity allowed greater scope for intervention by other family members than had been available in factory work and thereby allowed it to be far more regulated and controlled than the former had been. One result of this was the irregularity and meagreness of the earnings that many women reported.

## Negotiations over time and money

One point of intervention related to the hours of work women put into their homeworking activity. Unlike factory employment, where the length of the working day was an indivisible block of time contractually agreed with the factory owner, and paid for on a monthly basis, the hours that women put into homeworking could be decided at their own discretion as long as the orders were available. The allocation of time to homeworking was thus endogenous to the household and open to intra-household negotiation. Consequently, an important point of control in relation to women's earnings occurred prior to the entry of these earnings into the home and related to the hours of time they could put into their homeworking activity which in turn determined how much they would earn. The actual amount of time that women allocated to an activity reflected their own preferences and the extent to which these converged with those of dominant family members.

Conflicts within the household about the optimal use of women's time generally expressed conflicting views about the primacy of their domestic roles. There was consequently a life cycle dimension to these conflicts, since the primacy given to their domestic roles varied at different stages of a woman's life. They were least likely to occur among young, unmarried women who might be expected to help out with the housework, but were not expected to take primary responsibility for it. They were generally free to decide for themselves how much time they wanted to spend on the machine. While women who headed their own households usually had primary responsibility for housework, they were also in a position to decide for themselves how to allocate their time between housework and homeworking.

Conflicts over the allocation of women's time were thus reported most frequently by married women. Clearly married women who agreed with the view that their domestic role was primary were unlikely to report any conflict over the time they spent on the machine. They were also likely to be at the lower end of the spectrum as far as earnings from homeworking was concerned. Homeworking occupied the status of a residual activity in their day, undertaken once their primary commitment to their domestic obligations had been fulfilled:

> They give the work so you can do it in your spare time. You only take the amount of work that you have time to do. The work is convenient because I can fit it in with looking after my family and doing the housework. If I worked outside I couldn't do all these things. I find it convenient, it fills up my time when the children are at school.

There were other married women who did not necessarily subscribe to dominant gender ideologies about their domestic role, but nevertheless acquiesced to them because they did not feel able to challenge them. One of these was Mariam Bibi, the woman who had never raised the possibility of outside work with her husband because she knew he would never agree to it. She also expressed her resignation to the fact that she had primary, in fact, sole, responsibility for housework, regardless of the value of her earnings from homework and regardless also of the fact that her husband had been unemployed for several years:

> I do the housework myself. My husband sometimes helps with the hoovering but he doesn't do anything else . . . I see some men washing clothes or helping with the cooking, but my husband is not like that. If someone doesn't want to do something, you can't force them. Of course men should help women if they are not going out to work . . . but they don't do it because they don't feel like it.

Mrs Miah had secured her husband's consent to her taking up homeworking on the condition that she did not neglect her domestic duties. Her comments expressed her frustration at not being able to spend more time on the machine, but also her acceptance that the needs of her children came first:

> The middleman gave me work three days ago and I haven't been able to start on it yet. I've had guests and have not been able to sit down at the machine. I have to cook and look after the children, when can I get the chance to work? ... I should have done some work yesterday, but I couldn't do it, this person comes, that person comes and I have to give them tea and shupari, I have to cook and feed them, is it possible to machine?

Tahera Banu, who described a fairly harmonious relationship with her husband, still failed to persuade him to do a larger share of work around the house:

> My husband just does the shopping, I do the washing, cooking and cleaning ... Of course men should help with the housework if they see something needs doing. It's not just the wife's duty is it? I don't know why men won't do it, they must have some reason, it is not as if it is forbidden by the Koran.

And Zaheda, whose husband had retired a number of years ago, offered the following comment on the lack of assistance that Bengali men in general gave their wives around the house:

> Bengali men don't know that their religion tells them to help their wives and not send them outside the home. After his important works in the world, our Prophet went home and helped his wife. But Bengali men think they are superior to their wives, they don't understand their own responsibilities.

Although these women did not subscribe to the idea that domestic chores were solely their responsibility, their earning capacity was curtailed by their husbands' refusal to assist them in any way. Even so, there were a few enterprising women in this group who organised their daily routine in such a way as to maximise the time they spent on the sewing machine. Hajera Begum described how she

managed to do this without incurring accusations by her husband
that she was neglecting her domestic responsibilities:

> I cook enough to eat for two days, I make extra dishes, perhaps a vegetable,
> meat and *dal.* If I cooked at lunchtime, the food is enough for the next
> day's evening meal. I keep a plan like that. I tidy up the kitchen in the
> morning and take the children to school. Then I machine for about two
> hours. Then I collect the children for lunch and give them something to
> read or play with, they sit beside me while I work and I talk to them. I stop
> machining at 5 or 6 o'clock when my husband comes home from work.
> He would tell me off otherwise, he thinks the children will become bad-
> mannered if I machine too much.

Finally, there was a third group of around sixteen married women
who did not report any conflict over the hours they put into
homeworking hours because their husbands helped them out with
the housework. These women were at the higher end of the
earnings spectrum since they were able to allocate more regular
hours to homework. Nasreen hoped to find a job as a nursery
school teacher when her children were older, but in the meanwhile
earned money through her homeworking. Her husband had
worked as a waiter but was unemployed at the time of the interview.
He had been willing to help out around the house, even before
she started machining, but now took on a greater share in order to
let her concentrate on the machine:

> My husband used to help me with the housework even before I started
> machining. He helps me more now, he never did the cooking before but
> now he has to do it because sometimes I have too much work and can't
> stop machining. He doesn't do anything else. He helps me because he is
> unemployed and I don't have the time. Men don't help with the cooking
> in our country, do they? Not a bit. They should though. I don't know why
> they don't.

Ruxana's husband had not always been amenable to helping her
out with the housework but she reported that a change was
beginning to occur:

> My husband does the shopping and bathes the children. He doesn't do
> much housework. I do it because it's my duty, I never ask him. He often

does the cooking, but it depends on his mood. I do the cleaning and hoovering. I never ask him to cook, he just does it. He didn't help much when I started machining, I had to do everything myself. But housework and child care are not their responsibility, it is the woman's. If they had been taught from the beginning to share these duties, they would agree. You would say, 'You will do this and I will be responsible for that'. I think as days go by, he is improving, he is doing more out of choice.

## Mediated entitlements:
## management, consultation and control

The 'embeddedness' of homeworking in intra-household relations, and the embeddedness of the household in relationships within the wider ethnic economy, created other control points where intervention by family members had the effect of further diluting the impact of women's access to an income-earning opportunity on their status within the household. These stemmed from the role played by male family members in contacting middlemen or factory owners for orders, in arranging the collection and delivery of these orders and the payment for them.

Most men in the Bangladeshi community had links with the clothing industry, either directly because they worked in it, or indirectly because they knew others who did. Not only did this give them access to information about machining orders but also the scope for acting as informal middemen themselves. In many house-holds, it was male members, often husbands, who purchased or arranged for the hire of a sewing machine, picked up orders from the factory or middleman, delivered the finished product and collected the payment. Around eighteen women reported that their husbands had arranged their first contacts with factories or middle-men while nine reported other male relatives. Others had either organised it themselves or relied on another homeworker. While around nine husbands continued to remain directly involved in picking up orders and delivering the finished product, the rest now relied on a middleman of their acquaintance.

The scope for mediating women's access to orders obviously gave dominant family members the potential for exercising various forms of control. It allowed those for whom it mattered to minimise the need for women to move around in the public domain. Asia was one of the women who had ruled out the possibility of outside work because her husband would have disapproved. As a machinist in a garment factory, he was able to make all the necessary arrangements for her homeworking activity: 'My husband brings the work home once or twice a week, they provide all the materials, including the thread. I did not need to buy anything for the work nor did I need to go out. I hardly go out, I don't need to.' Mrs Islam, who had a very conflictual relationship with her husband, was only allowed to take up homeworking as long as he controlled the arrangements. Initially, these had been undertaken by a middle-man friend of his, but when they moved house, and this was no longer possible, he took on the responsibility himself.

Men's intervention in the homeworking process had the effect of 'blurring' women's entitlements to the income from their efforts. Rather than an activity undertaken by women on their own, it became a sequentially-shared labour process between women and men within the household so that entitlement to the proceeds from the work could also be seen as shared. Male medi-ation in the labour process also resulted in their ability to mediate women's access to their earnings. Men were often the first recipi-ents of women's pay packet since they were the ones to pick it up from the factory on behalf of women. Even where a male family member did not directly collect the woman's pay packet, middle-men were predominantly drawn from male social networks and it was easy enough to acquire the information about what women earned. It was difficult therefore for homeworkers to exercise the kind of covert control over any of their earnings that women factory workers reported in Dhaka. Official and actual accounts of management and control tended to converge in the London context.

The home-based location of homeworking thus gave men a strategic position from which to exercise various forms of control over the terms and conditions of women's homeworking activities. This structural advantage accrued to all men by virtue of their position as household heads. However, the extent to which individ-ual men actually sought to realise their advantage, and individual women sought to contest it, introduced important variations in the

extent to which women exercised some control over how their
income was handled and allocated.

In some cases, it was clear that women's entitlement to the
earnings from their homework was barely recognised to the extent
that they were totally bypassed in the payment process. They were
generally older and less educated women. While these women were
not necessarily at the lower end of the earning spectrum, and may
indeed have been the sole earner in their household if their
husbands were unemployed or retired, they appeared to attach very
little significance to their own contributions to the household:

> The guvnor gave me the money on Fridays, always with a wage slip. I gave
> it to my husband and took it from him when I needed it, we don't quarrel
> about it. He is the main earner in our family. I can't really say whose
> money is spent on what, we have a joint income.

As might be expected, women who had been totally bypassed in
payment procedures expressed ignorance about its disposal,
explicitly confirming or implicitly conveying that they had played
very little role in deciding its use:

> Sometimes they paid me and sometimes my husband would collect my
> payment on Fridays from the factory. He needed it to do the shopping . . .
> he hasn't been working and he would use the money for the groceries.

> My children collected the work. I don't know much about the money, their
> father collected the money. I never asked him for it, what would I have
> done with it? He spends it on the household.

Most women in this category did not express any resentment at
these arrangements and it was only in the rare cases that they did
that it was possible to establish whether they had actively consented
to these arrangements or merely acquiesced in them. One of these
exceptions was Mariam Bibi whose testimony made it clear that she
did harbour some resentment at not having any voice in how her
earnings were spent:

> Sometimes the money from my work is given to my husband, sometimes to
> me. When the factory owner gives me the money, I hand it over to my
> husband. If my husband is at home, sometimes he gives it straight to my

husband. He uses it for family needs. If money is left over from my income, it is kept by my husband in his bank account. I don't have an account. Even if I wanted an account of my own, my husband wouldn't let me because he keeps the money in his account ... I don't know how it is spent. He doesn't give me the chance to open my own bank account. I do feel some regret that I can't keep track of how he is spending the money after he takes it from me.

A second group of women were those who managed their own earnings and sometimes also managed the pooled earnings of the household. These were generally women who took pains to emphasise that their families recognised their entitlement to their own earnings. Even where some other member of the family picked up their pay packet from the factory or received it on their behalf at home, the accepted practice was that it would be handed over to the woman in question. The testimonies provided by this group of women highlighted the symbolic importance that they attached to this recognition of their entitlement:

> The factory owner is a friend of my husband. He delivers the work. The money is always given to my husband. But my husband then gives me the money anyway.

> The lady normally hands me the wages, but if I am not at home, she gives it to my husband and he put it on the mantlepiece for me.

> I am paid in cash, it is given to me, not to my husband. I do the work, I keep the money and spend it as I like. But I will give him some when it is necessary.

These were also women who played some role in the disposal of their earnings, a role which varied according to the temperaments of the individuals concerned and the quality of their relationships with dominant family members. Tahera Banu, for instance, managed the pooled finances of her household. She provided her husband with accounts on how his wages were utilised, but did not feel that she had to account for how she spent the weekly £25 she earned through her homework:

> Even if I look after my husband's money, he knows how much there is and how much is being spent. He always knows what is happening to his

money. If I bought something we need with his money, I'd tell him. But not if it is with my money.

However, the fact that many of the women in our sample earned irregular, and not particularly significant, amounts of money from their homeworking activities meant that actual control of these earnings was not of particular concern to many of them. What they emphasised instead was their right to be consulted on certain allocative decisions, regardless of who managed the income. Their testimonies suggested that they made a distinction between 'exceptional' decisions on which joint consultation was considered necessary and 'unexceptional' ones for which it was not. Unexceptional decisions related to more predictable and routine expenditures: regular daily needs or periodic 'lumpy' expenses, such as mortgage repayments or council taxes. They could be decided on unilaterally by whoever managed the income. 'Exceptional' expenditures referred to more discretionary items, often expensive. Consultation for such expenditures allowed the preferences of different members to be taken into account. As Parveen put it: 'I wouldn't buy expensive things without my husband's consent, he would also consult me before buying anything costly.'

Such distinctions worked as long as they were respected by other members of the household and it was evidence of men's power as the official household heads that they were less likely to be bound by this distinction than women. Husna spelt out her resentment at her husband's tendency to make unilateral decisions over expenditures where she felt she should have had the opportunity to express · her own preferences:

I have never gone out and bought something big for the house without asking my husband, how can you do anything like that? My husband has bought things, he can do what he likes. He came home one Sunday with a showcase. I knew that we were going to buy one, but didn't know which day it would be bought. I liked it a little but what difference does that make once it has been bought. Another day, he bought a sofa set. These were necessary things but two people have different preferences and he bought them according to his own tastes. You can't say anything after something has been purchased. It is his habit, he buys things without saying anything.

Thus, it would appear that women's ability to exercise 'voice' in allocative decision making was less linked to the management of household income, or their own earnings, and more to the quality of intra-household relationships. In situations of trust between family members, issues of management and control over income were less relevant. Thus, as we saw in the last chapter, Tahmina had defied her husband to take up homeworking and expressed a clear-cut entitlement to spend her earnings according to her own priorities. At the same time, she also saw her entitlement to do so as embedded within the mutual rights and obligations which made up the marriage relationship:

> My husband and I are both wage earners ... It is a great help if both husband and wife are working, the whole family is better off ... The English have a different culture, husbands and wives are independent of each other, although they live together, they each spend their wages separately. I don't like the way they live because I am used to my own culture. If I like something, I buy it, I don't have to always ask my husband. And if he buys something, I will complain if I don't like it. We don't argue too much about such things.

In Mrs Islam's marriage, on the other hand, where trust was clearly lacking, the struggle over the control of her earnings symbolised the deep antagonism which characterised her relationship with her husband. When she had first started homeworking, she had been able to retain a degree of covert control over her earnings because her husband's job usually kept him out of the house and her earnings were delivered straight to her by the middleman: 'That is how I saved money without my husband knowing, I hid it in secret places. And if I earned £500, I would say I had earned £200, he had no way of knowing the truth because he is a minicab driver and out all day.'

However, when they moved house, her husband took on the role of middleman picking up and delivering orders on her behalf and her scope for exercising covert control over her earnings, and indeed for deciding how much to earn, was radically reduced:

> Other people have work delivered to them. If I could, then I would be able to work regularly throughout the year. But my husband objects to

anyone else bringing the work to me. He feels that when I do work is up
to him and that I don't have any need to earn. I can't hide any money
from him anymore. He has a minicab, so he collects the money and he
always knows how much I have got.

Although her husband handed her earnings over to her, she
reported constant conflicts over how he wanted her to spend it:
'He wants to send money to Bangladesh, he knows about the £300
I got from work I have recently done. He wants to take it. Of
course, I feel bad when he takes away the little money I have saved
. . . But I don't say anything because I am too scared.'

## Assessing the impact of women's wages:
## the individual picture

What the analysis so far suggests is that homeworking as a labour
process lent itself to multiple points of intervention through which
other more powerful family members were able to determine the
magnitude, regularity, management and disposal of their earnings
from homework if they wanted to. However, despite evidence that
these controls were frequently exercised, women nevertheless continued to work as homeworkers. Indeed, the conflicts reported by
some women, not only over the amount of time they spent on the
machine, but also in some cases, over their desire to do homework
at all, suggested that family members, husbands and wives in
particular, assessed the utility derived from women's earnings very
differently. While men appeared to gain greater utility from the
time that their wives spent on domestic labour than from the
income they earned from homeworking, women appeared to have
needs, wants or interests which were not being addressed through
the existing sources of household income. We therefore turn to
the allocation of women's earnings, and their evaluation of its
impact on their lives, in order to assess what these might have
been.

We will start, first of all, with those who reported very little
impact at all and examine why this was the case. As might be
expected, these were the women who were either completely

bypassed in the payment process or else who handed over full control over their earnings to their husbands, presumably to meet the collective expenses of the household. They often did not earn very much, they played very little role in allocative decision making, they had very little idea of how their earnings were spent and they did not appear to attach a great deal of value to their earnings. Mariam Bibi, who had ruled out outside work for herself because she knew her husband and her in-laws would object, said: 'I don't see too much advantage in working, there isn't much profit or loss, we are just managing the way we are.'

There were other women who also made it clear that they did not attach a great deal of importance to their earnings:

> I have never done a lot of work and I have never earned a lot of money . . . it doesn't have much of an impact . . . I can't make claims for anything because of my money, I just haven't earned that much.

> I never keep track of the money, my husband takes it from me when it is necessary . . . we don't have any savings at all, we just live from one day to the next.

Homeworkers who either themselves subscribed to the primacy of their domestic roles, or else had deferred to their husbands' insistence on the primary of these roles, similarly did not give much value to their earnings from homeworking. They tended to describe their activity as a way of using up spare time. Sharifa Begum, who would not have considered outside work 'because she didn't want to' and 'because her husband would not have allowed it' found that her domestic obligations left her with very little spare time to earn money: 'I don't do it for the money . . . if you want money, you have to go out and work. It is difficult to work in the house with children around.' Mrs Miah, whose mobility had also been severely curtailed by her husband, described homeworking as a way of allaying the boredom of staying at home all day: 'I think it is better to work than sit around, I enjoy it. I only have the youngest child at home, I stop if she starts to cry.' Mila described her machining work as something 'to pay for extras. The money isn't very good, I just pass the time.' Sufia also worked to pass the time rather than because of any pressing economic need: 'I started machining because I was bored . . . Although I earned some money, I don't think I gained much from machining . . . I am not working for the money, I just need something to help me pass the time.'

Not surprisingly, women who saw homeworking in these second-ary terms tended to depict their earnings in similarly secondary terms, distinguishing between the essential necessities paid for by the male income and the discretionary expenditures made possible by their earnings. What was striking about many of their testimonies was the vocabulary of 'pin money', 'extras', 'bits and pieces', 'odds and ends' which they used to describe the uses to which they put their income. Given the limited amounts they generally earned, this description probably had some grounding in objective fact:

> The money isn't enough to save and I spend it on clothes and sweets and crisps for the children. My husband never asked me for it, it's not as if it was a lot. We just spent it on things to eat and clothes.

> I spend the money on sweets and things for the children, what else can you do with ten pounds in this country? You can't buy gold.

> The money was sometimes given to me, sometimes to my husband. I spent it on things I needed. I didn't save anything, what could I save from so little? I bought sarees and bangles, nothing large.

> My husband is the main earner of the family, he earns more than me. My income is spent on odds and ends.

However, there were other homeworkers, some of whom earned sums of money not significantly greater than those earned by the previous group, but who gave a rather different, and far more positive, interpretation to their capacity to earn. Within this group, we can distinguish three sub-categories. There was a first sub-category of women who emphasised the difference that their earnings had made in their household's efforts to secure a decent living standard, pointing to forms of consumption that the family would have otherwise had to forgo:

> If I can earn something we gain, if I can't, we don't lose anything. I work so that we can get nice things to eat. My husband's money is used for most things and on top of it, he has a car, he spends £200 a month on it . . . When I work, I sometimes contribute to the bills or buy clothes for the

children or I make sure that we have different types of things to eat. Eating and clothing has to be the same all the time for the children. You can't have any differences with them, you can't give them a lot to eat one week and less the next.

Talia Begum, whose husband worked in a car factory, said that she used her earnings from homeworking to purchase 'all the things we need for the house . . . we have a colour TV, video, washing machine, car', adding, 'If I didn't work, we wouldn't be able to maintain this standard of living.' Heera valued her earnings for the difference they made for her children's well-being:

> My family has grown and the children need extra things. I thought if I got a job I would be able to give them more things to eat and wear. Perhaps if only one of us worked, we wouldn't be able to afford private tuition for them. At the moment, they are studying Bengali and Arabic privately. Because I am working, they can have extra English lessons if they want.

Hira Begum, whose husband was unemployed, was very aware of how much they relied on her earnings: 'When I don't work, we have to be more careful with our money. We can't reduce the food we buy but we spend less on clothes and other things.' Sakera described her own income in supplementary terms: 'My husband is the main earner. He works permanently, I only work temporarily, on and off.' She too was aware of the difference made to their living standard by her earnings: 'When I stop working, we have less money and have to scrimp and save. We don't have to do this when I work.'

There was a second sub-category of women for whom their earnings constituted an independent source of purchasing power and who valued the ability it gave them to meet some of their own wants and preferences without constantly having to ask their husbands for money. Husna Khanam, who had continued her homeworking activities despite her husband's periodic objections, said:

> Of course if you work hard, you will find happiness, you earn a little money and eat something good or put your money to good use. If someone earns £20, that is good, isn't it, the family benefits . . . If your husband says to you, you can't do that, you can earn your own money and do it. Your

husband won't always be able to give you money because he needs it himself. If you work, you can do something you want, that's why women want to work.

Ruxana, whose husband had come around to her decision to take up homeworking after initial resistance, also valued the independent purchasing power her earnings gave her: 'My husband used to give me spending money. But I thought if I had my own income, then I could spend freely. This would also help my husband because then he could save something and it would be better for me.'

She described how she had become increasingly 'daring' about making decisions on her own as she got used to her new status as earner:

> I've started buying many things since I started earning without first telling my husband. I got the showcase and then told him, he paid for it afterwards. I got it with my Barclaycard, he didn't mind because it made the house look nice. I got the video recorder also without telling him. You become more and more daring once you start.

Similar sentiments were expressed by a number of other women:

> I started machining for the money. If you earn something yourself, you can spend it how you want, you can't do that with your husband's money.

> Women who work will be respected more in the community. They can move around freely and spend their money on whatever they want. They don't have to depend on their husbands for money.

> I feel that if I work, I occupy myself and earn some money to buy the things I want. That way I don't have to trouble him. He only buys me sarees when he feels like it. If I work, I can buy what I want when I want it.

Finally, there was a third sub-category of women who put aside some of their income to invest in their own or their family's future security. These were often the women we described in the previous chapter who had exercised a great deal of initiative in pursuing the opportunity to earn, often in the face of their husbands' resistance. Heera was one of the women who had managed to organise her domestic responsibilities so as to maximise her time in homeworking.

Her income had given some degree of economic autonomy within the household as well as allowing her to open a savings account in her own name.

Tahmina had overridden her husband's initial opposition to her homeworking, buying her own sewing machine and arranging her own delivery and collection of work. She used part of her income for the joint consumption needs of the family but also invested some of her income into land back in Bangladesh and jewellery (traditional sources of security in Bangladesh):

> The money has been extremely useful. I was able to buy some extra things for the children and for myself. I bought some land in Dhaka and quite a lot of gold jewellery. My husband has never bothered asking me how much I earned, he let me do what I wanted. I paid for the bed, the furniture, the showcase and anything else we needed.

Tulie, a young unmarried woman still living with her parents, saved her machining money to put down a deposit on a flat she was purchasing jointly with her sister. Talia Begum was able to remit money out of her income to her sister in Bangladesh. She also believed that her reduced consumption claims on her husband's income increased his ability to save, an ability that was in the collective interests of the household:

> I spend most of my money on my children's clothes. I have also bought jewellery for myself and some sarees. My husband has no objection to this. After all, it is not a lot of money. Sometimes I use the money to pay the bills and sometimes to send to my older sister in Bangladesh. My husband gives me money to spend as well. But I thought if I had my own income, then I could spend freely. This would also help my husband because he could then save some money and that would be better for me.

Finally, for Jamila Begum, whose husband was not well, her ability to earn gave her a sense of security about the future:

> Once the children are older, you need more money for the family. Also my husband is unwell. Both my daughter and I have learnt the work so we have some money to fall back on in times of crisis . . . If I can work today, I can make some provisions for the future and can have a business. If I can work, I can help my husband. He can't feed me all my life, can he? If he

becomes ill today, he won't be able to support us and the money we will get from the government won't be enough.

## Assessing the impact of women's wages: the larger picture

Given the very mixed evaluations that women gave to their ability to earn, it is not surprising that their views on its larger transformatory potential were similarly mixed. Obviously those who gave very little value to their own earning power tended to see the question as largely irrelevant since they defined their own roles in conventionally domestic terms. A few of the others subscribed to the view that what really counted for women was the quality of their relationships, particularly with their husbands, and that this had very little to do with their earning power. Despite valuing the purchasing power her earnings gave her, Husna Khanam said:

> If you have respect in the family, it won't depend on whether you are working or not. There are many women who don't know anything and yet their husbands give them all the money and say 'we will do everything together'. And there are men who earn hundreds and thousands of pounds but they don't ask their wives anything, they do just what they want.

However, the majority of the women in the London sample were of the view that women's capacity to earn was critical to the respect that they received within their families. As Talia Begum put it: 'Money is the root of everything. Women have an independent income when they work and they should have the right to spend it . . . The husband treats them with more respect and the money is of assistance to the family.' Where they differed was on whether earnings from homeworking were sufficient to bring about such respect. Sakera believed that it did. She pointed out that not only did women's earnings from homeworking obviate their family's need to scrimp and save, but it entitled them to a say in how it was spent and the right to be consulted on family matters:

> Women should have the right to spend their earnings how they want, they might want to give it to their parents, it's from their own hard work. They won't waste it, whatever they spend will benefit their families. Not all

women are the same, some spend it on the house, some will save it . . . Homeworking benefits women because they can earn. When women work, their husbands will consult when they want to use their money. Some women will be respected because they are earning: well, those who are worthy of respect will receive it but those who don't say anything will be ignored. When I work, I can offer to pay for something if my husband didn't have enough money. I will have some say then. If I didn't work, I wouldn't have that say.

Masuka, whose husband's illness made her the primary breadwinner in her family, also agreed with the view that homeworking had enhanced women's status within the family: 'By earning for the family, the woman's status increases. Bangladeshi women doing homework command more respect in the family. And since they earn their own money, they can spend it according to their own preferences.' Rajna valued the fact that homeworking had given her a skill that she could always fall back on, but she also felt that she needed to diversify her employment options for a better sense of self-reliance:

I think it is good to know different kinds of work, you never know what will happen. If something did happen, I would be able to work and earn my own living. I have one skill and would be able to use it. It would be even better if I knew other things. Of course women get more respect from men when they work . . . They used to think that Bengali women were completely useless but now they think they have brains and are able to achieve something . . . And if they do one thing, it is hopeful that they will be able to do another.

However, other women pointed to specific characteristics of homeworking which disqualified it as a source of status for women either within their own families or in the wider community. Along with the various disadvantages associated with the work, many simply did not see homeworking as a proper job, just as a way of passing the time. This was how Mrs. Riju put it: 'I can't remember the first day I started homeworking . . . it's not like it's a proper job, it's not like it is useful to keep a record, it's all within the home.'

Zohra Khanum maintained that the impact of women's access to earning opportunities varied according to their own individual personalities as well as those of their husbands, but she also believed that the social isolation of work within the home did little to boost women's self-confidence:

> Some women are able to benefit from homework, some aren't. Some women's husbands take their money and spend it, some women spend it how they want. Women are benefiting because they are able to buy more food or buy land, but they don't have more confidence when they work at home. It is up to the individual of course but if they went out to work, they would meet ten other people and learn useful things.

Sultana Begum gave a mixed verdict on the benefits of homeworking. On the one hand, she clearly valued the independent purchasing power it gave her: 'When I machine, I have money in my hands, I wouldn't have that otherwise. Women would not machine at home if there were no benefits from it. If only the husband is working, the woman may be reluctant to ask him for money to buy something she wants. If you have your own money, you can buy it.' On the other hand, however, she believed that the meagre earning potential of homeworking curtailed its impact: 'I don't think women are respected for working at home. It is not possible to save from that kind of money.'

Then there were those who were unequivocal in their view that homeworking did little to improve women's position within the home or within the community. According to them, only a 'proper' job, outside the home, earning a decent income, paying income tax would bring women any significant prestige or value in the eyes of their family or their community. Roushan Khanam, whose husband had returned permanently to Bangladesh, leaving her to look after their children on her own, was the sole breadwinner for her family. She had no education, spoke very little English and did not have the inclination or confidence to seek work outside. She prayed regularly and brought her daughters up to do so as well; her sons were more interested in computers. However, she believed that only 'proper' work outside the home would bring women respect from the community: 'Women don't get status by working at home. Those who go out and work in offices earn respect from the community. What status can you expect from sitting at home and churning out linings?'

Ruxana had recently moved out of homeworking into part-time youth work where she earned less money monthly but on a regular basis. It was clear that, while she saw many intangible gains from women's earning status, she believed these gains were more likely to be realised with work outside the home:

> If a woman works, she can be free, she can spend the money herself, buy things of her own choice. She is not dependent on anyone. She can lead a better life. I don't think women who work should waste their money on things they don't need or overspend. But they should have the right to spend their money freely or to have savings. The only advantage of working at home is that you can save a bit of money, that is all.

Tulie, the young woman who had saved enough from her machining work to put down a deposit on a house that she purchased jointly with her sister, had moved into youth work on a part-time basis and was using her earnings to finance driving lessons. Her ambition was to become a full-time youth worker. She made a strong link between women's dependency within the family and their lack of voice, but felt that homeworking was too badly paid to transform this dependency status.

> If a husband is running the family entirely with his salary, he will think, 'Who is she, I am everything'. But if there is a partnership and equal rights around money and everything else, then you can question him about how he is spending the money. Otherwise he will think, 'I am the one working, I have all the responsibilities' and he becomes narrow-minded. If people don't do anything with their lives, then even if they are educated, they become narrow-minded. Women are respected when they work, their husbands will always ask them before they do something, they will ask, 'Shall I do this with your money? Or shall I do that?' The person who doesn't work will always feel left out but if a person works, her opinions will be respected because she earns money. Everybody puts oil on a greasy head.

Finally, Mehrun, one of the few divorced women in our sample, also subscribed to the view that while women needed an income of their own, it was only through their experiences in outside employment that women would learn to stand up for themselves. In fact, she ascribed her husband's resistance to her desire to take up outside employment when their marriage had begun to deteriorate to a similar view on his part:

> He didn't want me to work outside because I would start to understand everything. When I stayed at home, I didn't understand anything but if I did begin to understand, then I would have started to stand up for myself instead of letting him abuse me the way he had. I found many possibilities for work outside – in factories or taking pregnant women to the hospital – but he wouldn't let me work. I had wanted to because he was not giving me any money and I needed to buy things for myself and my child. He didn't want me to work outside because he said his reputation would go and he didn't want me to do homework because then I would neglect the children and housework.

When her husband finally divorced her, Mehrun found herself isolated within the community and subject to gossip about her status as a divorced woman living on her own. She was doing homeworking intermittently when we interviewed her and was also working part time in a local child care centre, but she had applied and got a place at the local college to attend a course in shorthand, typing and computing skills to qualify her for an office job. She hoped that the course would be the start of a new life for her, giving her the economic independence that homeworking had never provided:

> It is my own idea, I am going to college. I thought I would get a good job if I did a course and got a good certificate. I will do typing, office studies and computing – that is five days a week from 9.30 to 4 so I can only start doing it when my younger son starts going to school ... I don't think women spoil their reputations when they work outside. Everybody should stand on their own feet.

## The broader conditions of choice

Clearly women's reasons for taking up homeworking, the magnitude of their earnings, the extent to which they had a say in its disposal and the meanings they invested in their earning capacity all combined to determine how individual women experienced the homeworking decision and the impact it had on their lives.

However, while it is important not to underestimate the importance of the value of the gains outlined above, however small they might appear in many of the cases, the overall conclusion from the analysis in this chapter must be that women's homeworking activity had a fairly limited impact on gender relationships within the household and in the wider community. Let me summarise some of the evidence from this chapter which would support such a conclusion.

In the course of this chapter, I have pointed to various 'control' points in the process by which women's earnings from homework was translated into impact within the household. The capacity to influence decisions at these points was significant in shaping the nature of the impact which finally resulted from women's access to homeworking opportunities. While some of these control points are generic to any hierarchically organised set of household relationships, others were very specific to the home-based nature of the labour process involved. The opportunity to intervene at these various points allowed dominant household members to regulate women's working hours, to keep track of their earnings and to ensure that their domestic responsibilities took precedence over their paid activity.

These restrictions on women's earning capacity made the actual power of disposal over income far less critical as a point of control. Where women did report having the power of disposal over their incomes, and an increase in their personal purchasing power, it was frequently within parameters laid down by these previous 'control' decisions. However, the most critical point of intervention by dominant household members was in relation to the homeworking decision itself. In other words, in those cases where women had expressed their preference for an alternative form of employment, one with perhaps greater transformatory potential than homeworking, it had been the preferences of dominant family members which had prevailed, confining them to a form of employment which offered very little challenge to power relations within the family: it paid very little, it had the status of a spare time activity and it kept them under the surveillance of the family and socially isolated within the community. A major reason why dominant preferences prevailed in this way related to the weakness of women's fall-back position in the event of family breakdown.

The case of Mrs Islam was instructive for what it revealed about the mutually-reinforcing relationship between the limitations of homeworking in altering women's bargaining position, on the one hand, and the weakness of women's bargaining position which confined them to employment with such limited transformatory potential, on the other. We encountered Mrs Islam earlier as one of the only two women in our London sample who reported openly conflictual marriages. She had been living in the UK for just three years when we interviewed her. Her relationship with her husband began to deteriorate soon after their marriage when she found out that he had lied to her about his previous marriage. Not only did his first wife turn out to be alive and living in Bangladesh, contrary to his assurance that he was a widower, but he was also in regular correspondence with her. Her husband proved to be a violent and jealous man. He prevented her from attending language classes to improve her English and forbade any form of outside employment in case she became 'bad' and had only acquiesced to her desire to take up machining on condition that the work was brought to her, initially by an acquaintance and subsequently by him.

She described the oppressiveness of her situation: 'If I go to someone's house, and he doesn't find me at home, he starts swearing at me. I feel suffocated if I stay at home too long. Once my father in law saw the state I was in and took me to their house for a few days. I stayed five days, there are children there and I enjoyed being surrounded by people and noise.' She had decided that she wanted to leave her husband and return to Bangladesh. Her goal in working was to save up enough money to buy her passage home. However, she was finding it difficult. As we saw, she had initially relied on a middleman to supply her with orders and it had been possible to hide how much she earned from her husband. She had begun to use it in ways to prepare for her eventual return to Bangladesh:

Sometimes I send money to my brothers in Bangladesh, they are very poor and earn their living, ploughing the land. My husband and I argue about this, I tell him that it is my own hard-earned money and nothing to do with him. Apart from that I need something to fall back on when I return to Bangladesh, that is why I have opened an account in Sonali Bank in Bangladesh without telling him. I have a distant relative in this country, I use his address for all my correspondence. I'll need this money when I go back to Bangladesh and I have my savings and this gold jewellery. The other reason for opening an account is that I won't be able to carry on homeworking when I go back to Bangladesh and I won't be qualified to do anything else. That is why I am relying on my savings.

However, her ability to control her earnings became increasingly undermined when her husband took over the role of middleman. She reported constant conflicts over how she used the money since he clearly felt that he had a right to her earnings. She made a very clear link between the helplessness of her situation as a recently arrived immigrant woman, who had few networks of her own in the UK, and her unwillingness to risk any open confrontation with him:

He always talks about things which will lead to arguments. He wants to send money to Bangladesh ... he knows about the £300 I got from work I have recently done. He wants to take it. Of course, I feel bad when he takes away the little money I have saved ... But I don't say anything because I am too scared. If I have an argument, I have nowhere else to go ... He hasn't taken the £300 because this time, I won't give it to him. Because I am scared of him, I'm not saying anything. If I did, it would lead to a full-blown argument. I am having an unspoken argument with him and I have decided not to give him the money. If I said anything, there would be an argument and he would hit me. And I can't hit him back, how can I? I just cry. I don't have any relatives in this country, I am the only person in my *gusthi* to have come here.

Mrs Khan's testimony reminds us of the vulnerability of some of the women in our sample, but it also draws attention to the social, rather than economic, basis of this vulnerability. Indeed, given the existence of a state-guaranteed social security system, the availability of better-paid employment outside and even the possibility of earning more from piecework by putting in more hours, it could be argued that Bangladeshi women could have survived economically on their own in the London context. The weakness of their bargaining position stemmed from their fear of the social isolation of their situation should they be rejected by their families. As we have noted, they were first-generation immigrants in the UK. Many had arrived relatively recently and were still cut-off from the wider society by their inability to speak English. And as we saw in the previous chapter, they were constructed as 'dependants' not only by their own culture, but also by immigration law. The social networks of family and community were their main source of social support in an environment which was marked by antagonism and violence towards people of their colour. A life of independence outside the protection and support of their family and community was not an appealing one for most women and they saw little to gain by going against the wishes of its head and jeopardising their position.

The testimonies from women in the London context therefore featured far less overt conflict than did those from Dhaka. Those who might have been prepared to consider outside work generally did not do so if their families were against it. We saw little evidence of the extended negotiations through which many of the women we interviewed in Dhaka had managed to overcome their family's resistance to their desire to work outside the home. And there was even less evidence of the open contestation of male authority within the household which led some of the women in Dhaka to walk out on violent, irresponsible or dishonest husbands. Indeed, it was one of the striking features of our London sample that with one exception, none of the ever-married women without husbands, were responsible for their state. They had either been abandoned or divorced or widowed. These women were often the ones who opted for outside employment, partly because of their desire to earn a decent income in the absence of male support, partly because an important source of constraints on their employment choices was not relevant in their case and partly to get away from the social isolation associated with homeworking.

## Conclusion

The analysis in this chapter has suggested that the relationship between women's access to an income through homeworking and its impact on intra-household relationships was not uniform, but depended on the motivations which led women to take up homeworking, the magnitude of their earnings and the degree of conflict or co-operation that they encountered in their desire. Their motivations ranged from those for whom homeworking was simply a way of using up spare time, and hence likely to have little impact, and those for whom the financial remuneration mattered and who consequently attached a certain amount of value to this use of their time. In the latter group, the motivations for wanting to earn money – to contribute to household welfare, to exercise some degree of purchasing power, to save or acquire independent assets – were further factors in shaping impact. However, we have also pointed to the various 'control' points in the labour process, largely arising out of the particular way in which homeworking was organised, which allowed dominant members to regulate their working time and control their earnings, thereby diluting the impact on their status within the household.

Consequently, despite the importance of the gains that some women undoubtedly made as a result of their homeworking earnings, we saw little evidence of the kinds of strategic choices that factory women in Bangladesh had been able to exercise as a result of their newly established earning capacity. The meagreness of the earnings, the mediated nature of their entitlement to them and the social isolation of their working conditions all served to curtail the extent to which women's participation in homeworking brought about any major shift in intra-household power inequalities. However, perhaps the more important point to come out of the analysis is that while homeworking did little to improve women's bargaining power within the household, it was their lack of bargaining power in the first place, the social weakness of their fall-back positions, which explained their presence in a form of employment with such limited transformatory potential, regardless of what their preferred option might have been. It is unlikely that their daughters will suffer from the same disadvantages. They will have been to school in this country, learnt the language, made their own social networks and developed a wider frame of reference than their mothers had. Whether this will lead to improved opportunities in the labour market will then depend on the extent to which the wider society is prepared to give them more space than it gave their parents.

# 9

# Exclusion and economics in the labour market: explaining the paradox

The starting point for the research in this book was the observance of the very differing ways in which Bangladeshi women were incorporated into the garment industries in Dhaka and in London at the end of the 1980s. Given that these were very different contexts, it was the paradoxical form that this difference took, rather than the fact of it, which appeared to merit further research. In other words, why were women in Dhaka, where powerful norms had served to constrain their presence in the public domain in the past, prepared to respond so rapidly to the availability of a new form of factory employment rather than continue in home-based forms of work as they had previously done? And why did the majority of Bangladeshi women in London, a context where public mobility for women was widely acceptable, opt for home-based piecework? The first aim of the book was therefore a straight-forward empirical one: an explanation for this paradox.

As I have pointed out, economic theories of choice would find it easy enough to explain women's decision to enter factory employ-ment in Dhaka in terms of a response to economic incentives, but less easy to accommodate their decision to do homework in Lon-don. Culturalist paradigms, on the other hand, would explain women's concentration in homeworking in the London context as evidence of the continuity of purdah norms, but find it harder to explain the apparent departure from such norms in the Dhaka context. One of the advantages of the comparative framework we have adopted in this study is that it allowed us to explore both contexts simultaneously, identifying common themes in the two sets of labour market decisions as well as the possible differences which might account for the counter-intuitive forms they took.

We are now in a position to pull together the findings from the preceding chapters in order to summarise what they tell us about the reasons for our labour market paradox. No single factor, or even any clearly dominant factor, emerges as the explanation. Instead our analysis throws up a cluster of mutually compatible mechanisms, each of which constitutes a piece of the puzzle and which, taken together, go some way towards constituting an explanation. Given that it is group-level differences in women's work patterns that are of interest here, rather than individual differences, the various causal mechanisms making up the explanation also operate through differences in group characteristics and structural contexts rather than through differences at the individual level.

## Group characteristics and differences in preferences

The first set of differences which feature in our explanation relate to differences in group characteristics and their implications for the kinds of preferences likely to prevail among the two groups of women. The first point to make is that the women we interviewed in London tended to be more homogeneous in a number of ways. We have pointed out that the overwhelming majority of the Bangladeshi community in London came from a single district in Bangladesh and indeed from specific villages within it. Secondly, they came from a particular economic class within these villages, small, landowning households who could afford the cost of the journey to Britain. The circumstances under which they migrated introduced a further degree of homogeneity to the group. Many of the men had migrated very much earlier and on their own, often entering Britain under the 'voucher system' in the 1960s. The majority of the women came much later. They had grown up in Bangladesh and had arrived in the UK to join, usually their husbands, but sometimes their fathers, in many cases only a few years before we interviewed them. The circumstances of their migration meant that most of the women in our sample, and in the community in general, were married.

The women in the Dhaka sample were a much more heterogeneous group than those in London. First of all, their regional origins were far more diverse. Some had been born in Dhaka, some had migrated into it at some earlier stage of their lives, others had come more recently, often in response to the opportunities offered by the garment industry. Those who had migrated into Dhaka city came from districts all over the country, but disproportionately from the poorer, more densely populated districts of Faridpur, Barisal, Comilla and Mymmensingh. These districts also provided much of the male migration and were characterised by a higher incidence of landlessness than the rest of the country. Women migrants in the garment industry tended to come disproportionately from landless or land-poor households. However, they were not uniformly poor. Many had completed primary education while others had gone on to secondary and higher education. The variety of circumstances which had brought women into Dhaka city, and into the garment industry, meant that there was also considerable diversity in their marital status. Although unmarried women were the single largest category, there was a sizeable number of married women in the industry and a significant minority of once-married women.

How would these differences in the characteristics of the two groups of women help to explain differences in their patterns of labour market participation? First of all, differences in their regional origins within Bangladesh might have accounted for some differences in the social construction of 'preferences', particularly in relation to what was considered acceptable behaviour for women. Given that the overwhelming majority of women, and their families, in the London context came from one of the most religious districts in Bangladesh, with lower rates of female labour force participation, it is highly likely that they were more conservative in their evaluations of what were acceptable forms of paid work compared to women, and their families, in Dhaka who had come from less conservative districts, with higher participation rates by women in paid activity.

However, our analysis of the testimonies of the two groups of women did not suggest that their interpretations of purdah diverged sufficiently to constitute the sole, or even the most important, explanation for the difference in their patterns of employment. A small minority of women in the London sample did explain their decision to do homework in terms of their own or their family's adherence to purdah, but equally, we came across women in the Dhaka context who believed that they were breaking purdah norms by their appearance in the public domain. Among the rest of the women in both groups, there were remarkable similarities in their interpretations of purdah, including their views about its compatibility with certain forms of outside employment.

Differences in the demographic composition of the two groups of women could also have had a role to play in explaining difference in their employment patterns. As we noted in Chapter 7, the general literature on homeworking in the UK suggests that its compatibility with child care responsibilities was a major factor in explaining the large-scale involvement of women from all ethnic communities, black, Asian and white. Since most of the Bangladeshi women who migrated to London were wives joining husbands, they were more likely to have children compared to women who joined the factories in Dhaka, many of whom were unmarried. Furthermore, fertility rates had declined less dramatically in Sylhet than in the rest of the country. Hence differences in the significance of the child care constraints may have been another source of the differences in the labour market choices made by women in London and Dhaka.

Certainly, the women in our London sample reported more children than married women in Dhaka; the age of their youngest child also tended to be lower. However, the larger statistical picture suggests that child care constraints only partly explained the concentration of Bangladeshi women in homeworking in the London context. We pointed out in Chapter 7 that in contrast to women from all other ethnic groups, for whom a major fall in levels of economic activity was associated with the presence of a young child, a far more dramatic fall in the labour force participation rates of women from the Bangladeshi community in London appeared to be associated with marriage. The evidence from Dhaka suggests that this 'marriage' effect was not as marked. Although, in general, currently married women, and women with young children, did have lower levels of labour force participation than women who had been married or were still unmarried (Paul-Majumder and Mahmud, 1994), surveys of the work force in the garment industry suggest between a third and a half of women were currently married. In addition, over half of women employed in formal manufacturing, and 40 per cent of those in the informal manufacturing sector were married in 1983/84; the rates had increased considerably in 1995/96 (Zohir, 1998).

This suggests that marriage carried somewhat different meanings in the lives of Bangladeshi women in London compared to those in Dhaka. These differences in the construction of marriage may have been a more relevant manifestation of the different geographical origins of the two groups of women than differences in their discourses about purdah. One aspect of this that we have already noted is that dowry practices had appeared very much more recently in Sylhet and were still far less widespread than they were in other parts of Bangladesh.

Differences in the economic backgrounds of the two groups of women also have implications for their labour market choices. As we saw, women in the London community were more likely to have come from small, landowning families than the women who made up the Dhaka sample. Such families are not generally accustomed to their women doing paid work and they are, in any case, far more status-conscious in their choice of jobs. Only a very small minority of women in our London sample had any experience of paid work before they came to England. By contrast, a much larger percentage of women in the Dhaka sample had come from poorer, landless families, the category providing most of the female waged employment in Bangladesh. Many of the women had already been previously employed, primarily as domestic servants, but also in factories, home-based cultivation and handicrafts.

These differences in the general characteristics of the two groups of women in our study are all likely to have contributed to part of the explanation for the observed differences in their labour market decisions. However, there is still an unexplained component. The differences we have discussed so far are relevant in explaining why women in London, and members of their family, were more likely to have *preferred* home-based employment compared to those in Dhaka. In other words, they help to explain differences in labour market decisions as long as the focus is on consensual decision making in the two contexts. However, when we turn to situations of conflict, where women's preference, or willingness to consider, outside employment diverged from the preferences of those in authority in their households, we find that women in the London study were less able to bargain successfully for their preferred form of employment. In other words, while conflicts over women's preferred labour market choices occurred in both London and Dhaka, they resulted in different outcomes, with women's preferences more likely to prevail in final outcomes in the Dhaka context than in London.

We have already noted why this could not be simply dismissed as an artefact of the way we defined our sample. Instead, it reflected a real difference in women's ability to make choices, and to bargain over the terms of familial contracts. We turn next therefore to differences in the contexts in which women were making their decisions in order to identify those which might help to explain these differences in women's bargaining power in the two contexts.

## Local labour markets and the competition for jobs

A major area of difference in the two contexts relates to the labour market opportunities facing the two groups of women. Given the importance of the clothing sector in both contexts as a key source of employment for women, the particular nature of the garment industry itself is likely to be an important component of this aspect of our story. As we have seen, it is an industry that has been characterised by the increasing subdivision of its production process, the intensiveness of its use of largely unskilled labour, the seasonal and fashion-related fluctuations in the demand for its product and its historical reliance on a labour force which can be paid low wages and flexibly managed to cope with fluctuations in the level of demand for clothing. An analysis of the characteristics of the labour force employed in the clothing industry at different times and in different places therefore appears to be essentially an exercise in exploring how 'disadvantage' is constructed in the labour market under different circumstances. As far as the objective of this book is concerned, such an analysis would uncover the specific disadvantages of Bangladeshi women in the contexts of London and Dhaka which led to their incorporation into the clothing industry in the two contexts and the particular forms it took. But we are also interested in finding out whether differences in women's positions in these two labour markets might have had any bearing on differing outcomes to intra-household conflicts over their labour market preferences.

In both the contexts under study, labour markets were characterised by marked segmentation, and by the marginalisation of disadvantaged groups. However, they differed in the nature of the social inequalities which formed the basis of labour market disadvantage. Gender inequality was common to both contexts, leading to the exclusion of women from mainstream opportunities and confining them to a limited number of occupations and activities. Limitations on women's labour market choices in both contexts reflected a combination of ideological norms and exclusionary mechanisms, although clearly these took culturally differentiated forms and also served to differentiate levels of female labour force participation. Women in Bangladesh had far lower rates of labour force participation than women in Britain. More significant for our story, however, was the fact that Bangladeshi women's status as disadvantaged labour was embedded in rather different sets of social relations in the two contexts, with very differing implications for the extent of their competition with relevant sections of the male labour force.

In Bangladesh, where women had been excluded from mainstream forms of employment as the result of long-standing structural constraints, and restricted to a very limited range of poorly paid activities, they constituted the major source of disadvantaged labour in the economy and the logical choice for employers seeking to meet the demands of an intensely competitive industry. Nor did women's recruitment into the garment industry lead them into direct competition with male labour. It was a new industry, generating a new demand for female labour, rather than putting men out of work. Men, in any case, generally had other choices and were not prepared to comply with the demands of factory discipline, the long hours of work, the compulsory overtime and generally exploitative conditions of an internationally competitive industry. Furthermore, with the increasing construction of the garment industry as a 'female' sector, there were even fewer inducements for men to seek employment in the industry.

In the British context, on the other hand, Bangladeshi women's concentration in the home-based sector of the clothing industry was also related to labour market segmentation but here it was produced by a double 'closure' (Parkin, 1979). Part of it related to the gender segmentation of the labour market. Over 80 per cent of the labour in the industry was female and the job of machining was widely perceived by the white male worker as 'women's work'. However, the gender segmentation of the labour market was crosscut by racial segmentation. As a number of authors have pointed out, the poor conditions of work which prevailed in the industry, its association with 'sweatshop conditions', the practice of piece-rate payment and the low level of the pay itself had led to a movement away from the industry by many of its white women workers as well as some of the second-generation of earlier immigrants, such as the Cypriots (Shah, 1975; Josephides, 1988), although it remained dominated by women from the ethnic minorities.

However, the other aspect of racial segmentation in the labour market was that it endowed men from the ethnic minorities, in this case, Bangladeshi men, with many of the characteristics of disadvantaged labour, undercutting their advantages as male labour by their racially disadvantaged status. Racially-based forms of closure in general, exacerbated by their lack of requisite language and educational qualifications, led to the widespread exclusion of members of the Bangladeshi community from mainstream labour market opportunities and confined them to a highly restricted range of occupations. The clothing industry, whose location in London coincided with the main area of Bangladeshi settlement, was one of the key industries to which the Bangladeshi community found itself confined. However, within the community, a second closure revolving around gender norms served to further limit the range of opportunities available to women from the community. It effectively retained outside, and somewhat better forms, of employment in the clothing industry for male members of the community, while women were confined to home-based piecework.

Thus the wider structures of the labour market shaped the distribution of possibilities available to the households which we studied and in turn shaped the choices that individual women within these households were able to make. What we found in Dhaka were large numbers of women who had either previously not worked at all or else worked largely from home prepared to take up work outside as new opportunities arose. What we found in London, on the other hand, was a scarcity of employment opportunities for the community in general, its confinement to a limited niche of the labour market and the mobilisation of ideologies of domesticity, marriage and gender propriety which served to confine women to home-based piecework, pre-empting the likelihood of direct competition with men from their families or from the community for the better-paid jobs in clothing. However, by itself this does not explain the differences in women's bargaining power in the two contexts. It does not explain why women in London did not succeed in overcoming male resistance to their desire to take up outside employment, as they had in Bangladesh. It also does not explain why, given high levels of male unemployment in the Bangladeshi community, the opposite incentive for women to seek better paid jobs did not prevail.

## The role of the state and the affordability of female dependence

We therefore turn to the next important difference which is likely to have been relevant to explaining some of the differences in the labour market options facing women workers, and their families, in the contexts of London and Dhaka. This relates to the role of the state. The state featured very intermittently in the women's testimonies in Dhaka and rarely as a source of direct material assistance. A number of women attributed their jobs in the garment industry directly to state intervention, possibly because of the constant pronouncement on women and development by successive government leaders; others spoke more generally of the references to women's equality and women's rights which had characterised state discourse since the mid-1970s. Otherwise there was little reference to the role of the state. By contrast, the state in various forms was very much more present in the lives of the women in the London context. There were references to the negative aspects of the state, particularly to the indifference of the police to racist attacks on the community, but many more direct and indirect references to its welfare aspects, the provision of a safety net for the unemployed, child benefits and the subsidised health and education system.

The absence/presence of the state provided an important backdrop to decisions about women's labour supply in the two contexts. In Dhaka, the absence of any safety net meant that basic survival imperatives outweighed status considerations for many families. However, even among better-off families, the need to secure household living standards and concerns about children's educational prospects were sufficiently important for women to be prepared to consider forms of employment which went against convention and for men to be persuaded to consent to such employment, despite initial reservations. By contrast, the presence of the welfare state in the British context placed an economic floor below which households could not fall. It removed economic desperation as a factor in women's work decisions and hence a motivation which might have been powerful enough to impel women into less conventional forms of employment. The availability of a subsidised state education system also removed the need to save for children's educational expenses, which had been an important factor motivating women from better-off families in Dhaka to enter the labour market. To that extent, the presence or absence of a welfare state is likely to have accounted further for some of the differences in preferences and strength of motivations to take up outside employment observed among women in London and Dhaka.

However, in addition, the availability of a state safety net may also have underpinned men's ability to resist women's desire to take up outside employment, regardless of their own unemployed status. It allowed considerations of male status and family standing in the community to take precedence over any earnings that women might be able to bring in from outside employment. This possibility is echoed in the wider literature for the British population at large. As Morris (1990) has pointed out, the existence of the welfare state is thought to have a bearing on the absence of any major renegotiation of gender roles in situations of male unemployment among families in both the US and the UK, as evidenced in the rarity of women taking on paid work in such situations and in male resistance to the contemplation of such arrangements. Indeed, in both societies, there appeared to be higher percentages of unemployment among wives of *unemployed* men than there was among wives of employed men.

For instance, in the UK in 1986, 25 per cent of wives of unemployed men were in work compared to 67 per cent of wives of employed men. In the US in 1983, the proportions were 20 per cent and 65 per cent respectively (cited in Morris, 1990, p. 69). While the 'disincentive' effect of the UK benefit system[1] has been partly held responsible for this polarisation in its working population between two-earner/no-earner households, the repetition of the pattern in the US, where the system does not contain this disincentive effect, suggests that additional factors may be implicated in explaining why women do not generally take on the role of breadwinner when their husbands are unemployed. Among the various factors considered by Joshi (1984) for the general population, those with particular resonance for the Bangladeshi community in the UK include the increased workloads of women as a result of the husbands' presence at home, resistance to the idea of women usurping the breadwinner role and the probability that

1. Both the UK and the US have contributory social security systems to which payments made during periods of employment entitle workers to benefits during periods of unemployment for a period of 12 months in the UK and 26 weeks in the US. What happens subsequently varies considerably between the two countries. In the US, despite some variation in the availability of means-tested benefits between the states, many of the long-term unemployed have no financial means of support, once they have exhausted their eligibility for unemployment benefit. In the UK, on the other hand, unemployment benefit is commonly supplemented by a means-tested benefit whch takes account of the workers' individual circumstances. When the period of unemployment benefit is over, supplementary benefit or 'income support' continues to be paid, usually in larger amounts. However, if the wife of the claimant is in paid employment, then a substantial portion of her earnings (all earnings over £5) is deducted from the claim.

where jobs were hard to find for men, they would be hard for women as well.

## The presence of 'the community' and the pressure to conform

Finally, differences in women's ability to assert their own employment preferences when these diverged from those of dominant household members can also be related to the differences in the kinds of community in which they were located in the two contexts. As Elster points out, movements from the countryside into the city tend to be characterised by the dissolution of the face-to-face enforcement of norms in a 'sea of anonymity': people find themselves spending a larger proportion of their lives with strangers who are not in a position to enforce such norms effectively and may not, in any case, have any desire to.

The story of migration into Dhaka conformed to this pattern. The urban community in which the women in Dhaka found themselves was a fragmented, dispersed and impersonalised community, one where neighbourhoods were constituted not only of non-related residents but often of migrants from different districts of Bangladesh. The ability of such communities to impose sanctions or express disapproval in relation to women's behaviour was very limited. Certainly women took precautions to avoid attracting the undue attention of their neighbours, but they did not attribute them with the power to constrain the choices that their kin and social peers in village society might have had. When women sought to negotiate permission from their family guardians to take up outside work, the opinion of the more impersonal and diffuse community did not count for a great deal in the negotiations for either party.

However, the process of migration by the Bangladeshi community into London was very different. Bangladeshi women found themselves as members of a community which had in many ways constituted itself as a version of the 'face-to-face' community of rural society that it had left behind. We have noted some of the factors which assisted in this process: the origins of the community from a restricted number of villages in one district in Bangladesh; the voucher system which reinforced the selectivity of the migration stream by encouraging migrants from the families and kinship networks of those who had already settled in the UK; the geographical concentration of the community in East London, reinforced over time by recession-related redundancies among those who had taken jobs in other parts of the UK and their gravitation to London; and finally, the institutionalised racism of British society which gave these processes of geographical concentration an added impetus.

In terms of the variations in situations of conflict resolution observed in the two contexts, therefore, we can see why differences in the presence of the community as a factor in the lives of women and their families might play an additional role in shaping final outcomes. While men in both contexts may have had a disproportionate influence in shaping women's labour supply behaviour, they were by no means autonomous actors. Like women, they were also influenced by the wider social relationships of which their families were a part and by the scope for choice that these wider relationships allowed them in pursuit of their own and their family's interests. The difference was that in Dhaka, the weight of community opinion counted for less because the community itself was a less effective presence in their lives as a bearer of resources or as a source of sanctions. Conflicts over women's labour supply decisions were far more likely to be settled on the basis of private negotiation revolving around private considerations.

In London, on the other hand, the community was not simply the backdrop against which the individuals lived their lives but was woven into the fabric of their everyday lives. Its networks were critical as a source of support, employment and a social life, but equally its norms formed the basis of their actions. Women's negotiations over their preferences with dominant members of their family thus not only had to deal with the reservations of the individual concerned, but also, beyond them, with the reservations of their community.

## Conclusion

By way of conclusion, it is important to reiterate that we have been looking at two groups of women in two very different parts of the world and at very particular moments in the history of their communities. The women we talked to in Dhaka were part of the first generation of women in Bangladesh to take up factory employment on a large scale, often migrating on their own from the countryside into the towns to do so. The women we talked to in London, on the other hand, were part of the first generation of women to have emigrated in large numbers from a rural area of Bangladesh to one of the world's largest cities, usually as dependants of fathers or husbands. In each context, one would expect the generation of women who came after them to confront a rather different set of constraints to those that they had faced.

Thus our analysis applies to a particular historical conjuncture and to the specific configurations of markets, states and communities which mediated these moments of change in the lives of two communities. It suggests that while the labour market decisions made by women in the two communities concerned might have appeared counter-intuitive at first sight, a more in-depth and context-specific investigation of the reasons that they were made – as well as the reasons behind these reasons – reveal them to be the logical working out of economic and social forces in the two different contexts. Like many paradoxes in the social sciences, they only appear to be paradoxical if the explanation is confined to either purely economic or purely sociological terms. Once both are integrated into the analysis, the paradoxical element evaporates.

# 10

# The power to choose and 'the evidence of things not seen':[1] revisiting structure and agency

My second objective in undertaking the research for this book was a theoretical one. It was to explore the extent to which women's own rationales for their labour market decisions meshed with those put forward in the theoretical social science literature on these questions. It was pointed out in Chapter 2 that mainstream economics casts a powerful light on the importance of choice in explaining patterns of human behaviour, but has little to say about power and how it might create inequalities in people's ability to choose. Structuralist theories, on the other hand, have emphasised the significance of social constraint in limiting the scope for individual choice, but fail to acknowledge how individuals seek to manoeuvre within these constraints, in the process, often transforming them. Both approaches contribute valuable insights to our understanding of how society works, but they address different levels of social reality. Economists locate their explanations at the immediate and observable level of experience while structural theories deal with deeper, often hidden, forces. The analytical approach in this book was to locate itself at the middle level, acknowledging structure without denying agency, in order to see their interaction in shaping how women's labour market decisions were actually made.

The women workers who emerged out of this approach were

1. This phrase by St Paul is taken from 'The Deptford Trilogy' by Robertson Davies.

neither the free-floating, atomised individuals of neo-classical analysis nor did they resemble the 'structural dopes' of certain sociological portrayals. Rather, they were 'persons-in-relations' (Nelson, 1996, p. 68), individuals whose preferences and priorities reflected their own unique histories and subjectivities, but also bore the imprint of the complex of social relationships to which they belonged and which determined their place in society. Equally, the 'households' described in the women's testimonies had little in common with social science descriptions of corporate entities, controlled by all-powerful heads, benevolent or otherwise, nor were they composed of essentially autonomous individuals, co-operating on the basis of a mutual-gain calculus and bargaining on the basis of their threat positions. Instead, they were largely made up of members of the same family, bound to each other by ties of blood or marriage, caring for each other and sharing projects in common, but whose ability to make choices and to influence collective decision making were significantly shaped by their contractually defined roles, resources, responsibilities and 'place' within the family and the wider community. In the rest of this chapter, I want to draw together some of the key insights which this more situated analysis of individuals and families might contribute to our understanding of gender, choice and power in relation to women's labour market decisions and to consider what they add to the explanatory power of the different social science approaches to the problematic of structure and agency.

## Power, choice and preferences: focusing on the individual

Let me start with preferences, a concept at the heart of economic theories of choice, and yet one of its most neglected. The underspecification of preferences within mainstream economics is symptomatic of the marginal role generally assigned to questions of culture and ideology in its understanding of human behaviour. The analysis in this book confirms that individual preferences are both an important dimension of choice as well as a key route through which wider social contexts – and the inequalities which they often embody – are 'endogenised' within the decisions that people make. Ideology and culture do not merely operate as externally-imposed constraints on people's choices; they are woven into the content of desire itself. Consequently, what people need and want, how they define their identities and their interests, partly reflects their own individual histories and subjectivities, but are also significantly and systematically influenced by the norms and values of the societies to which they belong.

The decisions facing an individual can be conceptualised in terms of a value-defined continuum, with those decisions which are governed by purely subjective preferences, i.e. idiosyncratic to the individual in question, at one end of the spectrum while at the other end are the more value-laden decisions, those in which their meta-preferences tend to come into play. These meta-preferences, the 'ought' factor in the evaluation of choice, are not immutable, but they tend to be slower to change than individualised preferences because they often express the collective beliefs and values of a society. Considerable social effort has been invested to ensure that they are reproduced over time. The observed resilience of norms and values about gender and gendered relationships in most societies, for instance, are a product of these collective social efforts, operationalised at the level of individuals through their shared understandings of what constitutes appropriate ways of 'being and doing' for women and men. Inasmuch as social values and beliefs embody the structural inequalities of the wider society, the preferences that individuals express are unlikely to be neutral in their content or implications.

For instance, the acceptance by some women in this study of their lesser claims on household resources can be seen as individual expressions of the collective values of a society which has long held that women are lesser beings than men and hence entitled to less. Such beliefs bear no logical relationship to the actual value of women's work and hence do not necessarily change with changes in women's productivity. As Razia Sultana from the Dhaka study told us: 'Garment work may be hard work, but it doesn't mean you should starting eating more . . . We tend to give more to the men in the house. My brother is older, he is a man, we have to give him more. If a woman eats less, it doesn't look so bad. If I don't get enough to eat, I wouldn't complain. But if he doesn't, it looks bad to me.'

The internalisation of social values and beliefs were also manifested in the very different considerations which came into play in labour supply decisions by gender. The fact that both men and women in our study subscribed to similar familial ideologies meant that they shared common perceptions about what constituted the optimal use of time by different family members, perceptions which were significantly influenced by gender and by the particularities of family relationships of the member in question: in other words, not only whether they were male or female but also whether they were defined primarily as a father or mother, husband or wife, son or daughter, brother or sister, son-in-law or daughter-in-law within that family. Areas of 'inertness', or 'non-decision making', in the allocation of the time of household members reflected these prior normative considerations within which calculations of 'comparative advantage' took place. In addition, intra-familial relationships, and the contractual obligations they embodied, also reflected the family's insertion into larger social hierarchies. Views about the optimal use of members' time were consequently also influenced by their family's class position, and the extent to which it valued, or could afford to value, dominant norms about the division of labour among family members, within and outside the household.

These meta-preferences about appropriate ways of 'being and doing' introduced gender asymmetries in attitudes to paid work. By and large, the role of breadwinner was so integral to men's identity as men that the decision to enter paid employment was generally taken for granted: their labour supply decision focused on *when* they would start work and *what* kind of work it would be rather than on *whether* they would work. As breadwinners, considerations of male gender identity were discernible in the kinds of work that men expressed a preference for and we noted examples of the very different considerations which came into play in the two study contexts in determining what constituted 'acceptable' forms of work for men. The other side of the coin to the construction of garment employment as 'women's work' in Bangladesh was its lack of attraction to male workers and their minority presence in its work force. Many of men we did interview expressed their discomfort at finding themselves in such unusual proximity to large numbers of women. Despite the gender segregation of tasks within the factories, men found the idea of working in a 'female' industry denigrating to their sense of manhood. In the UK, on the other hand, the garment industry was one of the few sources of work for women and men in the Bangladeshi community. Here, despite the fact that both women and men worked as machinists, men's identity as breadwinner was at least partly protected by their monopoly of 'outside' work in the industry and the confinement of women to 'inside' work. In addition, we noted the contrast that male machinists made between the skilled nature of the work they did compared to the unskilled 'flat' machining done by women at home.

For women, a different set of considerations came into play in their labour supply decision. Their contractual obligations within the family, particularly in their capacity as wives and mothers, defined the care of the family and domestic labour as their primary responsibility. Consequently, the decision to take up paid work had to take account of these prior claims on their time, and the extent to which they could be accommodated or renegotiated, along with more conventional calculations about relative returns to different uses of their time. For women, therefore, the labour supply decision included the question of *whether* to take up paid work as well as when and what kind of work. In other words, shared understandings about what constituted an appropriate division of roles and responsibilities between women and men gave rise to gender-differentiated meta-preferences, in terms of attitudes to the idea of paid work, and gender-asymmetrical terms of entry into the labour market.

A rational choice calculus would have failed to capture the interplay of factors which shaped women's decisions to take up employment because it would have focused on purely, or largely, economic considerations, whereas their own testimonies suggested that marginal productivity criteria often took second place to a range of other non-economic criteria, such as the gender propriety of work in question, its appropriateness to their class or cultural background and its compatibility with other socially-sanctioned demands on their time within the home. Their meta-preferences essentially served to define a normatively admissible set of employment options for women – their 'preference possibility sets' – before marginal productivity considerations came into play. Paid work within the home was least challenging in meta-preferential terms since it could be organised around their domestic roles as well as being compatible with norms about female seclusion. As we have seen, such considerations featured to a much greater extent in the testimonies of the women in London and explained their overwhelming concentration in home-based piecework.

The decision to take up paid work outside the home was more fraught for most women because of the public break it appeared to represent with the ideology of the male provider and of female seclusion. It was particularly fraught when it took women into occupations in the labour market traditionally associated with men as, for rather different reasons in the two contexts, factory employment had generally been. However, our story in the Dhaka context began at a time when a new form of factory employment had come into existence and, for reasons and through processes we have analysed, had been constructed as a 'female' industry. Its emergence had the effect of shifting the option of factory employment from the realm of non-decision making for most women, excluded from consideration by the weight of past custom, into the realm of admissible choice and hence of labour supply decision making.

Once outside employment was admitted into women's preference possibility sets, a rational choice calculus may have captured reasonably well the decisions of some of the women in our study to opt for factory work, but would have offered a very impoverished understanding of the decisions of others. In particular, it would have failed to distinguish between those for whom the decision was a response to a gap between their resources and aspirations, and consequently a genuine preference, and those who were responding to the gap between resources and need, where the question of 'choice' was less clear-cut. As we saw, the degree of agency exercised in these latter cases varied according to the nature of the need in question. For the poorer women in our sample, the decision to work was a matter of survival. Many had already been engaged in earning their own livelihoods in occupations which were lower down on their preferences orderings than factory employment (once it became available): the drudgery-factor may have been greater, returns to their efforts lower or less regular or the conditions of work may have been more menial and degrading. Whatever the contours of their particular calculus, factory employment offered these women tangible economic gains as well as the more intangible benefits of a contractually defined labour relationship and a new identity as 'proper' workers.

Consequently, although the decisions of some of the women who took up factory employment was in response to economic need, it was not necessarily a 'distress sale' of labour. Cases of 'distress sales' of labour in our study were generally less associated with poverty, and more often with the loss of male support, usually husbands' support. For women who had grown up expecting to live a sheltered life, looking after their husbands and children, and in turn being cared for, and protected by them, but, instead, found themselves on their own, abandoned, widowed, divorced, deceived, 'patriarchal risk' had materialised as harsh reality. They took up factory work as a response to a perceived contraction in their choices, not an expansion. What defined their 'distress' was consequently not poverty per se, but economic need mediated by gender disadvantage.

A very different picture emerged out of the testimonies of women who had been motivated to work in order to fulfil certain aspirations. These women came closer to the economic model of agents acting on their preferences, maximising their own utilities or the joint welfare of their households. Nevertheless, here too, a purely economic calculus would have failed to capture important dimensions of their choice. Some of their aspirations were conventional economic ones, directly linked to increased purchasing power, e.g. improving household living standards, financing children's education, saving for dowry or for general contingencies. Others, however, reflected less economistic gains and included the desire on the part of many to escape the overt as well as more hidden humiliations associated with their dependent status within the home. Quite often, more detailed investigation of decisions, which were initially described as a response to economic aspirations, were revealed to contain a powerful desire to have some degree of economic agency, to 'count' for somebody within the family. Furthermore, among women who decided to forgo the economic security of a second marriage in order to be able to keep their children from a previous marriage, it could be said that emotional priorities took precedence over material gains. These intangible gains had little to do with levels of household income or with changing marginal productivities. Rather they reflected the desire on the part of women to transcend the implications of their subordinate status within the family, a subordination which applied to all the women in our sample, regardless of their class background and regardless of whether they acknowledged it or not.[2]

Our analysis therefore confirms the importance of preferences in shaping choice and rejects the idea that they are stable over time or purely subjective to the individual and, hence, can be treated as exogenous to the decision making process. Instead, class, gender, race and social upbringing were all shown to introduce systematic variations in preferences, shaping how people viewed their choices and made their decisions. Such factors also led to different orders of preferences so that not all decisions could be taken to be equally reflective of 'choice'. Where survival imperatives dictated decision making outcomes, there was little scope for choice. They were qualitatively different from decisions made on the basis of genuine alternative choices. Renu's use of her salary to purchase drinking water in a situation where she barely earned enough for her family's basic needs was very obviously of a very different order of 'choice' to Delowara's use of her income to buy gifts for her parents.

When survival imperatives were no longer at stake, and there was some scope for real choice to be exercised, we distinguished between first-order preferences of the subjective, idiosyncratic or 'wanton' kind and second-order meta-preferences which were more akin to 'values' (Hirshman, 1985). Furthermore, our analysis also suggested a distinction between those meta-preferences which had evolved in the course of longer term socialisation processes, and had hence assumed a taken-for-granted 'doxa-like quality', and

2. I say regardless of whether they acknowledged it or not because although many of the women we spoke to did not use an explicitly feminist vocabulary to describe this desire, they often expressed sentiments that radical feminists might recognise. For instance, when we asked Renu, who had finally left her husband why she thought her husband was so abusive towards women, she replied bitterly 'Chele der jat' (i.e. it is in their genes).

meta-preferences which were the product of introspection, of conscious reflection on one's situation. It was meta-preferences in the former 'acquired' sense of the word, the product of a complex set of forces in the lives of individuals, including social upbringing, class background and cultural identity which accounted for recurrence of patterns of behaviour, the manifestation of the stability of the social order. And it was meta-preferences of the latter, more consciously adopted kind, that introduced the possibility of social change.

Both categories of meta-preferences played an important role in our analysis of women's labour supply decisions, leading them to favour certain employment options over others and to place still others in the realm of non-decision making. The complex deliberations which these women revealed in their accounts of their decision to take up particular kinds of paid work, deliberations which showed their awareness of the social, rather than purely individual, implications of their choice signalled clearly that this was a category of choice which belonged to the more value-laden end of the decision making spectrum. At the same time, however, particularly in the Dhaka context, their deliberations also suggested that for many, the values which had governed their time allocation preferences in the past no longer held the same, taken-for-granted status in their choices, but were being subjected to a process of critical reflection and re-evaluation. The structure of meta-preferences in these women's lives was undergoing a process of transformation.

## Power, choice and conflict: focusing on the household

Women's own values and preferences were thus important elements in explaining their labour supply decisions, helping to distinguish between admissible and inadmissible options in each context as well as their preference orderings over these options. However, they were not the only preferences which mattered in their decisions nor were they always the most important. The corporate organisation of the household, the recognised authority of the household head to define its welfare and enforce its interests, meant that women's decisions about the use of their labour were rarely taken in isolation. In most cases, they entailed consultation with other more powerful family members whose preferences could drive a wedge between women's own preferred uses of their labour time and those which finally prevailed. Decision, in other words, did not necessarily reveal choice, as presumed by mainstream economists.

The processes by which women's labour supply decisions were arrived at ranged between full consensus and outright conflict along with various compromise solutions in between. While an intuitive interpretation might associate consensus in household decision making with the likelihood of choice on the part of women and conflict with the exercise of power by men, in reality, the equation was more complex. To understand why this was the case, and what this revealed about the nature of consensus and conflict within the family, we need to first summarise what our analysis has told us about what differentiates, in the generic sense of the word, the family-based household from other collectivities in society. Secondly, we need to analyse what distinguished the different types of family-based households in our study from each other.

In generic terms, the household which emerged from our analysis was characterised by relations of *unequal interdependence* of a particular kind. *Interdependence* within the household was partly emotional. This is hardly surprising since the bonds of blood and marriage which bind people together as a family and the love, affection and loyalty which develops between those who have shared their lives over a period of time almost inevitably gives them some kind of stake in each other's well-being. We saw evidence of this emotional interdependence in the sense of common purpose described in the testimonies of many of the women workers in both our samples, particularly, and perhaps most movingly, illustrated in their shared struggles in times of economic adversity or in the face of social discrimination. Interdependence between household members also had a material basis, deriving from the division of roles and responsibilities within the family and the forms of exchange and co-operation which this required. While this co-operation may have often appeared to be voluntaristic, springing spontaneously from the affective basis of family relationships, it was also underwritten by implicit, but socially-sanctioned familial contracts which defined the mutual claims and obligations of different members to each other. These contracts consequently also allocated resources, activities, entitlements and privileges on the basis of these definitions.

*Inequality* within the household, and the potential for power and conflict, reflected the fact that the distribution of resources and responsibilities within the family was neither random, symmetrical, equitable nor necessarily efficient. Instead, it was explicitly hierarchical. Authority and responsibility were closely bound up in constructing this hierarchy: those responsible for the collective welfare of the family were also given the authority to decide how it should be defined. And because hierarchies within the family tend to coalesce along lines of age, gender and life cycle, it was most frequently men, in their capacity as fathers, husbands, brothers and sons, who occupied positions of authority over women in their capacity as daughters, wives, sisters and mothers. Male dominance within the family was thus underpinned by men's socially-sanctioned responsibility to represent the interests of family members, their authority to define what these interests might be and their privileged access to material resources to discharge their responsibilities and to back up their authority. Women took care of domestic matters, of home and family, and deferred to male authority within the household on most critical decisions. In return, they could expect to be provided for, their interests represented in the public domain, and their honour protected within the community.

The exercise of power within the family was thus unlike power in any other domain of life. No other power relationship offers the inducements and compensations to those deprived of power that familial relationships appear to offer and few are imbued with ideologies of love, affection and mutuality in quite the same way. However, none of this should disguise the fact that such power did not rest on consent alone, hence in principle alterable by the withdrawal of consent. It was also underpinned by the socially-sanctioned contracts governing family relations which were indisputably patriarchal in intent and effect and gave rise to marked gender inequalities in both opportunities and outcomes within the communities we have studied. On the other hand, although the highly asymmetrical terms of the patriarchal contract have led a number of observers to characterise it as among the least negotiable in the world, time has shown that the seeds of its own transformation lay precisely in the asymmetry between power and responsibility which constituted the core of the contract. As Cain et al. have pointed out, this asymmetry derived from the material base of male authority coupled with the normative nature of male responsibility. Women's vulnerability to patriarchal risk lay in the fact that normative responsibility, while persuasive, did not carry the same weight as material power and was more malleable in the face of economic imperative.

However, what Cain et al. overlooked is that the norms underpinning female dependence were neither immutable nor absolute. Female dependence was the other side of the coin to male responsibility and was, in principle, open to renegotiation in the event of men's abdication from their responsibility. Indeed, that has been one of the main findings of our study, particularly in the Dhaka context; the renegotiation of dependency norms in the context of a changing environment of male responsibility: the actual abdication from their responsibility by some men, the fear of many women that it might happen, and the problems faced by yet others whose male breadwinners were clearly finding it difficult to discharge their obligations. At the same time, women's continued reliance on men for social protection, the vulnerability of a woman without male support to different kinds of risk and threat, explained their reluctance to openly challenge the norms of patriarchal authority and thereby risk the breakdown of the family. Instead, they sought to renegotiate norms to expand their sphere of action in ways that threatened as little as possible the established hierarchy within the household.

Understanding the ideological association between authority and responsibility within the family, the relationships of unequal interdependence it generated and the contradictory incentives for co-operation and conflict in household decision making it engendered, helps to make sense of the different labour supply decision making processes which emerged out of the women's testimonies in our study. It also helps to explain why it proved so difficult to classify them within a simple dichotomous framework of consensus/choice, on the one hand, and conflict/power, on the other. Not only did apparently similar labour market outcomes conceal extremely different stories about the decision making process underlying them, but both consensual and conflictual decision making processes themselves concealed very different stories about the exercise of preference, power and choice in the context of women's labour supply decisions.

Consider, first of all, households that reported consensual decision making over the allocation of women's labour. If we disaggregate this category, we find that it comprised households in which consensus was an actively agreed outcome and households in which it merely reflected the absence of opposition. Clearly, these imply very different stories about the gender distributions of power, authority and choice within these households. In some households, for instance, consensus reflected the fact that the woman in question was the undisputed head of the household. She had no need to consult anyone else within the household because no one else had authority over her. In other households, consensus had been arrived at through a process of active consultation between the woman worker and those in authority over her. In either case, whether the consensus resulted in factory employment in Dhaka or home-based piecework in London, it reflected a shared belief within the household that the decision was in the best interests of the family, but resulted from very different configurations of gender and authority within the household.

In addition, however, there were a number of other cases of decision making which were ostensibly consensual in form, but where questions of power, choice and agency were far more difficult to establish. For instance, the women we discussed earlier, for whom the decision to take up factory employment represented a 'distress' sale of their labour, rarely encountered any opposition to their decision to take up factory work, but this lack of opposition was a reflection of their social isolation. No one cared enough, or could afford to care enough, to take on responsibility for them. While they could be said to have exercised agency in their decision to take up factory employment, it was an agency that had been thrust on them by their loss of male support and was seen as symbolic of their loss. Nevertheless, in taking up factory work, they were going against established conventions about women's work, and in many cases, against the expectations they had grown up with. To that extent, we described them as exercising an 'active' agency, however reluctant that agency might have been.

The question of agency was even more difficult to establish in those cases in the London context where women were classified in the analysis as having exercised a 'passive' form of agency, not because the decision in question appeared to conform to the conventional roles ascribed to women – this was the case for the majority of women in our London sample – but because of the reasons they gave for making the decision. These were cases where the preferences of more powerful 'others' appeared to have been so fully assimilated into women's own preferences that it became difficult to establish whether the decision to work at home had been a genuine act of choice or an expression of internalised constraint. The 'others' in question were either dominant members of their households or the more generalised 'others' of the wider community. We described their decision as 'passive' in order to distinguish them from those other women in the London study whose decision to work at home had been taken because of its compatibility with child care responsibilities or because of their perceived lack of qualifications for other kinds of work. While both decisions led to the same labour market outcomes, and both might be described as examples of 'constrained choice', they were qualitatively different. In one case, the possibility of outside employment had not even entered women's preference orderings; it had been ruled out *a priori* on cultural or religious grounds. In the other case, it had at least entered women's preference orderings but was either given very low priority compared to other uses of their time or else considered to lie outside their feasible (rather than admissible) opportunity set because of objective constraints.

Households where decision making over women's labour supply was characterised by some degree of conflict provided a different vantage point from which to view the operations of power, choice and agency within relationships characterised by 'co-operative conflict'. While coercion, threat and violence did surface from time to time in women's testimonies, the exercise of power in the context of conflicting preferences about women's labour supply rarely took the form of naked expressions of self-interest or the exercise of brute force. Instead it was conducted at the discursive level through contestations over what constituted the collective interests of the family and how women's time could be best allocated to achieve it. Men were more able to resort to officialising strategies, disguising self-interest through the discourse of family welfare, because they had the socially-sanctioned authority to define family welfare and their definitions carried legitimacy. Power was thus manifested in the intra-household negotiations in terms of a hierarchy of interpretative authority, with some interpretations of collective welfare carrying greater weight than others in deciding final outcomes. Our analysis therefore bears out the point made by Moore in relation to intra-household bargaining:

> inequalities of power are made manifest in the interpretation of the terms of the contract, and ... these give rise to material conflicts of interest between women and men. The ability to provide an interpretation of the terms of the marital contract, or indeed of any set of normative practices and understandings, is, of course, a political ability. It is political because the definition of terms, and interpretations of normative practices and understandings, can in principle be redefined and contested and these processes of definition, redefinition and contestation will always have material consequences. (Moore, 1994, p. 91)

We saw various examples of these discursive struggles in the attempts of those in authority in the household to invoke the collective welfare of the household to legitimate and 'officialise' their own preferences and to dissipate any potential threat to their privileges. In particular, husbands who felt that their gender identity as primary breadwinners and household heads was threatened by their wives working, or at least working outside, were able to invoke precisely the authority vested in them as primary breadwinner and household head to preclude such choices for their wives. In doing so they not only defused the potential threat to their authority but did so in the apparent interests of the whole family. We can see why Bourdieu's concept of officialising strategies is such a valuable contribution to the analysis of particular kinds of power relations.

Power in this sense therefore did not require open conflict to be exercised. It operated largely through tacit understandings among family members of social norms and conventions, about which forms of behaviour were acceptable and which were not, which would be permitted and which would not, which could be legitimately forbidden and which could not. This more implicit operation of power explains Sayarun Bibi's statement cited earlier, 'My husband's family haven't actually forbidden me to go out to work but yet in a way they have.' It also explains why, despite the fact that she herself did not subscribe fully to the dominant view of purdah within her family, she did not even raise the possibility of outside work with them, anticipating in advance that they would rule it out of the question.

Women's reluctance to openly defy male authority within their families partly reflected their acceptance of the legitimacy of this authority. However, it also reflected the benefits that they derived from their membership of the family, the claims inscribed in its implicit contracts, which would have been put into jeopardy by such open defiance. Indeed, it was only in those households where these implicit claims were clearly not being respected that they were prepared to push their disagreement into open conflict, and to accept the consequences: the exacerbation of violence or the breakdown of their marriage. Open conflicts over women's labour supply preferences were less frequently reported in the London context where most of the women in our sample reported a preference for a form of work which could be accommodated within pre-existing norms about women's place and the primacy of their domestic roles. In Dhaka, on the other hand, where the preference in question was for a form of employment which went against the grain of established custom and threatened men's position as primary breadwinners, the greater incidence of open conflict was to be expected. What was less predictable were the outcomes of these conflicts. In one or two cases, men managed to override women's preferences; in a few more cases, as we have just noted, where men had abdicated on their responsibilities as breadwinners, women asserted their preferences in open defiance of male authority. However, in the majority of cases of conflict, it was women's preferences that prevailed in the final outcomes although sometimes after a prolonged period of negotiation.

This presented us with a conundrum which was not easily explained by either economic or culturalist models of household power. Why did men, as the more powerful members of the family, agree to allow women, as the subordinate members, access to a form of employment which many social science theorists, as well as many of the male workers in our sample, believed would enhance women's bargaining power and undermine their own authority and privileges within the household? Such outcomes do not make sense within a dichotomous model of the division of power within the household. Instead, we have to take seriously the implications of households as relations of unequal interdependency and household decision making as a process of co-operative conflict.

The strategies through which women managed to obtain men's consent to their desire to take up outside employment in situations of conflict derived largely from the co-operative nature of the family and women's intimate and empathetic knowledge of who they were bargaining with. Such strategies were aimed at effectively 'talking up' the very real material benefits to be derived from their factory employment and 'talking down' its transformatory potential. These strategies were partly discursive, entailing the 'definition, redefinition and contestation' of the key concepts which under-pinned co-operation within the family: children's welfare, family interests, the shared consequences of economic adversity and joint resistance to the empty authority of 'moral community' which sought to police women's behaviour without taking the concomi-tant material responsibility this entailed.

They were also partly practical, a strategy of 'yielding' concessions on certain matters in order to 'wield' their preferences on others. In particular, women took steps to ensure that their employment in the factories constituted as little threat as possible to the estab-lished way of doing things within the household: ensuring that their domestic responsibilities did not impinge on male family members; handing over their wages to the household head; adopt-ing modesty of conduct and deportment in the street and making a point of never leaving the house unaccompanied, except to go to and from work.

Our analysis of women's testimonies therefore provides some general insights into the nature of power and choice within the household. First of all, it demonstrates the role of norms as an aspect of the implicit contracts of the family, shaping and constraining the behaviour of individual members. Norms are different from values in that they are not necessarily internalised in the way that values are. They function, as Folbre puts it, as a decentralised form of social authority, shared understandings about the way to behave. They may not be unanimously subscribed to by all members of a family and society, but are nevertheless sufficiently widely observed to reproduce a social patterning of behaviour. Women did not abandon norms when these appeared to go against their interests or the interests of the family because of social implications of such a rejection but, by their actions, demonstrated that norms were of a very different order of constraint from economic, physical or legal ones. These latter are examples of what Elster (1989) describes as 'hard' constraints: they make a clear distinction between what is a feasible action and what is not. Thus, 'hard' economic constraints mean that both rich and poor individuals can choose to sleep under the bridges of Paris but that only the rich can sleep at the Ritz.

Norms, on the other hand, are what we might call 'fuzzy' constraints. They can accommodate a range of interpretations and allow scope for a variety of possible actions. And, as the women's testimonies often showed, they also lend themselves to considerable creativity of interpretation. We have noted some of the ways in which women sought to reconstruct the meanings of various norms in order to accommodate their changing needs and preferences. Thus a great deal of bargaining within the household took the form of contestations over the meaning of norms, particularly the norms defining relationships between mothers and children, wives and husbands, daughters and parents, with women often invoking the authority of religious texts in imaginative ways to back up their own interpretations.[3] Thus, many of the women in Dhaka justified their entry into outside employment on the grounds that the Koran permitted women to go out to work in situations of 'exceptional

---

3. It should, of course, be noted that resort to the imaginative interpretation of religious texts by men to legitimate their individual and collective interests is a long-standing practice in many societies.

need'. A widow in London told us that it was written in the Koran that if a woman had no male household member, she could do her own shopping while another challenged her husband's assertion that men 'don't do' housework on the grounds that 'after all his important works in the world, our Prophet went home and helped his wife'.

Secondly, our analysis points out that, while male power within the household rested on men's control over household resources and their recognised authority over household members, it was not an absolute power, but conditional on their delivering their end of the patriarchal bargain. Male power rested on male responsibility. Conflicts over women's work preferences were most likely to spill into open defiance on the part of women when men were perceived to have failed in their obligations as primary breadwinners. Examples of this occurred more frequently in Dhaka and were more frequently directed at husbands than fathers, suggesting that the contractual element was much stronger in marriage than in parent–child relationships. Fathers were less likely to neglect daughters and daughters to walk out on fathers, although we came across one or two cases in the Dhaka context when this had happened. Open defiance was rare in the London context, partly because unemployed husbands could still bring in unemployment benefit and continued to be referred to as the primary breadwinner. To that extent, their authority remained intact.

The final general point to come out of our analysis is support for Hirschman's plea to give 'voice' a much more important role in shaping economic processes. The economic agent of orthodox theory is essentially, as he puts it, a 'silent scanner', surveying his full range of options, engaging in breathtakingly complex calculations and then making his decision, all apparently without uttering a word. Even where the decision is collectively taken, it is presented as an essentially wordless exercise, the tacit recognition of the superior bargaining power of some members leading silently and smoothly to greater weight being given to their preferences in decision making outcomes. Such depictions of decision making would find it difficult to explain why decision making outcomes might give greater weight to the preferences of weaker household members over those of more powerful members when the two were in conflict.

If, on the other hand, we incorporate Hirschman's point that the economic actor has 'considerable gifts of verbal and non-verbal communication and persuasion that will enable her to affect economic processes', then this apparently anomalous outcome becomes easier to comprehend. Women may, in general, have fewer material resources to call upon in their negotiations with more powerful family members, but they still have considerable intangible resources at their disposal, based on their tacit understanding of the rules and relations of the household, and they still have 'voice' in the very literal sense of the word. Our analysis has focused largely on their persuasive power, their empathetic understanding of the opposition, their skilled interpretation of shared discourses to support their own preferences, their invocation of the joint interests of household members. However, we also came across examples of the use of sexual bargaining by some women, like Hasina in Chapter 4, to secure their husband's compliance, while Islam (1998) has pointed to the weapons of mockery and ridicule, drawing again on an intimate understanding of what it meant to be a man which women in her study of an urban slum in Dhaka often used to get their own way in situations of conflict.

## Power, choice and fall-back positions: beyond the household

Our analysis of the processes of bargaining over women's labour supply decisions in the Dhaka context highlights the limitations of approaches which stress a purely rational choice calculus in household decision making as well as of sociological approaches which stress the immutability of cultural norms. However, a focus on intra-household relationships alone would fail to explain why conflicts in the London context had such different outcomes, suggesting that the analysis of bargaining power could not be restricted to intra-household analysis alone but had to take account of asymmetries of various kinds in the wider environment of decision making.

As we have noted, conflicts were less frequently reported in the London context where women were more likely to favour forms of employment which were compatible with male preferences and community norms. The fact that the overwhelming majority of them came from one of the most conservative districts in Bangladesh may have accounted for some of the differences in preferences compared to the more regionally heterogeneous sample of women, many of whom came from districts with a higher than average incidence of women in paid employment. Nevertheless, preference conflicts were not entirely absent from the testimonies of women in London. In some cases, they were suppressed. In others, they took ambivalent forms, merging choice and constraint. In addition, there were also cases of open conflict, sometimes over women's desire to take up outside employment and sometimes over their desire to do homework. By and large, women were more likely to contest objections to their desire to do homework because these were perceived as less legitimate. In most of these cases, they were able to implement their preferences by reassuring their husbands that they would not neglect their household responsibilities. But we noted cases where husbands had sold off their wives' sewing machines because they judged them to be spending too much time on the machine.

However, in those cases where women's desire to do outside work conflicted with the preferences of dominant members, they were almost invariably overridden. The small numbers of women in the London sample who had taken up outside work, or were actively looking for it, either had no male authority figure within their household to oppose their preferences or else had done it with the support of their families. There were no examples of open defiance or of the kind of protracted negotiations which we saw in Dhaka.

The differences in the incidence of conflict, and in the outcomes of conflict resolution, between London and Dhaka were difficult to explain in terms of differences in individual preferences alone. In fact, despite the differences in the geographical origins of the two groups of women, families in both contexts subscribed to remarkably similar views about gender and gender roles, while the women's views about purdah as a constraint on outside employment were also remarkably similar. Nor was there any reason to believe that women in the London sample were any less eloquent or articulate than those in Dhaka, or any less strategic in their thinking. Instead, it was to differences in the wider environment of choice that we looked for an explanation for this aspect of our findings. This larger context was critical in shaping the contours of intra-household conflict in a number of ways. On the one hand, it shaped the extent to which women were willing to act against the grain of cultural norm, to express dissent and to engage in nego-tiation to achieve their preferences. On other hand, it also influ-enced the extent to which dominant members were prepared to accommodate departures from conventional roles by women in their family and the costs of conceding to women's preferences when these conflicted with their own.

We pointed to particular aspects of the configurations of state, market and community in London and Dhaka which might have been significant in explaining differences in the incidence of conflict and in the outcomes of conflict resolution. As we suggested in the previous chapter, the differing role of the state in the two contexts was clearly one factor in differentiating the *affordability* of female dependency in the two contexts. However, it did not feature very directly in women's testimonies, acting more as a backdrop against which decisions about various aspects of the household economy were taken. A more central role was given to other manifestations of collective action in women's lives, suggesting that these constituted the more proximate explanation for differences in their bargaining power in the two contexts. What was of particu-lar relevance was the effects of collective action in defining the contours of labour market opportunities for men and women, the degree of overlap and separation between them, and the embed-dedness of both in 'chosen' or 'given' communities.

If we were to try to describe how normative constraints were experienced as 'lived reality' by the women in this study, it would be summarised in the idea of 'other people'. Norms, as we noted earlier, are a decentralised form of social authority, shared with other members of a community and sustained by their approval and disapproval (Elster, p. 113). The 'other people' who appeared in the women's testimonies were sometimes very close to the women in question, members of their families or their immediate neighbours. At other times, they were a more diffuse and general-ised category, 'the community' at large.

It was what these relevant others said or did which prompted certain forms of behaviour on the part of women, and of their families, and inhibited other forms. Indeed, in some cases, it was the opinions and actions of the more general category of 'other people' which prompted dominant family members to constrain the behaviour of the women. Consequently, an analysis of the relevant 'others' in the two contexts, the people whose opinions and actions 'counted' as far as the decisions of individual women were concerned, how effectively these people were able to express their approval or disapproval and the emotions of pleasure, shame or guilt that they were able to invoke in the women we interviewed, is a useful way of capturing the structures of constraint as women experienced them.

We have seen the effects of some of these collective actions, sometimes taken by 'chosen' groups and sometimes by 'given' groups, in shaping the nature of labour market segmentation in different contexts. The efforts of the white, male-dominated labour movement in the British context to defend their privileged position in the labour market through protective/protectionist legislation, exclusionary forms of behaviour and outright discrimination against various disadvantaged groups, often in collusion with white male employers, provided a clear example of a powerful 'chosen' group using tactics of social closure against less privileged sections. One of the critical effects of their action was to modify gender as a principle of segmentation within excluded groups, such as the Bangladeshi community in Britain, bringing its male and female members into potentially direct competition with each other. In the Bangladesh context, we saw examples of the informal, but equally powerful constraints imposed by 'given' groups of kinship and shamaj on women's labour market choices leading to lower levels of labour force participation as well as to their confinement to specific segments of the labour market. Here race was not relevant as a discriminatory factor in the labour market and there was a more straightforward demarcation between male and female segments in the labour market.

In addition, however, women's fall-back positions in the two contexts were also differentiated by the operation of cultural identities and affinities within the labour market in shaping the contours of opportunity. Thus, a major factor which differentiated most forms of outside employment in London from those in Dhaka was the extent to which employer and employee belonged to the same cultural group and shared similar views about norms of behaviour in the work place. We saw how both employers and employees in the Dhaka factories shared an interest in maintaining the norms of gender propriety as far as possible, observing principles of gender segregation on the factory floor and maintaining strict rules about interaction between women and men during working hours. It was this adherence to shared norms that reassured both women, and their families, as to the propriety of factory work and made a wider range of outside employment possible for women in the Dhaka context.

These reassurances about the maintenance of moral order in the work place were not available to women and their families in the London context where employers in general did not share their norms and values. Consequently, work places outside the orbit of the community were considered 'unsafe' for women for a variety of reasons. There were problems of the culture of the work place: the fact that they would have to work alongside men or alongside women from communities with different moral values. There were women's anxieties associated with the loss of cultural identity, of being forced to adopt forms of clothing and ways of behaving which were alien to their own upbringing. In addition, of course, there were the obstacles to labour market participation posed by women's lack of command over English, a factor which was not relevant in the Dhaka context. We noted also the experiences of racism reported by the one or two women in our sample who had sought work outside these accepted boundaries and who reported their lack of 'voice', their inability to exercise 'the power of language', in their encounters with co-workers from other ethnic groups.

Finally, and partly linked to the differing patterns of inclusion and exclusion in the labour market in the two cities, was the differing significance of community and *locale* in women's fall-back positions. In the absence of marked racial divisions in the society of the kind which characterised the London context, the garment workers and their families in Dhaka were dispersed across the city. They described neighbourhoods where no one knew them beyond their immediate neighbours and a wider urban community in which they were even more anonymous. While there were attempts by the self-constituted moral sections of the community to impose controls on women's labour market behaviour, they could be ignored because such attempts lacked both material sanction and moral authority. Women took precautions to avoid attracting undue attention in the public domain, particularly within their neighbourhoods, but it was private negotiations with their immediate family and kin, their 'given' groups, which mattered to them. Because marriage did not cut them off from their own natal families quite as dramatically as it did when international migration was involved, the possibility of returning to their families in the event of marital breakdown was physically more possible while their new status as earners made it economically more acceptable.

The constitution of community took a very different form in London because it was made up of a group of people who had arrived in London through their kinship networks and found themselves in a hostile environment where they had to define themselves *against* the majority culture. The community itself became their chosen group: Bangladeshi workers in clothing factories were often described as 'sticking together', a different kind of solidarity to that which the trade unionists we interviewed spoke about. However, the solidarity of the community, its self-chosen character in the face of exclusion from the mainstream of society, translated into very restrictive definitions of women's choices. Men from the community monopolised better paid outside forms of work while women were largely confined to paid work that could be carried out within the home. Although community work for the local council was considered acceptable for women, these were generally limited and women generally excluded themselves from jobs outside the community, hampered by language constraints and cultural anxieties. In addition, husbands preferred not to let their wives work outside because of the threat it was seen to present to their own role as breadwinners and their fear of loss of face with the rest of the community. Parents were also often unwilling to let daughters work for fear that they would compromise their reputations.

For younger Bangladeshi women, particularly those who had

arrived relatively recently and had enjoyed a degree of freedom in Bangladesh, life in London turned out to be far more 'closed' than the one they had left behind. As Tulie who was twenty-five years old when we interviewed her, and had left Bangladesh when she was seventeen, commented:

> If you see women in Dhaka and Chittagong university, they seem more advanced than the women here. Here we have to come home on time and close the doors after us. In Bangladesh everything is open, your brothers, your cousins come and go, people can do many things.

Thus, the closeness of the community, its face-to-face nature, and the importance of its networks as a source of social as well as economic resources made departure from community norms costlier for individuals and for their families than it had been in Dhaka. While men in the London context may indeed have had a disproportionate influence in shaping the labour supply behaviour of women in their families, they were by no means autonomous actors. They too in turn were influenced by the wider relationships into which they were inserted and the scope for action that these wider relationships allowed them in the public as well as in the private domain.

## Delowara and Rabia: daughters in Dhaka and London

The very differing weight given to the notion of 'community' in the labour supply decisions of the two groups of women can be illustrated by bringing together the testimonies of two of the women we encountered in earlier chapters. They were similar in many ways: both were young, unmarried, educated and articulate and both had sought to negotiate with their parents to gain access to new opportunities for themselves. However, one lived in Dhaka and the other in London. Delowara had been born and grown up in a village in Mymmensingh. She had been forced to give up education after Class 9, although she would have liked to have continued, because of her family's economic losses. She found out about the garment factories from cousins who worked in them and had come to visit her family in the village. Her parents were at first adamantly opposed to letting her migrate to Dhaka to work in a factory and we noted the protracted negotiations through which she was finally able to obtain their permission. I will repeat here some of the concerns they expressed and her counter-arguments:

> But my parents were against it because of what people might say, they were afraid I might go off and fall in love with someone, or do something like that. I said, it is better than me just sitting around here. I might be able to earn something. My father talked about loss of honour and chastity so I said to him Abba, if I am going to throw away my chastity, I can do that sitting right here. And if I am not going to do it, I can take care of myself even if I do go out to work ... They were mostly worried about my getting involved with some man. There were other things as well. For example, I had never been into town before. I might not be able to look after myself in this new environment. I had never been to Dhaka, so they worried about that as well. They said, 'These are not good times, you don't know what might happen. It might not be safe. Something bad might happen to you.'

Rabia had arrived in London two years before we interviewed her. She had completed Class 10 before she left Bangladesh and had hoped to go to college to obtain further qualifications to equip for a 'proper' job. However, her parents refused their permission. Instead, she was 'encouraged' by the rest of her family to help her mother out with her homeworking orders in order to alleviate her boredom. Rabia offered this account of her parents' concerns:

> I wanted to go to a language centre to learn English so that I could get a good job ... I want to do a job that requires academic qualifications, people respect those kinds of jobs, but my parents refused their permission. I think that they fear that I will become uncontrollable ... I don't like machining, I am not interested in working in a factory or a shop. I wanted to do a course at our local college but my parents won't let me go as there is no one to accompany me. I had found out about the course on my own initiative and I asked my parents for permission, but they have taken no notice. They ask who is going to take me there? My father is not that keen on me machining, he thinks that it is not necessary for me to do so much work at such a young age, but he won't let me go to college either.

However, although parental authority was the immediate constraint on Rabia's ability to make choices about her work options, she also recognised that her parents were themselves acting in response to constraints imposed by the extended family and the larger community:

> My parents would be willing to send me to a college or a language centre but we have older relatives and people from our village here who have told them that girls who go out to school become wild, run away with boys and forget their religion. My parents gave in to the pressure because they think that I am grown up now and so they worry. But they don't trust me. If they did, they would let me go to college.

In both these accounts, we see evidence of similar fears on the part of parents about the reputations of their daughters and the temptations they might be exposed to in the outside world. In both accounts, we see a similar emphasis on the part of daughters of the need for trust on the part of parents. However, the opinions of the wider community, and the fear of the unknown clearly counted for far more for Rabia's parents and there was the additional concern with loss of cultural identity, 'forgetting your religion'. As we have already noted, Delowara's parents eventually conceded to her pleadings. When we interviewed her in Dhaka, she had left her village and was living in a shared rented room with her cousins. The landlord kept an eye out for them, acting as surrogate guardian. On holidays, she either went back to her village or her brother came to visit her and they had recently started going out to the cinema.

Rabia, on the other hand, failed to persuade her parents to even consider letting her attend a course at the local college. At the time of the interview, she was studying from home, doing homeworking on a part-time basis. It did little to relieve her boredom and in her testimony, she spoke of how lonely and homesick she was:

> I study at home now. I write sometimes, I write short stories. I want to publish them in the newspapers but I don't know how it is done ... Machining helps me pass the time but I don't do it regularly because I get backache ... When there is no work to do, I just sit and think. There are so many things to think about. I think about Bangladesh and the reasons

for coming to this country. I think about my studies and my friends back
there.

## Power, choice and structuration: continuity and change

Finally, the analysis in this book also illuminates aspects of 'structuration' processes, the reconstitution of social structures over time,
in the two different contexts. Both groups of women, along with
their families, had lived through an era of considerable social
change. Both groups of families had experienced first-hand the
increase in poverty and the growth of landlessness in Bangladesh
and both had seen the movement of the rural population out of
the traditional agricultural sector into other, often urban-based
forms of livelihood. However, while one group had sought to
diversify its economic options within the national boundaries of
Bangladesh, the second group had opted to emigrate to the UK. At
first impression, the act of international emigration constituted
the more abrupt and radical form of change, one that held out the
potential for a major renegotiation of gender relations within
the family. However, as this book has documented, in fact, Bangladeshi immigrants into Britain sought to reconstitute family and
gender relations in the London context as closely as possible to the
model they had been accustomed to in the past. It was migration
within national boundaries, into Dhaka, which proved to be more
disruptive of past patterns of gender constraint. Women's employment patterns in the two contexts were both a product of, and
contributed to, the very different processes of structuration which
characterised them.

Structuration processes, as Giddens describes them, are produced by the continuous flow of activity by social actors, and of the
implications of these activities for the established patterns of habits,
customs, routines (and resource allocations) which characterise the
contexts in which they occur. In this book, we have been concerned
with a particular set of activities, those associated with women's
labour supply decisions. We have noted not only what was different,
but also what was paradoxical, about the form these activities took
in the two contexts. The striking difference we found in the extent

to which women were able to 'freeze' or 'cut out' the act of taking up different forms of paid work from the continuous flow of activities which made up their daily lives was a compelling indicator of the difference in the meaning and significance that they attached to the decision – as well as of its implications for social continuity and change.

Most of the homeworkers found it difficult to pin-point the day when they could say that they had started homeworking. The process of entry was too hazy and diffuse. They had usually spent some time practising on their sewing machines at home or on their neighbour's machine, moving gradually and almost imperceptibly to the point where they were taking in a few orders for payment and then, over time, increasing their speed on the machine and perhaps the number of orders they took. They described the activity itself as one that could not be clearly distinguished from the other activities which made up their daily routine. It was often presented in residual terms, organised around their domestic obligations. The meagreness of their earnings in many cases meant that they did not always try to keep track of how it was spent: 'it's not like it's a proper job'. The embeddedness of the homeworking process in intra-household relations, the reliance of most homeworkers on male family members to pick and deliver orders on their behalf, also blurred entitlement to the proceeds from the work. Other family members mediated their access to work and often their access to its proceeds, in some cases, totally bypassing them in the payment process.

By contrast, the decision to take up factory work constituted a definite break from their past lives for most of the women in Dhaka. It was a proper job. The entry process was remembered very clearly: most women were able to pin-point, if not exactly when the idea first came to them, then at least when they had started work, what they had been asked at the interview, who had accompanied them on their first day of work. The work itself entailed clearly understood terms and conditions, often in the form of a contract: it entailed fixed hours of work a day, with recognised overtime hours and it was carried out in a clearly demarcated location, away from the home and family. In place of the mediated and blurred entitlement described by the homeworkers, the factory

worker's entitlement to her wage was direct, clear-cut and individualised, symbolised by the pay packet that was handed to her
every month. However she chose to use her wages, her contribution
to the household and her status as a worker were undeniable.
Finally, while her domestic obligations remained largely intact, they
were now reorganised around her working day rather than, as in
the case of homeworkers, her paid work being organised around
her domestic obligations.

These striking differences in how women represented their entry
into paid work in the two contexts were symbolic of the differences
in the material reality of these decisions. We have already explored
some of the differences in the underlying patterns of constraint
which shaped the distribution of possibilities available to different
actors in different contexts and which determined women's labour
market decisions. What I would like to explore here are the
implications of these labour market decisions for the structures of
constraint within which they occurred, both in relation to the past
as well as in terms of the reconstitution of these patterns in the
future.

Women's decision to work from home in the London context
was described as a choice on their part, a response to their domestic
obligations, to child care constraints and to their lack of the
qualifications necessary for outside work or else a response to the
preferences of dominant families. However, behind the proximate
motivations which led them to opt for home-based work were larger
structural forces which served to restrict the range of possibilities
available to them, offsetting the impetus for changes in the patterns
of constraints which might have been expected to occur as the
result of their migration to a different cultural context. As we have
suggested, it was not the inflexibility of cultural values which
explained the predominance of Bangladeshi women in the home-
based sector in London – the Dhaka component of the study
reminds us that cultural norms were not immutable.

Nor could it be attributed primarily to the racism of their new
environment, and its constricting effects on the life chances of
ethnic minorities. Racism had not prevented women from some of
the other ethnic minorities from taking up employment in outside
forms of employment, including employment in the clothing factor-

ies of London. Rather, it was the interaction between the two that explained the gender differentiation in patterns of labour force participation within the Bangladeshi community. The specific beliefs and values of the Bangladeshi community were reinforced and strengthened by the hostile and racist environment in which it found itself and its restrictive cultural norms were enforced even more restrictively for Bangladeshi women in London than they were for women in Dhaka. Racism was thus mediated for Bangladeshi women in London by the simultaneously protective, and constraining, presence of the community.

While only a minority of the women in the London sample described their decision to take up homeworking purely in terms of their desire to conform to the dictates of purdah, the norms of the community entered their explanations through a number of different routes. For a significant number of women, the preference for homework was based on a particular, culturally constructed view of marriage and motherhood. Indeed, it was the remarkable fall in the numbers of Bangladeshi women in outside employment after marriage which distinguished the Bangladeshi (and Pakistani) women. Among women from other ethnic groups, there was some decline in the labour force participation rates of married women, but only after they had children.

Community norms also entered women's decisions through their assessments of what would be considered acceptable by 'other people' in their community. We saw the importance attached by women, and by their families, to the views of generalised 'others' in the community and how this anxiety shaped and constrained their behaviour in various aspects of their lives, acting as a constant reminder of the need to conform to community norms as much as possible. Even those who were willing to take up outside work restricted themselves to work within the community in activities which were considered appropriate for women. In this connection, the behaviour of other women like themselves provided an important model on which women based their own assessments of what was acceptable behaviour and what was not. Thus a common route into homeworking described by many of the women was their observance of their neighbours and relatives while Morjina's comment revealed the weight of past practice in constraining women's entry into factory work: 'Our women don't work in factories . . . they feel a lot of shame and they have never done it before.'

These various constraints ensured that Bangladeshi women in London were largely channelled into a form of work that effectively reconstituted this past practice and offered little scope for future transformation. As we argued in Chapter 8, and Mitter has also suggested, women's ability to earn through homeworking may indeed have shifted the balance of power within the family, 'but only slightly' (Mitter, 1986, p. 60). There was little evidence that it had expanded their domain of choice in any new and strategic way. Indeed it was precisely the lack of transformatory potential which explained the acceptability of homeworking for their guardians. The possibility for greater emancipation for women in the context of a society where emancipation could lead to the loss of cultural identity and to the assimilation into a culture whose morality and mores diverged so radically from their own was a threatening prospect for most family guardians. It was particularly threatening for husbands because such assimilation was also associated with the greater sexual permissiveness of this majority culture.

Women in Bangladesh, on the other hand, were making their labour market choices in a context where underlying structural changes were creating both the motivation for, as well as the possibility of, challenging the terms of the patriarchal bargain. Some of these changes were economic: we have pointed to growing impoverishment and landlessness over the past few decades, and the occupational diversification and migration into the cities which have occurred as a result. Some of these changes were social: the erosion of older forms of patron–client relationships, the break-down of community ties, particularly in the context of the city, the rise of dowry, the decline in family size and fertility rates and the growing economic marginalisation of women.

We noted the belief expressed by Cain et al. (1979) that because of the malleability of male responsibilities, which were defined by norms, compared to the resilience of male authority, which was grounded in a material base, the increasing deterioration of the terms of patriarchal bargain for women would be unlikely to be accompanied by a relaxation of patriarchal constraints on women. However, this prognosis was based on an overestimation of the monolithic nature of men's stake in women's dependence. Not all men benefited equally from keeping the women in their families in a state of economic dependence: many fathers benefited from their daughters' contributions to the family budget, particularly in the absence of sons; many husbands benefited from their wives' contribution, particularly when their own earning power was clearly inadequate; many brothers, who had assumed responsibility for the household on the death or departure of the father, found their burden eased by their sisters' financial contributions.

Moreover, Cain et al. had overlooked the possibility that, just as the norms of male responsibility proved to be malleable in the face of economic adversity, the norms of female deference might also prove to be malleable in the face of male irresponsibility. Women were able to point to the very real disjuncture that had opened up between community norms and economic reality to justify their action: the growing insecurities of marriage, the insufficiency of the single male income, rising aspirations for family living standards, for children's education, the cost of living in the city and so on. Finally, as in London, there was the frequency-dependent effect of other people's actions but while in London, the effect was to keep women working within the precincts of the home, in Dhaka, it led to women redefining their employment opportunity sets to admit the possibility of working in factories. As Delowara said, after having found out about garment work from cousins who were visiting from the city, 'If they could do it, why couldn't I?'

Transformation of past practice occurred in Bangladesh partly in response to the emergence of new opportunities and partly in the changes in relative returns to women's time, that these new opportunities entailed. In addition, however, our analysis of women's testimonies also pointed to changes in their meta-preferences, a possibility that has been given short shrift by both methodological individualists and structuralists. These changes were products of the possibility, pointed to by a number of social scientists, of the unique human capacity to step back from their immediate circumstances and the preferences associated with them to question its implications: 'to ask themselves if they really want these wants and prefer these preferences' (Hirschman, 1985; McCrate, 1988; and Folbre, 1994).

We have seen evidence how many of the women in the Dhaka context did precisely this. In the past, women's dependency status within the family and community had made them passive bystanders in some of the most important events in their lives: who and when they would marry, where they would live and with whom, when they would have children, who would feed them and hence whose authority they were under. The decision by women to take up factory employment, despite, or perhaps, because of the divergence it represented from past forms of behaviour, was a decision on the part of many to take control over their lives. It was not merely a change in tastes and preferences in the trivial sense of the word. What was occurring was a rethinking of values, as the practices which they had sustained in past became increasingly to be perceived as inefficient, unsustainable or simply unjust.

Consequently, although there were no large-scale and dramatic confrontations with patriarchy in the Dhaka context, our analysis suggests that access to wages had transformed the lives of women workers in important, possibly fundamental, ways. It also draws attention to the nature of the social transformation involved. Social change did not occur as a single identifiable moment of rupture with the past, the moment at which women entered the factories. Rather, women's entry into the factories could be seen as a significant moment in the larger processes of structural transformation which had created the antecedent conditions for them to come out of the home in large numbers, but also one that, in turn, set in motion other forces of social change.

We see these forces of change being set in motion by various practical actions taken by the individual workers to implement their decision to take up factory work, such as their decision to migrate to towns, to set up unconventional residential arrangements, to postpone their age of marriage. The forces of change were also set in motion by the repercussions which flowed from the goals which women sought to achieve through their new earning power: their attempts to secure a more central place within existing domestic relationships; to ensure a better life for their children and better life chances for their daughters; to renegotiate the terms of unsatisfactory relationships; to walk out of, or refuse to enter into, relationships which undermined their agency in unacceptable ways.

And finally, the forces of change also occurred as the intended and unintended consequences of these individual actions were aggregated into changes at the structural level: new configurations of labour market possibilities; novel householding arrangements; changing marriage practices and migration flows; and the increasingly routine presence of women in the public domain.[4] These various changes together have introduced a greater diversity into the social landscape in which women will be making their choices in the future.

## Conclusion

According to Connell, (1987, p. 95), 'To describe structure is to specify what it is in the situation that constrains the play of practice. Since the consequence of practice is a transformed situation which is the object of new practice, 'structure' specifies the way practice (over time) constrains practice'. Practice is always in response to a situation, it is the transformation of that situation in a particular direction. In this book, I have sought to identify what was different about the situations in which women, and their families, found themselves in London and Dhaka which led them to forms of social practice with very different implications for the reconstitution of these situations over time. I want to conclude here with a brief comment on the role of agency in shaping these social practices and the correspondence between agency at the individual level and patterns of continuity and change at the structural level.

While the reconstitution of cultural norms among the Bangladeshi community in the London context might appear from the outside to reflect the forces of 'inertia' within a tradition-bound community, this would be somewhat of a simplification. To reconstitute old ways in an entirely new, and often hostile, context can hardly be interpreted as the force of habit, routine and inertia. Not only did the act of international migration entail considerable effort, resources and willingness to take risk on the part of the

4. And, of course, in the composition and rates of growth in the country's GNP and foreign exchange earnings.

Bangladeshis, many of whom came from families who could only just barely afford the journey, so too did the reassertion of older ways of 'being and doing' in a totally new environment. It did not 'just happen'. The reasons why it happened may have been, in part, an unconscious reaction to the unfamiliar, an understandable need to re-establish the reassuring certainty that old routines can bestow, and in part, a conscious strategy of building an ethnic economy in the face of discrimination. But how it happened was the product of considerable effort and agency on the part of individual members of the community. The recreation of aspects of 'home' in the East End of London by the Bangladeshi community has therefore to be seen as an active reassertion of its identity, an act of choice in the face of particular constraints, rather than passive conformity with past tradition.

In Dhaka, on the other hand, for reasons we have discussed, old ways were under challenge from new material realities, but these older norms and meanings continued to shape and explain the form this challenge took. One of the interesting questions raised by our study of the Dhaka context is when does the re-negotiation of norms to accommodate an expanding range of practices cease to be a process of re-negotiation and become the emergence of a new set of norms. As I pointed out earlier, norms are 'fuzzy' constraints in that they do not clearly distinguish between what is possible and what is not. Consequently, it would be difficult to establish at what point the re-negotiation of purdah norms to accommodate an ever-expanding sphere of action ceases to be a process of re-negotiation and becomes the constitution of a qualitatively different set of constraints.

What we appear to be witnessing in Bangladesh is a situation where the current practices of women workers – in both discursive and material senses of the word – are pushing up against the boundaries of old structures and helping to reconstitute them in more enabling ways. They may not have managed to escape culture – ideologies of purdah and propriety continue to impinge on their choices and shape their behaviour, but they are in the process of redefining them in perhaps radical ways. If we listen to the voices of the women workers themselves, they are under no illusion that Bangladesh is undergoing a major social transformation in which they had played a part: 'Each event is overturning more of the old ways. Of the old rules, only a quarter remain, three quarters have gone. You have to move in step with the rhythm of change.' In such an environment, women's entry into factory work can be seen as both a response to past changes as well as a vehicle for future transformation.

# 11

## Weak winners, powerful losers: the politics of protectionism in international trade

Finally, returning to the concerns outlined in the first chapter, the analysis in this book offers one set of answers as to why many of those in the northern labour movement, who supported quotas on the import of clothing from Bangladesh on the grounds of the exploitative conditions which prevailed within the industry, remained silent on the equally exploitative conditions which prevailed for many in the British clothing industry. Women workers in Bangladesh were seen to be a legitimate focus for concern because their poverty made them vulnerable to exploitation by ruthless employers. Bangladeshi women in Britain, on the other hand, were seen to be expressing their cultural preferences by opting to work from home, even if the conditions of work were equally exploitative. While there is an element of truth in both explanations, I have sought to demonstrate why they offered very partial versions of the reality of women's lives in both contexts. In this chapter, I want to turn to the third and final objective of the book which was to consider how ethical standards in international trade might look when the perspectives of working people, particularly working women in the Third World, are taken into account.

## Women workers in London and Dhaka: ten years on

In the ten years that have passed since the fieldwork for this study was carried out, the changes associated with the restructuring of the international clothing industry have not been reversed. The UK clothing industry has continued to decline. The recession at the end of the 1990s saw an estimated loss of 500 jobs a week (*Guardian*, 2 December 1998). According to the Transport and General Workers Union, around 25,000 jobs had been lost in 1998 alone and a further 60,000 jobs were expected to be lost over the next two years. By the end of 1998, there were only 215,000 people still employed in the clothing industry in the UK, with around 140,000 in the machining sector where jobs were most vulnerable to overseas competition. However, data on jobs in the underground economy remain sparse. According to one estimate, there were around half a million homeworkers in Britain (Shaw, 1997) while another suggested 1 million.[1] In addition, it was estimated that around 20,000 people were working in around 1000 sweatshops in London (*Observer*, 23 June 1996).

For the Bangladeshi community in East London, some things have changed. An increasing percentage of the community is now born, brought up and educated in the UK and has a greater ability and self-confidence in communicating with the wider society than their parents. Racism has by no means vanished from the streets of the East End but the threat of physical attack that persisted through much of the 1980s has decreased. As Reverend Ken Leech, a local historian and anti-racist campaigner in the area for more than 40 years, observed, 'The Bangladeshis have succeeded where the Jews failed. They have broken through the barrier on the no-go area of Bethnal Green' (*Independent on Sunday*, 24 May 1998).

Another indicator of the improved situation in the community relates to the educational performance of girls within the community. Ninety-seven per cent of students in the Mulberry School for Girls located in Tower Hamlets were from the Bangladeshi community and references to the school had cropped up frequently

1. *Home Truths*, National Group on Homeworking, 1994.

during the interviews with the homeworkers, many of whose daughters attended it. It was generally regarded as one of the 'sink' schools which typify deprived inner city areas. However, its GCSE results are now proving to be consistently higher than other schools in the area, with 38 per cent of pupils gaining 5 A–C grade GCSEs in 1997 compared to 26 per cent for the borough as a whole. In a survey of *all* English state schools carried out by the Sunday *Observer* (December 6 1998), it came second in terms of its average GCSE points scores. The calculation controlled for the fact that English was a second language for the Bangladeshi girls who made up the overwhelming majority of the student body and that 74 per cent of the children came from families claiming benefits. Whatever else the *Observer* survey suggests – and there were queries raised about its sampling procedures by Tower Hamlets Council – the results do show that this generation of Bangladeshi girls are far better equipped to deal with the wider society than their mothers were.

However, other aspects of community life have not changed. Men and women from ethnic minority groups continue to have lower rates of economic activity than those from white households, with the difference particularly glaring among Bangladeshis. Although most estimates do not capture the extent of unofficial economic activity among the Bangladeshi community, they do testify to the resilience of racial segmentation within mainstream forms of employment. We have already noted the continued low rates of economic activity among men, but more particularly among women, in the community compared to other ethnic groups. According to the latest Labour Force Survey carried out in early 1997, 31 per cent of Bangladeshi and Pakistani households were classified as 'workless' (*The Asian Age*, 15 August 1998). In other words, they had no employed members. The equivalent estimate for white households was 17 per cent. Unemployment is around 17 per cent in general for the Tower Hamlets area but rises to 38 per cent among young Bangladeshis (*Independent on Sunday*, 24 May 1998). Not surprisingly, many of the unemployed youth have sought alternative forms of inclusion, some 'reverting' to Islam, others turning to drugs and gang identities. As Gaffar Choudhury, a Bangladeshi journalist cited in the latter article, put it, 'Today in Tower Hamlets all people care about is the hijab or heroin'.

In Bangladesh, by contrast, the export-oriented clothing industry has flourished. It has grown from around 700 factories, employing anything between 80,000 and 250,000 women workers, in the mid-1980s to around 2400 factories in 1995–96, employing around 1.2 million workers, still overwhelmingly women. These estimates do not, of course, include the additional 5 million people who according to one estimate in 1991, have benefited indirectly from work as a result of the industry (*Daily Ittefaq*, 25 November 1991, cited in Jackson, 1992, p. 24). In addition, the industry's contribution to the country's export earnings has grown from less than 1 per cent in 1982 to around 64 per cent today.

However, its growth trajectory remains circumscribed by the operational pattern of the MFA (Bhattacharya, 1995). The outcry against quotas on clothing imports from Bangladesh led to them being lifted by Britain and France in 1986 and the European market has remained quota free since then. However, almost all items of ready-made garments exported to the US remain governed by quotas as do exports into Canada. According to a cautious estimate by the Overseas Development Institute in 1992, a lowering of trade barriers would boost Bangladesh's overall export earnings by 13 per cent (Page et al., 1992).

## The current face of protectionism: the issue of child labour

The other trend which has not been reversed is the growth of protectionist sentiment in the north. Protectionist lobbies have benefited enormously from public support as a result of their growing sophistication in linking their demands to genuine humanitarian concerns. The issue of child labour is perhaps the issue par excellence in this strategy. Bangladesh found this out in 1993 when Senator Harkin of Iowa introduced his Child Labour Deterrence Bill into the US Senate, the stated aim of which was the prevention of imports into the US of any foreign products made partly or wholly with child labour. It is worth providing a brief summary of what unfolded in Bangladesh in the wake of this Bill because it captures in microcosm the politics of protectionism currently being played out on the international stage. The following account is drawn largely from Bissell and Sobhan (1996) and Bhattacharya (1995).

Humanitarian concerns with children's welfare explain why the Harkin Bill had wide-ranging support among a cross-section of the American public. However, it also benefited from less altruistic forms of support. The Child Labour Coalition (CLC), a Washington based consumer coalition, which was extremely active in its support of the Harkin Bill, included the International League of Garment Workers among its members and worked closely with the American-Asian Free Labour Institute (AAFLI), an international affiliate of the AFL-CIO, the largest labour union in the United States.

The efforts of these organisations were considerably boosted by an NBC Dateline programme which painted what many in Bangladesh saw as a 'highly unbalanced and sensationalised account' of the situation of children in the garment industry (Bissell and Sobhan, 1996). The programme had an immediate effect on US consumers and buyers, bolstering the CLC's calls for a boycott of Bangladeshi garments in the country. The programme's other message was clearly spelt out for its viewers by a prominent American labour unionist who declared that 'for every child working in a Bangladesh garment factory, there is an adult American out of a job'.

Given that the Bangladesh garment industry exported nearly half of its products to the US, this unwelcome publicity threatened to jeopardise the entire industry. Employers reacted immediately by laying off child workers en masse, presumably the effect intended by the Bill. However, it quickly became clear to development organisations within Bangladesh that the instant dismissal of children from the garment factories did not end child labour, but merely pushed it into far more hazardous and exploitative forms of work. Concern with the fate of retrenched children led UNICEF and a number of local non-governmental agencies to call for some kind of 'holding' operation until a more satisfactory alternative to immediate dismissal could be worked out. A National Child Labour Working Group (NCLWG), bringing together the Bangladesh Garment Manufacturers and Exporters Association, UNICEF, the International Labour Organisation, government representatives, trade unions and local non-governmental organisations, was set up under the auspices of the Department of Labour in order to develop 'a measured response for the phased abolition of all forms of child labour'. A protracted process of negotiation was begun to work out what such a response might be.

AAFLI and CLC sought to play an active role in influencing the outcome of these negotiations. AAFLI flew a former garment worker from Bangladesh to the US to testify on child labour before a Senate Committee (see testimony of Nazma Akhter in US Senate (1994). An AAFLI representative now arrived in Bangladesh seeking to open up a field office in Dhaka in order to play a more direct role in the negotiating process. AAFLI's initial goal was to try and take over the monitoring cell of the NCLWG, a role which would have given it strategic access to the garment factories. However, this was resisted by local NGOs who felt it was inappropriate for a foreign organisation with no clear cut status or history within the country to be exercising such a function.

After prolonged negotiation, a draft Memorandum of Understanding (MOU) was prepared for signature by the BGMEA, AAFLI, UNICEF, the Centre for Development Research, Bangladesh and the American-Bangladesh Economic Forum. However, the Extraordinary General Meeting of the BGMEA convened to consider the agreement refused to endorse it, objecting in particular to a provision which would allow factory inspection by an NGO, a role for which the US Embassy were promoting AAFLI. For obvious reasons, the industry was not willing to be monitored by an agency whose track record had already shown it to have interests other than the prosperity of the local industry at heart. In reaction to the BGMEA's decision, AAFLI and CLC announced that they were going ahead with a call for a boycott of Bangladesh garments in US markets.

As Bissell and Sobhan pointed out, the CLC may have had a genuine commitment to the abolition of child labour, but it was poorly informed about prevailing economic conditions in Bangladesh and the implications of their actions. A successful boycott would not simply have led to the widespread sacking of the remaining children, but would have also threatened the jobs of the one million women who were employed by the garment industry, depriving them of their livelihoods and possibly increasing the likelihood of even more children being sent out to work. Furthermore, what both AAFLI and CLC failed to appreciate was that BGMEA members were, in fact, under no obligation to sign the MOU. Indeed, the first instinct of the garment employers to dismiss all their child workers would have secured compliance with the Harkin Bill and averted the threat of a boycott. They had been dissuaded from doing so by UNICEF who were concerned to prevent the children who were sacked from simply disappearing into the ranks of the 'nowhere children' who eke out a living on the margins of the urban economy.

The attempts by AAFLI and the CLC to shape the course of negotiations roused the ire of several national and international organisations within Bangladesh who questioned the credentials of 'outsiders', with little knowledge or understanding of local conditions, to be in a position to determine what constituted the best interests of children in Bangladesh. There was particular mistrust of AAFLI. Like the American Insitute for Free Labour Development (AIFLD), another international affiliate of the AFL-CIO, it had been created in the 'Cold War' years as part of the American government's fight against communism. Both were widely believed in their respective regions of operation to have strong links with the CIA. Many in Bangladesh were well aware of the subversive role played by AIFLD in anti-communist operations in Central America and few believed AAFLI to have the interests of Bangladesh's garment workers at heart. The Field Director of Save the Children Fund (UK) was quoted in the local papers as asking: 'Who are they, where do they come from and where do they get their funding from . . . Their agenda is not entirely clear to me and I don't know what UNICEF is doing with an organisation like AAFLI'. The Country Representative of Oxfam also questioned AAFLI's motives: 'This is naked protectionism. If it was really about helping children then they wouldn't have pushed the children out on the streets. . . . It is very clear now that whatever the BGMEA does here, there is a whole lobby in the US which doesn't want Bangladeshi garments' (*Daily Star*, 24 May 1995).

The position of most NGOs in Bangladesh on the issue of child labour was far less black-and-white than the position adopted by the American child rights lobby (Bhattacharya, 1995). The Shishu Adhikar Forum, a coalition of 70 Bangladeshi NGOs for children's rights, was critical of the conditions which gave rise to child labour and of the government for not enforcing child labour laws. However, they proposed the gradual, rather than drastic, elimination of child labour and accepted the possibility of allowing children in light work until better options had been made available.

The BGMEA did agree to return to the negotiating table, but on condition that AAFLI was excluded. The negotiations were resumed between the BGMEA, the ILO and UNICEF. However, the memorandum which was finally signed was not, in fact, the one that had met with the unanimous approval of all three signatories. Their preferred version would have permitted some light, part-time regulated factory work for children in the 12–14 age group along with school attendance. This would have eliminated the need to compensate them for loss of livelihood. However, this time, the draft MOU was rejected by Western buyers on the basis of what they referred to as 'the perceptions of the Western consuming public' who, it was claimed, would not be able to comprehend the merits of a solution which combined work and study and would be satisfied only with the complete elimination of all child labour from the factories. The version that was finally signed in 1995 stated as its intention the removal of all children under the age of fourteen from BGMEA factories and their placement in education programmes run by two Bangladeshi NGOs with a track record in this field. Stipends of 300 takas a month were provided to those child workers attending school programmes in recognition of the loss of income involved. On the basis of the 10,000 children still remaining in the factories at this time, this entailed a monthly expenditure of $50,000 a month on stipends alone. The ILO was made responsible for the verification component of the MOU.

## Who decides the best interests of the child?

Debates about child labour crystallise the complexities of ethical concerns in international trade in a far more emotionally loaded way than more general debates about labour standards. As Stalker

(1996) put it, child labour 'fuses many issues and ideas – political, economic and humanitarian – into a set of powerful and disturbing images that dramatise and personalise subjects that might otherwise seem technical and remote'. The photograph of a little Honduran boy apparently asleep through exhaustion while stitching tennis balls on the cover of UNICEF's 1997 report on the state of the world's children; the title – 'By the sweat and toil of children' – given to the US Department's 1994 report on the use of child labour in American imports; televised images of children hunched over machines in dimly lit factories and sweatshops in far-off places in the world, illustrate poignantly and powerfully why there is such a widespread and gut-level reaction to the idea of children being put to work. Not only do children symbolise innocence and vulnerability for many, but because they are also seen as too young to make choices for themselves, their interests are seen to be a collective social responsibility and hence open to definition by a variety of different social groups.[2]

However, despite its potency as a rallying cry for action by child rights campaigners, there is no clear cut consensus on what should be done about child labour. There appears to be a wide gulf between those whose interest in the issue has been shaped by the images brought to them by the television or by various activist campaigns and those whose commitment is influenced by an understanding of ground level realities. Indeed, it was its proximity to ground level realities which led to the horrified attempts by the UNICEF office in Bangladesh to seek to halt the overnight dismissal of all children from the garment factories. To understand the reasons for UNICEF's response, and the response of most of the local NGOs and trade unions, to the consequences of the Harkin Bill, we would have to understand who these children were, why they were in the factories and the options available to them outside factory work.

---

2. There is a certain analogy in the double-edged paternalism adopted by northern trade unions towards women and children in the south. As far as the ICFTU is concerned, women workers in the south constitute an 'underclass of international capital' forced to work in appalling conditions by the TNCs. Depictions of this kind have allowed trade unions in the north to assume responsibility for the welfare of women and children in the south in ways that often coincide with their own self-interests.

Estimates as to the incidence of child labour in the garment industry have varied widely between 200,000, before the glare of publicity was focused on the industry, to around 10,000 in 1995, when a team acting on behalf of the signatories to the MOU carried out its own survey. Children worked mainly as 'helpers', running errands, cutting threads, hand-stiching, ironing, sewing on buttons and other finishing work. The vast majority, not surprisingly, came from poorer families. Some of their fathers were unemployed, others worked in casual daily labour and yet others had abandoned their families (Paul-Majumder and Chowdhury, 1993). Mothers tended to work in badly paid domestic service or else in the garment industry, often in the same factory as the child. Around 80 per cent of child labourers were found to have a relative in the same factory. Indeed, employers claimed that it raised the productivity of the mother if she did not have to worry about leaving her children to fend for themselves. Many of these women had to leave the factories when their children were dismissed since there was no one at home to look after them.

Consequently, it was possible to distinguish between two categories of children in the factories. At the younger end were those who had come into the industry because there was no one to look after them at home. Accompanying working mothers or siblings to the factories, they had drifted into casual labour, working as helpers and packers (Bissell and Sobhan, 1996). At the older end were the 'hard-core' child labourers who had been driven into employment by the poverty of their families. Most had been in some form of informal sector employment prior to their entry into the factories and were to return to these jobs when they were ejected from the factories.

What were these other jobs? A UNICEF/ILO survey carried out in 1994 found children in urban Bangladesh to be working in around 300 different occupations (cited in Stalker, 1996). In Dhaka alone, it was estimated that anywhere between 200,000 and 1 million children, mainly girls, worked in domestic service. While the glare of publicity focused largely on child labour in the garment industry, where children tended to be around 12–14 years old, children as young as 6 and 7 worked as domestic servants. Girls also worked in waste collection, making up around a third of the

100,000 children working in this occupation in Dhaka. The other
main alternatives for girls were prostitution and begging. Boys
worked in petty trade and small informal factories, brick-breaking
and rickshaw pulling. Children working full time in urban areas
earned around 797 takas a month as self-employed workers and
around 492 in informal factories. According to Rahman (1992),
female domestics aged less than ten received food and lodging, but
no salary; those aged 10–12 earned around 100 takas a month,
while those aged 13–15 earned 200 takas. Prostitution paid between
as much as 1,500 daily for girls working independently to nothing
for those working for pimps.

On financial grounds alone, therefore, the garment factories
paid relatively well at around 700–800 a month. However, it was a
preferred option for children for other reasons as well, some of
which we have touched on in the course of the book. There was
the question of working hours. Working hours were undeniably
long in the garment factories. Although the standard working day
reported in interviews with children was eight hours long, overtime
meant that many children sometimes worked up to 12–14 hours a
day (UNICEF, 1996). However, working hours were even longer in
some of the other occupations. Children in domestic service were
worst off in this respect, working longer hours than in any other
occupation, seven days a week, often from 6 am to midnight with
little break.

In addition, there was the question of the dignity and respect
associated with different kinds of jobs. Working children are vulnerable to physical, psychological and sexual abuse by the adults they
work for. Once again, domestic servants reported the worst conditions with child domestics often locked up in the house by their
employer when the family went out. In her interviews with seventy-
one female children in domestic service, with an average age of
eleven, Blanchet (1996) found that 25 per cent had been sexually
harassed by employers, with seven girls reporting rape. Child
domestics also had more immediate and daily reminders of their
socially subordinate position than most other working children:

> While admitting that there is a wide range of attitudes among employers,
> child domestic servants are undoubtedly one of the most abused categories

of children. This is not only the researcher's appreciation, but it is also what the children think. In the sample as a whole, half of the girls and a third of the boys considered themselves to be physically abused by their employers. They are slapped, beaten with a bamboo stick, or with an iron tool in a way that they feel is incommensurate with their 'mistakes'. They compare their treatment with the way parents punish their own children, and they feel a class apart. They remark that, for them, punishment is never followed by gestures of affection as parents commonly dispense to their own children. (Blanchet, 1996, p. 118)

In contrast to these forms of work, the garment factories were perceived by children, by parents and even by the local trade union movement as a relatively safe and regulated environment. For young girls in particular, the likelihood of sexual harassment was far lower on the factory floor where they worked alongside hundreds of other women, including members of their own family, than it was in most other forms of employment available to them (Delap, 1998). Finally, the study by the ILO/ACPR found not only that children working in the garment industry earned higher wages than their counterparts working elsewhere, but that they were better fed and had a more diverse diet as well as having more spent on their health (Paul-Majumder and Chowdhury, 1993).

It was against this background of the options available to working children that the groundswell of protest against the dismissal of children from the garment factories has to be understood. Such concerns have drawn accusations of complacency from advocates of labour standards like Charnovitz (1995): 'It is said for example that if an 11-year-old girl were not working in a rug factory, she might be out on the street, homeless, and working as a prostitute. This defence of the increasing use of child labor is not immoral; but it is complacent' (p. 176). However, it is both misleading, as well as indicative of the polarised nature of the debate, to suggest that such concern amounts to complacency towards child labour. Very few who express such concern would argue that children working in factories was an ideal outcome. However, until better alternatives have been put in place, putting children out on the streets is hardly conducive to their welfare by any stretch of the imagination.

Even the phased elimination allowed for in the MOU, with

provisions for part time school attendance and the payment of stipends, failed to soften the blow for children most in need. Of the 200,000 children estimated to have been working in the garment factories at the time of the Harkin Bill, only 10,000 children were enrolled in the non-formal education programmes set up under the MOU. Many of these children combined school attendance with some form of waged work, obviously outside the factories, but by 1998, their numbers had dropped to 5000 (Bissell, 1999). Families found they could not survive without the child's earnings. The MOU scheme also failed to capture the unknown thousands of children who had been retrenched in the immediate wake of the American boycott as well as immediately after the signing of the MOU[3] by employers seeking to limit their involvement in the MOU.

The negotiations over the MOU were, as we noted above, very revealing of the stakes of various national and international actors in the question of child labour, stakes which had moral, economic, political and social dimensions. However, as in the debates about the MFA quotas documented in Chapter 1, conspicuously missing from the international debates, once again, were the voices of the primary stake-holders, this time the children working in the factories. Yet if politically expedient or morally naïve universalisations are to be challenged, these voices are critical. As one UNICEF publication in Dhaka pointed out:

> What seems a straightforward social or moral issue for an adult in the United States or Europe looks very different through the eyes of a working child in Asia, Africa or Latin America. A young girl working in a factory in Bangladesh, for example, has her own distinctive view. She may not want to be forbidden to stitch shirts if her only alternative is destitution or even prostitution . . . Rather than waiting for deliverance from exploitation, she is more frightened of finding herself on the street, and out of work. (Stalker, 1996, p. 4)

However, the perspectives of working children were not sought out by those who campaigned on their behalf with the American consumer. When American public opinion was being galvanised by

3. Over 40,000, according to Bhattacharya (1995).

the CLC against the use of child labour in Bangladesh factories, the American consumer was not told of the thousands of Bangladeshi children who lobbied the government for their jobs to be protected. Nor were they provided with a copy of the petition published by child workers in a local newpaper: 'If you find child workers in any hazardous/heavy work, you can bring them back to light work and you can even stop new recruitment of young workers in the garment industry, but don't throw away on the streets those of us who are already involved in some kind of light work'. Nor were they informed that the vast majority of children sacked from the industry did not go onto the MOU schooling scheme, but joined the ranks of the thousands of others who fend for themselves in far more hazardous and exploitative forms of employment: breaking bricks, pulling rickshaws, sorting rubbish, selling their bodies or just begging. Instead, the intervention of the CLC was presented for American public consumption as the triumph of consumer conscience over employer's greed (Ross, 1997).

In the end, the Harkin Bill foundered on the resistance of the free trade lobby within the US Senate. Those who had campaigned for the end to the use of child labour in the garment industry generally lost interest in the fate of the children once their goal had been achieved. They did not seek to find out how the dismissed children had fared nor to take up the cause of those other children working in far more hazardous and exploitative forms of work than those in the garment factory. Such work was outside the sectors which threatened northern jobs and, hence, appeared not to attract the same level of moral outrage at the international level. It was literally, as Bissell and Sobhan put it, a case of out of sight, out of mind.

An interesting exception to this was AAFLI. It changed its name to the Solidarity Centre and, with USAID funding, helped to set up the Bangladesh Independent Garment Workers Union (BIGWU) in 1996. The new union is led largely by women, many of them former garment workers, including the woman who had testified against child labour in the American Senate. An early activity by the Solidarity Centre and BIGWU was to try and raise funds from individuals in Dhaka to set up its own schools for the sacked children, cast aside, as its leaflets put it, by ruthless employers. No mention is made in these leaflets of AAFLI's own role in engineering these sackings.

BIGWU has played a constructive role in the area of workers' rights. With generous funds from USAID channelled through the Solidarity Centre, it has been able to hire the services of the Bangladesh Association of Women Lawyers who provide legal education to the workers and help them to take their complaints against management to court. However, these are expensive activities, not ones that can be afforded by some of the other activist organisations in the city, and it is not clear how BIGWU will manage if AAFLI pulls out. Its membership funds are not sufficient and till now, AAFLI has been reluctant to let BIGWU seek funds anywhere else. In the meanwhile, BIGWU can correctly portray itself as independent of political parties, unlike most of the other trade unions, which are wings of the main parties in Bangladesh. However, it is widely seen as being under the tutelage of AAFLI and regarded with some suspicion by other NGOs and trade unions in the country. Nevertheless, it is worth bearing in mind that, just as women workers have been able to carve out areas of autonomy for themselves, despite the disciplining efforts of the employers, so too BIGWU may end up championing the genuine interests of women workers in Bangladesh, regardless of what AAFLI's intentions might be.

### 'Officialising' strategies in international trade: protectionism with a human face

I have gone into some detail into the campaign around child labour in the garment industry of Bangladesh, not only because it echoes some of the issues raised for me by the labour movement's support for MFA quotas on Bangladesh garment exports in 1985, but also because it captures even more potently what is at stake in current controversies over labour standards. As Amsden (1994) points out, there was a time when the question of labour standards was fairly straightforward. Employers and right-of-centre social scientists, especially mainstream economists, were against them, while labour unions and their left-of-centre allies were for them. The first group argued that the premature introduction of labour standards would introduce economic distortions in the market place, inhibiting employment and income. The second maintained that they would improve the motivation and physical capacity of workers and hence their productivity.

However, as the twentieth century draws to a close, the labour standards issue has become a great deal 'murkier'(Amsden, op. cit.). While conservatives remain opposed to them, there has emerged a geographical division between some 'neo-institutionalists' or 'internationalist' labour advocates in the north, particularly in the United States, and much of the south, not simply southern governments but also many southern trade unions and non-governmental organisations. Interestingly, the United States government has played a leading role on *both* sides of the divide. It has acted as the world's most vigorous champion of free trade, taking sanctions against countries which operate trade barriers and using its influence within the international financial institutions to press for the opening up of the world's economies to international capital. And it has simultaneously led attempts, supported by the American labour movement, to link trade to labour standards, thereby seeking to protect American jobs from competition with low-wage labour elsewhere.[4]

A common strategy used by advocates for global labour standards has been to present it in 'win–win' terms. The first Director of ILO spelt this out during a debate on international economic policy during the 1930 conference:

What a strange idea ... to find a contradiction between the 'labour protectionism' of the International Labour Office and the theory of free or freer trade for which the League (of Nations) stands. You talk of labour protectionism. Yet surely the attempt at nationalist labour protectionism is

4. As far back as 1953, it sought to include the proviso that unfair labour standards would nullify or impair benefits from free trade to the international agreement on this matter. In 1960 a Working Party of GATT was set up, primarily at the behest of the United States, to look at ways of avoiding 'market disruption' believed to be caused by imports from the newly industrialising low-wage economies, a concept which was steamrollered through the Working Party even before it had been defined (Jackson, 1992). The MFA was one of the effects of this concern.

in contradiction with the attempt to secure common labour standards
which we are pursuing here'. (cited in Charnowitz, 1987, p. 581)

In 1986, the American delegation to the Preparatory Committee of
GATT argued that consideration of ways of dealing with workers'
rights issues in the GATT was essential 'so as to ensure that
expanded trade benefits workers in all countries' (Charnowitz,
1987). Northern labour advocates have also supported this win–win
view, seeing no contradiction between their purported commitment to international labour solidarity and their demands for
tougher labour standards for the south (Amsden, 1994). They
argue that such standards would benefit labour in both north and
south. Workers in the north would benefit from standards which
increased the price of exports from late-industrialising countries
and which reduced their attractiveness as low-cost production sites
for northern investors. Workers in the south would benefit from
higher wages and better working conditions which would in turn
lead to increases in aggregate demand and employment. A version
of this argument was made by Cavanagh (1997) during a conference organised in New York in 1996 in connection with the 'No
Sweat' campaign against sweatshops launched by UNITE, the
American garment workers union and the National Labor Committee. He pointed out that a war on sweatshops in the apparel
trade had been declared by the American unions because of the
growing recognition 'that their own interests now lie in helping
workers elsewhere. As long as sweatshops exist in El Salvador or
Indonesia, US firms will use their ability to source production there
to bargain down US wages and working conditions to sweatshop
levels' (p. 40).

The politics of representation has come to the foreground in
the promotion of this win–win advocacy because consumer conscience is now seen as the most powerful weapon available to the
northern labour movement. As Charnowitz suggests (1995), the
American public is solidly behind the idea of restricting the import
of goods which use child labour, an assertion which is backed up
by surveys, such as that carried out by Washington's Marymount
University which found that 78 per cent of polled consumers
declared that they would be willing to pay more for clothes which

had not entailed sweated labour (cited in Ross, 1997, p. 29). One of the successes attributed to this strategy of 'banking on consumer conscience' by UNITE activists is the campaign against child labour in the Bangladesh garment industry where the Child Labor Coalition is given credit for 'upwards of 25,000 children' being moved out of the garment industry and into schools. Such accounts, inaccurate though they might be, help to persuade consumers of the humanitarian payoff to their support for trade boycotts. Yet Bissell (1999) has estimated that the actual numbers of children initially enrolled was no more than 10,000 (dropping to 5,000 within the year), while UNICEF's own maximum estimates are 8,200.[5]

Boycotts are, by their very nature, blunt instruments. Their success rests on their ability to portray Third World factories as 'showcases of horrors for the labor abuses sanctioned by the global free trade economy, where child labor, wage slavery, and employer cruelty are legion' (Ross, 1997, p. 10). There is little mileage in presenting nuanced, balanced and differentiated accounts of ground-level realities in low-income countries, distinguishing between situations where the problems are largely poverty and underdevelopment and those which entail the flagrant violation of basic human rights. Certainly, the CLC's threat to organise a boycott of Bangladeshi garments was taken seriously by the BGMEA because both parties knew how easily a single unfavourable exposé could sway American public opinion against Bangladeshi garments. What remains unclear is how American consumers would have reacted if they had been better informed of the wider context in which the employment of children or women occurred and the consequences of their boycott on the lives of thousands of poor families.

Yet the likelihood of such information reaching them is remote. Although organisations like the CLS claim that 'the simple truth' is their greatest weapon in the war against sweatshops (Krupat, 1997, p. 51), the 'truth' that reaches the consumers of the West is a highly partial one, tailored to stir their moral outrage. A graphic

5. The UNICEF estimate comes from a pamphlet brought out by UNICEF, in April, 1997 with assistance from the BGMEA and the ILO in Bangladesh.

example of this monochromatic approach to the truth is to be found in a contribution by Spielberg, a member of UNITE, on the question of child labour in the Bangladesh garment industry. She begins with the extraordinary claim that 'there's a saying among the girls in the slums of Bangladesh: if you are lucky, you'll be a prostitute – if you're unlucky, you'll be a garment worker' (p. 113). She then goes on to describe a young girl she encountered during a visit to Bangladesh who had been sold into a brothel when she was 11 and had ended up in a garment factory by the age of 13:

> the foreman came on to her all the time. No doubt he could sniff out her background. But that wouldn't have made a difference. No, not for a pretty one like that in a garment factory. Just threaten to fire them and they're yours. A girl in the labor force means that she's unprotected: either her family has abandoned her, or the family men are too poor and desperate themselves to make trouble. (p. 112)

However, the most extraordinary aspect of Spielberg's account is the following detailed description of the condition of the *feet* of another young garment girl, a description she includes on the basis of some tenuous connection with working conditions in the garment factory:

> Whatever early malnutrition had started doing to her chances of marriage, the garment trade had finished off. The mind cannot register, in the first few seconds, that these appendages are attached to a creature that walks upright on the ground. They have flattened and spread out to such a degree they seem more suited to one that propels itself in the water. Like fins. Like flounders, but curved in toward each other: bottom fish that got trapped, and grew, inside a kidney-shaped pan. The mind tries to grasp hold of something more noble, something scientific perhaps, to explain why a child, a child who is now admiring her new plastic bangles and smoothing the hem of her best dress, has been cursed with feet like that on which to toil. Compensation: now that's a scientific word. The bones of her feet were too weak to support the weight of the body, so they accommodated the floor. (p. 114)

First of all, I found absolutely no support for Spielberg's claim that prostitution was considered preferable to factory work among researchers and activists who have been working in the urban slums of Bangladesh. Indeed, the claim was greeted with incredulity. Research conducted in the urban slums in recent years has explicitly made the point that the garment industry is considered to be among the more respectable options open to young girls and women to the extent that many are willing to pay a bribe for the possibility of such a job (Islam, 1998). Interviews carried out during a UNICEF-supported study on working children, including sex workers, also reiterated the finding that jobs in the garment factories were 'coveted' because they were considered 'prestigious and well-paid' (Chalwa, 1996). A more recent study found that most parents preferred their daughters to be in garment factories precisely because they were *less* likely to be sexually harassed than in other occupations open to girls (Delap, 1998).

As far as Spielberg's horrified fascination with the state of the young garment worker's feet, its relevance to her account may be tenuous but it does have the effect of establishing her own credentials as a caring moral being, at the same time reducing the young girl to the status of 'the other', deserving of sympathy perhaps, but also a living testimony to the dehumanising conditions that American workers are battling to combat. This interweaving of fact and fiction is characteristic of a great deal of the populist discourse around labour standards and indeed, a leading NLC activist makes a virtue of the fact that 'he (was) not a professional – not a trained organizer, economist or academic' (cited in Krupat, p. 74) and that the NLC relied instead on 'human stories . . . anecdotal examples and accessible language' to win consumer support. Young workers from Third World factories are considered by the NLC to be its best asset and are frequently flown over to testify in their campaigns: 'We wanted the most authentic, direct, virtually naïve workers we could find. We had faith that these young kids would simply tell the truth and that would be more damaging than anything an academic could say.' Yet, as the essay goes on to reveal, the NLC does not deal in simple, spontaneous and unmediated truths but rather on what is described as 'intensive educational techniques' to ensure that their 'authentic, direct, virtually naïve' workers make 'eloquent witnesses':

They stay in our apartment. We're together constantly, talking and learning from one another. In my opinion, it's filthy and rude to bring a young
worker up from Central America and just say, 'Here's a speech. Go ahead'.
She'd say, 'We're oppressed'. What does that mean? No one ever asked
her to define it. Why? How? Name it. We do that. We really press them to
be specific. 'They yell at us'. 'What do they say'. 'How?' They call us
chicken heads, we're born of whores'. 'They hit us'. 'Well how do they hit
you?' 'They hit us on the head'. 'How?' 'With their knuckles'. We make
them write it down and practice their delivery till it's polished. They're so
elevated by the fact that someone has given them their own voice and the
chance to speak for all their co-workers, they dig inside themselves and
they're unstoppable. (cited in Krupat, 1997, p. 75)

One could view these 'intensive educational techniques' as yielding
'the truth', as the National Labor Committee clearly believes they
do, or as a way of ensuring that the workers in question produce
the 'correct' story in their testimonies. Moreover, 'the facts' produced by the NLC have been disputed by journalists writing in the
Los Angeles Times ('Stitching together a crusade') and the *New
York Times* ('Hondurans in "Sweatshops" see opportunity') who
suggest that many of the workers in the very factories that the
NLC targeted evaluated their jobs rather differently to the one-
dimensional picture the NLC sought to project (see footnote 18 in
Krupat, 1997). This, of course, has also been the gist of many of
the testimonies of the women workers interviewed for this book.

### Deconstructing 'win–win': counter-claims in the labour standards debate

While recognising the genuine nature of the concern expressed by
many about the exploitative conditions facing Third World workers,
we can also see powerful evidence of an 'officialising' strategy at
work in the positive sum gains claimed for labour standards by
northern governments and trade unions. The chequered history of
attempts to link trade and labour standards suggests that these
'win–win' arguments have not been entirely successful. There are a
number of reasons why this might be the case.

First of all, the actual benefits of linking trade and labour standards have by no means been empirically established and are likely to differ for different countries. As Amsden (1994) points out, in larger wage-led economies like India, a link between wages and productivity, one of the examples of the labour standards package frequently promoted, is unlikely to be particularly effective. Such countries have large domestic markets and their export sector is not particularly significant. On the other hand, the overwhelming number of developing countries are small (measured by population or GDP) and increasingly rely on international trade to gain access to wider markets and reap some of the benefits of scale economies. While linking wage increases to productivity gains in their export sectors may increase domestic demand, it would be unlikely to offset the fall in demand from the price-sensitive, rest-of-the-world. Instead, rising costs in the export sectors would hurt their profitability and most certainly reduce their long-term growth. Singapore, for instance, experimented briefly with a high wage policy in the 1980s in an attempt to shift output towards more capital and technology intensive industries, but had to abandon it in the face of decreasing international competitiveness.

A second point, one that is not often highlighted in debates about labour standards, is that trade restrictions have costs for consumers, particularly poorer consumers, in the countries imposing restrictions. It forces them to switch from cheaper imported products to the more expensive domestic versions. The National Consumer Council in Britain pointed out that by restricting the availability of low-cost clothing, the poorest sections of the British population, particularly those who are single parents, were hit hardest by the MFA. It acted as a regressive tax on these sections since they spent a greater proportion of their income on clothing than the better-off: the average British consumer was spending around 7 per cent of their disposable income on clothing and footwear while low-income, single parents spent 12 per cent (National Consumer Council, 1990). According to Silberston (1989), the abolition of the MFA would have led to a 5 per cent reduction in shop prices, while the total cost of the MFA to British consumers was reckoned to be around a billion pounds a year at 1988 prices. In other words, the average British consumer was spending £44 a year extra on its clothes bill in order to keep Third

World imports out. Trade restrictions in textiles and clothing were estimated to cost rich countries around $22 billion a year (Trella and Whalley, 1990).

Furthermore, restrictions on competition with cheaper foreign goods removed incentives to improve efficiency within domestic industries and to move into higher quality and more skill intensive forms of production where richer countries would have a more obvious competitive advantage. Indeed, the only way that the UK and the US have been able to continue to compete on labour costs has been through the super-exploitation of their ethnic minorities. The lowering of labour costs through social exclusion has constituted the basis of their comparative advantage. In 1996, the *Observer* (23 June) carried a photograph of a dress with the accompanying headline: '£45 buys this pretty summer dress from Next. The woman who made it earned £1 an hour. In Hong Kong or Bangladesh? No, in the East End of London.' The article pointed out that while Oxfam's recently launched clothes code campaign sought to raise public awareness about the exploitative working conditions in overseas garment factories that supplied the high street outlets in the UK, in Britain itself, machinists were being paid as little as £1 an hour to work in conditions that did not meet basic health and safety regulations: old machinery, overcrowding, blocked fire escapes, lack of ventilation, men and women often sharing a single toilet, few written contracts; compulsory overtime and dismissal if absenteeism exceeds three days, even for illness.

It is popular among those commenting on such conditions in the London rag trade to liken it to Third World conditions and indeed an ex-clothing factory owner is cited in the *Observer* article saying, 'This government has created a Third World economy in manufacturing in the UK in order to keep our prices competitive with the Far East.' These commentators have yet to come to terms with the fact that what they refer to as 'sweatshops' in the Third World are often models of modernity compared to those found in the underground economies of New York, Los Angeles or London: orderly, well-ventilated, spacious and equipped with up-to-date machinery and paying wages which, while deemed extortionate by Western standards are not necessarily so from the perspective of those who earn them. Moreover, as we noted in Chapter 6, these so-called

'Third World' conditions have always been a part of the clothing trade in the East End, able to flourish because of the industry's capacity to capitalise on the vulnerability of those who are excluded from the wider labour markets. Only the profile of the work force changes over time. The brief reference in the *Observer* article to the identities of those who were working in these East End sweatshops in 1996 will not come as a surprise: Turkish and Kurdish refugees, Greek Cypriot and Asian immigrants, overwhelmingly female.

However, possibly the main reason why there has been little progress on attempts to institutionalise labour standards in international trade rules, is the suspicion on the part of many in the south, and some in the north, as to the real reasons for such advocacy.[6] The south has seen too many examples of how powerful countries seek to impose rules, define them selectively and then to bend or break them when it suits their interests. Indeed, the history of the textile and garment industry is quintessentially a history of such behaviour. Britain was able to nurture its own textile and garment industry at the start of the industrial revolution through an elaborate system of protectionism: as we saw, the textile industry of Bangladesh was at the receiving end of Britain's transition from a strategy of colonial plunder to colonial protectionism. In time, the US put in place its own protectionist system to promote import substitution and developed an effective system of tariffs and embargoes over the nineteenth century (Ross, 1997). It was subsequently able to use its political power to impose voluntary restraints on Japan's textile export trade in the 1940s.

6. Ethical concerns have always been somewhat selectively applied by governments as far as their trade relations are concerned. Legislation passed in the US in 1890 to ban imports of foreign goods made by convict labour, and extended in 1930 to also cover 'forced' and 'indentured' labour, nevertheless made exceptions for those items where domestic production fell short of consumer demand. Consequently the US government was able to rule against the request of the United Mine Workers of America to ban the import of low-sulphur coal from South Africa where it was produced by indentured labour under penal sanctions because it was calculated that domestic sources were insufficient to meet American needs. The British Parliament also promoted this selective version of ethics when, in 1897, it prohibited the import of goods produced in foreign prisons, gaols, houses of correction and penitentiaries – unless that type of good was not manufactured in the UK. South Africa passed similar 'ethical' legislation in 1913, legislation which remained on its books right through the apartheid era.

Later it joined up with the European producers, with whom it shared a 'gentleman's agreement' to waive all import duties, in order to ensure that the textile and apparel trade, the one area of manufacturing in which it was likely to face future competition from the poorer countries, was exempted from the key rules of GATT. As Ross (1997, p. 19) points out:

> From its 1947 inception to the Uruguay Round in 1994, GATT rules against discrimination (most favoured nation treatment), tariff protectionism, and quantitative restrictions on imports were all relaxed for textile and apparel, and a series of international accords culminating in the 1973 Multi Fibre Arrangement sought to manage the trade flow from developing countries to Western markets through an elaborate system of bilateral agreements concerning import quotas and trade routes.

In other words, the MFA controlled 70 per cent of world trade in clothing and textiles, placed strict limits on what poorer countries can export to the rich but no controls on what richer countries export to each other. Marcelo Raffaelli, Chairman of the GATT Textiles Committee in 1992, had this to say about the MFA:

> From the beginning it was a game with a foregone result. Both the Cotton and the Multi-Fibre Arrangement were supposed to deal with an economic concept: market disruption; unfortunately for the developing countries, almost all developed countries applied these arrangements with politics, not economics in mind, and developing countries being less able to retaliate, were sacrificed to appease the protectionist lobbies. (1990, pp. 263–264)

It is, of course, no coincidence that it was the textile and garment sector alone which was made subject to such regulation. It was these sectors which had spearheaded the industrial revolution in the major industrialised countries in the past and they remained the key sectors in which today's poorer countries had a competitive advantage. Jackson (1992) summarised the matter bluntly: the MFA 'allowed the rich to change the general free-trade rules for clothing and textiles, because it was the one sector where they thought they might lose to the poor' (p. 10).

Defending US demands for the global setting of labour standards, Charnowitz makes the point that 'while workers everywhere would benefit from the further division of labour made possible by international commerce, freer trade is stymied whenever any trading partner questions the underlying fairness of the labour practices used by another' (p. 581). However, southern governments, trade unions and activist groups might equally ask who gets to decide what is 'fair'. The Third World Network (1996) makes an obvious point in relation to this when it asks: 'And if there is to be a trade-social clause link, who will take action against the United States (or for that matter the UK) at the World Trade Organisation – where whatever the theory, only the powerful can take retaliatory measures against the weaker partners and not vice-versa . . . in the current power structure and relations in the world, all these instruments only work to the advantage of the powerful and the dominant, and make the world more oppressive'.

Nor are concerns about the loaded rules of the game in international trade confined to southern networks. A recent report by Oxfam[7] published in preparation for Seattle round trade talks shows that northern governments have systematically reneged on past commitments to open their markets to poor countries. They have cut their tariffs by less than poor countries during the Uruguay Round of trade negotiations, which ended in 1993. As a result, tariffs facing developing countries are now around one third higher than those facing industrialised countries. These barriers today cost the world's poor some $700bn a year, fourteen times what they receive in aid.[8] Commenting on the report, an editorial in the *Independent on Sunday* (7 November 1999) said:

> The double standards applied by governments now parading their free market credentials on the WTO catwalk defy belief. America imposes quotas on steel imports from Latin America yet at the same time demands that poor countries open their markets to agricultural exports produced

7. 'Loaded against the poor', Oxfam, 1999.

8. An earlier econometric study of the workings of the textile and clothing trade worldwide estimated that the MFA alone cost the Third World around $26 billion a year, using 1986 figures, and that all trade restrictions in this sector put together cost $31 billion (Trela and Whalley, 1990). Assuming that the potential benefits to the Third World grew in line with the overall growth in the trade, the barriers cost it around 450 billion dollars a year, nearly as much as all Western aid put together (Jackson, 1992).

in the US with heavy subsidies. Likewise the EU spends taxpayers' money on aid for rural development in Africa and then destroys livelihoods on a huge scale in the very same areas by dumping produce from Europe's food mountains on Africa's local markets . . . When it comes to removing trade barriers at home, the rich world has developed feet-dragging into an art form. Five years ago, we pledged to phase out the Multi Fibre Arrangement (MFA) which places restrictions on textiles, the developing world's single biggest manufacturing export. But we have so far done nothing.

Similar sentiments were expressed in the *Guardian* (8 November 1999):

The problem with the specialised division of labour between nations, wrote the Uruguayan historian, Eduardo Galeano, is that some nations specialise in winning and others in losing. He might have added that the winners also specialise in fixing the rules to ensure that the losers stay where they are and nowhere more effectively than in international trade.
    . . .
    Take the case of textiles, which accounts for about one fifth of all Third World manufacturing exports. Under agreements made during the Uruguay Round, the industrialised countries should by now have removed over one-third of restrictions on imports. In fact, the EU and the US will only have removed around 5 per cent. The costs of protectionism to the world's poorest countries are not widely appreciated. The world's 48 poorest countries now account for only 0.4 per cent of world trade, and their share is shrinking. For developing countries as a whole, export earnings could rise by $700bn a year if rich countries opened their markets, raising GDP by about 12 per cent. This represents around ten times what the developing world receives in aid.

Countries who opened up their economies to liberal trade regimes on the advice of powerful multilateral agencies like the World Bank and the IMF have been bitter at finding themselves facing restrictions on their traded goods by the very countries which dominate these organisations. Indeed, it has been argued that it was the adjustment policies imposed on many countries in the south which have caused a general deterioration in labour standards in these countries. To then penalise them in trade agreements for these labour standards would be 'doubly discriminatory' (Shaw n.d.). The terms of the MFA gave the advanced industrialised countries a special allowance of some thirty years to adjust in just one industrial sector to new competition from the Third World. Under IMF sponsored adjustment programmes, debt-strapped countries in the Third World and Eastern Europe get barely two years to make painful changes across whole economies.

## Stepping back in history: from the 'golden age of growth' to the 'lost decade of development'

If calls for the imposition of international labour standards continue to be resisted by most countries of the south as a disguised form of protectionism, is unregulated trade, and an inexorable 'race to the bottom', the only option available? I have argued that the positive sum benefits claimed by those who are currently promoting global labour standards are largely spurious. Making trade conditional on such standards may benefit many of the workers in the north and a few in the south but it is also likely to further marginalise large sections of the world's poor, particularly in the south. A win–win solution in international trade may still be possible, but it is unlikely to arise out of ad hoc, piecemeal and self-serving demands for universal labour standards which take no account of differences in the capacity of different countries to observe them. It also requires us to step back from the zero-sum politics which dominates current negotiations over trade rules and to take a more historical perspective on why workers in wealthy, northern countries find themselves pitted in competition for low-wage, low-skill jobs with workers from the poorer south.

The inter-war experience was profoundly important in shaping post-war institutions at both international and national levels. Despite world-wide recession, western countries, still dominated by the classic laissez-faire belief in reliance on 'equilibrating' market mechanisms, engaged in ever-more competitive devaluations, deflationary expenditure cuts and protectionist strategies, but merely succeeded in deepening the slump and adding to mass unemployment. The value of world trade fell by 65 per cent between 1929 and 1933 (Singer, 1989). The experience of the inter-war years, together with the catastrophe of the Second World War, explains the growing influence of Keynesian thinking about the need for the state to manage the economy in the interests of full employment.

What was instituted after the war in the economies of North America and Europe was a form of 'social compact' between workers, employers and government. Workers' organisations practised wage restraint in return for a commitment by employers to share the fruits of technical change and productivity growth and to contribute to a system of universal social security through the welfare state. Governments committed themselves to maintaining full employment by encouraging high rates of investment through their fiscal and monetary policies. At the international level too, there was co-operation over trade and monetary arrangements within the Bretton Woods agreement under the leadership of the US.

The period between 1945 and 1973 has been described as the 'golden age' for the industrialised countries. They enjoyed exceptionally high rates of investment and productivity growth and a concomitant rise in real wages. The trend growth rate during this period was around 5 per cent a year, nearly twice the trend rate of the previous 100 years (South Centre, 1996). The engine of economic growth was expanding world trade. The 'rents' generated for the richer countries on the basis of their comparative advantage within monopolistic trade relations with the developing world were shared between various domestic interest groups through the distributional mechanisms of the welfare state (Jordan, 1996).

However, the long period of continuous full employment and prosperity in the post-war period also contained the seeds of its own destruction (South Centre, 1996). As supplies of labour grew more scarce, the share of wages in these economies grew, and profits fell (Kindleberger, 1967), but expectations had been fostered among workers that there would be continued increases in their wages and benefits. When growth in productivity began to slow down towards the end of the 1960s and there was a rise in oil and commodity prices in the 1970s, they proved unwilling to accept a decline in their real wages commensurate with the squeeze on profits. Increased levels of industrial action by trade unions seeking to protect their 'job rents' through collective action resulted in an intensification of the profits squeeze and in spiralling inflation. Capital in the advanced industrialised countries began to look overseas for more profitable investment opportunities. These became increasingly possible with the emergence of new technologies, better communications, new organisational systems and the hospitable climate for foreign investment offered by the governments of south-east Asia.

The end of the 1970s saw the abandonment of Keynesian demand-management policies. Commitment to full employment was abandoned in favour of the fight against inflation and the liberal market model based on restrictive monetary policies and the deregulation of financial, commodity and labour markets became the new orthodoxy. The reasons why the era of post-war prosperity came to an end in 1973 have not yet been satisfactorily explained, but the contractionary macro-economic policies of northern countries undoubtedly contributed to the problem rather than to the solution. As Maddison put it (cited in Amsden, 1994):

(What) reinforced the sharpness of the slowdown (after 1973) was the basic change in the 'establishment view' of economic policy objectives. The new consensus emerged as a response to events, but it also helped to mould them. The shock of inflation, the new wave of payments problems, and speculative possibilities brought a profound switch away from Keynesian type attitudes toward demand management and full employment. Most countries gave over-riding priority to combating inflation and safeguarding the balance of payments. Unemployment was allowed to rise to pre-war levels. Even when oil prices collapsed and the momentum of world inflation was broken in the early 1980s, the new orthodoxy continued to stress the dangers of expansionary policy in spite of widespread unemployment and strong payments positions. (p. 35)

Unemployment has grown in most OECD countries since the 1980s, despite strong and nearly continuous economic growth. The deflationary bias built into multilateral arrangements set up under Bretton Woods to deal with imbalances of payments between different countries was one factor believed to have contributed to the pattern of 'jobless growth'. Although the IMF constitution enjoined it to put equal pressure on both deficit and surplus countries, it was not been able to exert pressure on surplus countries, such as Japan and Germany. The burden of adjustment fell almost entirely on deficit countries who were required to undertake deflationary measures without any equivalent pressure on countries with surpluses to contribute to the adjustment process by expanding their own demand. Even among deficit countries, pressure was selective and the IMF had little impact on the United States, the country with the largest balance of payments deficit during this period.

The deflationary bias of the Bretton Woods agreement had no serious effects during the golden years of the post-war boom. The economic policies of the US provided sufficient liquidity to the international economy, initially through spending under the Marshall Plan, and subsequently through its military expenditure and foreign investments, to allow adequate expansion of world demand and hence faster growth and full employment in the industrialised countries. Balance of payments problems between countries could be resolved without undermining either. Indeed, pressure on deficit countries in general could be justified in the interests of controlling inflationary pressures within the world economy.

However, the relative competitive decline of US industry, the emergence of serious balance of payment deficits between a number of industrial countries as well as their growing concerns about the 'overheating' of their economies led to the disintegration of the Bretton Woods system, symbolised by President Nixon's decision in 1971 to suspend the free convertibility of the US dollar into gold at an internationally agreed fixed rate. In the era of slow growth, unemployment and recession which followed in the wake of the assertion of oil power by OPEC in 1973, the IMF did not, or could not, exert any pressure on surplus countries in order to mitigate these undesirable deflationary consequences (Singer, 1989).

A second factor in contributing to jobless growth has been the deregulation of the international financial markets and its implications for the real economy. Up to the 1980s, the turnover in the global financial markets corresponded roughly with the total volume of trade. Today, according to estimates compiled by the

Solidar Campaign[9] (Solidar, 1998), the annual capital flow is thirty times larger than the amount of goods and services traded. However, it is of a very different kind. While there has been a huge increase in profitability and in share prices on the world's stock markets in the post-1980 period, there has also been a rise in the longer-term cost of capital. Long term real interest rates in many of the leading OECD countries, including the US, averaged 1.7 per cent between 1956 and 1973 but have risen to over 5 per cent a year since the 1980s (South Centre, 1996). This has had a negative effect on capital flows which are responsive to the 'fundamentals' of trade and longer-term investment in infrastructure. Instead, international financial flows are dominated by short-term speculative capital movements resulting in enormous volatility in exchange and interest rates. Transactions in foreign exchange markets now amount to $1.2 trillion a day, over *fifty* times the level of world trade, dwarfing the flows of foreign trade and direct investment (Gray, 1998).

All of this has had devastating effects on labour markets and the lives of working people in the OECD countries. The highly leveraged *virtual* economy in which currencies are traded for short-term profits has enormous potential for destabilising the underlying *real* economy (Gray, 1998). The major shift from manufacturing and the provision of services as central economic activities in the OECD countries to trading in financial assets has led to the shrinking in the size, as well as the economic significance, of the industrial working class. However, with the growth of part-time jobs, contract work and portfolio employment, insecurity has also become a way of life for many middle-class professionals. Although the US has had much lower unemployment rates than Western Europe in the post-1980 era, this partly reflects the fact that it also has much lower levels of public social security provision for its citizens, obliging its workers to take up whatever jobs were available. Not surprisingly, US workers are far more likely to find themselves chasing jobs in low-wage sectors of production and hence more directly affected by lower-wage competition.

9. A European alliance of development, humanitarian aid and social welfare NGOs linked to the trade union movement and social democratic parties.

Real wages of US workers have not increased on average for nearly 20 years and those of blue collar workers have actually fallen since 1973. US public policies have intensified internal inequalities in other ways. The failure to invest in the country's human capital explains why Siemans pay its German workers much higher wages than its US workers: the productivity of German workers is twice as high as those of the US. At the same time, US tax and fiscal policies ensure that CEOs in the US earn roughly 150 times the average US workers' salary in 1990; the differentials were just 21 in Germany and 16 in Japan (Gray, 1998).

However, workers in other countries have also fared badly. Between 1978 and 1989, real manufacturing wages increased in just 6 out of 20 industrialised countries and fell in 26 out of 33 non-Asian developing countries. The wage share in manufacturing value-added increased, or remained constant, in 4 out of 21 developed countries and 20 out of 40 non-Asian developing countries (Amsden and van der Hoeven, 1994). The poorer, oil-reliant countries of the world have fared worst. The 1980s began with a constellation of circumstances, each of which reinforced the negative effects of the others: reduction in their capacity to export, with the recession and protectionism in the north reinforcing each other; highly unfavourable terms of trade as a result of higher oil prices and deterioration in the prices of other commodities relative to manufactured imports from the north; a cessation in private sector lending and a rise in real interest rates; increasing debt burdens as a result of higher service payments and lower export earnings. Per capita GNP fell for most categories of developing countries, as did the share of industry and investment ratios, while debt service payments rose to around 4.3 per cent of GNP, absorbing up to 30 per cent of exports in sub-Saharan Africa (Singer, 1989). Not surprisingly, the 1980s have been described as a 'lost decade' development for many of the poorer countries of the world.

## 'Win–win policies' in an interdependent world: economic competition and social co-operation

Clearly, there are no simple solutions to the challenge of maximising the opportunities, and minimising the risks, associated with increasing globalisation. However, financial and economic crises in Latin America, and more recently in East Asia, together with continued crisis in much of sub-Saharan Africa, has led to the search for alternative strategies to replace the current emphasis on global deregulation. One proposal has been to abandon the overriding commitment to inflation control in the advanced industrialised countries in favour of demand-based growth strategies (South Centre, 1996; Amsden, 1994). However, its proponents recognise that in order to avoid the inflationary distributional struggles of the past, such a growth strategy would have to take place within a framework of co-operation between countries at the international level and between employers, governments and workers within countries. At a time when the earlier neo-liberal hostility to the state is gradually giving way to a recognition of the importance of an active state for mediating the relationship between global forces and local citizens, this may not be as utopian as it sounds.

What is proposed essentially entails a new social contract between the state, civil society and the corporate sector to ensure a balance between wages and profits and to provide a social benefit system to cushion those who lose out in times of crisis and transition. However, there is greater unanimity on the need for increased co-ordination at the global level since the ability of individual countries to carry out their policies is strongly interdependent with the policies undertaken by other countries. A global governance structure is considered essential to regulate international financial flows, to ensure that balance of payments problems are tackled by both surplus as well as deficit countries and to put in place a global social policy regime based on negotiated agreements of labour and environmental standards.

Negotiations around global social policy are likely to involve responsibilities as well as rights. Some commitment to redistributive measures will be critical. Without a basic social safety net in place for all citizens of a country, their willingness to take whatever form of work comes their way, no matter how exploitative, is difficult to challenge or combat. In any case, the richer countries of the world will need to share part of the burden of enabling poorer countries to implement labour standards which entail costs, since they would also benefit from the elimination of these 'international public bads' (Lee, 1997; Deacon, 1999). If a consensus is reached at the global level that child labour is one of these international public 'bads', then its progressive elimination will have to be accompanied by investments in the expansion and improvement of educational provision, together with some form of compensation to the affected families. Otherwise, the ethical standards of the world's richer countries will directly penalise the children and families of the poor.

Co-ordinated macro-economic expansion by the leading industrial countries would, it is suggested by its advocates, come closest to the possibility of a genuine win–win outcome. It would benefit workers and consumers in the richer countries by making employment a priority once again. It would also benefit workers and consumers in the poorer countries. Unlike aid, trade generates the self-reliant growth, employment and investment needed to reduce poverty. With the transition from what Amsden calls 'labour-sweating' to 'labour-friendly' growth regimes, the need for workers in wealthy industrialised countries to engage in wage competition with workers from poorer countries would be seen for the anomaly that it is. As Wark (1997) has pointed out 'the First World campaign against Third World sweatshops would have more credibility if it were combined with a frank recognition that the adjustment of clothing and textile industries in the overdeveloped world is not something that can be put off forever. Low-skill, labour-intensive, and low value-added industrial employment does not have a future in high-wage countries' (p. 230).

Once the discussion about labour standards ceases to be dominated by coalitions of 'powerful losers' in the north seeking to claw back the gains made from international trade by 'weak winners' in the south, we would be in a better position to consider what forms of regulation do need to be put in place to ensure that the benefits of global trade are shared more equitably with workers rather than being monopolised by the transnationals. International and domestic capital has benefited from various concessions to promote investment in these industries; they must also bear certain responsibilities for ensuring a minimum bundle of rights for their workers. What are these rights?

Despite the fact that there is 'a deep fault line of distrust between industrialised and developing countries' (Lee, 1997, p. 177), most countries across the world have signed up to what the ILO describes as the three 'core' labour conventions (Mehmet et al., 1999). These include freedom of association, the right to collective bargaining and the absence of forced labour. These rights were chosen in order to reflect a balance between economic and social development. If the parameters of trade sanctions were removed, then the core standards would be expanded by the ILO to include equal pay for equal work, freedom from discrimination and elimination of exploitative forms of child labour. What is distinctive about the three core conventions is that they focus on *rights*, not *standards*. They do not presume a certain level of development for their implementation, but they are fundamental to democratising the struggle for improved labour standards, both nationally and internationally. They allow workers in different countries to determine their own priorities, to fight for them and to accept the risks that such a struggle might entail.

In a world that is characterised by highly uneven development, building an inter-national system that is committed to universal human rights is extremely difficult to reconcile with one that also respects the rights of others to decide things for themselves. But, as Edwards (1997, p. 32) points out, societies have developed in different ways. They have had to make their own trade-offs between economic, political and social objectives. The world economy is not a level playing field and globally agreed improvements in labour standards will still have to be graduated according to conditions within each country: 'the only instances where flexibility is not legitimate are when the most basic of human rights are denied – the right to human integrity, the right to have rights and an equal voice on their application'.

## Women workers and labour standards:
## the missing voices in international debates

Finally, of course, and this is a point that feminists have been making, we have to recognise that the interests represented in negotiations around labour standards have not only been largely northern, but also largely male. Nowhere in the world have trade unions been known for their sensitivity to the needs of workers outside formally organised factory production. Yet this is where many of the poor and disadvantaged sections of their societies are based. It is also where women workers are largely based.

Historically, the response of the British and American trade unions to homeworking has been to call for its abolition. From its inception, the International Ladies' Garment Workers' Union in the United States has maintained, and won, the outlawing of homeworking (Howard, 1997). This negativity is still in evidence today. Reagan's attempt to lift the fifty-year ban on homeworking in the women's apparel industry was successfully resisted by the unions. In Britain, trade union opposition to homeworking has not been as absolute, but attitudes have been marked by extreme suspicion and the conviction that homeworkers were impossible to organise (Rowbotham, 1993). Even today, homeworking continues to operate under a tangle of legal restrictions.

Yet the fact remains that for many women, burdened by domestic division of labour, restricted by norms from opportunities in the public domain or by the absence of such opportunities, homeworking may be their only, or even their most preferred, option. To ignore this section of the working population from the labour movements' attempts to win a better deal for working people reflects badly on the notion of workers' solidarity and social justice. For the many women from the ethnic minorities who predominate in the garment homework in the UK, including the Bangladeshi women in East London, the insecurities engendered within their communities by racism has also bred a reluctance to engage in the adversarial politics of conventional trade unionism. What has worked better for them has been community-based associations which take cognisance of the full range of problems that they face, not simply those related to their working lives (Aekta, 1999).

However, leaving homeworking to one side, workers do not always share uniform interests even within the organised sectors of production. Gender-specific constraints and responsibilities mean that women workers do not always seek to conform to the norm of the full-time, life-time industrial worker, the norm which has traditionally informed trade union struggles in the past, and continues to do so in the present. Women are likely to value flexibility more than men, to define issues of social security differently and to prioritise a different set of demands (see, for instance, Razavi, 1999; Chhachhi and Pittin, 1996; Elson, 1996).

We are seeing a gradual emergence of a newer kind of organisation among women workers in Bangladesh, somewhat different from the traditional party-dominated politics of trade unions. Along with the new model offered by BIGWU, a number of other organisations have also set up community-based activities with women workers, organised around where they live rather than the work place and seeking to contact them during their holidays rather than insisting on meetings during working hours. Shireen Akhter, a trade union activist with a long history of working with women in the garment industry, believes that women workers are far more willing to confront management with their grievances than they had been when she first began working with the industry. However, despite many more examples of sporadic strikes, 'downing of tools', group bargaining with management and other forms of collective action (see, for instance, Dannecker, 1998), women workers in the Bangladesh garment industry have remained difficult to organise on a large scale. They are far more likely to give their support to the incremental accretion of rights at work than to the kind of confrontational tactics which led to male workers in the industry being replaced by women.

Part of the problem of large scale organisation is women's fear of losing jobs in a labour surplus economy where they have few opportunities anyway (Dannecker, 1998). Part of it is the high turnover within factories as women move from factory to factory seeking better pay. Part of it is the fact that most of the women are recent rural migrants with little history of paid work. A belief in the right to work, let alone in rights at work, is likely to evolve gradually rather than to come into existence overnight. And finally, part of it is the fact that while women may complain bitterly about conditions in the work place, access to factory employment has provided them with something positive in their lives, something that they would be reluctant to jeopardise without a very clear idea of what they are likely to gain.

Since carrying out the fieldwork for this book, there have been a number of other studies on the women workers in the Bangladesh garment industry. These have been cited at various stages in this book. They generally confirm that labour standards in the factories remain low and that complaints about hours of work, irregularity of pay, disrespect from management continue to crop up frequently in interviews with women workers. At the same time, they also confirm that most women workers, nevertheless, evaluated their factory jobs in largely positive terms, which included job satisfaction, new social networks, greater voice in household decision making, greater freedom from physical and verbal abuse, an enhanced sense of self-worth and self reliance as well as greater personal freedom and autonomy (Newby, 1998; Amin et al., 1997; Zohir and Paul-Chowdhury, 1996; Kibria, 1995 and 1998; Dannecker, 1998).

This paradox of negative objective conditions and positive subjective evaluations is not unique to Bangladeshi women workers. It also characterised the experience of industrialisation for women workers in Europe and America. As Fraser points out, feminists who have equated early capitalist employment with 'wage slavery' have missed out on the contradictory and gender-specific implications of such employment in the lives of workers in much the same way as current campaigners who perceive only the negative aspects of female employment in the Bangladesh garment industry:

> To be sure, it was painfully experienced in just that way by some early-nineteenth century proletarianized (male) artisans and yeoman farmers who were losing not only tangible property in tools and in land but also prior control over their work. But their response was contextually specific and gendered. Consider, by way of contrast, the very different experience of young single women who left farms – with open-ended work hours,

pervasive parental supervision, and little autonomous personal life – for mill towns, where intense supervision in the mill was combined with relative freedom from supervision outside it, as well the increased autonomy of personal life conferred by cash earnings. From their perspective, the employment contract was a liberation. (Fraser, 1997, p. 230)

## Conclusion

Whatever the truth of the matter is about the relationship between labour standards and the interests of Third World workers, and there is clearly no consensus on this question, it will be abundantly clear by now that the battle over labour standards is essentially a struggle over jobs being fought out in the terrain of representation, discourse and meaning. Protectionists have found consumer conscience a powerful resource for their cause and language a powerful weapon for mobilising it. As one campaigner points out 'the repugnance attached to the term "sweatshop" commands a moral power, second only to slavery itself, to rouse public opinion into a collective spasm of abhorrence' (Ross, 1997, p. 11). However, the juxtaposition of terms like sweatshop and slavery should not obscure important differences between them. Very few slaves described slavery as an opportunity and a route to greater personal autonomy as did so many of the women that I, and others, have interviewed in the Bangladesh garment industry.

The garment industry has historically made its profits through exploiting the labour of excluded sections of society, whether in the First World or the Third. There is, however, a very real difference in the situation of the two groups. The Bangladeshi women who worked in home-based piecework in London, like ethnic minority workers in the garment industry in New York and Los Angeles, obtained these jobs as members of socially excluded groups. These were jobs that had been rejected by the more privileged sections of the working class in these countries and the predominance of ethnic minority women in these jobs was symbolic of both the discarded status of the jobs and the excluded status of those who performed them. The Bangladeshi women who worked in the factories of Bangladesh, by contrast, *aspired* to such employment because it moved them from their position at the margins of the labour market to a more central, better paid and more visible place in the economy. Their jobs can be seen as an expression of a new, if problematic, inclusion.

# Appendix 1

# Methodological note

As I pointed out in the preface, one of the initial aims of the research was to evaluate the fit between 'actual' decision making processes, focusing in particular on women's labour supply decision making, and the formal neo-classical depiction of such decision making. Subsequently, this objective was expanded to include the significance of cultural constraints on women's actions. The methodology adopted for the research can be described as 'testimony-based' hypothesis testing. In other words, rather than relying on statistical correlations to support or reject the hypotheses about women's labour market behaviour thrown up by the social science literature, I focused on asking women for their own accounts of how their labour market decisions were made and the impact it had on their lives. I used these explanations to establish the extent to which the considerations which influenced women's decision to work, and the type of work they opted for, echoed those put forward in different social science theories.

These personal accounts were taken as an immediate level of explanation, based on what women knew and how they perceived their options. I was interested in the extent to which their perceptions about their opportunities and constraints were based on their values and beliefs, the cultural dimension of decision making, and the extent to which it was supported by the empirically verifiable data. In addition, however, I wanted to explore the 'explanation for their explanations' (Lawson, 1997), the underlying configuration of factors which gave rise to the opportunities and constraints that the women workers considered important. Consequently, along with women's personal testimonies, I have also incorporated secondary information which helps to illuminate this deeper level

of analysis. The sequence of research activities followed in each city
was the following:

- A literature survey to obtain as full a picture as possible on the
  structure of the garment industry, labour force patterns and
  trends and existing explanations of women's labour supply
  behaviour in the two contexts which were to be studied.
- Interviews were carried out with 12 employers in garment factories scattered across Dhaka to get their views on their employment
  strategies. It was more difficult to do the equivalent in London
  because the relationship between the homeworkers and their
  employers was far more tenuous. In fact, women often did not
  know who their employers were. However some employers in the
  East End of London had already been interviewed prior to the
  study as part of the research for the World Development Movement Campaign and this material has been utilised to some
  extent in the research. Interviews were also conducted with trade
  unionists in both contexts.
- In-depth interviews with 60 women workers in Dhaka and 53 in
  London. The approach adopted to identify women in the two
  contexts necessarily had to be different. In Dhaka, we asked the
  employers we interviewed to provide us with factory files on their
  work force. Using the information they provided, we purposively
  selected a sample of women who came from both poor and
  better-off households, were married, single as well as either
  divorced, abandoned or widowed. These interviews were carried
  out within the factories; employers provided us with a private
  space, either an unused office or sometimes the store room.
  However, interviews were often continued in their workers'
  homes. In London, on the other hand, we used a variety of
  methods: we knocked on doors, used our respondents to help us
  identify other homeworkers in the building as well as relying on
  a range of informal contacts in the community. These interviews
  were obviously carried out in the homeworkers' homes. Although
  we had intended to interview 60 women in London as well, the
  greater difficulties of tracking down homeworkers made this
  impossible to do in the time available.
- Interviews with key members of the families of the women

workers. In Dhaka, we asked the women workers if they minded us visiting their homes to talk to another member of their family for their views. (Obviously this did not apply to women living on their own.) None refused and the majority were enthusiastic about being visited at home. In principle we wanted to interview whoever was seen as the household head, but it proved to be too complicated to arrange. Instead we interviewed whichever adult member of the family was at home at the time we arranged to visit. Consequently, family members interviewed included mothers, fathers, husbands, brothers and sisters. It proved to be far more difficult to interview other members of the family in the case of the London homeworkers. Most lived in nuclear households so that it would generally be husbands that we would have been interviewing. However, the men were extremely suspicious about their wives being interviewed about their homeworking activities and generally refused to be interviewed themselves. Consequently, while we have some of the voices of other family members in the London research, they are far fewer and generally belong to female family members.
• Interviews with 30 male workers in each context. These were briefer than those with the women but covered similar ground.

The interviews were all taped with the permission of those being interviewed and transcribed afterwards. Since the interviews with the women workers constituted the core of the research, I will describe the approach adopted for the interviews with them.

It was clear from the outset that attempting to study 'the labour market decision' by asking women workers direct questions about it would not be a particularly fruitful approach, likely to elicit 'normative' answers as to who made the decision and why. Instead, we opted for a life history approach, using free conversational format but trying to make sure that a previously worked-out checklist of key issues were covered in the course of the conversation. We were not always successful, hence the summary statistics on the women workers reported in Appendix 2 and 3 contain a number of missing values.

We began the interviews by asking women to tell us a little about themselves, about their lives, where they had been born, where they had grown up, had they gone to school and so on, right until the present day. In addition, we asked them their views and opinions on a number of matters, including the meaning of work in their lives. Clearly this provided us with a lot of information that was not immediately relevant to the research, but did help to provide some insight into each woman's background and previous history, information that was critical to interpreting how their labour market decisions were made and what their implications were. It also helped to provide insights into the operation of 'structures' in the lives and decisions of the women.

The check-list of issues that we ensured were covered in the course of our conversations with the women related primarily to their decision to enter the factory or to take up homework. They were divided into three phases of the decision:

Pre-entry information
1) Key events in her household's history which might have a bearing on its current economic status (including migration history).
2) Changing labour strategies over the household lifecycle.
3) Prior domestic division of labour.
4) Previous occupational history and reasons for participation, or absence of participation, in paid work at this stage.

Entry information
1) Who initiated the idea of paid work, who supported it, who objected and what were the reasons for each.
2) Were there any particular events which led to the decision.
3) How was information acquired about the paid work in question, what was the process by which this information was then acted on. In the case of factory jobs, this involved questions about how the application for the job was made, the interviewing process, training and job assignment. In the case of homework, this involved questions about how homeworking arrangements were set up.

Post-entry information
1) Changes in the household composition and structure as a result of women taking up factory/homework.

2) Changes in the domestic division of labour.
3) Management of household income flows and assignment of women's earnings.
4) Women's own perceptions of the changes effected in intra-household relations as a result of their paid work as well as the perceptions of other household members.
5) Society's perceptions of women's paid employment.

Because 'the decision' of interest in the study was recognised from the outset to be one that entailed the broader household member-ship, rather than the individual woman alone, we used our inter-views with other household members to seek out the complex reactions by the key members of the family to different aspects of women's labour market decisions. Interviews with male workers, carried out in the factories in Dhaka, and in their homes in London, were used to throw light on some of the different factors which came into play in the case of male employment decisions as well as their views about women's paid work.

The analysis was conducted using a number of different tech-niques. First of all, and most important, it entailed a close reading and re-reading of what the women workers were saying and what their families were saying. I became aware in this process of how easy it is to fall into the trap of 'hearing' those voices which confirm one's own favoured interpretations and discounting those that did not. I had gone into the research, unsure and curious about the factors which led to women's very different work patterns in Dhaka and London, but also deeply influenced by some of the feminist literature which suggested that 'merely' earning wages would do little to alter women's subordinate position within the household. However, repeated readings of the interviews with women workers in Dhaka persuaded me that this view was not reflected in how the women talked about their new capacity to earn and its impact on their lives. Similarly, while the interviews with the homeworkers in London confirmed the view that home-based work did little to transform women's structural position within the home, it also became clear that their ability to earn did have certain important implications at the individual level which it was important not to miss.

Consequently, in terms of the structure-agency duality which constitutes the theoretical core of this book, I began writing it as someone who was positioned closer to the 'structuralist' end of the continuum, but have come out of it far closer to the 'agency' end. My conversations with women workers was my first experience of such a methodology. It has convinced me of the importance of hearing the 'voices' of those who are often mute within academic research and policy debates and has influenced a great deal of my subsequent research. At the same time, the experience of writing this book, and becoming aware in the course of it how much my own preconceived explanations biased who and what I heard, also served to remind me of the importance of 'counting', even for such a small and purposively selected sample.

The responses given by the women workers made it clear that no single explanation for either the decision to take up employment or the implications of employment sufficed in either context. Instead, the explanations reflected the current circumstances of the women's household, their own individual characteristics, particularly their life-cycle status, and finally, something unique to each woman, their subjective interpretations of their options and the degree of agency they brought to bear on different aspects of their lives.

While we had pre-coded some of the basic socio-economic facts about the women workers in order to get a basic statistical description of them, I decided also to classify and count the responses I was getting to the key research questions. By 'counting' the incidence of different responses, I was able to distinguish between those which reflected the situation or opinion of a minority of women and those which were more widespread. I was also able to guard against giving undue importance to those responses which confirmed my own preconceptions and politics. A description of the basic socio-economic characteristics of the women workers in Dhaka, along with their responses to the key questions of the research, is provided in Appendix 2 while Appendix 3 provides a statistical summary of the London community and the responses of the homeworkers to the key research questions.

A final aspect of the methodology adopted for the research was to explore the extent to which the premises on which women's explanations of their labour market behaviour rested were borne out by other sources of data. While not doubting that women were able to explain their labour market decisions based on what they knew, it is also the case that people generally operate with less than perfect information about the wider decision making environment in which they live. Thus, while some of the women workers in London explained their decision to work from home in terms of their lack of education or inability to speak the language, it was clear from the interviews with the male workers that the same factors had not prevented them from finding jobs outside the home. Clearly, while it may have explained the decisions of individual women, it was only part of the explanation. It was by seeking to delve beyond the immediate explanations given by the women workers to what lay behind these explanations, and by locating their accounts in their broader contexts, that we were able to obtain a view of the 'structures of constraint' in which they lived their lives. However, it is important to add that the effects of these structures were not only indirectly observable. We also saw them directly referred to in many of the women's accounts.

I have, of course, for reasons of confidentiality changed the names of the women and men who appear in this book. It was critical to do so, particularly in the London context, where the community is so much smaller and its members so much easier to identify. However, this was not easy to do. Although the interviews were undertaken around a decade ago, I still have their voices on tape, I have read and re-read what they said and they have remained real people, with their own identities and their own histories. Their names were an important part of their identities and I waited till the very end before I reluctantly changed them.

# Appendix 2

# Statistical background to
# the Dhaka study

The aim of this study, and hence the methodology adopted, was the exploration of meaning and motivations for particular courses of action rather than the production of statistically generalisable findings. However, other studies have been carried out on women garment workers in Bangladesh which used survey data as well as more qualitative approaches. Their findings have been cited at various points in the course of the book because they help to establish the extent to which the various studies are all telling broadly similar or contradictory stories. Consequently, they also help to place my own, smaller-scale and more in-depth study on a more firm empirical basis. In this appendix, I want to provide some basic data on the socio-economic characteristics of the Dhaka women workers reported by other quantitative studies as a background to this study. In addition, I have included tables containing information on the women in my sample along with frequencies on various aspects of their responses which relate to the analytical points made in the book. This is intended as a simple numerical check rather than having any statistical significance.

An early survey of 1,000 women workers in the Dhaka garment industry carried out in 1985 (Commission for Justice and Peace, 1985) found that around 10 per cent of the workers were under the age of 16; 60 per cent of the workers were between 16 and 20 years; 23 per cent were between 21 and 25 and around 7 per cent were above 26. As far as marital status was concerned, the survey found that 78 per cent of the women were single, but there was a substantial minority of married women (20 per cent). Most workers had some education: 17 per cent had studied at primary level; 50 per cent had reached secondary education and 31 per cent had reached or completed higher education. For the vast majority of the women (92 per cent), this was their first job. Of the 8 per cent who had worked before, the majority had been working in another garment factory. The remainder had been domestic servants.

A later survey of 428 females and 245 males was carried out by Zohir and Paul-Majumder (1996) in 1990. They also found a youthful work force of whom 70 per cent were younger than 24. Women workers tended to be on average younger than men: about 45 per cent of women were younger than 20 compared to 26 per cent of men. Sixty-six per cent of men and 54 per cent of women were unmarried. However, a larger percentage of women appeared to be married than in the previous survey: 38 per cent as compared to 34 per cent of male workers. Less than 1 per cent of men were in the widowed/divorced/abandoned category compared to 7 per cent of women. Thirty per cent of the men and only 7 per cent of the women had been previously employed, men as labourers or in petty trade and women in domestic service or in sewing/tailoring. In terms of education, a third of the women were just literate in the sense of being able to sign their names compared to 10 per cent of the men. Thirty-five per cent of women had reached primary education (compared to 14 per cent of men); 27 per cent had reached secondary education (compared to 39 per cent of men); and 9 per cent had reached higher education (compared to 36 per cent of men). There were fewer educated women in the later survey and it is worth noting that Zohir and Paul-Majumder report that employers were finding it difficult to find educated women to fill some of the supervisory positions.

Finally, the survey found that 70 per cent of women and 83 per cent of men had come from the countryside. Sixty-five per cent of the female migrants were unmarried compared to 60 per cent of male migrants and 17 per cent of women who had migrated had done so on their own compared to 40 per cent of men. Although it is still much lower than that of men, the rates of individual migration by women are remarkably high for a country where women have traditionally only migrated with their families. Not surprisingly, most of the migrant workers came from districts with high levels of population density and landlessness (Dhaka, Barisal, Faridpur) which were also the districts supplying much of the migrant population in Dhaka city in general (Paul-Majumder, 1993).

A still more recent survey by Newby (1998) in 1997 found that 78 per cent of garment workers were below the age of 25, with the largest numbers in the 15–19 group, followed by the 20–24 group. About 50 per cent had been married, of whom the majority were still married. The majority came from landless or land-poor households. Forty-eight per cent had no education at all while only 14 per cent had more than five years of education. Thus there were even fewer educated women in the latest sample. The majority of garment workers were classified as migrants. Sixty-four per cent had migrated in search of work, 63 per cent had entered garment work within a year of arriving in Dhaka. Of those who stated migrating in search of garment work, 80 per cent had found such work within a year of arrival in the city. She also noted that garment workers lived in a wide range of household arrangements, including around 40 per cent who lived in non-conventional households.

Let me turn now to some of the main socio-economic characteristics of the sample of women interviewed for this study. Household size reported by these women varied between one and thirteen with most households but most were in the range of two and five members. Household organisation varied considerably. Seventeen households were made up of nuclear families, another eight were supplemented nuclear, i.e. a nuclear family plus one other member. Three households were made up of a single person, living on her own. The rest were made up of female-headed households (six), women living in 'mess' arrangements (four) and finally around sixteen households that were made up of a mixture of relatives that made them difficult to categorise. These were often young girls from villages who had come into the town to live with some close or distant relative.

The fact that we had a cut-off point in both components of our study of sixteen as the minimum age of workers we would interview, our Dhaka sample misses out on the 10 per cent or more of the work force which were found in larger samples to be below this age. Nevertheless, it confirms the youthfulness of the garment work force. Since they were selected with a view to getting an equal representation of single, married and women in the divorced/abandoned/widowed category, we find roughly a third of our sample in each of these categories. Similarly the sample was purposively divided into equal numbers of women who came from poor and non-poor households.

Of the forty-three ever-married women in the sample, eleven had no children, while the rest had around one or two. Only seven women had more than three children. Around half of the women with children reported that their youngest child was five or younger. For the rest, the age of the youngest child was between five and ten. Around sixteen women in our sample had migrated to Dhaka within the five years prior to the study. A total of thirty-five had migrated within the last ten years. However, only eleven had been born in Dhaka city, while five came from a neighbouring area. Of the forty-five women who had migrated into the city at some stage in their lives, twelve had come specifically in search of garment work, six had come in search of any work, twenty-seven had come with their families.

The occupational profile of the fathers and the mothers of the women workers, of the male breadwinners in their households, along with their own previous occupational histories, all serve to highlight a key point of the study: the gender segmentation of the labour market. Thus the thirty male breadwinners currently reported as working were in twenty-one different types of activities. Fifty-four of the women reported their fathers' occupations which ranged across eighteen categories of work. However, the seventeen mothers who had worked, or were still working, were engaged in just seven different types of occupations, of which four were home-based. Thirty-seven women workers had previously been involved in home-based paid work in just seven different types of activities; ten had been involved in outside work in five different activities. Finally, women's preferred occupations provide some evidence on how cultural factors shape their own preferred opportunity sets. Of the thirty-five women who responded to this question, the preference was either not to work (six), to work in a home-based occupation (five), or else in a government job.

It should also be noted that twenty-seven women in the sample

reported breadwinners with irregular sources of earning, suggesting
that in these cases, at least, women's earnings formed the stable
component of household livelihoods. Thirty-one of the women in
our sample were currently machine operators; twenty-nine had
begun as helpers and another sixteen as trainee operators. Thirty-
eight women had been in the factory for between 1 and 3 years;
the rest for longer. The average starting salary reported by women
was around 300 takas a month while their average current salary
was 840.

We also purposively selected a roughly equal proportion of
women from poor and non-poor households. Given the very loose
distinction between poor and non-poor women that features frequently in the main analysis, it is worth noting some of the other
characteristics of the women in the two groups.

- Out of the thirty-five women in our sample who had no more
  than 5 years of education, twenty-seven of them came from
  households classified as 'poor'.
- Out of twenty-two who had fathers who were illiterate, seventeen
  came from poor households.
- All eight of the women in the sample whose mothers had worked
  as domestic servants came from poor households.
- All nine women in the sample who had been domestic servants
  themselves came from poor households; the three who had been
  involved in other factory work (shrimp packing and ceramics)
  came from poor backgrounds.
- Of the fourteen households headed by the garment workers
  themselves, ten were classified as 'poor'.

**Table 1:** *Household size*

| | |
|---|---|
| 1 | 3 |
| 2 | 13 |
| 3 | 5 |
| 4 | 12 |
| 5 | 7 |
| 6 | 9 |
| 7 | 6 |
| 8+ | 5 |

**Table 2:** *Household type*

| | |
|---|---|
| Single | 3 |
| Sub-nuclear | 6 |
| Female-headed | 6 |
| Nuclear | 17 |
| Supplemented nuclear | 8 |
| 'Mess' | 4 |
| Other | 16 |

**Table 3:** *Age distribution of women workers*

| | |
|---|---|
| 16–19 | 10 |
| 20–24 | 22 |
| 25–29 | 14 |
| 30+ | 2 |
| Missing | 12 |

**Table 4:** *Marital status of women workers*

| | |
|---|---|
| Single | 17 |
| Married | 17 |
| Divorced | 6 |
| Deserted | 5 |
| Separated | 4 |
| Widowed | 5 |
| Co-wife | 6 |

**Table 5:** *Children ever born to ever-married women*

| | |
|---|---|
| 0 | 11 |
| 1 | 10 |
| 2 | 11 |
| 3 | 4 |
| 4 | 4 |
| 5 | 3 |

**Table 6:** *Number of years resident in Dhaka by women workers*

| | |
|---|---|
| 1–5 years | 18 |
| 6–10 years | 12 |
| 11+ years | 19 |
| Born in Dhaka | 11 |

**Table 7:** *Father's occupation*

| | |
|---|---|
| Farmer | 12 |
| Government clerk | 6 |
| Clothing trade | 3 |
| Food vendor/vegetable seller | 4 |
| Medical assistant | 1 |
| Tailoring | 1 |
| Rice trade | 3 |
| Cart puller | 1 |
| Own shop | 4 |
| Factory job | 2 |
| Contract labour | 1 |
| Agricultural labourer | 6 |
| Guard/police | 4 |
| Mason | 3 |
| Sell animals | 1 |
| Transport business | 1 |
| Casual labour | 1 |

**Table 8:** *Mother's occupation*

| | |
|---|---|
| Domestic servant | 8 |
| Home-based farming | 1 |
| Home-based handicrafts | 3 |
| Home-based tailoring | 2 |
| Office | 1 |
| Agricultural labourer | 1 |
| Ration card business | 1 |
| No employment | 32 |
| Not stated | 11 |

**Table 9:** *Male breadwinner's primary occupation*

| | |
|---|---|
| Rickshaw-wallah | 1 |
| Government clerk | 5 |
| Private tuition | 2 |
| Clothing trade | 1 |
| Pharmacist | 1 |
| Tailoring | 1 |
| Rice trade | 2 |
| Cart puller | 1 |
| Own shop | 2 |
| Factory job | 2 |
| Contract labour | 1 |
| Agricultural labourer | 6 |
| Waiter | 2 |
| Casual labour | 1 |
| Mechanic | 1 |
| Bus conductor | 1 |
| Guard/police/army | 3 |
| Mason | 1 |
| Sell animals | 1 |
| Transport business | 1 |
| None/not stated | 24 |

**Table 10:** *Typical examples of female employment prior to emergence of garment industry*

| | |
|---|---|
| Family planning/health visitor | 6 |
| Domestic servant | 12 |
| Nurse | 2 |
| Menial government job | 1 |
| Home-based farming | 5 |
| Other factory work | 2 |
| Home-based handicrafts/ piecework | 12 |
| Home-based tailoring | 4 |
| Government clerical | 1 |
| Begging | 3 |
| Office/bank | 3 |
| Brick-breaking | 1 |
| Agricultural labour | 2 |
| Training/tuition | 2 |

**Table 11:** *Previous paid work by women workers*

| | |
|---|---|
| Family planning worker/ health visitor | 2 |
| Domestic servant | 9 |
| Menial government | 1 |
| Other factory | 3 |
| Tailoring shop | 2 |
| Office | 2 |
| Home-based farming | 4 |
| Home-based handicrafts/ piecework | 11 |
| Home tailoring | 6 |
| Training/tuition | 4 |
| Agricultural labour | 1 |

**Table 12:** *Occupations preferred by women*

| | |
|---|---|
| Family planning/health visitor | 6 |
| Menial government job | 6 |
| Nurse | 3 |
| Home-based farming | 1 |
| Home-based handicrafts | 2 |
| Home-based tailoring | 2 |
| Government clerical | 4 |
| Teaching | 3 |
| Office/bank | 3 |
| No employment | 6 |

**Table 13:** *Women workers' reasons for working\**

| | |
|---|---|
| Basic survival | 18 |
| Specific event | 16 |
| Irregularity/insufficiency of male wages | 14 |
| Improve living standards | 2 |
| Daughter's dowry | 3 |
| Children's needs/education | 14 |
| Own dowry/own future | 13 |
| Help parents | 4 |
| Own consumption | 8 |
| Own savings | 6 |
| Bad relations with family | 6 |
| Other demands on breadwinner's income | 3 |
| Inflation | 1 |
| Likes to work | 1 |

**Table 14:** *Advantages of garment factory work\**

| | |
|---|---|
| Gender segregation of factory/ female predominance | 4 |
| High wages | 9 |
| Possibility of advancement/ increment | 4 |
| Friendships | 3 |
| Place to pray | 2 |
| Proximity to home | 8 |
| Good toilet/washing facilities | 1 |
| Prestige | 1 |

\* Women may give more than one reason/advantage/disadvantage

**Table 15:** *Disadvantages of garment factory work\**

| | |
|---|---|
| Men in factories | 2 |
| Overtime hours | 12 |
| Working conditions | 2 |
| Wages (too low, too irregular, not been raised) | 9 |
| Health problems | 2 |
| Mixing of different social classes | 1 |
| Hard work | 4 |
| Breaks purdah | 6 |
| Bad reputation | 5 |
| Distance from home | 2 |
| Inadequate toilet/washing facilities | 3 |
| Cannot look after children | 1 |
| No holidays/benefits | 1 |

**Table 16:** *Information about garment opportunities*

| | |
|---|---|
| Non-related garment worker | 5 |
| Related garment worker | 6 |
| Garment workers on street | 1 |
| Friend of family | 5 |
| Relative of factory manager | 1 |
| General information/'everyone knew' | 4 |
| Neighbours | 5 |
| People in the village | 5 |
| Garment girls from own village | 3 |
| Newspaper | 5 |
| Other | |

\* Women may give more than one reason/advantage/disadvantage

**Table 17:** *Labour market decision making category*

| | |
|---|---|
| Reluctant/consensual | 7 |
| Active/uncontested | 18 |
| Active/consensual | 14 |
| Active/negotiated | 10 |
| Active/conflictual | 9 |

**Table 18:** *Use of income: categories of choice*

| | |
|---|---|
| Basic survival | 10 |
| Joint welfare maximisation | 13 |
| Practical gender needs | 14 |
| Strategic gender interests | 23 |

**Table 19:** *Assessment of impact of garment work at personal level*

| | |
|---|---|
| Positive | 44 |
| Mixed | 11 |
| Negative | 5 |

**Table 20:** *Assessment of impact of garment work for women in general*

| | |
|---|---|
| Positive | 34 |
| Mixed | 16 |
| Negative | 10 |

# Appendix 3

## Statistical background to the London study

Given the dearth of data on Bangladeshi homeworkers in London, I have drawn on two categories of data to provide some kind of statistical background to this section of the study: data on clothing homeworkers in the UK and data on the Bangladeshi community. However, both sources of information are highly imperfect. There was, and still is, very little reliable data on the incidence of manufacturing homework in the UK. According to the 1981 Labour Force Survey, the Department of Employment concluded that there were 660,000 homeworkers in England and Wales, but this also included sales people and professionals working from home (GLC, 1985). The Low Pay Unit's report *Sweated Labour*, published in 1984, estimated that if these were excluded, there would be 251,000 homeworkers of whom 72,000 were engaged in manufacturing. However, it added that this was likely to be an underestimate given that ignorance about their rights and fears about their liabilities made many homeworkers reluctant to declare themselves.

Homeworking in the present study refers to the supply of machining work to be performed by individuals in domestic premises, usually for piecework payment. There were (and still are) no official statistics for the number of homeworkers in London at the time of the study, but it was known to have a higher proportion of homeworkers relative to in-firm employment compared to the rest of the country, and homeworking was disproportionately concentrated among women from the ethnic minorities, especially South Asia and southern Europe (mainly Cyprus). A survey of the Cypriot clothing industry in London in 1984 found that homeworkers made up 60 per cent of its work force. It was likely to be as high, or higher, in other sections of the industry. In 1981, registered employment in London clothing industry, which excluded home-workers and many smaller factory employees, was 29,000. This gave a conservative estimate of 30,000 to 40,000 homeworkers in the London clothing industry alone (GLC, 1985).

The Low Pay Unit's report estimated that hourly rates in 1984 ranged between 7 pence to £4 an hour, while one quarter of manufacturing homeworkers earned 50p. or less an hour. The statutory minimum was £1.50. Homeworkers tended to be paid less than workers doing equivalent tasks within the factories. Employers did not simply flout minimum wage regulations, but also avoided overhead costs. By not giving homeworkers employee status, they were able to avoid responsibility for paying National Insurance or providing sickness or maternity pay. The homeworker was respon-sible for purchasing or hiring her own sewing machine, paying her own heating and lighting bills and the costs of powering her machine.

A 1994 survey of homeworking in a wide variety of manufacturing and clerical work found that conditions had not changed much. Women worked a median of 33 hours a week, with no sickness or pension entitlement for an average of £1.28 an hour but with some earning as little as 30p. an hour. They were described as people with the 'least time, least opportunity and least cash to take action about the manner in which they are exploited' (Jean Lambert, cited in the *Guardian*, 13 September 1994). The survey also found that over 90 per cent of homeworkers tended to be women and more than three-quarters had school age children. Forty per cent of the surveyed population were Asian. Most reported financial hardship combined with the need to be at home with their children for taking up homework. The irregularity of the supply of work meant that they tended to work highly irregular hours, often working all night and at the weekend to meet deadlines. They had no job security and were afraid to question the amount of work or pay for fear of losing the work.

However, it should be noted that the conditions of workers in the clothing sweatshops were not much better. By late 1984, attention had been drawn to the dangerous conditions which prevailed in many when five workers were killed in a fire in a sweat-shop in East London while various reports drew attention to the illegally low wages in this sector. Although the then Tory government declared a 'campaign against sweatshops' to be waged by factory and wages inspectors, they had cut the relevant staff by one third since coming to power so that every factory could expect a visit once every 19 years (Phizacklea, 1990).

As far as data on the London community was concerned, the main source was a recent report by the HMSO (1996), but I have backed it up where possible with one or two other sources. Ballard (1983) has shown that migration processes characterising the Bangladeshi as well as the Pakistani community (mainly concentrated in Bradford) differs from that of most other ethnic communities, including those from other parts of the Indian sub-continent. While most groups chose the 'family reunion' option, so that, for instance, Sikh wives had begun joining their husbands in the late 1950s, Bangladeshis opted to become 'international commuters', working in Britain, saving and making a long visit home. This pattern was repeated several times and it was only in the early 1980s that their wives began to join them in Britain.

HMSO data from the mid-1990s confirms this pattern. First of all, it reminds us that the Bangladeshis are a relatively small proportion of the ethnic minority population in the UK and still largely concentrated in London. Indians make up the largest proportion, about 26 per cent of the ethnic minority population. Pakistanis and Caribbeans made up around 15 per cent each while Bangladeshis make up about 5 per cent. However, it is worth noting that the Indian group included many from East Africa, making it more heterogeneous than at first apparent. For instance, while 85 per cent of Bangladeshi women said that they *always* wore the clothing of their country of origin (compared to only 7 per cent of men), 43 per cent of Indian women from the sub-continent said they did, compared to just 27 per cent of East African Asians.

While immigration from the Caribbean, the other major immigrant ethnic group in the UK, peaked in the early 1960s, immigration from South Asia did not peak till the early 1970s. The Bangladeshi community consequently has a youthful population with just under half under the age of 16 and around three-quarters under the age of 35 (1991 figures). Combined with Pakistanis, its child dependency ratio was higher than most ethnic groups (72 compared to 37 among the Indian community and 33 among whites) while its elderly dependency ratio was lower (5 compared to 26 among whites). While nearly half of the ethnic minority population had been born in the UK in 1995, the figure among Bangladeshis was 40 per cent compared to 60 per cent among Caribbeans. Consequently, a lower percentage of the community spoke English than other ethnic minorities, although differences were far less among the younger sections. Focusing simply on South Asians, the largest ethnic group for whom English was not a first language, only 74 per cent of Bangladeshi males of all ages reported the ability to speak English in the mid-nineties compared to 92 per cent of Indian males and 88 per cent of Pakistani. The equivalent figures for males aged 16–29 were 92 per cent, 96 per cent and 95 per cent. Only 59 per cent of Bangladeshi women spoke English compared to 77 per cent of Indian women and 54 per cent of Pakistani. The figures among the 16–29 age group of women were 68 per cent, 89 per cent and 78 per cent.

The Bangladeshi community had a larger household size than the rest of the population with an average of more than 5 members compared to around 2 among the white population and 4 in the Indian. Only 7 per cent of Bangladeshi/Pakistani households were made up of a single person compared to 27 per cent of white. Sixty-seven per cent of the Bangladeshi population aged 16–64 was married, 25 per cent was single and 4 per cent separated or divorced. The equivalent estimate for the white population was 57 per cent, 26 per cent and 7 per cent while for the black population it was 33 per cent, 45 per cent and 13 per cent. The mean age at marriage for Bangladeshi women was younger at 21 than all other communities; it was about 23 for Pakistanis and 27 for whites.

Sixty per cent of households in the community were made up of a couple with dependent children compared to 20 per cent of black households and 50 per cent of Indians. Eighty-nine per cent of Bangladeshi children under the age of 16 lived with married parents compared to 78 per cent of white children. The majority of lone mothers in the Bangladeshi community (only 8 per cent of households) were married women (i.e. their husbands were abroad) while the rest were divorced or widowed.

Sixty-three per cent of Pakistani/Bangladeshi families were concentrated in council estates and low income areas compared to 42 per cent of the black population and 40 per cent of the Indian. Whites were more likely to be found in affluent suburban and rural areas (20 per cent) and mature home-owning areas (27 per cent). Fifty-nine per cent of Bangladeshi families were in housing rented from the social sector compared to just 8 per cent of Indians and 22 per cent of whites. Thirty-six per cent of Bangladeshis owned their own home outright or on mortgage compared to 83 per cent of Indians. Fifty-two per cent of Bangladeshis lived in flats compared to only 16 per cent of whites, the majority of whom lived in semi-detached or detached houses. Forty per cent of Bangladeshis expressed dissatisfaction with their housing compared to 20 per cent of the black population and around 8 per cent of the white.

Rates of economic activity in 1995 were much lower, at 66 per cent, in the Bangladeshi community than in other ethnic groups. They were 80 per cent for men from both the Afro-Caribbean and the Indian community. Bangladeshi and Pakistani men were most likely to be in skilled and semi-skilled manual labour, unlike Indians, who were also likely to be found in professional occupations. Like other South Asian women, Pakistani/Bangladeshi women were mainly in semi-skilled work (but this is not likely to include those in homeworking). Bangladeshi men were also more likely than other communities to be in temporary or casual employment (around 13 per cent of the community compared to 7 per cent of white community) and in self-employment (22 per cent compared to just over 10 per cent of the white community). Female activity rates in the Bangladeshi community were even lower. Using national statistics, Smith (1977, cited in Stone, 1983) estimated that 74 per cent of Afro-Caribbean women were in employment in the early 1970s compared with 45 per cent of women from the white community and 43 per cent of Asian women. However, among *Muslim* Asian women (largely from Bangladesh and Pakistan), the rates were around 17 per cent.

These figures do not appear to have changed much, according to the report of the Office of National Statistics cited above.

According to 1995 figures, only 20 per cent of women in the Bangladeshi community were economically active so that there has been only a marginal increase of 3 per cent since 1977. By contrast, activity rates among Afro-Caribbean women and white women at the other end of the spectrum were 70 per cent. Twelve per cent of Bangladeshi/Pakistani women were in full-time employment (compared to 37 per cent of Afro-Caribbean women), 6 per cent were in part-time work and 7 per cent were classified as 'unemployed', i.e. were seeking work. The overwhelming majority of Bangladeshi women registered as employed were in 'public administration, education and health', i.e. in local government social services (HMSO, 1996, Table 4.6). However, significantly, none were classified as working in the manufacturing sector so clearly the official statistics failed to pick up homeworking.

Many of the key characteristics of the Bangladeshi community reported in the national data were echoed in the sample of homeworkers and of their families included in the London side of this study. Since a lower cut-off age of 16 was used in selecting women in both components of the study, neither sample had women younger than this. However, there was no upper cut-off point and this resulted in many more older women in the London sample than we found in our Dhaka sample, a reflection of the wider age distribution of women generally involved in the homeworking sector in London compared to the greater concentration of younger women in the garment factories in Dhaka. Of the 53 women who made up the London sample, 7 were aged 16–24; 18 were in the 25–29 age group; 21 in the 30–39 age group and around 7 were aged between 40 and 50.

Forty-four of the 53 women in our sample were married, 4 were single, 4 were divorced/separated and there was 1 widow. Of the 49 ever-married women in the sample, 3 had no children, 33 had between 2 and 4 children, and 13 had more than four children. The median age of the oldest child was between 10 and 11 years while for the youngest, it was between 2 and 3 years. Households were primarily nuclear: 42 out of the 53. Only 4 were extended in some way while 7 were sub-nuclear. Like the rest of the community, household sizes reported by the women in our sample were large by British standards. Ten had between 3 and 4 members, 18 had 5 members and 19 had more than 5. Most households (40) were headed by the homeworkers' husbands; 9 were headed by the homeworker herself; the rest by her father most often, or her son. Confirming the recent arrival of the community, only 3 of the homeworkers had been born in the UK. The rest had been born and brought up in the Sylhet district of Bangladesh, and were mainly rural in origin. Forty-three had migrated to join husbands, while 7 had migrated with their parents. Twelve of the women in the sample had migrated within the last 5 years, 21 within the last 10. The remaining 20 had lived in the UK for more than 10 years. By contrast, 42 of the 47 male household heads had lived in the UK for more than 10 years, while 32 had lived in the UK for more than 20 years.

The women were in general less educated than their husbands. Twenty of the women in the sample had 5 or less years of education, 24 had between 6 and 10 years of education while 8 had between 11–12 years of education. By comparison, 5 of the husbands of currently married women had less than 5 years of education; 14 had between 6 and 10 years of education and 11 had between 11–12 years of education. Younger women tended to be somewhat more educated than older women. Only 8 out of the 25 women under the age of 29 had completed less than primary education compared to 12 out of the 26 who were older than 29.

The next set of tables provides some idea about employment patterns among men and women in the community. Twenty-five of the household heads were employed, 19 were unemployed, the rest were retired or in between jobs. Looking at the distribution of occupation by head of household (which would include women themselves, their fathers and their husbands) it appears that the garment industry was a source of employment for 23 heads and catering for 11. Six were, or had been, employed in other factories. The occupational profile of their fathers is more varied, reflecting the fact that many of these men were still in Bangladesh, or had started out their working lives in Bangladesh and then come to the UK. The overwhelming majority of the women had only ever done homeworking. In terms of their preferred occupations, there was greater evidence of variability among those that responded. Seven would have liked to stop working, 3 to continue in homeworking. Other preferred options included teaching, shops, offices/banks, creches, community work and 'outside work'. Over half of the women interviewed had been in homeworking for 5 or more years.

**Table 1:** *Household size*

| 1 | 1 |
|---|---|
| 2 | 3 |
| 3 | 5 |
| 4 | 5 |
| 5 | 18 |
| 7 | 4 |
| 8+ | 7 |

**Table 2:** *Household type*

| Single | 1 |
|---|---|
| Sub-nuclear | 1 |
| Female-headed | 4 |
| Nuclear | 42 |
| Supplemented nuclear | 4 |
| Other | 1 |

**Table 3:** *Age distribution of homeworkers*

| 16–19 | 2 |
|---|---|
| 20–24 | 5 |
| 25–29 | 18 |
| 30–34 | 15 |
| 40+ | 7 |

**Table 4:** *Marital status of women workers*

| Single | 4 |
|---|---|
| Married | 41 |
| Divorced | 3 |
| Deserted | 1 |
| Widowed | 1 |
| Co-wife | 3 |

**Table 5:** *Children ever born to ever-married women*

| 0 | 3 |
|---|---|
| 1 | 0 |
| 2 | 8 |
| 3 | 11 |
| 5 | 5 |
| 6 | 2 |
| 7–9 | 6 |

**Table 6:** *Years of residence in London: male household heads*

| 1–5 years | 3 |
|---|---|
| 6–10 years | 2 |
| 11–20 years | 16 |
| 21+ years | 26 |

**Table 7:**  *Years of residence in London: homeworkers*

| | |
|---|---|
| 1–5 years | 12 |
| 6–10 years | 21 |
| 11–15 years | 18 |
| 16–20 years | 2 |

**Table 8:**  *Father's occupation*

| | |
|---|---|
| Farmer | 10 |
| Government service | 2 |
| Clothing business | 1 |
| Bank manager | 4 |
| Cement business | 1 |
| Fakir | 1 |
| Furniture business | 1 |
| Ship chef | 1 |
| Grocery shop | 5 |
| Factory job | 6 |
| Contract labour | 1 |
| Agricultural labourer | 6 |
| Police | 1 |
| Restaurant business | 2 |
| Sailor | 2 |
| School caretaker | 1 |
| School teacher | 1 |

**Table 9:**  *Male household head's occupation*

| | |
|---|---|
| Minicab driver | 1 |
| Garment worker | 22 |
| Other factory job | 5 |
| Waiter/chef | 7 |
| Homeworker | 1 |
| Grocer shop | 1 |
| Teacher | 1 |
| Driving instructor | 1 |
| Restaurant owner | 4 |
| Office | 2 |
| Community service | 1 |
| Currently employed | 25 |
| Currently unemployed | 19 |
| Retired | 2 |

**Table 10:**  *Homeworkers' preferred occupation*

| | |
|---|---|
| Homeworking | 3 |
| Teaching | 4 |
| Shop | 3 |
| Office/bank | 4 |
| Creche | 6 |
| Voluntary/community work | 3 |
| No work | 7 |
| Not stated | 23 |

**Table 11:** *Homeworkers'*
*education levels*

| | |
|---|---|
| None | 7 |
| Class 1–5 | 13 |
| Calss 6–10 | 24 |
| Matric+ | 8 |
| Not stated | 1 |

**Table 12:** *Reasons for taking up*
*paid work\**

| | |
|---|---|
| To save | 5 |
| Own purchasing power | 11 |
| Children's expenses | 9 |
| Necessities | 5 |
| Improve households' standard of living | 4 |
| Otherwise household income inadequate | 6 |
| Greater security | 4 |
| Other demands on breadwinners' income | 3 |
| Inflation | 1 |
| Likes working | 1 |

**Table 13:** *Advantages of*
*homework\**

| | |
|---|---|
| Compatibility with domestic chores | 13 |
| Compatibility with child care | 29 |
| Husband forbids outside work | 11 |
| Uses up spare time | 15 |
| Everyone is doing it | 11 |
| Flexibility | |
| Flexibility of work | 5 |
| Can say prayers | 1 |
| Keeps reputation intact | 2 |
| Cannot find other work | 2 |
| Looking for other work | 5 |

**Table 14:** *Reasons for not taking*
*outside work\**

| | |
|---|---|
| Language problems | 16 |
| Education | 6 |
| Child care constraints | 15 |
| Purdah | 4 |
| Family objections | 12 |
| Domestic obligations | 5 |
| Has never considered it | 1 |
| Has done it | 4 |
| Prepared to do it | 2 |
| Actively looking for outside work | 7 |

\* Respondents may give more than one reason/advantage

**Tables 15:**  *Advantages of outside work (problems with homeworking)*

| | |
|---|---|
| Better for health | 8 |
| Meet people | 6 |
| Better pay | 9 |
| Free from interruption | 5 |
| Work will be less hard | 2 |
| Recognised as work | 1 |
| Work more regular | 2 |
| Has more status | 2 |

**Table 16:**  *Information about homeworking*

| | |
|---|---|
| Neighbour | 35 |
| Landlady | 2 |
| Newspaper ad | 3 |
| Husband | 2 |
| Knock on door | 1 |
| Relative | 6 |
| Everyone does it | 4 |

**Table 17:**  *Who arranged work*

| | |
|---|---|
| Husband | 18 |
| Factory owner/middleman | 4 |
| Other relative | 8 |
| Another homeworker | 5 |
| Son | 1 |
| Daughter | 1 |
| Neighbour | 6 |
| Self | 10 |

**Table 18:**  *Decision making categories*

| | |
|---|---|
| Passive agency/consensual decision making | 6 |
| Suppressed agency/conflictual decision making | 5 |
| Negotiated agency/conflictual decision making | 8 |
| Active agency/consensual decision making | 34 |

**Table 19:**  *Use of income: categories of choice*

| | |
|---|---|
| Basic needs | 9 |
| Individual preferences | 21 |
| Reduced dependence on husbands | 9 |
| Joint household welfare | 7 |
| Future security | 6 |

**Table 20:**  *Assessment of impact of homeworking for the individual woman*

| | |
|---|---|
| Negative | 10 |
| Mixed | 43 |

**Table 21:**  *Assessment of impact of homeworking for women's position in general*

| | |
|---|---|
| Positive | 8 |
| Little impact | 45 |

# Bibliography

Abdullah, T.A. (1974), *Village women as I saw them*, The Ford Foundation, Dhaka.

Abdullah, T. and S. Zeidenstein (1982), *Village Women of Bangladesh: prospects for change*, Pergamon Press, London.

ACPR/ILO (1993), 'A survey of economically active children in Bangladesh', Associates for Community and Population Research, Dhaka, mimeo.

Adams, C. (1987), *Across Seven Seas and Thirteen Rivers*. THAP Books, London.

Adnan, S. (1988), '*"Birds in a cage"*: institutional change and women's position in Bangladesh', paper presented at conference, 'Women's Position and Demographic Change in the Course of Development', Asker, Norway, 15–18 June.

Adnan, S. (1990), *Annotation of Village Studies in Bangladesh and West Bengal: a review of socio-economic trends over 1942–88*. Bangladesh Academy for Rural Development, Comilla.

Agarwal, B. (1997), '"Bargaining" and Gender Relations: within and beyond the household'. *Feminist Economics*, vol. 3, no. 1, pp. 1–51.

Ahmad, A. and M.A. Quasem (1991), *Child Labour in Bangladesh*, Al-Afser Press, Dhaka.

Ahmad, R. and M. S. Naher (1987), *Brides and the Demand System in Bangladesh*, Centre for Social Studies, Dhaka.

Ahmed, M., P. English, S.Feldman, M.Hossain, E. Jansen, F. McCarthy, K. de Wilde and R. Young (1990), *Rural Poverty in Bangladesh: a report to the Like-Minded Group*. Dhaka, University Press Limited, Dhaka.

Alam, S. (1985), 'Women and Poverty in Bangladesh', *Women's Studies International Forum*, vol. 8, no. 4, pp. 361–371.

Alam, S. and N. Matin (1984), 'Limiting the women's issue in Bangladesh: the Western and Bangladesh legacy', *South Asia Bulletin*, vol. 4, no. 2, pp. 1–10.

Allen, S. and C. Wolkowitz (1987), *Homeworking: myths and realities*, Women in Society Series (ed. J. Campling), Macmillan, Basingstoke, UK.

Amin, A.T.M.N. (1986), 'Urban informal sector: employment potentials and problems', in R. Muqtada, and M. Islam (eds.), *Selected Issues in Employment and Development*, ILO-ARTEP, New Delhi.

Amin, S., I. Diamond, R.T. Naved and M.Newby (1998), 'Transition to adulthood of female garment factory workers in Bangladesh', *Studies in Family Planning*, vol. 29, no. 22, pp. 185–200.

Amsden, A.H. (1994), 'Macrosweating policies and labour standards' in W. Sengenberger and D. Campbell (eds.), *International Labour Standards and Economic Interdependence*, IILS, Geneva, pp. 185–193.

Amsden, A. and R. van der Hoeven (1994), 'Manufacturing Employment and Real Wages in the 1980s: labour's loss till century's end', report of ILO.

Anwar, M. (1979), *The Myth of Return*, Heinemann, London.

Ariffin, J. (1983), 'Women workers in the manufacturing industries', in CAP (ed.), *Malaysian Women: problems and issues*, CAP Publications, Penang, pp. 49–62.

Arizpe, L. and J. Aranda (1981), 'The "Comparative Advantages" of Women's Disadvantages: women workers in the strawberry export agribusiness in Mexico', *Signs*, vol. 7, no. 2, pp. 453–473.

Arrow, K. (1990), 'The Pioneers', in R. Swedberg (ed.), *Economics and Sociology: redefining their boundaries*, Princeton University Press, Princeton.

Arthur, B. and G. McNicoll (1978), 'An Analytical survey of population and development in Bangladesh', *Population and Development Review*, vol. 4, no. 1, pp. 23–80.

Ballard, R. (1983), 'The context and consequences of migration: Jullunder and Mirpur compared', *New Community*, vol. 11, no. 1/2, pp. 117–136.

Ballard, R. and C. Ballard (1977), 'The Sikhs: the development of South Asian settlements in Britain', in J. L. Watson (ed.), *Between Two Cultures*, ed. Basil Blackwell, Oxford.

Bangladesh, Commission for Justice and Peace (1986), 'Women garment workers' study', report of the Catholic Bishop's Conference, Commission for Justice and Peace, mimeo.

Becker, G.S. (1976), *The Economic Approach to Human Behaviour*, Chicago University Press, Chicago.

Begum N.N. (1988), *Pay or Purdah: women and income-earning in rural Bangladesh*, Winrock International Institute for Agriculture Development and the Bangladesh Agricultural Research, Dhaka.

Begum, S. and M. Greeley (1983), 'Women's Employment and Agriculture: extracts from a case study', seminar papers, Women for Women, Dhaka.

Beneria, L. and M. Roldan (1987), *The Cross-Roads of Class and Gender*, University of Chicago Press, Chicago.

Berry, S. (1984), 'Households, decision-making and rural development: do we need to do more?', Harvard Institute for International Development, report no. 167.

BGMEA (1992), *The garment industry: looking ahead at Europe of 1992*, Bangladesh Garment Manufacturers and Exporters Association, March.

Bhattacharya, D. (1995), 'International trade, social labelling and developing countries: the case of Bangladesh's garments exports and use of child labour', Bangladesh Institute of Development Studies, December, mimeo.

Birnbaum, B. (n.d.), 'Women, skill and automation: a study of women's employment in the clothing industry, 1946–72', mimeo.

Birnbaum, G. et al. (1981), 'The clothing industry in Tower Hamlets: an investigation into its structure and problems', Tower Hamlets Council, mimeo.

Bissell, S. (1997), 'Working children in Bangladesh', University of Queensland, October (unpublished report).

Bissell, S. (1998), ' "I go to school": a child-centred assessment of MOU implementation', mimeo.

Bissell, S. (1999), 'Concepts and constructs of childhood in South Asia: a perspective from Bangladesh', proceedings from a conference on 'Needs versus rights: social policy from a child-centred perspective', New Delhi.

Bissell, S. and B. Sobhan (1996), 'Child labour and education programming in the garment industry of Bangladesh: experience and issues', report from UNICEF, September.

Blanchet, T. (1996), *Lost Innocence, Stolen Childhoods*, University Press Limited, Dhaka.

Blei, T. (1990), 'Dowry and bridewealth presentations in rural Bangladesh: commodities, gifts or hybrid forms?' Chr. Michelsen Institute DERAP, working paper 10.

Blood, R.O. and D.M. Wolfe (1960), *Husbands and Wives*, Free Press, New York.

Bolts, W. (1772), *Considerations on India Affairs*.

Booth, C. (1902), *Life and Labour of the People in London*, Macmillan, London.

Boserup, E. (1970), *Women's Role in Economic Development*, St Martin's Press, New York.

Boserup, E. (1982), 'Introduction', in T. Abdullah and S. Zeidenstein, *Village Women of Bangladesh: Prospects for change*, Pergamon Press, London.

Bourdieu, P. (1977), *Outline of a Theory of Practice*, Cambridge Studies in Social Anthropology Series, Cambridge University Press, Cambridge.

Bowley, A. (1921), 'Earners and dependants in English towns in 1911', *Economica*, vol. 2.

Buchanan, J. (1988), 'Contractarian political economy and constitutional interpretation', *American Economic Review: Papers and Proceedings*, vol. 78.

BUP (1990), 'A study on female garment workers in Bangladesh', Bangladesh Unnayan Parishad, mimeo.

Cain, M., S. R. Khanam and S. Nahar (1979), 'Class, patriarchy and women's work in Bangladesh', *Population and Development Review*, vol. 5, no. 3, pp. 405–438.

Carey, S. and A. Shukur (1985), 'A profile of the Bangladeshi community in East London', *New Community*, vol. XII, no. 3, pp. 405–417.

Cavanagh, J. (1997), 'The global resistance to sweatshops', in A.

Ross (ed.), *No Sweat: fashion, free trade and the rights of garment workers*, Verso, London and New York, pp. 39–50.

Chalwa, N. (1996), 'In search of the best interests of the child: a first step towards eliminating child labour in the Bangladesh garment industry', report from UNICEF.

Charnowitz, S. (1987), 'The influence of international labour standards on the world trading regime', *International Labour Review*, vol. 126, no. 5, pp. 565–584.

Charnowitz, S. (1995), 'Promoting higher labour standards', *The Washington Quarterly*, vol. 18, no. 3, pp. 167–190.

Chen, M. (1986), *A Quiet Revolution: women in transition in rural Bangladesh*, Schenkman Publishing House, Cambridge, MA.

Chen, M. and R. Ghuznavi (1979), 'Women in food-for-work: the Bangladesh experience', report from the World Food Programme.

Chhachhi, A. and R. Pittin (1996), 'Multiple identities, multiple strategies', in A. Chhachhi and R. Pittin (eds.), *Confronting State, Capital and Patriarchy: women organising in the process of industrialisation*, Macmillan (with ISS, The Hague), Basingstoke.

Chiplin, B. and P.J. Sloane (1976), *Sex Discrimination in the Labour Market*, Macmillan, London.

Chisolm, N. et al. (1986), *Linked by the Same Thread: the Multi-Fibre Arrangement and the Labour Movement*, Tower Hamlets International Solidarity and Tower Hamlets Trade Union Council, London.

Cleland, J. et al. (1994), *The Determinants of Reproductive Change in Bangladesh: success in a challenging environment*, World Bank, Washington DC.

Connell, R.W. (1987), *Gender and Power*, Polity Press, Cambridge.

Coyle, A. (1982), 'Sex and skill in the organisation of the clothing industry', in J. West (ed.), *Work, Women and the Labour Market* Routledge and Kegan Paul, London.

Dannecker, P. (1998), 'Between conformity and resistance: women garment workers in Bangladesh', Faculty of Sociology, University of Bielefeld, PhD thesis.

Deacon, B. (1999), 'Globalisation, social policy and social development at the end of the 1990s: new economic and intellectual conditions undermine the future for equitable social welfare', proceedings from conference, 'Revisioning social policy for the 21st century: challenges and opportunities', Institute of Development Studies, Sussex.

Delap, E. (1998), 'The determinants and effects of children's income generating work in urban Bangladesh', report from Centre for Development Studies, October, mimeo.

Dex, S. (1985), *The Sexual Division of work: conceptual revolutions in the social sciences*, Wheatsheaf Books, Brighton.

Dreze, J. and A. Sen (1995), *India, Economic Development and Social Opportunity*, Oxford University Press, Oxford.

Duesenberry, J.S. (1960), 'Comments', in National Bureau of Economic Research (ed.), *Demographic and Economic Change in Developed Countries*, Princeton University Press, Princeton, pp. 231–234.

Duffy, P. (1979), 'Bengali Action Research Project, Tower Hamlets', report of the Commission for Racial Equality, unpublished.

Duffy, P. (1981), 'The employment and training needs of the Bengali community in Tower Hamlets', report of the Commission for Racial Equality.

Dutt, R.P. (1940), *India Today*, London Left Books, London.

Dyson, T. (1996), 'Birth rate trends in India, Sri Lanka, Bangladesh and Pakistan: a long comparative view', proceedings of conference, 'IUSSP Seminar on Comparative Perspectives on the Fertility Transition in South Asia', Islamabad, Pakistan.

Edwards, M. (1997), 'The future of foreign policy: promoting international co-operation for development and human rights', proceedings from conference, 'Foreign Policy in the Twenty-first Century', One World Action, London.

Elson, D. and R. Pearson (1981), 'The subordination of women and the internationalisation of factory production', in K. Young, R. McCullagh and C. Wolkowitz (eds.), *Of Marriage and the Market: women's subordination in international perspective*, CSE Books, London.

Elson, D. (1983), 'Nimble fingers and other fables', in W. Enloe and C. Chapkis (eds.), *Of Common Cloth: women in the global textile industry*, Transnational Institute, Amsterdam pp. 5–14.

Elson, D. (1996), 'Appraising recent developments in the market for "nimble fingers"', in R. Chhachhi and A. Pittin (eds.), *Con-*

*fronting State, Capital and Patriarchy: women organising in the process of industrialisation*, Macmillan, Basingstoke.

Elster, J. (1989), *Nuts and Bolts for the Social Sciences*, Cambridge University Press, Cambridge.

Enayet, F. (1979), 'Women in the economic sphere: urban', in Women for Women (ed.) *The Situation of Women in Bangladesh*, Women for Women, Dhaka, pp. 183–224.

Farouk, A. (1976), 'The vagrants of Dhaka city', report of the Bureau of Economic Research, Dhaka University.

Feldman, S. (1993), 'Contradictions of gender inequality: urban class formation in contemporary Bangladesh', in A. W. Clark (ed.), *Gender and Political Economy: explorations of South Asian systems*, Oxford University Press, New Delhi.

Fernandez-Kelly, J. and M. P. Nash (1983), *Women, Men and the International Division of Labor*, Anthropology of Work Series (ed. J. Nash), State University of New York Press, Albany.

Folbre, N. (1986), 'Hearts and spades: paradigms of household economics', *World Development*, vol. 14, no. 2, pp. 245–255.

Folbre, N. (1994), *Who Takes Care of the Kids? Gender and the structures of constraint*, Routledge, London and and New York.

Fraser, N. (1997), *Justice Interruptus: critical reflections on the 'postsocialist' condition*, Routledge, London and New York.

Gardner, K. (1995), *Global Migrants, Local Lives: travel and transformation in rural Bangladesh*, Clarendon Press, Oxford.

Gerard, R. (1979), 'Foreword', in Women for Women (ed.), *The Situation of Women in Bangladesh*, Women for Women, Dhaka.

Giddens, A. (1979), *Central Problems in Social Theory: action, structure and contradiction in social analysis*, Macmillan, London.

Government of Bengal (1940), 'Report of the Land Revenue Commission', Bengal Government Press, Bengal.

Gray, J. (1998), *False Dawn: the delusions of global capitalism*, Granta, London.

Greenhalgh, S. (1985), 'Sexual stratification: the other side of "growth with equity" in East Asia', *Population and Development Review*, vol. 11, no. 2, pp. 265–314.

Haddad, L., J. Hoddinott and H. Alderman (1997), *Intrahousehold Resource Allocation in Developing Countries*, Johns Hopkins University Press, Baltimore.

Hakim, C. (1984), 'Homework and outwork: national estimates from two surveys', *Employment Gazette*, vol. 92, pp. 7–12.

Hakim, C. (1987a), 'Homeworking in Britain: key findings from the national survey of home-based workers', *Employment Gazette*, vol. 95, pp. 92–104.

Hakim, C. (1987b), 'Home-based work in Britain: a report on the 1981 National Homeworking Survey', report of Department of Employment, research paper no. 60.

Hartmann, B. and J. Boyce (1983), *A Quiet Violence: a view from a Bangladesh village*, Zed Press, London.

Hashemi, S.M., S.R. Schuler and A.P. Riley (1996), 'Rural credit programs and women's empowerment in Bangladesh', *World Development*, vol. 24, no. 4, pp. 635–653.

Hirschman, A.O. (1985), 'Against parsimony: three easy ways of complicating some categories of economic discourse', *Economics and Philosophy*, vol. 1, no. 1, pp. 7–21.

HMSO (1986), *Bangladeshis in Britain*, report from House of Commons, vol. I.

HMSO (1996), *Social Focus on Ethnic Minorities*, Government Statistical Office, London.

Hodgson, G.M. (1988), *Economics and Institutions: a manifesto for modern institutional economics*, Polity Press, Cambridge.

Hoffman, K. and H. Rush (1985), 'Microelectronics and clothing', report of Science Policy Research Unit, Sussex.

Hossain, M.M. (1980), 'The employment for women', proceedings from conference, 'Thoughts on Islamic Economics', Islamic Economics Research Bureau, Dhaka.

Hossain, H., R. Jahan and S. Sobhan (1988), 'Industrialisation and women workers in Bangladesh: from homebased work to the factories', in H. Heyzer (ed.), *Daughters in Industry: work, skills and consciousness of women workers in Asia*, Asian and Pacific Development Centre, Kuala Lumpur.

Hossain, H., R. Jahan and S. Sobhan (1990), *No Better Option? Industrial women workers in Bangladesh*, University Press Limited, Dhaka.

Howard, A. (1997), 'Labour, history and sweatshops in the new global economy', in A. Ross (ed.), *No Sweat: fashion, free trade and the rights of garment workers*, Verso, London and New York, pp. 151–172.

Humphries, J. (1980), 'Class struggle and the persistence of the working-class family', in A. H. Amsden (ed.), *The Economics of Women and Work*, Penguin, Harmondsworth, pp. 140–165.

Huq, J. (1979), 'Women in the economic sphere: rural', in Women for Women (ed.), *The Situation of Women in Bangladesh*, Women for Women, Dhaka, pp. 139–182.

Islam, F. (1998), 'Women, employment and the family: poor informal sector women workers in Dhaka city', Social Anthropology, University of Sussex, PhD thesis (in progress).

Islam, F. and S. Zeitlin (1989), 'Ethnographic profile of Dhaka bastees', *Oriental Geographer*, vol. 31, no. 1–2.

Islam, M. (1979), 'Social norms and institutions', in Women for Women (ed.), *The Situation of Women in Bangladesh*, Women for Women, Dhaka, pp. 225–264.

Islam, N. (1996), 'From city to mega city', report of Urban Studies Programme, Department of Geography, University of Dhaka, Bangladesh Urban Series no. 1.

Islamic Economics Research Bureau (1980), *Thoughts on Islamic Economics*, Islamic Economics Research Bureau, Dhaka.

Jackson, B. (1992), *Threadbare: how the rich stitch up the world's rag trade*, World Development Movement.

Joekes, S. (1982), 'Female-headed industrialisation: women's jobs in Third World export manufacturing – the case of the Moroccan clothing industry', IDS Research Report no. 15, Institute of Development Studies, Sussex.

Joekes, S. (1987), *Women and the World Economy*, Oxford University Press, Oxford.

Jones, G. S. (1971), *Outcast London*, Oxford University Press, Oxford.

Jordan, B. (1996), *A Theory of Poverty and Social Exclusion*, Polity Press, Cambridge.

Josephides, S. (1988), 'Honour, family and work: Greek Cypriot women before and after migration', in P. Bhachu et al. (eds.), *Enterprising Women: ethnicity, economy and gender relations*, Routledge, London, pp. 34–57.

Joshi, H. (1984), 'Women's employment in paid work', HMSO, Department of Employment Research Paper 45.

Kabeer, N. (1985), 'Do women gain from high fertility?', in H. Afshar (ed.), *Women, Work and Ideology in the Third World*, Macmillan, London, pp. 83–108.

Kabeer, N. (1988), 'Subordination and struggle: the women's movement in Bangladesh', *New Left Review*, no. 168 (March/April).

Kabeer, N. (1994), *Reversed Realities: gender hierarchies in development thought*, Verso, London and New York.

Kabeer, N. (1996), *Gender, Demographic Transitions and the Economics of Family Size: Population Policy for a Human-centred Development*, UNRISD Occasional Paper no. 7.

Kabeer, N. (1998), 'Ideology, economics and family planning programmes. Explaining fertility decline in Bangladesh', mimeo.

Kabeer, N. (1998), 'Money can't buy me love? Re-evaluating gender, credit and empowerment in rural Bangladesh', IDS Discussion Paper 363, May.

Kandiyoti, D. (1987), 'Women, Islam and the State', Richmond College, May, mimeo proposal.

Kandiyoti, D. (1988), 'Bargaining with patriarchy', *Gender and Society*, vol. 2, no. 3, pp. 274–290.

Kessinger, G. (1979), *Vilyatpur 1848–1968: social and economic change in a north Indian village*, University of California Press, Berkeley.

Khan, A. A. (1982), 'Rural–urban migration and urbanization in Bangladesh', *Geographical Review*, vol. 72, no. 1, pp. 379–394.

Khor, M. (1998), 'The WTO and the south: implications and recent developments', Third World Network briefing paper.

Khor, M. (1999), 'Issues and positions for the (1999) Ministerial Process', speech at the Seminar on the WTO, Developing Countries and Finland's EU-Presidency, Parliament House, Helsinki, May 28.

Kibria, N. (1995), 'Culture, social class and income control in the lives of women garment workers in Bangladesh', *Gender and Society*, vol. 9, no. 3, pp. 289–309.

Kibria, N. (1998), *Becoming a garment worker: the mobilization of women into the garment factories of Bangladesh*, UNRISD Occasional Paper no. 9.

Kindleberger, C.P. (1967), *Europe's Post-War Growth: the role of labour supply*, Harvard University Press, Cambridge, MA.

Krupat, K. (1997), 'From war zone to free trade zone', in A. Ross (ed.), *No Sweat: fashion, free trade and the rights of garment workers*, Verso, New York and London, pp. 51–78.

Ladbury, S. (1984), 'Choice, chance or no alternative? Turkish Cypriots in business in London', in R. Ward and R. Jenkins (eds.), *Ethnic Communities in Business: strategies for economic survival*, Cambridge University Press, Cambridge, pp. 105–124.

Lawson, A. (1997), *Economics and Reality*, Economics as Social Theory Series (ed. T. Lawson), Routledge, London.

Lee, E. (1997), 'Globalisation and labour standards: a review of issues', *International Labour Review*, vol. 136, no. 2, pp. 173–189.

Lily, F.B. (1985), 'Garment industry and its workers in Bangladesh', *ISIS Women's Journal*, vol. 4, pp. 41–47.

Lim, L. (1978), 'Women Workers in Multinational Corporations: the case of the electronics industry in Malaysia and Singapore, University of Michigan Occasional Papers no. 9, Women Studies Program, Michigan.

Lim, L. (1983), 'Capitalism, imperialism and patriarchy: the dilemma of Third World women workers in multinational factories', in M. P. Fernandez-Kelly and J. Nash (eds.), *Women, Men and the International Division of Labor*, State University of New York Press, Albany, pp. 70–92.

Lim, L. (1990), 'Women's work in export factors: the politics of a cause', in I. Tinker (ed.), *Persistent Inequalities: women and world development*, Oxford University Press, Oxford, pp. 101–122.

Lindenbaum, S. (1981), 'Implications for women of changing marriage transactions in Bangladesh', *Studies in Family Planning*, vol. 12, no. 11, pp. 394–401.

Mather, C. (1985), 'Rather than make trouble, it's better just to leave', in H. Afshar (ed.), *Women, Work and Ideology in the Third World*, Macmillan, London, pp. 153–177.

McCarthy, F.E., T. Abdullah and S. Zeidenstein (1979), 'Program assessment and the development of women's programs: the views of action workers', in R. Papanek and H. Jahan (eds.), *Women and Development: perspectives from South and South East Asia*, Bangladesh Institute of Law and International Affairs, Dhaka.

McCarthy, F. and S. Feldman (1984), 'Rural women and development in Bangladesh: selected issues', report from NORAD, January.

McCrate, E. (1988), 'Gender difference: the role of endogenous preferences and collective action', *American Economic Review*, vol. 78, no. 2, pp. 235–239.

McElroy, M.B. (1990), 'The empirical content of Nash-bargained household behaviour', *Journal of Human Resources*, vol. 24, no. 4, pp. 559–583.

Mehmet, O., E. Mendes and R. Sinding (1999), *Towards a Fair Global Labour Market: avoiding a new slave trade*, Routledge, London.

Mernissi, F. (1975), *Beyond the Veil: Male-female dynamics in a modern Muslim society*, John Wiley and Sons, New York.

Miranda, A. (1982), 'The demography of Bangladesh', report of Chr. Michaelson Institute, DERAP Publications no. 144.

Mitter, S. (1986), 'Industrial restructuring and manufacturing homework: immigrant women in the UK clothing industry', *Capital and Class*, vol. 27, winter issue, pp. 37–80.

Mohanty, C.T. (1991), 'Under western eyes: feminist scholarship and colonial discourses', in C. T. Mohanty, A. Russo and L. Torres (eds.), *Third World Women and the Politics of Feminism*, Indian University Press, Bloomington and Indianapolis.

Moore, H. (1994), *A Passion for Difference: essays in anthropology and gender*, Polity Press, Cambridge.

Morokvasic, M. (1983), 'Women in migration: beyond the reductionist outlook', in A. Phizacklea (ed.), *One Way Ticket: migration and female labour*, Routledge and Kegan Paul, London, pp. 13–32.

Morris, J. (1986), *Women Workers and the Sweated Trades: the origins of minimum wage legislation*, Gower, Aldershot.

Morris, L. (1990), *The Workings of the Household*, Polity Press, Cambridge.

Moser, C.O.N. (1989), 'Gender planning in the Third World: meeting practical and strategic gender needs', *World Development*, vol. 17, no. 11, pp. 1799–1825.

Mukherjee, R. (1974), *The Rise and Fall of the East India Company*, Monthly Review Press, New York.

Nelson, J. (1996), *Feminism, Objectivity and Economics*, Routledge, London.

Newby, M.H. (1998), 'Women in Bangladesh: a study of the effects of garment factory work on control over income and autonomy', Department of Social Sciences, University of Southampton, Ph.D. thesis.

Ong, A. (1987), *The Spirits of Resistance and Capitalist Discipline: factory women in Malaysia*, SUNY Press, Albany.

Osmani, S.R. (1990), 'Structural change and poverty in Bangladesh: the case of a false turning point', Bangladesh Development Studies, vol. 18, no. 3, pp. 55–74.

Page, S. et al. (1992), 'The GATT Uruguay Round: effects on developing countries', report of Overseas Development Institute.

Pahl, J. (1983), 'The allocation of money and the structuring of inequality within marriage', *Sociological Review*, vol. 31, no. 2, pp. 237–262.

Parkin, F. (1979), *Marxism and Class Theory: a bourgeois critique*, Tavistock Publications, Oxford.

Parmar, P. (1982), 'Gender, race and class: Asian women in resistance', in Centre for Contemporary Cultural Studies (ed.), *The Empire Strikes Back: race and racism in 70s Britain*, Hutchinson University Library, London, pp. 236–275.

Parpart, S. and J. L. Stichter (1990), 'Introduction', in S. Parpart and J. L. Strichter (eds.), *Women, Employment and the Family in the International Division of Labour*, Macmillan International Political Economy Series (ed. T. L. Shaw), Macmillan, London.

Paul-Majumder, P. and J. H. Chowdhury (1993), 'Child workers in the garment industry of Bangladesh', Associates for Community and Population Research, mimeo.

Pearson, R. (1992), 'Gender issues in industrialization', in T. Hewitt, H. Johnson and D. Wield (eds.), *Industrialization and Development*, Oxford University Press in association with Open University, Oxford, pp. 222–247.

Pearson, R. (1998), '"Nimble fingers" revisited: reflections on women and Third World industrialisation in the late twentieth century', in R. Pearson and C. Jackson (eds.), *Feminist Visions of Development: gender analysis and policy* Routledge, London, pp. 171–188.

Phelan, B. (1986), *'Made in Bangladesh'? Women, garments and the Multi-Fibre Arrangement*, Bangladesh International Action Group, London.

Phizacklea, A. (1990), *Unpacking the Fashion Industry: gender, racism and class in production*, Routledge, London.

Raffaelli, M. (1990), 'Some considerations in the Multi-Fibre Arrangement: past, present and future', in C. B. Hamilton (ed.), *Textiles Trade and the Developing Countries: eliminating the MFA in the 1990s*, World Bank, Washington DC.

Rahman, R.I. (1986), 'The wage employment market for rural women in Bangladesh', Bangladesh Institute of Development Studies research monograph no. 6.

Rahman, H. (1992), 'Situation of child domestic servants', report of UNICEF, mimeo.

Rahman, Z.H., M. Hossain and B. Sen (1996), '1987–1994 Dynamics of Rural Poverty in Bangladesh', Bangladesh Institute of Development Studies, final report of the Analysis of Poverty Trends project.

Razavi, S. (1999), 'Export-oriented employment, poverty and gender, contested accounts'. *Development and Change*, vol. 30, no. 3, pp. 653–684.

Rosenzsweig, M.R. (1986), 'Program interventions: intrahousehold distribution and the welfare of individuals: modeling household behaviour', *World Development*, vol. 14, no. 2, pp. 233–243.

Ross, A. (1997), *No Sweat: fashion, free trade and the rights of garment workers*, Verso, New York and London.

Ross, A. (1997), 'Introduction', in A. Ross (ed.), *No Sweat: fashion, free trade and the rights of garment workers*, Verso, New York and London, pp. 9–38.

Rowbotham, S. (1993), *Homeworkers Worldwide*, Merlin Press, London.

Safa, H. (1990), 'Women and Industrialisation in the Caribbean', in S. Parpart and J. Stichter (eds.), *Women, Employment and the Family in the International Division of Labour*, Macmillan International Political Economy Series (ed. T. Shaw), Macmillan, London, pp. 72–97.

Salaff, J. (1981), *Working Daughters of Hong Kong: filial piety or power in the family?*, Cambridge University Press, New York.

Samuelson, P.A. (1956), 'Social indifference curves', *Quarterly Journal of Economics*, vol. 70, no. 1, pp. 1–22.

Sanghatana, S. S. (1989), *We Were Making History': women and the Telengana Uprising*, Zed, London.

Sapsford, D. and Z. Tzannatos (1993), *The Economics of the Labour Market*, World Bank, Washington DC.

Sattar, E. (1974), *Women in Bangladesh: a village study*, report of the Ford Foundation.

Schuler, S.R., S. M. Hashemi, A. P. Riley and A. Akhter (1996), 'Credit programs, patriarchy and men's violence against women in rural Bangladesh', *Social Science and Medicine*, vol. 43, no. 12, pp. 1729–1742.

Schultz, T.W. (1973), 'The value of children: an economic perspective', *Journal of Political Economy*, vol. 81, no. 2, part II, S2–S13.

Scott, J. (1985), *Weapons of the Weak: everyday forms of peasant resistance*, Yale University Press, New Haven.

Scott, J.W. and L.A. Tilly (1980), 'Women's work and the family in nineteenth-century Europe', in A. H. Amsden (ed.), *The Economics of Women and Work*, Penguin, Harmondsworth, pp. 91–124.

Sen, A. (1982), *Choice, Welfare and Measurement*, Cambridge University Press, Cambridge, MA.

Sen, A. (1990), 'Gender and cooperative conflicts', in I. Tinker (ed.), *Persistent Inequalities*, Oxford University Press, Oxford, pp. 123–149.

Shah, S. (1975), 'Immigrants and employment in the clothing industry: the rag trade in London's East End', report of the Runnymede Trust, September.

Shankland Cox and Partnership (1981), 'Dhaka Metropolitan Area Integrated Urban Development Project', report of the Planning Commission, Government of Bangladesh.

Shaw, L. (1997), 'The labor behind the label: Clean Clothes Campaign in Europe', in A. Ross (ed.), *No Sweat: fashion, free trade and the rights of garment workers* Verso, London and New York, pp. 215–220.

Shaw, L. (n.d.), 'Global labour standards and trade', report of One World Action.

Silberston, Z.A. (1984), 'The Multi-Fibre Arrangement and the UK economy', report of HMSO.

Silberston, Z.A. (1989), 'The future of the MFA: implications for the UK economy', report of HMSO.

Singer, H. (1989), 'Lessons of the post-war development experience: 1945–1988', IDS Discussion Paper no. 260, Institute of Development Studies, Sussex.

Smith, D. J. (1977), *Racial Disadvantage in Britain: the PEP Report*, Penguin, Harmondsworth.

Smith, H. (1989), 'Integrating theory and research on institutional determinants of fertility', *Demography*, vol. 26, pp. 171–184.

Solidar (1998), 'Workers' rights are human rights: the case for linking trade and core labour standards', report of Solidar.

South Centre (1996), 'Liberalisation and Globalisation: drawing conclusions for development', South Centre, Geneva.

Spielberg, E. (1997), 'The myth of nimble fingers', in A. Ross (ed.), *No Sweat: fashion, free trade and the rights of garment workers* Verso, London and New York, pp. 113–122.

Spitalfields Working Party (1983), 'A short report on the Asian population of Tower Hamlets', report of London Borough of Tower Hamlets.

Stalker, P. (1996), 'Child labour in Bangladesh: a summary of recent investigations', UNICEF, Education Section Occasional Papers.

Standing, H. (1991), *Dependence and Autonomy*, Routledge, London.

Stigler, G. J. and G. S. Becker (1977), 'De gustibus non est disputandum', *American Economic Review*, vol. 67, no. 2, pp. 76–90.

Stone, K. (1983), 'Motherhood and waged work: West Indian, Asian and white mothers compared', in A. Phizacklea (ed.), *One Way Ticket: migration and female labour*, Routledge & Kegan Paul, London.

Third World Network (1996), 'Barking up the wrong tree: trade and social clause links', personal communication.

Townsend, J. H. and J. Momsen (1987), *Geography of Gender in the Third World*, Hutchinson, London.

Trella, I. and J. Whalley (1990), 'Internal quota allocation schemes and the costs of the MFA', report of UNCTAD.

UNDP (1996), 'A pro-poor agenda: poor people's perspectives', UNDP's 1996 Report on Human Development in Bangladesh.

UNICEF/ILO (1995), 'Rapid Assessment Survey', ILO and UNICEF, mimeo.

US Senate (1994), 'Child labor and the new global market place: reaping profits at the expense of children?', report of the US Senate Committee on Labor and Human Resources, hearing before the Subcommittee on Labour, mimeo, September 21.

Van Schendel, W. (1981), *Peasant Mobility: the odds of life in rural Bangladesh.*

Villareal, M. (1990), 'A struggle over images: issues on power, gender and intervention in a Mexican village', University of Wangingen, PhD thesis.

Viramma, J. Racine, and J-L. Racine (1997), *Viramma: Life of an Untouchable,* Verso, London.

Visram, R. (1986), *Ayahs, Lascars and Princes: the story of Indians in Britain 1700–1947,* Pluto Press, London.

Ward, R. and R. Jenkins (1984), *Ethnic Communities in Business: strategies for economic survival,* Cambridge University Press, Cambridge.

Wark, M. (1997), 'Fashion as culture industry', in A. Ross (ed.), *No Sweat: fashion, free trade and the rights of garment workers,* Verso, London and New York, pp. 227–248.

Westergaard, K. (1983), *Pauperization and Rural Women in Bangladesh: a case study,* Bangladesh Academy for Rural Development, Comilla.

Westwood, S. and P. Bhachu (1988), *Enterprising Women,* Routledge, London.

Whitehead, A. (1981), ' "I'm hungry, Mum": the politics of domestic budgeting', in K. Young, C. Wokowitz and R. McCullagh (eds.), *Of Marriage and the Market: women's subordination in international perspective,* CSE Books, London, pp. 88–111.

Whitehead, A. (1985), 'Effects of technological change on rural women: a review of analysis and concepts', in I. Ahmed (ed.), *Technology and Rural Women,* George Allen and Unwin, London, pp. 27–61.

Wilson, G. (1991), 'Thoughts on the cooperative conflict model of the household in relation to economic method', IDS Bulletin, vol. 22, no. 1, pp. 31–36.

Wolf, D. L. (1992), *Factory Daughters: gender, household dynamics and rural industrialisation in Java*, University of California, Berkeley.

World Bank (1983), 'Bangladesh: current trends and development issues', World Bank Country Study, Washington DC.

World Bank (1990), 'Bangladesh strategy paper on women and development', Asian Country Department, Washington DC.

World Bank (1990), 'Bangladesh strategies for enhancing the role of women in economic development', World Bank, Washington DC.

World Food Programme (1979), 'Women in food-for-work: the Bangladesh experience', report of World Food Programme.

Wright, P. (1985), *On Living in an Old Country*, Verso, London.

Zohir, S. C. (1998), 'Gender implications of industrial reforms and adjustment in the manufacturing sector of Bangladesh', Economics and Social Studies, University of Manchester, PhD thesis.

Zohir, S.C. and P. Paul-Majumder (1996), *Garment workers in Bangladesh: economic, social and health conditions*, Bangladesh Institute of Development Studies, Research Monograph 18, Dhaka.

# Index

Agarwal, B.
  women and household
    decisions 29
agency and choice
  bargaining models 120
  conclusion 410
  contracts and men 40–43
  'cultural dopes' 34–6, 326–7
  duality between individuals and
    structures 46–9
  forces of change 360–63
  gap between aspirations and
    resources 331–2
  Giddens on agency 38
  habitus and social change 43–6
  homeworkers 305–9
  household decision making
    117–20
  individual preferences and
    social context 21–3
  London household bargaining
    models 261–8
  preferences and power within
    the household 23–30
  the 'rational fool' 17–20
  social context 30–33
  social values and meta-
    preferences 327–34
  women make concessions to
    gain preferences 342–3
  women's own explanations
    51–3

Ahmad, A. 68n
Akhter, Shireen 401
Alam, S. 40
Allen, S. 14, 235
American-Asian Free Labor
  Institute (AAFLI) 368–71,
  377–8
American-Bangladesh Economic
  Forum 369
American Institute for Free
  Labour Development 370
Amsden, A. H. 378, 385, 398
Anwar, M. 216
Arthur, B. 59
Asda 211
'Asian tiger' economies 1
associations and societies
  voluntary membership 31–2
Awami League 57

Ballard, C. 228
Ballard, R. 224, 228, 423
Bangladesh
  absence of state social security
    net 320–22, 322n
  class 38–9
  entrepreneurs choose as 'quota-
    free' 3
  flourishing garment trade
    367
  gender relations in social
    change 60–70

Bangladesh (*cont.*)
  greater freedom for women
    than London immigrants
    350–51
  history of textile trade  54–6
  literature on rural women
    37–40
  loss of faith in the patriarchal
    bargain  179–80
  and Pakistan  56–7
  patriarchal contracts  40–43
  post-colonial economy  56–60
  poverty  61–2, 67–8
  quotas imposed by MFA  9
  social change  354
  strength of community  323–5
  women moving from margins
    403–4
Bangladesh Independent
    Garment Workers Union
    (BIGWU)  377, 401
Bangladeshi immigrants
  age statistics  423–4
  attitudes to outside work  236–8
  availability and sources of jobs
    317–20
  breadwinning women and
    outside work  251–5
  choosing outside work  255–61,
    303–5
  community model  354, 361–3
  compared to Dhaka workers
    313–17
  cultural images of women
    219–23
  cultural solidarity  275–9,
    323–5, 350–51
  decision to do homeworking
    242–51
  employers of different culture
    349
  experience outside cultural
  group  212, 216–19, 254,
    268–75
  factory work rejected by women
    238–42
  fear of official bureaucracy
    221–2
  gender hierarchy  278–81
  gender inequalities in British
    context  282–3
  household bargaining models
    261–8
  household negotiations over
    time and money  285–9
  household population average
    224
  housing  425
  interviews  406–11
  language skills  222–3, 224,
    232–4, 251
  less contestation of male
    authority  309
  living conditions  270–71
  marriage statistics  424–5
  occupational statistics  425–6,
    427–31
  presence of state social security
    net  320–22
  profile of London homeworkers
    223–7
  progress of second generation
    310–11, 365–6
  purdah  236
  racism decreased  365
  standard of living  232
  statistical analysis  421–31
  support networks  271–2
  ties to Bangladesh  225
  unemployment  366
Becker, G. S.
  New Household Economics  18
Begum, S.  37, 171n
Beneria, L.  143
Berry, S.  92

Bhattacharya, D. 368
Birnbaum, B. 206
Bissell, S. 368, 369, 377, 381
Blei, T. 60
Booth, Charles 204n
Boserup, E. 4–5, 37
Bourdieu, Pierre 340
  habitus and social change 43–6
  symbolic capital 44
Bowley, A. 204n
Bretton Woods agreements 392,
  393–4
Britain
  publicity about exploitation
    386
  response to immigration 197
  state social security net 320–22,
    322n
  textile industry in Bangladesh
    55–6
British Home Stores 208
British Medical Association 201
Broadhurst, Henry 203
Buchanan, J. 23–4

C & A 211
Cain, M. 41, 42
  female dependence 337
  male responsibilities 358–9
  on women in factory work 70
  women's distance to work 63
Canada
  trade with Bangladesh 10
Carey, S. 196, 270, 272
Caribbean immigrants 209, 270n
  statistics 423–6
Cavanaugh, J. 380
Centre for Development
  Research, Bangladesh 369
Charnowitz, S. 375, 380, 389
Child Labour Coalition (CLC)
  368–71, 381
Child Labour Deterrence Bill

  (Harkin Bill) 367–8, 376,
    377
children
  abused by employers 374–5
  arrangements for care 79
  Bangladeshi immigrants
    424–5
  comparison of Dhaka and
    London women 315–16
  custody in re-marriages 165–6,
    332–3
  daughters contributing to
    household 167–9
  desire to work 376–7
  of Dhaka women workers 79
  education 375–6
  fathers' concern about neglect
    245, 247
  and homeworking 233–4, 255
  labour 398
  mothers and daughters 179–83
  obstacle for working mothers
    260–61, 287, 357
  protectionist lobbies against
    child labour 367–71
  statistics of workers 373–4
  women's anxiety about
    childlessness 162–4
Chisolm, Nick 13, 216–17
Chittagong 3, 195
choice see agency and choice;
  decision making
Choudhury, Gaffar 366
class 119
  Bangladeshi women 38–9
  education 75
  influence on choice of job 93
  see also poverty
Commonwealth Immigrants Bill
  1962 197
Connell, R. W. 361
crime 270n
  see also racism

Cypriots 209, 319, 387
  homeworkers 214, 421–2
  self-employment 220, 222

Dannecker, P. 401
decision making
  active and consensual 106–9,
    249–51
  active and uncontested 103–7,
    158–61
  choosing homeworking 323–5
  in conflict 113–17, 339–45
  consensual 338
  economic bargaining 129–35
  London household bargaining
    models 261–8
  London women 242–51
  negotiated 110–13, 247–9
  non-verbal and verbal
    bargaining 344–5
  passive and consensual 242–3
  processes 99–100
  rational choices 17–20
  reluctant and in conflict 243–7
  reluctant and uncontested
    100–103, 130–31, 154–8, 339
  theories of choice 117–20
  women's reasons for working
    85–92
Department of Employment
  Homeworking Survey 215–16
Dhaka
  availability and sources of jobs
    317–20
  characteristics of women
    workers 76–80
  community constraints
    compared to London 345–51
  Delowara's story 351–2, 353,
    359
  entrepreneurs' choice 3
  interviews with women workers
    406–11

migrant population 58
  public disapproval of women
    working outside 82–5
  social change 361, 362–3
  statistical background to study
    412–20
  workers compared to London
    immigrants 313–17
dowries 190
  demands sour love match
    177–8
  not a factor in London women
    231
  social change in Bangladesh
    60–62
  women working for 164–5, 166,
    167, 169–71, 332
Duesenberry, J. S. 16, 17
Duffy, Patrick
  Bangladeshi immigrants in
    London 213
  cultural images 219–20

economics
  choice 23–4
  household labour 18–20
  post-colonial Bangladesh 56–60
  rational choice 17–20
education 231
  adult training 3–5, 258–9
  Bangladeshi immigrants 271,
    427
  barrier for London workers
    232–3
  employers prefer literate
    women 72–3
  families' fear of 352–3
  household fears for immigrant
    women in London 247
  increased promotion prospects
    75
  mothers' ambition for
    daughters 179–80, 181–3

education (*cont.*)
  progress of London daughters
    365–6
  statistics 413, 414
  women workers 76–7, 78
  working children 375–6
Edwards, M. 399
Elson, D. 6, 11–12
Elster, J. 323, 343, 347
employers *see also* garment
  industry
  attitudes towards immigrant
    workers 216–19
  preference for women 98
Enayet, F. 38
ethics and values
  global versus value-laden norms
    21–3
  moral order of community 64
  public disapproval of working
    women 82–5
ethnicity
  attitudes of trade unions and
    employers 216–19
  entrepreneurs and their work
    forces 211
  homeworking 212–19
  male authority 235
  minorities exploited in rich
    countries 386–7
  variety of peoples in London
    209, 212
  *see also* racism
European Union
  trade with Pakistan 11

Feldman, S. 66–7, 76, 77
Folbre, N. 343
  social structures of collective
    constraint 31–2
Fraser, N. 402
Fullerton, William 55

Galeano, Eduardo 390
Gardner, K. 196, 197, 225
garment industry
  child labour 367–71
  clarity of job status 355–6
  constructed as 'female' industry
    in Bangladesh 331
  cut-and-make-trim (CMT) firms
    208–12
  Dhaka women's choice 92–9
  employment practices and tax
    evasion 213–14
  estimates of child workers 373
  First and Third World 398
  flourishes in Bangladesh 367
  haute couture and short runs
    208
  history in London 200–12
  homeworking compared to
    factory work 284–5
  international labour standards
    403–4
  international restructuring 2–4
  invention of sewing machine
    200
  key job source for immigrants
    319–20
  labour standards and
    protectionism 378–84
  London factories rejected by
    Bangladeshi women 238–42
  London loses factories 211
  men's access to 289–95
  protectionism and poorer
    countries 367–71, 384–91
  publicity about exploitation
    386
  relocation to cheaper areas in
    Britain 207–8
  rumours of scandal and
    impropriety 84, 94, 186
  shift to low-wage Asia
    209

garment industry (*cont.*)
  skilled men and unskilled
    women  202, 206, 207,
    279–80, 330
  small subcontractors  206, 209,
    210
  statistics for homeworkers
    421–2
  tight profit margins  211–12
  urban locale  138–9
  wage differences for men and
    women  281
  women and racial minorities in
    London  205–12
General Agreement on Tariffs and
  Trade (GATT)  379n, 380
  and MFA  388
Gerard, R.  37–8
Germany
  labour  396
  trade with Bangladesh  10
Giddens, Anthony  52
  locale  269
  people as automatons  38
  structuration processes  354
  voluntarism  16
Greer, Germaine  267n
*The Guardian*
  trading double standards  390

habitus
  and social change  43–6
Hackney Trade Union Support
  Groups  211
Hakim, C.  215
Harkin, Tom  367–8, 370, 376,
    377
Hirschman, A. O.  23, 344–5
Hodgson, G. M.  21
Hoffman, K.  215
homeworking
  combining with domestic duties
    234–5, 243

community constraints in
  Dhaka versus London
    345–51
compared to factory work
  284–5
different ethnic rates  220–21
employment practices of small
  firms  212–19
fear of official bureaucracy
    221–2
history of in London  200–12
Homeworking Survey by DoE
    215–16
household negotiations over
  time and money  285–9
indistinctness of job status  355
invisibility  14
London workers' factors in
  decision  232–5
men's mediating in women's
  work  289–95
post-war London  208–9
prior to manufacturing  78
safety within immigrant
  community  275–81
statistics  421–2, 426–31
Hong Kong  1
Hope  325
households
  active and consensual decision
    making  106–9, 158–61
  child care  79
  as corporate organization
    334–5
  Dhaka models for decision
    making  117–20
  economic bargaining  129–35
  family honour  125
  gender divisions of labour  26
  group solidarity  30–33
  hierarchy  336–7
  homeworkers' choices  305–9
  implicit contracts  25–30

households (*cont.*)
  individual preferences 21–3
  interdependent inequality
    335–45
  London models for decision
    making 261–8
  migrants' unconventional
    79–80
  negotiated decision making
    110–13
  parental influence 246–7,
    263–4
  preference for homeworking
    243–7
  rejection or acceptance of
    women's pay 144–9
  shift in power relations 49–50
  social context 30–33
  statistics 414, 416, 428
  wives incorporated into
    husband's family 160
  women make concessions to
    gain preferences 342–3
  women's increased strength
    189–91
Huq, J. 39
Hussein, Ashraf 194–5

identity
  men's resistance to women
    working 122–9
  *see also* ethnicity
immigration
  hopes to return home rich 198
  increase in women to Dhaka 68
  Jewish garment workers 204–5
  renegotiation cultural rules
    267
  rural to urban areas 58, 77
*Independent on Sunday*
  trading double standards
    389–90
Indians 270n

household population average
  224
smaller entrepreneurs 212
statistics 423, 424, 425
Indonesia 6
industry
  old-style 1–2
  women fit 'flexible' demands
    5–6
International Labour Office
  (ILO) 371, 373
  labour protectionism
    379–80
  three core conventions
    399
International League of Garment
  Workers 368
International Monetary Fund
  (IMF) 393–4
Islam
  broken safety nets for women
    89
  cultural images of women 220
  permits women in need to go
    out 343–4
  religious differences of
    immigrants 194–5
  women's inner strength 91
  *see also* purdah
Islam, F. 135n, 138, 345
Islam, M. 38

Jackson, B. 388
Japan
  textile trade 387
Jews
  immigrant garment workers
    204–5, 206
  larger entrepreneurs 212
  men and women's jobs 281
Jhuli, Thakur Ma-er 193n
Joekes, S. 51
Joshi, H. 322

Kabeer, Naila  216–17
Kandiyoti, D.  34, 42
Keynesianism  391–3
Krupat, K.  384
Kurds  387

labour
    agriculture versus
        manufacturing  769–70
    children  398
    clarity versus indistinctness of
        job status  355–6
    Dhaka occupational statistics
        415–20
    employers' preference for
        women workers  70–76
    global 'win–win' policies  397–9
    intensive industries  1–2
    international labour standards
        378–84
    Keynesian years  392–3
    men at 'women's work'  98
    'new international division'  1
    occupations of immigrants in
        London  425–6
    options for women in London
        237–8
    skilled tailors exclude unskilled
        women  202
    'sweated'  201, 205
    three core conventions  399
    see also homeworking; pay and
        wages
Ladbury, S.  221
Lambert, Jean  422
The Lancet (British Medical
    Association)
    sweated labour  201
language
    Bangladeshi immigrants  222–3,
        224
    barrier to outside work  232–4,
        251, 319
    excuse for racism  257
    key to opportunity  258–9
    lack of voice without  349
    reluctance to attend classes  245
    second-generation Bangladeshi
        children  272
    self-teaching  248
    social barrier  309
law
    protection for women against
        men  185
    restrictions on married women
        working  105
leisure
    male choice  18
Liberal Party, Tower Hamlets  271
Lim, Linda  x
Littlewoods  208, 211
London
    attitudes and treatment of Asian
        immigrants  268–75
    Bangladeshi commerce
        199–200
    Bangladeshi immigration to
        193–200
    community constraints
        compared to Dhaka  345–51
    decline of garment industry
        207–8, 365–6
    history of the garment industry
        200–212
    Rabia's story  352–4
    see also Bangladeshi immigrants
Low Pay Unit
    Sweated Labour  421–2

Malaysia
    patriarchal traditions  6
Marks & Spencer  208
marriage
    as barrier to work  357
    comparison of Dhaka and
        London women  314–16

marriage (*cont.*)
conjugal contract 40–43
differences in London customs
231
effect of instability and divorce
179–80
emergence of dowries 60–62
female workers in Dhaka 77
holding out for better terms
177–8
impact of women working
190–91
loss of husbands 100–103,
119
statistics 226, 412–13, 414
worries about instability 161–4
*see also* dowries
Marymount University 380–81
Mather, C. 6
Matin, N. 40
Matlab Demographic Surveillance
Report 68
McCarthy, F. E.
feminine tasks 65–7, 70
McCrate, E. 23
McElroy, M. B. 27
McNicoll, G. 59
men
authority accepted 130
as breadwinners 85–6, 112,
127, 171, 203, 262–3, 337,
340, 344
controlling women's money
124–5, 308
discomfort at working with
women 329–30
domestic duties 122–4, 286–9,
343–4
effect of loss to wives 100–103
employment in London 226–7
expect domestic comfort 262
factory roles 98, 279–80

fear of London's permissive
culture 358
gender hierarchy of community
278–81
household hierarchies 336–7
household loss of 86, 100–103,
119, 131–2, 154–8, 252, 303,
309, 332
husband's influence on
homeworking 243, 245–6
interviews 407
Jewish skilled workers 207
malleability of responsibilities
358–9
marital anxiety 125–6, 129, 265
masculine tasks 74
mediation in women's
homeworking 289–95
migrants in city 77
occupational statistics 418, 427,
429
other choices of work in
Bangladesh 318–19
patriarchal bargain 344
previous wives and families
163–4, 175–6, 307
reason for women's rejection of
London factories 238–42
refusal to accept women's pay
146–7
resistance to women working
121–2
social values of gender
inequalities 328–30
threatening gaze 277
trouble for employers 71–2
underemployed 203–4
women lose faith in the
patriarchal bargain 179–80
women suspect of greed 171–2
women's acceptance of
authority 130

men (*cont.*)
    women's language for authority
        235
Mernissi, F. 36
methodology 405–11
Mitter, Swasti 14, 358
    contributions to homeworking
        221
    employment practices 214, 215
    homework as safer 276
Moore, H. 45, 340
Morokvasic, M. 220
Morris, J. 199
Morris, L. 322
Moser, C. O. N. 161
Mujib, Sheikh 57
Multifibre Arrangement (MFA) 2,
    367, 385
    contradictions of policy 10
    and GATT 388
    imposes quotas on Bangladesh 9

National Child Labour Working
    Group 368
National Front 270, 271, 273–4
National Garment Workers,
    Bangladesh 13
National Group for Homeworking
    235
National Labor Committee (NLC)
    383–4
National Union of Tailors and
    Garment Workers 211
nationalism and group solidarity
    32–3
Newby, M. H. 80, 414
Nixon, Richard M. 394
non-governmental organizations
    (NGOs)
    training for women 66

Ong, A. 7
Organization for Economic Co-
operation and Development
    (OECD) 395
Organization of Petroleum
    Exporting Countries (OPEC)
    394
Oxfam 370, 386

Pahl, J. 143
Pakistan 56–7
Pakistani immigrants
    childcare restraints 261
    male authority 235
    smaller entrepreneurs 212
    statistics 423–6
Parmar, P. 220
patriarchal bargain 6–8, 40–43,
    61–2, 118, 179–80, 332
Paul-Majumder, P. 77, 79, 413
    men and domestic work 122n
pay and wages
    acceptance or rejection 144–9
    averages for homeworkers 422
    choosing outside work 303–5
    as contribution to household
        158–61
    daughters' perspective 167–9
    effect of London homeworkers
        295–301
    effect on Dhaka workers 183–7
    effect on needy and 'optionless'
        women 154–8
    empowerment for women 8,
        172–4, 298–9, 302–3
    enhances status within
        household 301–3
    impact on household 142–4
    male control 149–51, 290–95,
        308
    meagre earnings evaporate 355
    minimum at CMT firms 211
    mother's perspective 178–83
    perception of women's
        'supplement' 201–2

pay and wages (*cont.*)
  potential for transformation
    152–4
  production costs  2
  saving  299–300
  shift in household power
    relations  49–50
  strategic gender needs  161–6
  wives' perspective  171–8
Pearson, R.  6, 7–8
Phizacklea, A.  199, 204
  different rates of self-
    employment  220–21
  flaws in Homeworking Survey
    215–16
  London loses factories  211
  small subcontractors  209,
    210
poverty
  child labour  373
  economy of Bangladesh  58–60
  opportunities in Bangladesh
    67–8
  'patriarchal risk'  61–2
  social change  136
  women driven to work  184
Powell, Enoch
  'rivers of blood' speech  197
prostitution
  automatic labelling  83
  children  375, 376
  Shefali's story  105–6
  Spielberg's claim of preference
    382–3
  as supplemental income  157
public opinion
  threatened by working women
    in Dhaka  82–5
purdah  37, 362
  factor in decision of London
    workers  323
  internal  236, 245
  interpretations  315

London women  244
patriarchal contracts  41
reinterpretation by women
  workers  87–92
social structure  34–6
women reject London factories
  238–42
women's distance to work  63

Quasen, M. A.  68n

racism
  Bangladeshi experience in
    London  270–75
  decrease  365
  effect on London labour
    market  319–20
  job discrimination  256, 257
  other minorities as well  356–7
  violence  222
Raffaelli, Marcelo  388
Rahman, H.  374
Rahman, R. I.  68n
religion
  authority over women's
    behaviour  64
Roldan, M.  143
Rosa, Kumudhini  12–13
Ross, A.  388
rural life *see* urban versus rural
  life
Rush, H.  215

*samaj*
  defines the rules  87–8
secrecy
  holding back earnings  150–52,
    172–3, 294
  working without telling  248
security
  *see* women: loss of men
self-respect  117, 189–90

Sen, A. 16
    household decision making
        27–8
sexuality
    abuse of child workers 374–5
    discomfort of men working with
        women 329–30
    fear of London's permissive
        culture 358
    men's anxiety 125–6, 263
    reputation of garment factories
        84, 94, 186
    strictness in workplace 73
    veiling women 35–6
    women's fear on streets 273–4
Shah, S. 217, 219
Shakur, A. 270, 272
shalish 64
shamaj 64
Shukur, A. 196
Sikhs 228, 423
Silberston, Z. A. 10, 385
Singapore 1
Sobhan, B. 368, 369, 377
social security
    presence/absence 320–22
society
    among the English 268–75
    change in Bangladesh 191–2
    comparison of constraints in
        Dhaka and London 345–51
    context of household decision
        making 30–33
    Delowara's story 351–2, 353
    effect on decision making
        357–8
    forces of change 360–63
    global social policy 397–9
    habitus and social change 43–6
    importance to Bangladeshi
        immigrants 234–5
    moral order of community 64

strength of community in
        Dhaka and London 323–5
    structuration process 354
    structure and individual choice
        33–6, 46–9
    wider changes for urban women
        135–9
    women's ambivalence about
        working 188
    women's internal social values/
        beliefs and meta- preferences
        327–34
South Korea 1
Spielberg, E. 382–3
Stalker, P. 371–2
structuration process 354, 360–61
Sweated Labour (Low Pay Unit)
        421–2
Sweden
    trade with Bangladesh 10
Sylhet 194–8

tailors
    exclude unskilled women from
        status 202, 206
Taiwan 1
taste 23
tax evasion 213–14
Tesco 211
textile industry
    Asian investment in Bangladesh
        69
    historical perspective in
        Bangladesh 54–6
    trade quota 9–14
Third World Network 389
trade and tariffs
    anti-quota campaign 9–14
    disadvantage to consumers
        385–6
    double standard protectionism
        384–91
    'ethical' legislation 387n

trade and tariffs (*cont.*)
  garment industry's reliance on
    international trade 385
  historical perspective of
    international economy 391–6
  MFA's 'anti-surge' agreement
    2–3
trade unions
  attitudes towards immigrant
    workers 216–19
  BIGWU 377–8, 401
  men's sphere 203
  Third World workers 12–13
  women's organisation 400–403
Trevelyan, Sir Charles 56

UNICEF 368, 369, 370
  children's point of view 376
  image of exhausted child 372
UNITE 381, 382
United Kingdom
  fall in clothing production 3–4
  reaction to MFA quotas 9–14
United Nations Conference for
    International Women's Year
    (1975) 5
United States
  international labour standards
    379, 381, 396
  self-interest in child labour
    debate 368, 370
  trade strategies 387–8
urban versus rural life 323,
    413–14
  Bangladesh 58
  labour statistics 69–70
  urban opportunities for women
    137–9

Van Schendel, W. 61
Villareal, M. 133–4
violence
  abusive husbands 333n

acceptance of 187
conflict at home over outside
    work 113–17
effect of women's
    independence 173–4
irresponsibility worse for
    women 131
racial 222, 273–5

wages *see* pay and wages
Wark, M. 398
Whitehead, A. 40–41
Wolf, D. L. 52–3
Wolkowitz, C. 14, 235
women
  active and uncontested decision
    making 103–7
  ages of workers 413
  agriculture versus waged work
    4–8, 69–70
  anxiety over childlessness
    162–4
  characteristics of Dhaka workers
    76–80
  choosing the garment trade
    92–9
  community influence 82–5,
    275–81, 323–5, 345–51
  comparison of Dhaka and
    London workers 313–17
  concessions to gain preferences
    342–3
  conflict over decision making
    113–17
  contracts and men 40–43
  controlling wages 149–52
  as 'cultural dopes' 34–6, 326–7
  daughters contributing to
    household 167–9
  deception about money
    150–52, 172–3, 294
  decision to work in
    manufacturing 85–7

women (*cont.*)
  discovery of previous wives and
    children 163–4, 175–6, 307
  domestic duties 133–4, 284–9,
    341
  economic aspiration 332–4
  effect of community 357–8
  effect of income on lives
    152–4, 295–301
  employers prefer 70–76, 98
  fear of going out at night 273
  fertility rates in Bangladesh 67
  forces of change and choices
    360–63
  gender inequalities 318,
    328–30
  gender role identity 122–9,
    278–81
  homeworking 78
  hopes for daughters 179–83
  household hierarchies 26–30,
    336–7
  images of Bangladeshi
    immigrants 219–23
  incorporated into husband's
    family 160
  individual with social values and
    meta-preferences 327–34
  inner strength 91
  labour organisation 400–403
  legal rights 185, 203
  limited distance to work 63
  literature on rural Bangladeshi
    women 37–40
  London women's reasons to
    work 230–32
  loss of male support 86,
    100–103, 119, 131–2, 154–8,
    252, 303, 309, 332

marriage as barrier to work
    357
  men's fears about public
    behaviour 129
  negotiated decision making
    110–13
  occupational statistics 415–20
  own explanation of choices
    51–3
  patriarchal bargain 6–8, 40–43,
    61–2, 118, 179–80, 332, 344
  patriarchal traditions 6–8,
    118
  'proper' work for 65–6
  reinterpretation of purdah
    87–92
  reluctance to defy 341
  reluctant and uncontested
    decision making 100–103
  sense of self-worth 189–90
  strategic gender needs 161–6
  types of jobs 201n
  viewed as 'supplemental'
    income 201–2, 203
  working for dowries 164–5,
    166, 167, 169–71
  *see also* households; marriage;
    purdah
Women in Development (WiD)
    63
World Development Movement
    (WDM) 216–17
  anti-quota campaign 11, 12
World Trade Organization
    (WTO) 389

Zohir, S. C. 77, 79, 413
  men and domestic work 122n,
    123n